The Travails of the Eurozone

Also by David Cobham

EUROPEAN MONETARY UPHEAVALS (*editor*)

FROM EMS TO EMU: 1997 to 1999 and Beyond (*editor with G. Zis*)

THE MAKING OF MONETARY POLICY IN THE UK, 1975–2000

THE ECONOMICS OF PALESTINE: Economic Policy and Institutional Reform for a Viable Palestinian State (*editor with N. Kanafani*)

The Travails of the Eurozone

Economic Policies, Economic Developments

Edited by

David Cobham

on behalf of the Money, Macro and Finance Research Group

palgrave
macmillan

First published 2007 by
PALGRAVE MACMILLAN
Houndmills, Basingstoke, Hampshire RG21 6XS and
175 Fifth Avenue, New York, N.Y. 10010
Companies and representatives throughout the world

PALGRAVE MACMILLAN is the global academic imprint of the Palgrave Macmillan division of St. Martin's Press, LLC and of Palgrave Macmillan Ltd. Macmillan® is a registered trademark in the United States, United Kingdom and other countries. Palgrave is a registered trademark in the European Union and other countries.

ISBN 13: 978–0–230–01892–1
ISBN 10: 0–230–01892–0

This book is printed on paper suitable for recycling and made from fully managed and sustained forest sources.

A catalogue record for this book is available from the British Library.

Library of Congress Cataloging-in-Publication Data

The travails of the Eurozone / edited by David Cobham.
p. cm.
ISBN 0–230–01892–0 (cloth)
1. Monetary policy–European Union countries. 2. Economic and Monetary Union. 3. European Union countries–Economic policy.
I. Cobham, David P.
HG925.T735 2007
339.5′3094–dc22 2006044690

10 9 8 7 6 5 4 3 2 1
16 15 14 13 12 11 10 09 08 07

Printed and bound in Great Britain by
Antony Rowe Ltd, Chippenham and Eastbourne

Contents

List of Tables

List of Figures

Notes on the Contributors

Ali Al-Eyd is Research Officer with the National Institute of Economic and Social Research (NIESR). He joined the National Institute World Economy team in 2004 after completing his PhD at Imperial College, London.

Christopher Allsopp is Reader in Economic Policy at the University of Oxford and editor of the *Oxford Review of Economic Policy*. He was an external member of the Monetary Policy Committee of the Bank of England from 2000 to 2003. He has published extensively on monetary, fiscal and exchange rate issues.

Michael Artis is Professor of Economics at Manchester University where he directs the Manchester Regional Economics Centre in the Institute of Political and Economic Governance, and a Professorial Fellow of the European University Institute. He is a Fellow of the British Academy and Research Fellow of the Centre for Economic Policy Research.

Katrin Assenmacher-Wesche joined the Research Department of the Swiss National Bank in 2004. Her research interests lie in the areas of monetary economics and applied econometrics. Much of her recent work has focused on analysing business cycle indices, estimating interest rate reaction functions using Markov switching techniques and modelling the role of money in the inflation process.

Ray Barrell has been the Senior Research Fellow at NIESR directing the National Institute World Economy team since 1990. He was previously an Economic Advisor at HM Treasury and a university lecturer at Stirling and Brunel. He has published over 100 papers since 1990, with about half in refereed journals ranging from the *European Economic Review* to *Economic Modelling*.

Miroslav Beblavý received his PhD in Economics at the University of St Andrews in Scotland. He was State Secretary of the Ministry of Labour, Social Affairs and Family in Slovakia from 2002 to 2006. Prior to this appointment, he served as the Executive Director of the Slovak Governance Institute and advisor to the Deputy Governor of the National Bank of Slovakia. He has been a visiting lecturer at the Comenius University since 2000. His principal research interests are monetary policy, social policy and governance issues.

Ansgar Belke is Professor of International Economics at the University of Stuttgart-Hohenheim. Previously, he held positions at the University of Bochum, the University of Essen and the University of Vienna. He has been visiting scholar at the Center for Economic Research (CentER) Tilburg, at the Centre for European Policy Studies (CEPS) Brussels, and at the Kiel Institute of World Economics. He is a member of the ECB watcher group 'ECB Observer' and of the Euro Area Business Cycle Network (EABCN), and research fellow of the Institute for the Study of Labor (IZA), Bonn.

Atanas Christev is Lecturer in Economics at Heriot-Watt University. His research areas are macroeconomic dynamics and fluctuations, growth and institutions and labour market imperfections in transition and emerging economies, and applied and time series econometrics. He is also a Research Fellow at IZA, Bonn.

David Cobham is Professor of Economics at Heriot-Watt University. His main research area is UK monetary policy, but he has also worked on European monetary integration, central bank independence, financial systems and the economies of the Middle East. He was a Senior Houblon-Norman Fellow at the Bank of England in 2001.

John Driffill is Professor of Economics at Birkbeck College, University of London. He previously worked at the University of Southampton, Queen Mary and Westfield College (University of London), and Tilburg University. Most of his research has been in the area of macroeconomics and monetary policy, and he has also worked on labour markets and macroeconomic performance.

Jayasri Dutta is Professor of Economics at the University of Birmingham. Professor Dutta's research interests are primarily in the areas of dynamic economics, growth and development, income and wealth distributions and in monetary economics.

Marco Ercolani is Lecturer in Economics at the University of Birmingham. He is an applied econometrician, with experience in cross-section, panel and time-series data. His general research interest is to 'bring theories to the data'. Dr Ercolani's current research interests include: sickness absence among UK workers, modelling seasonal and non-seasonal economic cycles, price changes at the introduction of the euro and estimating consumer demand functions.

Carlo Favero has been Professor of Economics at Bocconi University since 2002, before which he was Associate Professor of Econometrics from 1994 to 2001. He is a research fellow of CEPR, a member of the scientific committee of the Euro Area Business Cycle Network, and a member of the Centro

Interuniversitario Italiano di Econometria (CIDE). He has published in scholarly journals on applied econometrics, monetary policy and time-series models for macroeconomics.

Stefan Gerlach is Head of Secretariat of the Committee on the Global Financial System at the Bank for International Settlements, Adjunct Professor at the University of Basel and a Research Fellow of the CEPR. Between 2001 and 2004 he served as Director of the Hong Kong Institute for Monetary Research and Executive Director (Research) at the Hong Kong Monetary Authority. Before joining the BIS in 1992, he was Associate Professor of Economics at Brandeis University.

Bernd Hayo is Professor of Macroeconomics at the University of Marburg in Germany. He received an MSc from the University of Bristol and a doctorate from the University of Bamberg. His research focus is on empirical monetary economics, political economy and socio-economics.

Bernhard Herz is Professor of International Economics at Bayreuth University. He holds a doctoral degree in Economics from Tübingen University. He was Visiting Scholar at Stanford University and UC Berkeley and worked as a Research Fellow at the IMF and the Fed. Previously, he held academic positions at Tübingen University and Greifswald University.

Dawn Holland is Research Fellow at NIESR. She has worked at NIESR with the Institute's Global Econometric Model, NiGEM, since 1996. She manages NIESR's quarterly world economic forecast, which is produced using NiGEM. Her primary research focus has been in the economics of transition and European enlargement.

Philip R. Lane is Professor of International Macroeconomics and Director of the Institute for International Integration Studies (IIIS) at Trinity College Dublin. He is also Research Fellow and member of the steering committee on the Macroeconomics of Global Interdependence at the CEPR. He holds a PhD in Economics from Harvard University and was previously an Assistant Professor of Economics and International Affairs at Columbia University.

Campbell Leith is Professor of Macroeconomics at the University of Glasgow. He has written extensively on the interactions between monetary and fiscal policy in both closed and open economies. He also acts as a consultant to HM Treasury.

Manfredi La Manna is Reader in Economics in the School of Economics and Finance at the University of St Andrews. He has previously taught at the London School of Economics (LSE), and at the Universities of Leicester and

Swansea. He has published in the area of industrial organisation, game theory and R&D. He is currently working on the theory of optimal organisation as a complex system.

Fabrizio Mattesini is Professor of Economics at the University of Rome, Tor Vergata. Previously he worked at the University of Molise (Campobasso) and LUISS. His research interests are in monetary economics, finance, economic growth and Italian economic history.

Jacques Mélitz is currently Professor of Economics at Heriot-Watt University, Research Fellow at ENSAE in Paris and with the CEPR in London. He has been a contributor to the discussion of European macroeconomic policy and EMU in particular for many years.

Robert Mochrie is Lecturer in Economics at Heriot-Watt University. He has research interests in the history of thought and the microeconomics of finance. Recently he has been engaged in research on the impact of business owners' membership of financial and other networks in rural areas.

Charles Nolan is Professor of Economics and Director of the Centre for Dynamic Macroeconomics at the University of St Andrews. He worked for eight years as an economist at the Bank of England. His research interests are quantitative general equilibrium macroeconomics and monetary theory, international finance and business-cycle analysis.

Luca Onorante works in the Fiscal Analysis Division of the European Central Bank. He is a graduate of Bocconi University and a PhD candidate at the European University Institute, Florence. His research interests are focused on the analytical and empirical evaluation of fiscal and monetary policy and their interraction.

Gulcin Ozkan is Reader in Macroeconomics at the University of York and a CEPR Research Affiliate. Her research interests include international macro-economics and finance, political economy and macroeconomics in emerging markets.

Daniel Popov Gould was Research Assistant at the Institute for International Economics in Washington, DC. He is currently working on risk management of debt securitisation for Morgan Stanley in New York.

Adam S. Posen is Senior Fellow at the Institute for International Economics in Washington, DC. He is the author or co-author of a number of studies in applied monetary economics, including on central bank independence, inflation targeting and deflation. He has been a Visiting Fellow at central banks worldwide, including the Bank of England, Deutsche Bundesbank, European Central Bank and the Federal Reserve Board.

Michael Sumner is Emeritus Professor of Economics at the University of Sussex, where he has worked since 1983. Previous appointments were in the Universities of Salford, Guelph, Manchester, Essex and Sheffield. His principal research interests are in macroeconomics and public economics.

Paolo Surico is a Research Economist at the Monetary Assessment and Strategy Division of the Bank of England, and fellow of the Economics Department of the University of Bari. He holds a PhD from Bocconi University. He works on applied macro and monetary economics, and his research interests include determinants of the Great Moderation, consequences of multiple equilibria in sticky-price models and identification of asymmetric central bank preferences.

David Vines is Professor of Economics at the University of Oxford and a Fellow of Balliol College. He is also Adjunct Professor of Economics in the Research School of Pacific and Asian Studies at the Australian National University, and a Research Fellow of the Centre for Economic Policy Research. His research focuses on macroeconomics and international economics, in particular European monetary union and the theory of fiscal policy.

Lukas Vogel studied economics at Leipzig University, the Institut d'Etudes Politiques in Paris, and the College of Europe at Bruges. He completed his doctoral studies at Bayreuth University and has recently moved to the OECD. In his studies he focuses on international macroeconomics and European economic policy.

Sébastien Wälti is Lecturer in Economics and Research Associate at the Institute for International Integration Studies (IIIS) at Trinity College, Dublin. He holds a PhD in International Economics from the Graduate Institute of International Studies, Geneva, Switzerland. His research interests focus on the international transmission of shocks, monetary and financial integration, exchange rate regimes and the political economy of fiscal policy.

Acknowledgements

The papers on which the chapters of this book are based were first presented at 'The Travails of the Eurozone' conference at Heriot-Watt University in Edinburgh on Friday 24 March 2006, under the auspices of the Money, Macro and Finance Research Group (MMF) and the University Association for Contemporary European Studies (UACES). Funding for the conference was provided by the MMF, UACES and Heriot-Watt. The editor wishes to record his gratitude to Alex Cobham and George Zis for support and advice at different points in the project, and to John Sawkins for his help at the conference.

1
Introduction

David Cobham

The European Central Bank (ECB) was established in June 1998, European Monetary Union (EMU) came into operation in January 1999, Greece joined the 11 original members of EMU in January 2001 and euro notes and coin were introduced in January 2002. While all of these operations have arguably been carried out with considerable success, the economic performance of the eurozone has been less than outstanding and attitudes towards the ECB and EMU, especially in countries outside the eurozone, have become less favourable. In particular, the eurozone is generally considered to be experiencing poor economic growth: there was a strong recovery in 1999–2000, but the slowdown of 2001–03 was succeeded by only a weak recovery in 2004–05 (though it seems that a stronger pickup in growth is coming through now). At the same time, both the operation of monetary policy and the coordination (or lack of it) between monetary and fiscal policy have been subjected to a variety of criticisms. This book is designed to examine economic developments in the eurozone since 1999 and to assess the criticisms commonly made of the ECB and the EMU project. It brings together leading European and American macroeconomists to discuss issues in monetary policy, fiscal policy and structural reform, and a number of other questions which are important for the evolution of the eurozone.

It is useful to start by looking at some data. Figures 1.1–1.4 show real GDP growth, consumer price inflation, standardized unemployment and long-term government bond yields in the eurozone as a whole, other members of the EU15 (Denmark, Sweden and the UK), other Western European countries (Norway and Switzerland) and the USA from 1996 to 2005. Table 1.1 gives the averages for 1999–2005. What comes out of these comparisons is straightforward. First, economic growth in the eurozone has been slower than in the USA or the other EU15, but more or less the same as in the other Western European countries, while the cycles of all of these have been broadly in line, particularly since 1999. Second, eurozone inflation has been lower than in the US but higher than in the two other

European groups. Third, eurozone unemployment has remained, as it has been since the mid-1990s, consistently much higher than in the US and the other EU15, which in turn have had higher unemployment than the other Western European countries. And fourth, the credibility of monetary policy as measured simply by government bond yields has been broadly comparable with that in the two other European groups, and often better than that of the US. The large difference here is therefore unemployment rather than economic growth (or inflation or credibility): the main problem in the eurozone (as a whole) seems to be that growth has not been enough to bring unemployment down into line with other countries, rather than that growth has been very poor in itself.

While there is scope for a more detailed examination of these issues, including a disaggregation of the eurozone into its member countries, these data provide a useful background perspective to the substantial chapters of the book, of which the first three discuss monetary policy, the next two fiscal policy and the Stability and Growth Pact (SGP), the next two macroeconomic policy and structural reform, and the four others discuss financial integration, the notes and coin changeover, the new accession countries and the dollar/euro exchange rate.

The strongest criticism levelled at monetary policy in the eurozone has been that the ECB's monetary policy strategy is an unsatisfactory mix of monetary targeting and inflation targeting, with too much attention paid to monetary growth. In this book, Katrin Assenmacher-Wesche and Stefan Gerlach present a model in which trend monetary growth affects inflation in the long term while the output gap and cost-push shocks affect shorter term inflation. They use band spectrum regressions to test the model, and succeed in identifying the different frequencies of these various effects. Their chapter therefore provides a rationale for the ECB's emphasis on the

Table 1.1 Basic data for the eurozone, 1999–2005

	Real GDP growth	*Consumer price inflation*	*Standardized unemployment*[c]	*Government bond yields*
Eurozone	1.9	2.1	8.5	4.5
Other EU15[a]	2.5	1.6	5.2	4.5[d]
Other Western Europe[b]	1.8	1.5	3.6	4.0
USA	3.0	2.6	5.0	4.8

Notes: [a] Other EU15 = Denmark, Sweden, UK (unweighted average); [b] Other Western Europe = Norway, Switzerland (unweighted average); [c] 1999–2004; [d] Denmark and UK only.

Sources: growth from Eurostat (website); consumer price inflation and standardized unemployment from OECD *Economic Outlook*, December 2005; bond yields from *International Financial Statistics*.

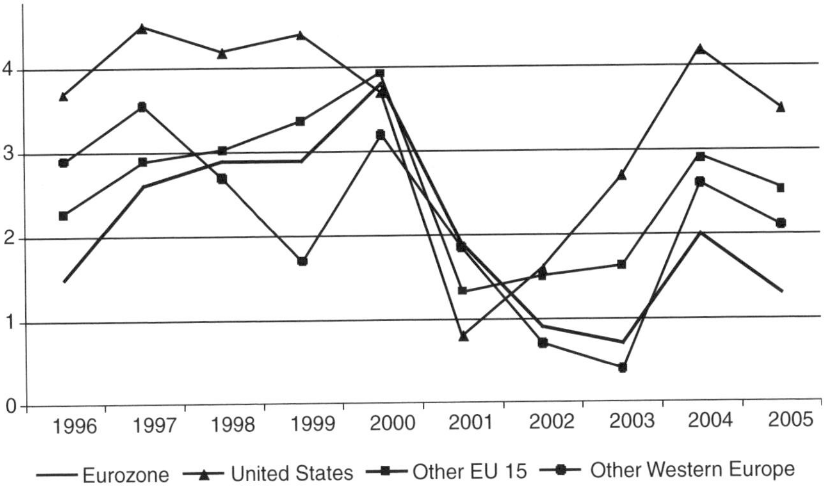

Figure 1.1 Real GDP growth
Notes and *Sources*: see under Table 1.1

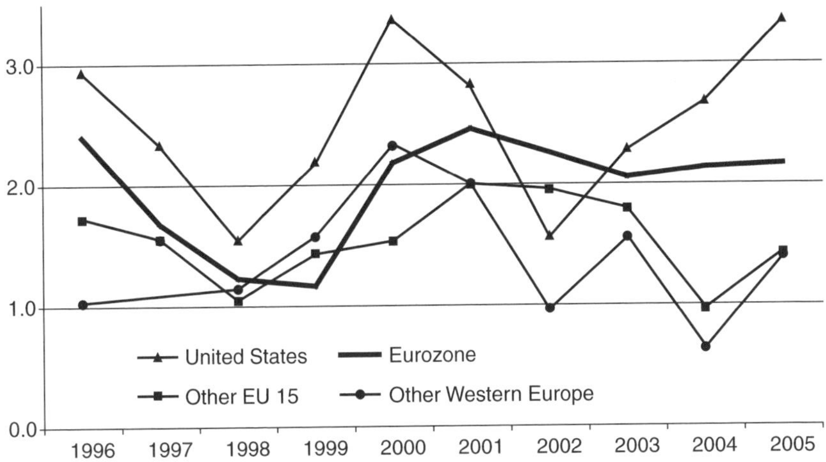

Figure 1.2 Consumer price inflation
Notes and *Sources*: see under Table 1.1

importance of monetary growth as well as other determinants of inflation, though they leave open the question of whether this emphasis should be reflected in a separate 'monetary pillar'. Michael Sumner makes the point in his comment that the Bundesbank's monetary framework, which was similar to the ECB's, was not criticised in the same way, and asks why.

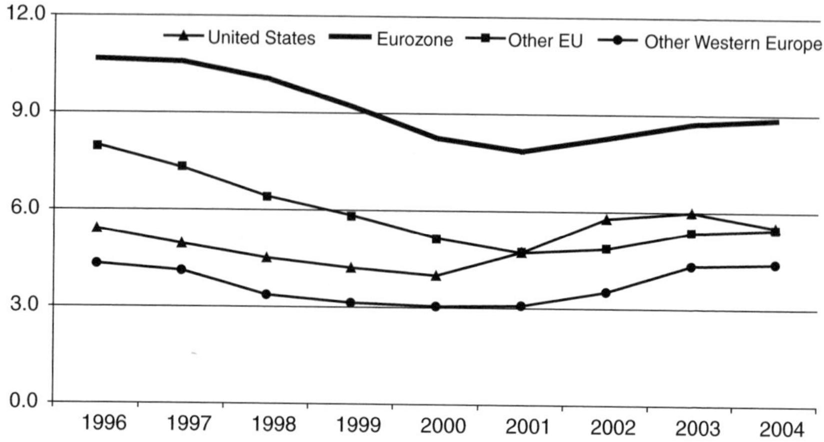

Figure 1.3 Standardised unemployment rates
Notes and *Sources*: see under Table 1.1

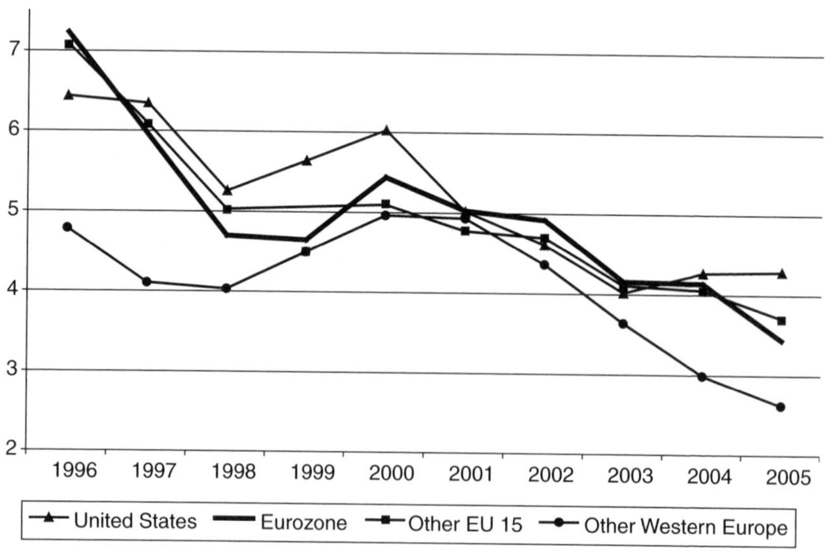

Figure 1.4 Government bond yields
Notes and *Sources*: see under Table 1.1

Paolo Surico focuses on the question of the determinants of inflation in a different perspective, by examining the New Keynesian Phillips curve (NKPC). He uses Monte Carlo simulations of a model where inflation is entirely forward-looking to show that, in a situation where the monetary authority does not ensure that real interest rates rise in response to a rise in inflation, econometric estimates of the NKPC will find, spuriously, a significant backward-looking component. But if the monetary authority responds more than one for one to inflation movements the estimates will correctly find no such significant component. While his emphasis is on how to interpret estimates of the NKPC, and on the nature of inflation persistence, his empirical work on actual data for the eurozone gets essentially the same results as his work on recent data for the UK and the US: inflation seems to be entirely forward-looking, which in his model can be construed as a reflection of the sound anti-inflationary tendency of the monetary policy of all three central banks. Fabrizio Mattesini in his comment raises a number of questions regarding the model-dependence of Surico's 'indeterminacy bias', the extent of the change in US monetary policy between the 1960s–1970s and the later years, and the relation between indeterminacy and inflation persistence.

Bernd Hayo addresses the question of whether interest rates would have been different if EMU had not been created and individual countries had continued to set their own rates in the same way as they did in the preceding decade or so. He does this by regressing Taylor rule equations for each eurozone member and then using the results to predict interest rates on the basis of post-1999 national data on inflation and the output gap. The results are that for almost all countries national interest rates would on average have been higher in the non-EMU case; the exception is Germany where rates would on average have been slightly lower. The clear implication is that low growth in the eurozone cannot be attributed to excessively high interest rates set by the ECB. In his comment on the chapter, Carlo Favero argues that Hayo's Taylor rule estimates are sufficiently imprecise that it may be difficult to put much weight on these conclusions.

Christopher Allsopp and David Vines argue that the ECB's monetary policy is broadly comparable to that in the US and the UK in terms of its focus on price stability and its willingness to allow output to vary around the natural rate in order to control inflation. However, they then focus on the issue of inter-country adjustment within EMU, presenting an informal model to analyse how, in the presence of asymmetric shocks, countries need to use national fiscal policy to adjust their national price levels and hence their real exchange rates *vis-à-vis* other members of the eurozone, and arguing that the constraints of the SGP make the appropriate use of fiscal policy very difficult. In some respects their chapter is a restatement of optimum currency area theory in the context of modern macroeconomic policy thinking, and they offer a highly pessimistic view of the future of EMU. However, as Charles Nolan points out in his comment, they may be dismissing the potential contribution of structural reform along the lines of the Lisbon agenda rather too easily, while asymmetric shocks may be less common than they imagine. It is also worth noting that Paolo Surico's work has shown that under EMU inflation is essentially forward-looking, which would also ease some of Allsopp and Vines's concerns.

Michael Artis and Luca Onorante address the issue of fiscal policy and the SGP from a very different angle. They estimate a structural VAR for the deficit/GDP ratio, the growth rate and inflation in each of the eurozone member countries, and undertake simulations to analyse the likely effects of the original SGP and the recent modifications to it on the variability of output in each country. Their historical analysis finds that discretionary fiscal policy did rather little to stabilise (or destabilise) output in the 1993–2004 period. Indeed they argue that, given the resources and information required to run an optimal fiscal policy and the limited gains from it, in practice it might be sensible to approximate the best policy 'by not using discretionary fiscal policy and simply letting the automatic stabilisers work freely'. Artis and Onorante then show through their simulations that the cost in terms of stabilisation of the original SGP was limited, but the recent modifications to the SGP offer relatively little additional freedom to national fiscal policy. Campbell Leith in his comment argues that there are a number of ways in which the Artis–Onorante analysis may underestimate the potential for fiscal policy to play a useful stabilising role.

Adam Posen and Daniel Gould investigate the extent to which EMU has affected 'wage restraint', that is the difference between real wage growth and productivity growth. They identify the change in wage restraint between 1991–98 and 1999–2004, discuss a range of relevant hypotheses, provide a cross-section analysis of wage restraint in relation to labour market institutions and EMU membership, and then undertake time-series analyses of Germany and Italy. They find that wage restraint did not change much post-EMU in member countries and increased by more in some non-EMU countries. Hypotheses that focus on labour market institutions seem to have little to contribute, and the change in monetary credibility, proxied by the change in the long-term bond rate – particularly large for some countries under EMU – turns out to be the most important determinant of the change in wage restraint. John Driffill's comment offers a wider perspective on the concept and measurement of wage restraint and on possible reasons for some of the results.

Ansgar Belke, Bernhard Herz and Lukas Vogel address the issue of whether EMU has encouraged structural reform of different kinds, by examining the relationship in two wider samples of countries between exchange rate fixity, which they interpret as a lack of monetary policy autonomy, and structural reform. While they find some support from their 'world' sample for the hypothesis that commitment encourages reform, there is little evidence of this in the smaller sample of OECD countries. In other words, EMU should not have been expected to stimulate structural reforms in the member countries and the low level of reform should be understood in that light. Gulcin Ozkan in her comment raises some important questions about the measures of reform used and the different types of reform considered, the relevance of the world sample, and the interpretation of exchange rate fixity as monetary discipline.

Philip Lane and Sébastien Wälti investigate the impact of EMU on financial integration, using both volume-based indicators and evidence from asset prices. They find that financial integration between EMU members has increased significantly, but they also identify a wider process of financial globalisation affecting non-EMU members as well. By examining carefully the time-varying correlation of returns they show that, other common things being equal, returns in EMU countries became more highly correlated from 1998 with a 'rapid, significant and persistent disconnect of correlations'. On the other hand, there are still major barriers to integration in banking at the retail and corporate levels. They also examine the international role of the euro, which has increased importantly in some dimensions but remains much smaller than that of the dollar. Robert Mochrie in his comment provides some useful perspective on and qualifications to the different results the authors have obtained, but emphasises the novel findings on stockmarket correlation as the chapter's key contribution.

Jayasri Dutta and Marco Ercolani provide a detailed study of the extent to which the changeover to euro notes and coin in January 2002 led – as widely believed in some EMU countries – to significant increases in prices and inflation. Using data disaggregated by countries and products, they first find only weak evidence of increases at the aggregate level, but go on to examine data for individual product groups and sub-groups. They confirm previous findings and common beliefs that restaurant prices were particularly affected in many countries, and find comparable results for a number of other sub-groups including cinemas and hairdressing salons, mainly but not exclusively in the service sector. Manfredi La Manna in his comment picks up on their discussion of the possible causes of these effects. He dismisses the menu cost explanation but presents a simple Bertrand duopoly model for a local oligopoly which offers some predictions in line with Dutta and Ercolani's results, but also emphasises the issue of the substitutability/complementarity of the products involved.

Miroslav Beblavý analyses the issues and problems involved in EMU accession for the Central and East European new members of the European Union. Beblavý shows that public opinion is by no means entirely favourable to EMU entry, but these countries have in effect signed up to entering EMU when they fulfil the Maastricht conditions, so his analysis then focuses on those conditions. It turns out that for most countries the most difficult conditions are the fiscal deficit and inflation conditions rather than the debt or interest rate ones. Beblavý relates countries' fiscal deficits to their fundamental political choices with regard to the size of the welfare states which they are trying to create, on the one hand, and their willingness and ability to levy taxes on the other. Inflation is something of a lottery (partly because the critical level is low and somewhat erratic, since it depends on the levels in the lowest members of the EU, rather than EMU), and is particularly problematic for some of the Baltic countries where the use of currency boards has prevented nominal appreciation of a kind which could help to minimise inflation in the context of strong tendencies to appreciation of the (equilibrium and actual) real exchange rate. The exchange rate stability criterion, on the other hand, is viewed in the new accession countries as unavoidable but irrelevant or potentially dangerous. In his comments on the paper, Atanas Christev notes the advantages of a wider, micro-founded and welfare-based assessment of alternative exchange rate regimes, and stresses the importance of popular support for accession to EMU.

Finally, Ali Al-Eyd, Ray Barrell and Dawn Holland investigate one of the most striking macro phenomena of the EMU period, the euro's initial depreciation against the dollar and its later stronger appreciation. They explain the background in terms of movements in sectoral balances and different types of capital flows, and then, using a portfolio-balance approach, try to identify influences upon the *ex post* risk premium in the uncovered interest parity relationship between the US and the euro area. Although changes in net foreign asset positions and monetary and fiscal policy 'news' can explain some of the movements in the risk premium, there remains a large element of pure noise. However, their analysis leads them to conclude that the exchange rate movements were driven largely by US rather than eurozone developments (which goes against much of the early commentary on the euro's depreciation). Jacques Mélitz in his comment argues that the analysis would be more convincing if it included Japan and China, the US's two largest net creditors, rather than just the US and the eurozone.

What overall judgment can we reach on the travails of the eurozone in its first seven years? It seems clear that on the monetary side the judgment of the EMU project so far has to be strongly positive: the institutional changes (including the notes and coin changeover) were made efficiently, the ECB operates monetary policy broadly like other competent modern central banks, and it is hard to claim that excessively tight monetary policy has impeded growth. Moreover, there is some evidence that the strong swings in the euro's exchange rate have reflected US policy actions and developments rather than eurozone ones. Fiscal policy remains a more controversial issue: in this volume Allsopp and Vines emphasise a problem to which other economists have so far paid relatively little attention, while Artis and Onorante write with a very different (and less apocalyptic) focus and perspective. On structural reform there is widespread agreement that there has so far been less reform than is desirable (though financial integration has deepened significantly), and there is slightly less widespread agreement that the low level of reform is a major contributor to the slow growth of the eurozone. However, it is important here to separate actions from words, since governments (for example in Germany and Italy) do not always act in accordance with their pronouncements, and in any case the aggregate development of the eurozone has been rather better than some commentators suggest.

Furthermore, in evaluating the achievements of the EMU project so far it is essential to choose the appropriate counterfactual (a point well made by Jacques Mélitz at the conference): if EMU had not taken place the member countries would almost certainly not be operating good modern monetary policy like the Federal Reserve Board or the post-1997 Bank of England, nor would they even be doing just what they were doing in the period between 1993 and 1998. Instead, it is likely that in many (but not all) of the EMU member countries monetary and fiscal policy would be less disciplined, inflation higher, output more variable and growth lower. Moreover, the existence and implementation of the EMU project has without doubt provided an important focus and anchor for the new accession countries in Central and Eastern Europe. In this light some of the criticisms made of the EMU project are only of second order importance, and the emphasis placed upon them underlines the progress made on first order issues.

Those favourable to EMU will inevitably feel more comfortable when there is firmer evidence of economic recovery and successful structural reform. But in the meantime the travails of the eurozone should be kept in perspective: they may be deeper and more prolonged than predictable teething problems, but they cannot detract from what is clearly a strong and successful project.

2

Understanding the Link between Money Growth and Inflation in the Euro Area

*Katrin Assenmacher-Wesche and Stefan Gerlach**

Introduction

In preparation for the establishment of European Monetary Union in January 1999, the European Central Bank (ECB) decided to adopt a monetary policy strategy consisting of two main elements or 'pillars'. The first of these was *'a prominent role for money with a reference value for the growth of a monetary aggregate'*, subsequently defined to be 4.5 per cent annual growth of M3, and the second *'a broadly-based assessment of the outlook for future price developments'.*[1] From the outset this two-pillar framework was controversial. One explanation for this might have been that the ECB provided neither an explicit representation of the inflation process nor a motivation for why it necessitated a two-pillar framework. Whatever the reasons, many observers misinterpreted the two pillars as combining monetary and inflation targeting, and criticised the framework for being inconsistent and lacking clarity.

Recently several authors have presented empirical models that provide a formal interpretation of the two pillars by incorporating money growth in a reduced-form Phillips-curve model for inflation. The monetary and the economic pillars of the ECB's framework are in these models viewed as reflecting different time perspectives on the determination of inflation. While money growth impacts on inflation in the long run, real economic indicators such as the output gap and cost-push factors influence inflation in the short run. This notion of different time horizons in the determinants

*We are grateful to Michael Sumner (our discussant) and conference participants for helpful comments and to Björn Fischer for data. The views expressed are solely our own and are not necessarily shared by the SNB or the BIS. Contact information: Katrin Assenmacher-Wesche: SNB, Börsenstrasse 15, Postfach 2800, CH-8022 Zürich, Switzerland, Tel +41446313824, email: Katrin.Assenmacher-Wesche@snb.ch; Stefan Gerlach: BIS, CH-4002 Basel, Switzerland, tel: +41612808523, email: Stefan.Gerlach@bis.org.

of inflation is emphasised by the ECB in its recent review of the monetary policy strategy. For instance, in an article in the June 2003 *Monthly Bulletin* on the outcome of its evaluation of the strategy, the ECB (2003, p. 87) writes:

> An important argument in favour of adopting the two-pillar approach relates to the difference in the time perspective for analysing price developments. The inflation process can be broadly decomposed into two components, one associated with the interplay between demand and supply factors at high frequency, and the other connected to more drawn-out and persistent trends. The latter is empirically closely associated with the medium-term trend growth of money.

Of course, the ECB is not the only central bank that finds it useful to distinguish between frequency bands in analysing inflation. In discussing the new monetary concept introduced by the Swiss National Bank in 2000, Jordan, Peytrignet and Rich (2001, p. 48) emphasise the importance of the time horizon in analysing inflation:[2]

> The SNB... continues to monitor two sets of indicators providing leading information on future price developments ... The first set of indicators is useful for forecasting short-run price developments ... It includes various indicators on the cyclical state of the economy, notably the output gap and supply and demand conditions in the labour market, as well as the real exchange rate of the Swiss franc. The second set of indicators comprises the monetary aggregates, which provide useful leading information on long-run price developments... Both sets of indicators are used together with the forecasts from various econometric models to produce a broadly based consensus inflation forecast, which now forms the centre stage of Swiss monetary policy.

In this chapter we review the literature that seeks to formalise this understanding of the inflation process and present some additional evidence on the determination of inflation in the euro area. The chapter is organised as follows. The next section starts by providing a highly stylised example of why it may be difficult to detect the impact of money growth on inflation. The essence of the argument is that changes in the average (or 'trend') growth rate of money over some period of time determine the average rate of inflation in the same period. However, changes in this trend occur gradually and may therefore be difficult to identify. Moreover, since only a small part of the variations in 'headline' money growth are due to changes in the trend, it is not surprising that 'headline' money growth tends to be insignificant in inflation equations. Thus, econometric work may underestimate the importance of money for inflation. The section goes on to review the papers of Gerlach (2003), Neumann (2003), Neumann and Greiber (2004), Gerlach (2004) and Assenmacher-Wesche and Gerlach (2006), which focus on this mechanism. The following two sections presents the econometric methodology, the data and the results.[3] Extending previous work, we offer new empirical evidence on the determinants of inflation at different time horizons. We find that changes in the exchange rate, the price of oil and import prices are statistically highly significant in euro-area inflation equations but that they do not appear to change the earlier findings that money growth and the output gap matter. While the output gap is informative for frequencies above one year, our analysis shows that the cost-push variables can explain inflation at higher frequencies. The final section concludes.

Modelling the two pillars

As a preliminary, it is useful to consider a simple empirical Phillips curve of the form:

$$\pi_t = \alpha_0 + \alpha_\pi \pi_{t-1} + \alpha_g g_{t-1} + \varepsilon_t \tag{2.1}$$

according to which inflation, π_t, depends on its own lagged value, the lagged output gap, g_{t-1}, and a residual, ε_t, which can be interpreted as capturing cost-push shocks. Next, we consider the average (or 'trend') rate of inflation in a time span which is sufficiently long for the output gap and the residual to average to zero:

$$\bar{\pi}_t = \alpha_0 / (1 - \alpha_\pi) \tag{2.2}$$

where a bar denotes the average value. Before interpreting equation (2.2), note that the deviation of inflation from its average rate in the time period in question is given by:

$$(\pi_t - \bar{\pi}_t) = \alpha_\pi (\pi_{t-1} - \bar{\pi}_t) + \alpha_g g_{t-1} + \varepsilon_t \tag{2.3}$$

According to equation (2.2) and provided that the persistence in the inflation process, α_π, is constant, the average rate of inflation over the period considered is captured by the constant in the Phillips curve, α_0. Thus, in periods when inflation was high, such as in the 1970s and the early 1980s, estimates of equation (2.1) will yield a relatively large constant. Furthermore, in periods when the average rate of inflation was relatively low, such as the late 1990s and early 2000s, the constant will be small. Econometrically, this model may 'explain' movements in inflation quite well if estimated in a sample period in which the average rate of inflation is well-defined and constant. Economically, however, it will be much less satisfactory in that it is unable to account for changes in the average rate of inflation over time. For it to be able to do so, some hypothesis about the determination of α_0 must be added. To anticipate the discussion below, models that seek to motivate the use of the two-pillar strategy argue that the average growth rate of money, perhaps adjusted for the average growth rate of output and changes in velocity, plays an important role in determining α_0.[4] Thus, changes in the average rate of inflation are attributed to changes in monetary conditions.[5]

Equation (2.3) holds that variations of inflation around its mean are due to movements in the output gap and to supply shocks. Interestingly, if the average rate of inflation is constant in the sample, perhaps because detrended data are used, variables that determine average inflation will be insignificant if included in the regression, leading the econometrician to infer incorrectly that they play no role in the inflation process.

With this as background we turn to a discussion of the different models that have been proposed as interpretations of the two-pillar strategy.

Gerlach (2003)

In what may be the first paper that sought to provide a formal description of the two-pillar framework, Gerlach (2003) used a simple exponential filter to compute an estimate, $\tilde{\pi}_t$, of $\bar{\pi}_t$ and to compute a similar estimate, $\tilde{\mu}_t$, of the average or trend growth rate of money $\bar{\mu}_t$. For some time series x_t, the filter is given by

$$\tilde{x}_t = \tilde{x}_{t-1} + \lambda\,(x_t - \tilde{x}_{t-1}) \tag{2.4}$$

or

$$\tilde{x}_t = \lambda \sum_{j=0}^{\infty} (1 - \lambda)^j x_{t-j} \tag{2.5}$$

Equation (2.5) warrants four comments. First, Cogley (2002) shows that depending on the choice of the smoothing parameter, λ, the filter removes the high-frequency variation of a time series. Gerlach (2003) consequently thinks of $\tilde{x}_t$ as an estimate of the low-frequency component of the series. The smoothing parameter captures the speed by which a once-and-for-all change in x_t impacts on $\tilde{x}_t$. In particular, $\ln(2)/\lambda$ captures the half-life of this adjustment. Gerlach (2003) conducts the analysis under the assumption that $\lambda = 0.075$, which corresponds to a half-life of about 9.2 quarters.

Second, there is no reason to assume that this estimate of $\bar{x}_t$ is optimal. In fact, much of the work in the subsequent literature has aimed at constructing better estimates of, or using better methods to model, the low-frequency components of inflation and the other variables involved in the analysis.

Third, since the estimate of the trend is an infinite moving average of the data, it evolves slowly over time. Given the value of the smoothing parameter used by Gerlach (2003), the ratio of the variance of changes in $\tilde{x}_t$ to the variance of changes in x_t is trivially small.[6] Headline data therefore contain little information about fluctuations in the trend.

Fourth, this filter is one-sided in that it only uses past information to form an estimate of the low-frequency component of the series. This has the notable advantage of making the filter operational in real time.

Using synthetic quarterly data for the euro area for 1980–2001, Gerlach goes on to estimate a version of equation (2.3) that incorporates two lags of inflation and the contemporaneous output gap among the regressors, and finds that the output gap has a large impact on $\pi_t - \tilde{\pi}_t$, which he interprets as a measure of the high-frequency component of inflation. Next he assumes that the inflation trend is determined in accordance with the quantity theory:

$$\tilde{\pi}_t = \theta_0 + \theta_1 (\tilde{\mu}_t - \tilde{\gamma}_t) + \zeta_t \tag{2.6}$$

where $\tilde{\mu}_t$ denotes the low-frequency component of money growth and $\tilde{\gamma}_t$ that of output growth, and where $\theta_1 = 1$ if shocks to velocity are uncorrelated with money growth. By combining equations (2.3) and (2.6), Gerlach obtains the estimate $\hat{\theta}_1 = 0.84$ (with a standard error of 0.09), which is compatible with the notion that trend money growth determines the average rate of inflation in some time span.

To understand the link between this model and the two-pillar strategy of the ECB, note that the model augments a standard reduced-form empirical Phillips curve with a measure of the low-frequency component of money growth, which is obtained by filtering money growth. Sustained changes in money growth will shift the Phillips curve vertically, generating changes in the steady-state rate of inflation. The ECB's monetary pillar can therefore be best seen as an approach to predict the average rate of inflation over some time period. By contrast, changes in the output gap, which by construction are temporary, will generate variations in inflation around that steady state. The economic analysis, the ECB's second pillar, can thus be seen as a method to predict short-run movements in inflation around its average level at a point in time, which highlights that the two pillars pertain to different time horizons.

Neumann (2003)

Neumann (2003) follows the analysis of Gerlach (2003), but sharpens it in important ways. In particular, he assumes that current inflation depends on inflation expectations formed last period:

$$\pi_t = \pi_t^e + \alpha_g g_{t-1} + \varepsilon_t \tag{2.7}$$

and adds an expectations-formations mechanism of the form:

$$\pi_t^e = \bar{\pi}_{t-1} + \alpha_e (\pi_{t-1} - \bar{\pi}_{t-1}) \tag{2.8}$$

where $\bar{\pi}_t$ is referred to as the 'core' rate of inflation. From a standard money demand relationship, he derives that:

$$\bar{\pi}_t = \bar{\mu}_t - \alpha_\gamma \bar{\gamma}_t \tag{2.9}$$

Thus, the core rate of inflation depends on the 'core' rate of money growth minus the 'core' rate of output growth, multiplied by the income elasticity of money demand, α_γ. Thus, he relaxes the assumption that the income elasticity of money demand is unity. This leads to an inflation equation of the form:

$$\pi_t = (1 - \alpha_e)(\bar{\mu}_{t-1} - \alpha_\gamma \bar{\gamma}_{t-1}) + \alpha_e \pi_{t-1} + \alpha_g g_{t-1} + \varepsilon_t \quad (2.10)$$

To fit this equation, estimates of the core rates of money and output growth are required. To obtain these Neumann (2003) uses the Hodrick–Prescott (HP) filter. Since this filter is two-sided, incorporating both past and future values of the filtered variable, it seems plausible that it leads to better estimates of the low-frequency component than a one-sided filter. Of course, if the purpose is to analyse the role of money growth for inflation in the past, this is desirable. By contrast, if the purpose is to forecast future inflation, a one-sided filter may be better.[7]

A second reason why a one-sided filter may be preferable is that a two-sided filter can lead to inconsistent estimates of the model's parameters. Least-squares estimators are only consistent if the error term is uncorrelated with the explanatory variables. In the case of a two-sided estimate of $\bar{\mu}_t$, this requires future observations of μ_t to be uncorrelated with π_t. Thus, there may be no feedback from inflation to money growth. This problem does not arise with a one-sided filter.[8]

Neumann (2003) proceeds to estimate the model on quarterly data for the period 1986–2002 and finds that it fits well, in particular when he controls for the change in velocity observed in the second half of 2001.

Neumann and Greiber (2004)

Neumann and Greiber (2004) extend the analysis in Neumann (2003) by incorporating oil prices as a measure of cost-push shocks, and find them to be highly significant. More importantly, they use four methods to compute core money growth: the Hodrick-Prescott filter, the exponential filter of Cogley (2002), the band-pass filter of Baxter and King (1999) and wavelet analysis.[9] They conclude that these filters lead to similar estimates of core money growth, but conclude that the exponential filter performs less well since it leads to an implausibly high estimate of the income elasticity of money demand.[10] Interestingly, the output gap is only significant when the exponential filter is used, and it is therefore dropped from the other regressions. Neumann and Greiber (2004) also study what frequency bands of money growth are most important and conclude that fluctuations of a periodicity of less than eight years do not seem to matter for inflation.

Gerlach (2004)

Gerlach (2004) provides a more refined version of the Gerlach (2003) model. First, the Phillips curve is extended to include expectations of future inflation, π^e_{t+1}:

$$\pi_t = (1 - \alpha_\pi)\pi^e_{t+1} + \alpha_\pi\pi_{t-1} + \alpha_g g_{t-1} + \varepsilon_t \tag{2.11}$$

Second, and as asserted by the ECB, the expected future rate of inflation is assumed to depend on trend money growth, $\tilde{\mu}_t$, using the exponential filter discussed above.[12] Under these assumptions it is possible to derive an inflation equation of the form:

$$\pi_t = \beta_1\mu_{t-1} + \beta_2 g_{t-1} + \beta_3\pi_{t-1} + \beta_4 g_{t-2} + \beta_5\pi_{t-2} + e_t \tag{2.12}$$

where the β-parameters are functions of the α-parameters in equation (2.11) and the smoothing parameter λ in equation (2.5), and where the residuals obey a first-order moving-average process with a coefficient of –(1–λ). The smoothing parameter can consequently be estimated jointly with the other parameters of the model. Fitting the equation on the sample period 1992–2003, Gerlach (2004) does not reject the overriding restrictions and finds that inflation in the euro area appears to be entirely forward looking. The estimated value of the smoothing parameter is 0.09, with a standard error of 0.02, which is close to the value assumed by Gerlach (2003). Furthermore, the data prefer a specification in which past money growth rates, rather than past inflation rates, determine inflation expectations.

Of course, the assumption that money growth determines inflation expectations should be taken with a grain of salt, and the equation is arguably best interpreted as a reduced-form forecasting model. However, it establishes that past low-frequency movements in money growth contain information that is useful for understanding inflation, and that this information is not embedded in past inflation rates.

Assenmacher-Wesche and Gerlach (2006)

The studies reviewed above use relatively simple approaches to construct measures of the 'trend', 'core' or 'low-frequency' components of inflation, money growth and output growth. Moreover, with the exception of Gerlach (2004), these measures are all computed in a step preliminary to estimation. Since the ECB has motivated the two-pillar strategy by arguing that the determinants of inflation vary by time horizon or frequency, Assenmacher-Wesche and Gerlach (2006), AWG in what follows, find it natural to use band spectral regression methods that integrate the filtering and estimation stages. More importantly, the use of advanced econometric techniques makes it possible to study the inflation process in the euro area at specific frequencies and thus permits a better understanding of the role of money in the inflation process.

Since we extend AWG's analysis below, it is useful to review it in some detail. AWG start by decomposing inflation, π_t, into low-frequency (*LF*) and high-frequency (*HF*) components:

$$\pi_t = \pi_t^{LF} + \pi_t^{HF} \tag{2.13}$$

and hypothesise that the high-frequency movements of inflation are related to movements in the output gap:

$$\pi_t^{HF} = \alpha_g g_{t-1} + \varepsilon_t^{HF} \tag{2.14}$$

By construction, the output gap has no low-frequency variation, which implies that it can at most explain temporary changes in the rate of inflation. Next, AWG assume that the low-frequency variation of inflation can be understood in terms of the quantity theory of money:[12]

$$\pi_t^{LF} = \alpha_\mu \mu_t^{LF} + \alpha_\gamma \gamma_t^{LF} + \alpha_\nu \nu_t^{LF} + \varepsilon_t^{LF} \tag{2.15}$$

where ν_t denotes the rate of change of velocity, which they assume depends on the change of the long-term interest rate, ρ_t:[13]

$$\nu_t^{LF} = \tilde{\alpha}_\rho \rho_t^{LF} + \varepsilon_t^{\nu,LF} \tag{2.16}$$

Equation (2.15) warrants three comments. First, at low frequencies, the growth rate of real output is identical to the growth rate of potential. AWG therefore define the output gap as the (logarithmic) difference between current output and the low-frequency component of output. In this chapter, we use the Hodrick–Prescott filter to compute potential output and show that the results are not affected by the particular definition of the output gap. Second, under the quantity theory, and provided that money growth is uncorrelated with velocity shocks at low frequencies (that is, μ_t^{LF} and $\varepsilon_t^{\nu,LF}$ are orthogonal), we expect that $\alpha_\mu = -\alpha_\gamma = 1$. Third, since velocity is defined using the levels of money, output and prices, equation (2.15) is in fact an identity and can be written $\pi_t^{LF} \equiv \mu_t^{LF} + \gamma_t^{LF} - \nu_t^{LF}$. It is the assumption that changes in velocity depend on changes in the long-term interest rates that renders the relationship inexact.

The full model is given by:

$$\pi_t = \alpha_g g_{t-1} + \{\alpha_\mu \mu_t^{LF} + \alpha_\gamma \gamma_t^{LF} + \alpha_\rho \rho_t^{LF}\} + \varepsilon_t \tag{2.17}$$

where $\varepsilon_t = \varepsilon_t^{LF} + \alpha_\nu \varepsilon_t^{\nu,LF} + \varepsilon_t^{HF}$ and $\alpha_\rho \equiv \alpha_\nu \tilde{\alpha}_\rho$. According to this model, the average rate of inflation during some period is given by the term in curly brackets, { }, that is, by the low-frequency part of money growth relative to real output growth and changes in the long-term interest rate, which AWG think of as the first pillar. Variation in inflation around that average is determined by movements in the output gap, which is seen as shorthand for the second pillar. In analysing and forecasting inflation it is appropriate to consider low-frequency, as opposed to 'headline', movements in money growth.

Since the present chapter extends the analysis in AWG, the results are similar and we therefore do not discuss the details of that paper here.[14] In brief, AWG find that money growth relative to output growth matters at low frequencies, and the output gap at high frequencies, for inflation. Furthermore, testing in the frequency domain, they find that these correlations in both cases reflect causality (in the predictive sense).

Estimation

As noted above, AWG show that quantity-theoretic variables (that is, money and real output growth, and changes in long interest rates) determine inflation in the long run, whereas the output gap accounts for short-run variations of the inflation rate. Neither group of variables, however, is able to account for movements in inflation in the euro area at periodicities of less than 1 or 2 years. One likely explanation is that in the very short run inflation is affected by a range of cost-push shocks stemming from exchange rate movements, changes in oil prices or import prices. It is therefore desirable to extend the analysis by incorporating also these factors.

Following AWG, we hypothesise that the high-frequency movements of inflation are related to once-lagged movements in the output gap, g_t, but also include cost-push factors, c_t:

$$\pi_t^{HF} = \alpha_g g_{t-1} + \alpha_c c_t + \varepsilon_t^{HF} \tag{2.18}$$

Since the transmission from the output gap to inflation takes time, we assume a one-quarter lag.[15] Though we hypothesise that cost-push factors influence inflation at high frequencies, at lower frequencies reverse causality seems plausible. Thus, a change in the overall inflation environment is likely to lead to a depreciation of the exchange rate, and thus to rising import prices, including for oil. We therefore expect to find the cost-push variables also to be significant, but not necessarily causal for inflation, in the low-frequency regressions.

The full model is given by:

$$\pi_t = \alpha_g g_{t-1} + \alpha_c c_t + \{\alpha_\mu \mu_t^{LF} + \alpha_\gamma \gamma_t^{LF} + \alpha_\rho \rho_t^{LF}\} + \varepsilon_t \tag{12.9}$$

where $\varepsilon_t = \varepsilon_t^{LF} + \alpha_v \varepsilon_t^{v,LF} + \varepsilon_t^{HF}$ and $\alpha_\rho \equiv \alpha_v \tilde{\alpha}_\rho$.

The data

The availability of long time series for the euro area is still limited. To investigate cost-push factors we are therefore restricted to the series available in the database for the ECB's area-wide model (Fagan *et al.*, 2005).[16] The sample period runs from 1970Q1 to 2003Q4. As a preliminary step to the formal econometric analysis below we review the raw data. Since the original HICP data are not seasonally adjusted, we first deseasonalised the rate of inflation by removing a frequency band around the seasonal peaks.[17] This obviates the need to model the seasonal dynamics in the regressions below.

The first column of Figure 2.1 presents a plot of the quarterly rate of inflation using the seasonally adjusted data, the quarterly rate of money growth as measured by M3, the quarterly change in the government bond yield, and the quarterly rate of real income growth, all for the period 1970Q2 to 2003Q4. The figure shows that inflation rose in the early 1970s and remained high and volatile before declining in the early 1980s. Since

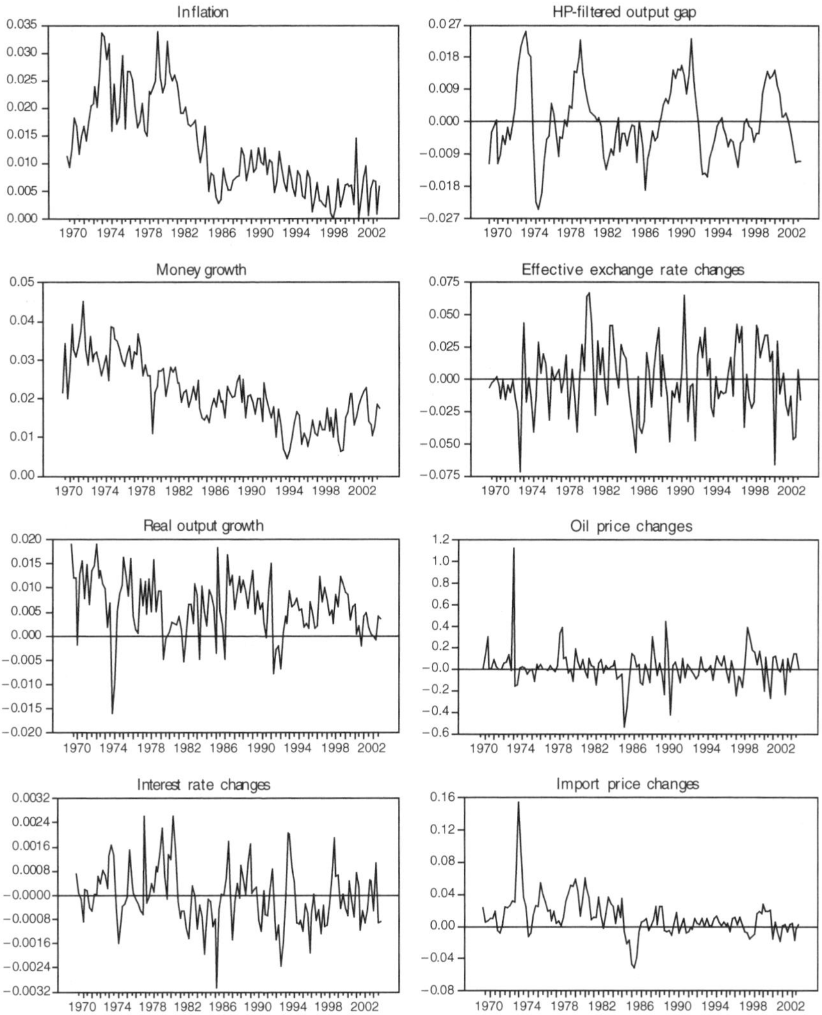

Figure 2.1 Data

the mid-1980s, inflation has fluctuated around a roughly constant level. It is evident that the fall in inflation was associated with a gradual decline in money growth over the sample as central banks took measures to disinflate after the sharp increase in inflation during the 1970s. The change in the long-term interest rate lies slightly above its mean in the 1970s and below thereafter, with persistent fluctuations.[18] Finally, real income growth was quite volatile over the sample. However, there is some evidence that the rate of growth of output has declined, as evidenced by the fact that output growth was below average in most quarters in the 1990s. Next we turn to the output gap, using the Hodrick–Prescott (HP) filter to construct a measure of the trend output.[19] The main movements of the output gap are associated with the large recession around 1974 following the first oil shock, and the recession in 1992–93.

The last three panels in Figure 2.1 show the cost-push variables, which are all measured as log first differences. While the average change of the nominal effective exchange rate was almost zero in the sample considered, the rise and the subsequent fall of the US dollar against the European currencies in the 1980s can be seen in the mainly positive changes during the early 1980s and negative changes in the second half of the 1980s.[20] The graph for oil prices, measured in terms of (synthetic) euros, shows several spikes in the early 1970s, and a peak in 1979 corresponding to the second oil shock.[21] The collapse in oil prices in 1986, which was associated with a sharp fall in inflation in the euro area, is also readily apparent. Turning to the rate of change of import prices, we see clearly the impact of changes in oil prices, suggesting that the series contain similar information. In contrast to the oil price series, the rate of change of import prices shows a slight downward trend, corresponding to the reduction in global inflation during the past thirty years.

Long-run and short-run characteristics of the data

To obtain an impression of the cost-push data and their relation to the rate of inflation, Figure 2.2 plots the low-frequency and high-frequency part of the series separately. The cut-off between low and high frequencies is chosen to be 4 years. While this choice is arbitrary, AWG show that it provides a reasonable distinction between the long run and the short run.

We consider first the low-frequency behaviour of the cost-push variables in the left-hand panel. Note that in the long run neither exchange rate changes nor oil price changes are closely tied to inflation. By contrast, the rate of change of import prices declines over time in much the same way as inflation. Turning to the high-frequency band in the right-hand panel, we note that there appears to be a strong positive correlation with inflation. This is compatible with the notion that changes in exchange rates, oil prices and import prices exert cost-push effects on inflation. We next proceed to a more formal analysis of the determinants of inflation at different frequencies.

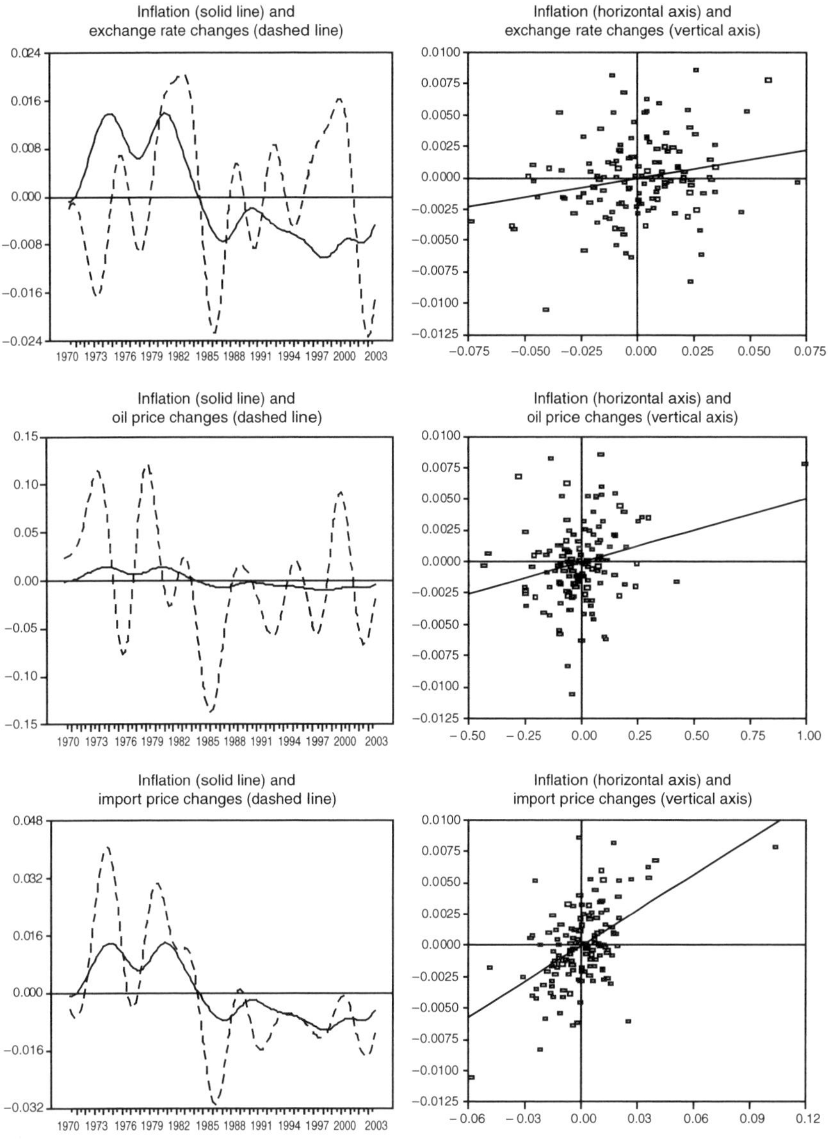

Figure 2.2 Changes in cost-push variables and inflation at low and high frequency

Unit-root tests

Figures 2.1 and 2.2 suggest that inflation and money growth may be non-stationary but that the other series appear stationary. Since stationary variables, which by definition do not experience permanent shocks, cannot

Table 2.2 Cointegration analysis

Rank	*Eigenvalues*	*Trace test*	*95% critical values*
$r = 0$	0.136	20.81	20.26
$r = 1$	0.014	1.78	9.16
Parameters	*Inflation*	*Money growth*	*Constant*
β unrestricted	1	−1.093	0.023
	(–)	(0.149)	(0.003)
β restricted	1	−1	0.021
	(–)	(–)	(0.001)
α (for restricted β)	−0.200	0.133	–
	(0.048)	(0.071)	

Note: The model includes a constant that is restricted to lie in the cointegration space. The sample period is 1970Q2 to 2004Q4. The Akaike criterion suggests the inclusion of 5 lags. A likelihood-ratio test does not reject the overidentifying restriction on the cointegration vector, β ($\chi(1) = 0.35$ and a p-value of 0.56). The adjustment coefficients are denoted with α and r is the rank of the long-run matrix, Π.

and money growth at the zero frequency using the band spectral estimator proposed by Phillips (1991) for nonstationary time series. The advantage of the strategy pursued here is that it is considerably easier to implement.

Results

Cointegration results

Table 2.2 shows the results from the cointegration analysis of the nonstationary variables, inflation and money growth.[24] The trace statistic indicates the presence of a single cointegrating relation at the 95 per cent significance level. Since the coefficient on money growth is close to one, we test the hypothesis of a unit coefficient with a likelihood-ratio test and find that the restriction is not rejected ($\chi^2(1) = 0.35$, $p = 0.56$). The loading coefficients, α, imply that inflation increases if the linear combination $\mu_{t-1} - \pi_{t-1}$ is positive. In contrast, there is no adjustment from money growth towards equilibrium.[25] We therefore impose the unit restriction on money growth and continue the analysis of the long-run determinants of inflation using the difference between inflation and money growth as the dependent variable.[26] Since output growth, changes in interest rates, the lagged output gap and changes in cost-push variables appear stationary, standard frequency domain methods can be applied.

Band spectrum regression: low frequencies

Next we turn to the estimates that are obtained using the band spectral regression method of Engle (1974). In Table 2.3 we consider the results at

Table 2.3 Band spectrum regressions: low-frequency band (4 years to infinity)

	Dependent variable: $\pi_t - \mu_t$				
Quantity-theoretic variables					
Output growth	−1.07**	−0.87**	−0.92**	−1.21**	−0.99**
	(0.19)	(0.27)	(0.18)	(0.19)	(0.20)
Interest rate change	4.05**	1.97	3.50**	2.91*	1.95
	(1.07)	(1.18)	(1.19)	(1.35)	(1.40)
Output gap (lagged 1 quarter)		0.02	0.02	−0.08	−0.02
		(0.10)	(0.07)	(0.06)	(0.06)
Cost-push variables					
Exchange rate changes		0.11*	0.13**		
		(0.05)	(0.05)		
Oil price changes ($\times 10^2$)		−0.31		2.65*	
		(2.06)		(1.18)	
Import price changes		0.09			0.11**
		(0.05)			(0.04)
$\bar{R}^2$	0.52	0.53	0.56	0.51	0.55

Note: All regressions include a constant which is not shown. Standard errors in parentheses; * indicates significance at the 5% level, ** significance at the 1% level. The sample period is 1970Q2 to 2003Q4. The number of degrees of freedom is 14 for the regression in the first column, 10 for the second column and 12 for the other columns.

low frequencies, defined as the frequency band corresponding to periodicities of between 4 years and infinity. As discussed above, the dependent variable in these regressions is the difference between inflation and money growth. The first column shows the results for a regression in which only the quantity-theoretic variables are included. We obtain a coefficient on output growth that is significantly different from zero but not from minus unity. The coefficient on the change in the interest rate is positive and highly significant. This suggests that higher interest rates reduce the demand for money so that, given the rate of money growth, inflation rises.

Of course, the finding that inflation, money growth, output growth and changes in interest rates are closely linked at low frequencies could simply reflect a money demand relationship. If so, the correlation between money growth and inflation would reflect causality from inflation to money. To explore whether this is indeed the case, we next investigate the feedback patterns, relying on the notion of causality introduced by Granger (1969). In the bivariate case, a variable is said to cause inflation if it contains information about future inflation that is not contained in past realisations of inflation. The extent and direction of causality can differ between frequency bands (Granger and Lin, 1995).[27] The empirical analysis below is based on the frequency-wise measure of causality suggested by Geweke (1982) and Hosoya (1991). Since it is important to account for possible feedback from third variables, we include, in addition to money growth and inflation, the other quantity-theoretic variables in the analysis.[28] For causality tests the lag length should neither be too short, since this may cut off significant coefficients, nor too long, since in this case the tests may lack power. We perform the tests with a lag length of 12.[29]

Figure 2.3 shows the frequency-wise measure of causality, where on the x-axis we have plotted the frequency, ω, measured in fractions of π (so that periodicity, measured in quarters, is given by $2\pi/\omega$).[30] At low frequencies money growth clearly causes inflation while there may be causality from inflation to money growth at periodicities higher than 1 year (that is, 0.5π).[31]

In the second column of Table 2.3 we include the output gap and all the cost-push variables in addition to the quantity-theoretic variables in the low-frequency regression. The results show again that output growth is significantly different from zero and that the hypothesis that the coefficient is minus unity, as the quantity theory would lead us to expect, cannot be rejected. Furthermore, the output gap is insignificant, indicating that it does not account for inflation at low frequencies. Turning to the cost-push variables, we note that, except for the change in the exchange rate, they are insignificant, as is the change in the interest rate.

Since the three cost-push variables are likely to be correlated, we consider them individually in columns 3 to 5. We find that the parameter on output

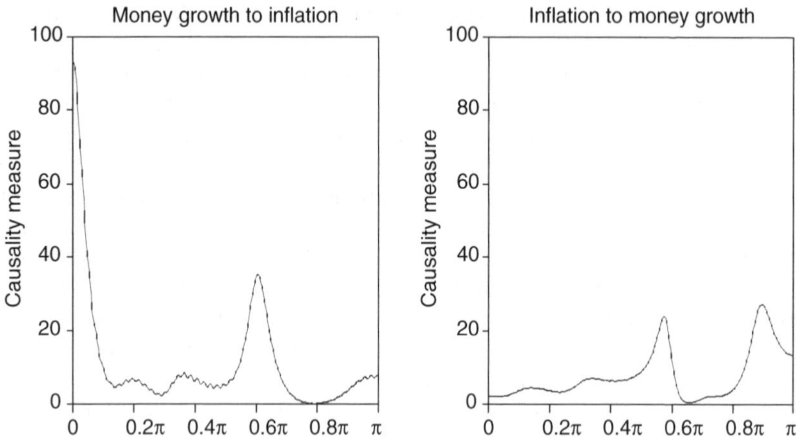

Figure 2.3 Money growth: frequency-wise causality measure

growth remains significant and close to minus unity. Furthermore, the parameter on the change in the interest rate is positive and significant, except in column 5 in which import prices are used to capture cost-push shocks. Interestingly, the cost-push variables are all significant when included separately.

Again, we investigate the pattern of causality between inflation and the variables that we expect to determine inflation in the medium to short run.[32] Since including all variables together is not possible, we include one cost-push variable at a time. Moreover, when examining the role of the

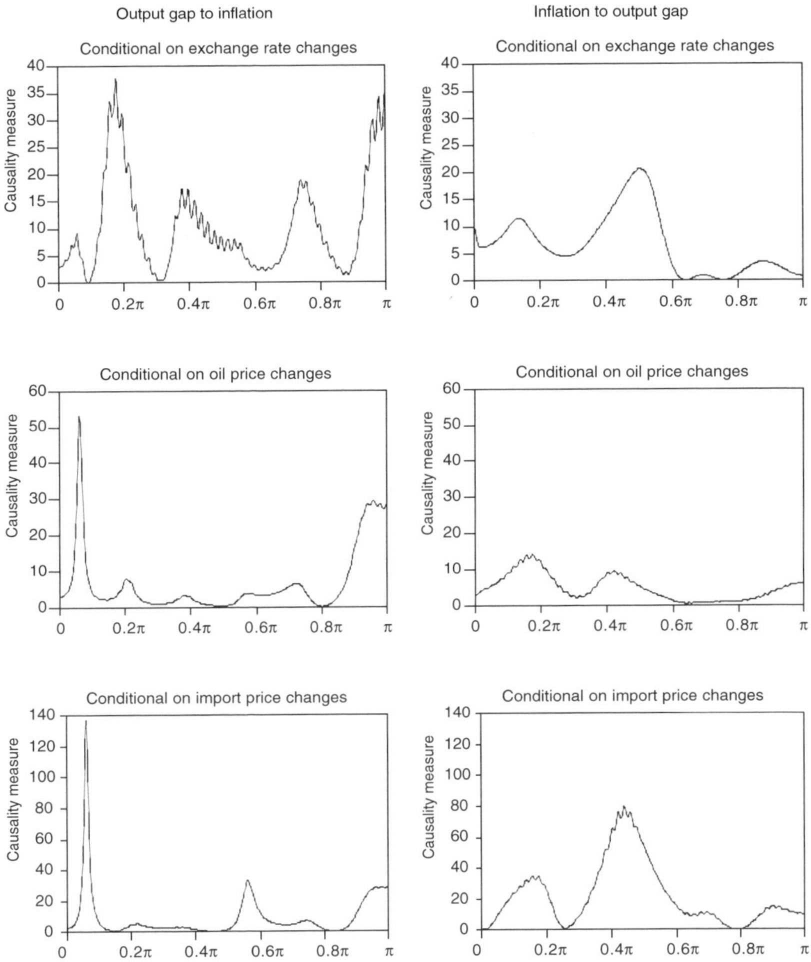

Figure 2.4 Output gap: frequency-wise causality measure

output gap we do not consider output growth since these variables are correlated at higher frequencies. Figure 2.4 shows that the output gap causes inflation at business cycle frequencies of 0.075π (which corresponds to a periodicity of about 7 years). In contrast, inflation causes the output gap mainly at the annual frequency.

Rapid money growth in the euro area is likely to lead to both inflation and exchange rate depreciation. Since the cost-push variables all depend on the evolution of the exchange rate, the finding that they are significant at

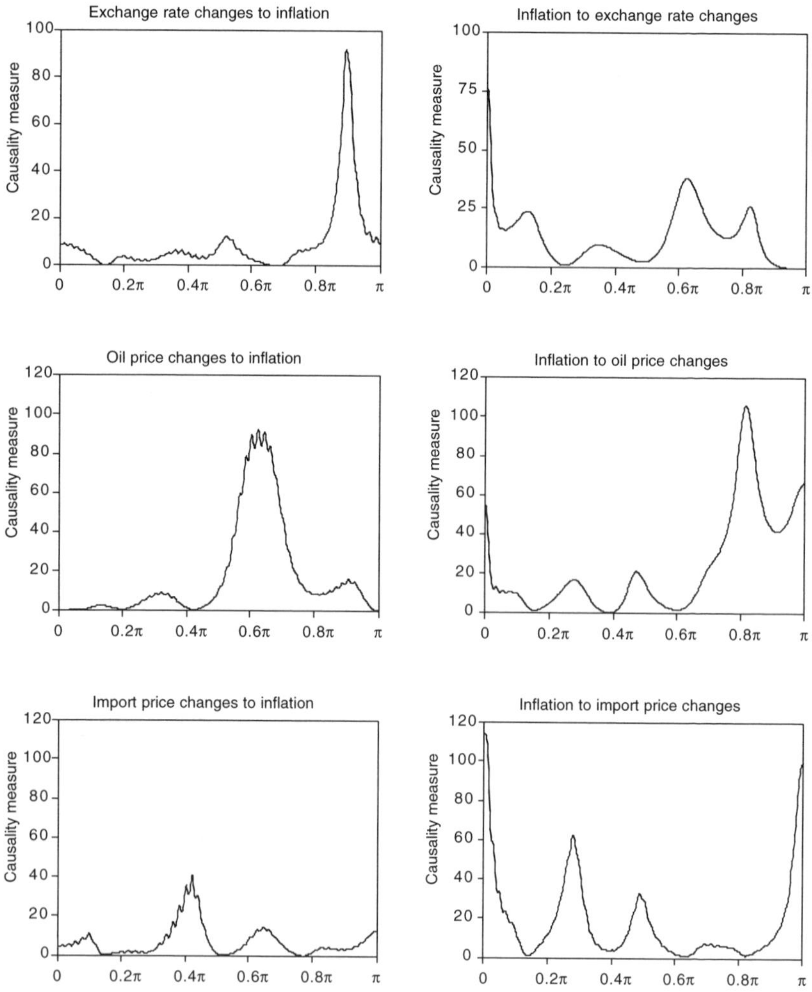

Figure 2.5 Cost-push variables: frequency-wise causality measure

low frequencies may therefore reflect the impact of the exchange rate rather than an independent causal effect. Figure 2.5 shows that the causality measure from exchange rate changes to inflation peaks at $\omega = 0.9\pi$, which corresponds to a periodicity of 2.2 quarters. In contrast, the causality measure from inflation to the exchange rate is high at the zero frequency and again at high frequencies. A similar pattern of causality from inflation at the zero and high frequencies, and to inflation at high frequencies, is present also for changes in oil prices and import prices. It is difficult to know whether these findings for the highest frequencies are structural or spurious.[33]

Band spectrum regression: high frequencies

Next we turn to the high frequency regressions. Table 2.4 shows the results when the short run is defined as including frequencies between 0.5 and 4 years.[34] By excluding the zero frequency, inflation and money growth become stationary. However, because they are correlated at the zero fre-

Table 2.4 Band spectrum regressions: high-frequency band: 0.5 to 4 years

	Dependent variable: π_t			
Quantity-theoretic variables				
Money growth	–0.07	0.41	0.30	–0.16
	(0.72)	(0.63)	(0.59)	(0.77)
Output growth	–0.01	0.12	0.11	0.03
	(0.14)	(0.12)	(0.11)	(0.15)
Interest rate change	0.13	0.55	0.38	0.11
	(0.16)	(0.30)	(0.35)	(0.26)
Output gap (lagged 1 quarter)	0.13	0.30*	0.27*	0.10
	(0.16)	(0.12)	(0.12)	(0.17)
Cost-push variables				
Exchange rate changes	0.01	0.03**		
	(0.01)	(0.01)		
Oil price changes (× 10²)	0.08		0.38	
	(0.20)		(0.24)	
Import price changes	0.07**			0.08**
	(0.02)			(0.03)
$\bar{R}^2$	0.44	–0.07	0.09	0.42

Note: All regressions include a constant which is not shown. Newey-West (1987) corrected standard errors in parentheses; * indicates significance at the 5% level, ** significance at the 1% level. The sample period is 1970Q2 to 2003Q4. Money growth is instrumented with its first lag. The number of degrees of freedom is 111 for the regression in the first column and 113 for the other regressions.

quency (as evidenced by the finding of cointegration), and because of leakage from the zero frequency into all other frequencies, they are correlated also at high frequencies. Thus, this leakage introduces correlation between the regressor and the error term at high frequencies. We therefore use instrumental variables estimation and instrument money growth with its first lag.[35] Interestingly and in contrast to the results for the low frequencies, the quantity-theoretic variables are insignificant at high frequencies. The regression in column 1, in which all cost-push variables are included, shows that changes in import prices, which by construction capture oil price shocks and exchange rate changes, help to account for high-frequency movements in inflation. In columns 2 to 4 we include a single cost-push variable at a time, and find again that import prices appear to be more important than the other variables (as evidenced by the $\bar{R}^2$). When they are included, however, the output gap is not significant.

Because the regressions in Table 2.4 include many insignificant parameters, we re-estimate the regressions by excluding the quantity-theoretic variables. Since there is no longer any need to take into account the correlation of money growth with the error term, we use the Engle (1974) estimator. The results, which are shown in Table 2.5, are similar to those in Table 2.4 except that the output gap is significant in all regressions. Again it appears that import price changes contain more information for inflation than changes in exchange rates or in oil prices.

In the analysis below we have defined the high-frequency band as fluctuations of a periodicity of between 0.5 and 4 years and have found the

Table 2.5 Band spectrum regressions: high-frequency band: 0.5 to 4 years

	Dependent variable: π_t			
Output gap (lagged 1 quarter)	0.14** (0.04)	0.21** (0.05)	0.20** (0.05)	0.13** (0.04)
Cost-push shocks				
Exchange rate changes	0.005 (0.01)	0.03** (0.01)		
Oil price changes (× 10^2)	0.07 (0.14)		0.52** (0.09)	
Import price changes	0.07** (0.01)			0.08** (0.01)
$\bar{R}^2$	0.44	0.28	0.31	0.45

Note: All regressions include a constant which is not shown. Newey-West (1987) corrected standard errors in parentheses; * indicates significance at the 5% level, ** significance at the 1% level. The sample period is 1970Q2 to 2003Q4. The number of degrees of freedom is 114 for the regression in the first column and 116 for the other regressions.

Table 2.6 Band spectrum regressions: high-frequency band: 0.5 to 1.5 years

	Dependent variable: π_t			
Output gap (lagged 1 quarter)	0.07 (0.05)	0.06 (0.05)	0.05 (0.05)	0.07 (0.05)
Cost-push shocks				
Exchange rate changes	0.01 (0.01)	0.02* (0.01)		
Oil price changes ($\times 10^2$)	0.14 (0.13)		0.41** (0.11)	
Import price changes	0.05** (0.02)			0.07** (0.02)
$\bar{R}^2$	0.14	0.05	0.08	0.15

Note: All regressions include a constant which is not shown. Newey-West (1987) corrected standard errors in parentheses; * indicates significance at the 5% level, ** significance at the 1% level. The sample period is 1970Q2 to 2003Q4. The number of degrees of freedom is 63 for the regression in the first column and 65 for the other regressions.

output gap to be highly significant. Next we re-estimate the regressions in Table 2.5, but consider increasingly narrower frequency bands in order to assess the role of the cost-push variables in accounting for the highest-frequency movements in inflation. Thus, Table 2.6 shows the results under the assumption that the high-frequency band contains periodicities of 0.5 to 1.5 years. While the output gap is insignificant in these regressions, the cost-push variables remain significant if they are considered individually. These findings suggest that they contain information about inflation at higher frequencies than the output gap.

Overall, our results confirm the findings in AWG that the quantity-theoretic variables explain inflation at low frequencies, whereas the output gap provides information about inflation at business-cycle frequencies. The novel finding here is that for frequencies from 0.5 to 1.5 years the cost-push factors, in particular import prices, are important for understanding the dynamics of inflation.

Two-pillar Phillips curve

So far we have studied the determination of inflation in different frequency bands. Next we return to the issue of how to model headline inflation (that is, inflation at all frequencies) and consider three sets of explanatory variables. The first of these are the quantity-theoretic variables. Since the econometric analysis above indicated that only the low-frequency variation of these variables mattered, we use only the frequency band of 4 years to infinity. We think of these variables as the empirical counterpart to the

ECB's 'first pillar' or the 'monetary analysis'. The second set is given by the output gap. Since it did not appear important at the highest frequencies, we focus on the frequency band of 1.5 to 4 years. The third set of regressors contains the variables capturing cost-push shocks, for which we focus on the frequency band of 0.5 to 1.5 years. We interpret the output gap and the cost-push variables as constituting the 'second pillar' of the 'economic analysis'. This leads to an inflation equation of the form:

$$\pi_t = \beta_0 + \{\beta_\mu \mu_t^{4-\infty} + \beta_\rho \rho_t^{4-\infty} + \beta_\gamma \gamma_t^{4-\infty}\} + \beta_g g_{t-1.}^{1.5-4} + \beta_c c_t^{0.5-1.5} + \varepsilon_t \qquad (2.20)$$

which can be thought of as a more refined version of the 'Two-Pillar Phillips Curve' studied by Gerlach (2003, 2004) and AWG.

Table 2.7 shows the results, which are obtained by OLS. In the first column we tabulate the estimates of a conventional regression in which all frequencies are included. While the coefficient on money growth is significant, it is significantly smaller than unity. Furthermore, the coefficient on output growth is far away from the expected value of minus unity and only significant at the 6 per cent level. A Wald test clearly rejects the hypothesis that money and output growth have coefficients of unity and minus unity, respectively.[36] Changes in oil prices are significant with the wrong sign, whereas the coefficient on changes in import prices is large, positive and significant.

The estimates in column 1 appear difficult to reconcile with the ECB's views of the inflation process. But those views emphasise that the determinants of inflation vary across frequencies and we therefore proceed by estimating the equation using different frequency bands for the regressors. The results are shown in columns 2 to 5 in the same table. Note that since the frequency bands are not overlapping, the regressors in one frequency band are orthogonal to those in another.[37] The parameters on the quantity-theoretic variables and the output gap do not therefore change as we consider the different measures of cost-push shocks. Consequently, we comment on the parameters by frequency band.

In the lowest frequency band, the quantity-theoretic variables are all highly significant, and the parameters on money and real output growth are close to unity and minus unity, respectively. Indeed, a Wald test does not reject this hypothesis. However, while money growth is statistically highly significant, it is likely to explain at most a small fraction of the variance of quarter-to-quarter changes in inflation since low-frequency variables evolve gradually over time.

Turning to the economic analysis, in the intermediate frequency band the output gap is highly significant, and in the highest frequency band changes in oil prices and, in particular, import prices help explain inflation. The fact that the significance of these variables depends on what frequency bands are considered is expected, given the ECB's view that the inflation process varies across frequencies.

Sensitivity analysis

The inflation equations presented in Table 2.7 are estimated under the assumption that the low-frequency band contains fluctuations of periodicities of between 4 years and infinity, the intermediate frequency band (in which the output gap is relevant) periodicities of between 1.5 and 4 years, and the high frequency band periodicities of between 0.5 and 1.5 years. Next we explore whether better results could be obtained by separating between the different bands at other frequencies. To this end, we re-estimate

Table 2.7 Two-pillar Phillips curves

Quantity-theoretic variables	*All frequencies*	*Periodicity: 4 to ∞ years*			
Money growth	0.49**	0.89**	0.89**	0.89**	0.89**
	(0.05)	(0.06)	(0.06)	(0.06)	(0.06)
Output growth	–0.18	–0.97**	–0.97**	–0.97**	–0.97**
	(0.10)	(0.23)	(0.23)	(0.23)	(0.23)
Interest rate change	0.41	4.45**	4.45**	4.45**	4.45**
	(0.52)	(1.32)	(1.32)	(1.32)	(1.32)
	All frequencies	*Periodicity: 1.5 to 4 years*			
Output gap (lagged 1 quarter)	0.04	0.25**	0.25**	0.25**	0.25**
	(0.86)	(0.08)	(0.08)	(0.08)	(0.08)
Cost-push shocks	*All frequencies*	*Periodicity: 0.5 to 1.5 years*			
Exchange rate changes	–0.01	0.01	0.02		
	(0.02)	(0.01)	(0.01)		
Oil price changes (× 10^2)	–0.93**	0.14		0.41**	
	(0.25)	(0.18)		(0.15)	
Import price changes	0.21**	0.05*			0.07**
	(0.03)	(0.02)			(0.02)
$\bar{R}^2$	0.72	0.78	0.78	0.78	0.78

Note: The dependent variable is the inflation rate. All regressions include a constant which is not shown. Standard errors in parentheses; * indicates significance at the 5% level, ** significance at the 1% level. The sample period is 1970Q2 to 2003Q4. The first column shows the results from a conventional OLS regression. Columns 2 to 5 include the low-frequency part of money growth, output growth and the interest rate change and the high-frequency part of the output gap. Newey-West corrected standard errors are reported.

Table 2.8 Optimal frequency bands

	Cost push variable	*Output gap*	*Quantity theoretic variables*
Exchange rate changes	0.50–1.68	1.73–5.33	5.45–∞
Oil price changes	0.50–1.21	1.23–5.45	5.57–∞
Import price changes	0.50–1.98	2.00–5.33	5.45–∞

Note: The table gives the optimal frequency band in years.

the two-pillar Phillips curve in equation (2.20), but vary the exact frequency at which we distinguish between low frequency and intermediate frequencies from 2 to 8 years, and the frequency at which we distinguish between intermediate and high frequencies from 0.5 to 2 years.

To judge the fit, we use the resulting R^2s. The frequency bands for which these maxima are attained are listed in Table 2.8. While the quantity-theoretic variables explain inflation at a frequency above 5.5 years, the output gap has explanatory power at business cycle frequencies between approximately 1.5 and 5.5 years (depending on what cost-push variable is considered), and the cost-push factors matter at the remaining frequencies. Not surprisingly, it appears that changes in oil prices provide information on the highest-frequency movements in inflation. Since the use of the optimal frequency bands identified in Table 2.8 leads to parameter estimates that do not differ much from those reported in Table 2.7, except of course for the higher R^2, in the interest of brevity we do not report them.

Conclusions

In this chapter we have reviewed several recent papers that have sought to provide an empirical representation of the ECB's views of the determination of inflation in the euro area. We have argued that these views can be given a natural interpretation in terms of an augmented Phillips curve in which the parameters vary across frequencies. Thus, the 'monetary' analysis is seen as a way of understanding the determination of inflation at low, and the 'economic' analysis at high, frequencies. Furthermore, we have presented empirical evidence that suggests that euro-area inflation can be decomposed into three frequency bands, each with a separate set of determinants. At the lowest frequencies the quantity-theoretic variables – money and output growth, and changes in long-term interest rates as determinants of changes in velocity – play important roles in determining inflation. In the intermediate frequency band the output gap appears to be the main causal variable, while at still higher frequencies cost-push shocks, in particular import prices, are of primary significance.

This view of the inflation process warrants three comments. First, although low-frequency factors are evolving more slowly over time than high-frequency variables and therefore have more gradual and long-lived effects on inflation, at any point in time all three sets of variables are operational. The fact that money growth is important only at low frequencies does not therefore mean that it can be disregarded when analysing current price pressures.

Second, monetary analysis is sometimes thought of as a way of cross-checking the findings of the economic analysis of inflation, implying that these approaches are substitutes. The interpretation of the monetary and economic analysis as pertaining to different frequency bands suggests, by contrast, that they should be thought of as complements. The two pillars are thus best seen as a way to 'build up' an overall assessment of inflation at the current juncture.

Third, while our results confirm that money growth contains information about inflation pressures, they are silent on the question whether this information is best incorporated in the policy analysis using a two-pillar framework or by integrating the pillars in a single analysis of inflation. The choice of a monetary policy strategy has two objectives: to frame the internal decision-making process on the basis of an analysis of all relevant information, and to facilitate the communication of policy decisions to the public. Judging how the two-pillar strategy satisfies these criteria is beyond the scope of this chapter.

Notes

1 See the ECB's press releases of 13 October 1998 and 1 December 1998, which are available at www.ecb.int.

2 The Deutsche Bundesbank (2005) also argues that low-frequency fluctuations in money growth impact on the long-term evolution of inflation, in contrast to high-frequency swings, which are much less informative about price developments.

3 Jaeger (2003) also analyses the relation of money growth and inflation across different frequencies but he includes the money gap, not the low-frequency part of money, in his inflation equation.

4 It has been shown for different countries and time periods that money growth and inflation are closely related, see Benati (2005), Fitzgerald (1999) or Haug and Dewald (2004).

5 Two-pillar Phillips-curve models do not explain why monetary conditions may have changed. For the Federal Reserve, Ireland (2005) argues that changes in the target level of inflation have been caused by a series of negative supply shocks in the 1970s and positive shocks in the 1990s.

6 For instance, using the data of Gerlach (2004), the ratio is 0.014 for inflation and 0.006 for money growth.

7 Bruggemann *et al.* (2005) show that a two-sided filter is also feasible for real-time analysis of monetary data when the data are augmented with forecasts from money demand models.

8 See for instance Ashley and Verbrugge (2005).

9 See Crowley (2005) for a discussion of wavelet analysis in economics.
10 The discussion in Gerlach (2004) suggests that this result arises because filtered real output growth is correlated with the output gap.
11 See European Central Bank (2001, p. 42) for a discussion of money growth and inflation expectations.
12 Lucas (1980) presents frequency-domain evidence for US data in support of this proposition.
13 Reynard (2005) shows that accounting for changes in velocity is critical for understanding the relationship between money growth and inflation in the euro area and in the US since the 1970s.
14 In another paper, Assenmacher-Wesche and Gerlach (2005) cast the two-pillar framework into a state-space framework in which trend money growth and trend output growth (and consequently the output gap which is defined as actual output less trend output) are treated as unobservables.
15 Experimentation with lagged and contemporaneous output gap and cost-push factors showed that a lagged output gap and contemporaneous cost-push variables provided the best fit.
16 M3 is not included in the dataset for the ECB's area-wide model. The monetary data used were provided separately by the ECB.
17 See AWG for a detailed discussion of the adjustment.
18 The interest rate is expressed at a quarterly rate by defining it as $0.25\ln(1+i/100)$, where i is the interest rate in per cent per annum. This makes it comparable to inflation, which is also measured at a quarterly rate.
19 The HP filter is applied with the usual smoothing parameter of $\lambda = 1{,}600$ for quarterly data. Kaiser and Maravall (2001) show that the HP filter can be viewed as a band-pass filter. By setting $\lambda = 1{,}600$, fluctuations with a periodicity of more than 40 quarters are retained.
20 Since the original exchange rate data showed a large spike in the first quarter of 1990 which possibly is related to statistical effects due to German reunification, we removed this spike by regressing the series on a dummy. The results are not affected by this adjustment.
21 The oil price data is the US dollar price per barrel for UK Brent oil from the *International Financial Statistics* of the International Monetary Fund. The exchange rate used to convert the series into euros is the euro/US dollar exchange rate from 1999 on and the ECU/US dollar exchange rate from 1979 to 1998. For the time before 1979 an exchange rate series has been constructed by using the exchange rates for the Belgian franc, the Danish crown, the Dutch guilder, the French franc, the German mark, the Irish punt, the Italian lira and pound sterling with the ECU basket weights from 1975, see European Navigator (2004).
22 The unit-root tests are discussed in Maddala and Kim (1998).
23 However, the results are not all completely unambiguous. For instance, the PP test accepts trend stationarity for inflation and money growth, and the KPSS test rejects stationarity for output growth and import prices.
24 The model is specified with a constant that is restricted to lie in the cointegration space. The results are insensitive to other assumptions regarding the deterministic components in the model.
25 This corresponds to the finding that in the long run money growth causes inflation, which we discuss below.
26 Superconsistency of the cointegration parameters assures that the asymptotic distribution of the other parameters is not affected.

27 Though the component of a series in a certain frequency band cannot be estimated without the use of a two-sided filter which destroys the temporal aspect of the causal definition, it is possible to deduce causal relationships at different frequencies without estimation of the series' components, as is done in the band spectrum regressions.
28 We follow the approach suggested by Hosoya (2000) to test for causality in a multivariate system.
29 The approach is described in more detail in AWG.
30 While elsewhere in the paper we let π denote the rate of inflation, in discussing frequencies we let it denote the irrational number defined by the ratio of the circumference of a circle to its diameter.
31 Breitung and Candelon (2005) argue that in a bivariate cointegrated system the causality measure approximately follows an F-distribution with 2 degrees of freedom. It is not clear, however, if the critical value provides a good approximation for a multivariate system where some variables are $I(1)$ and others $I(0)$. We therefore do not include a critical value in Figures 2.3 to 2.5.
32 Since inflation is nonstationary whereas the other variables are stationary, the latter cannot cause inflation at the zero frequency. Since excluding the zero frequency makes a nonstationary variable stationary, causality at other frequencies is possible.
33 For instance, one would expect that the exact construction of the synthetic euro area data (for instance, whether the quarterly data is to be thought of as an average for the quarter, or taken at a point in time within the quarter) would matter for the highest frequencies.
34 The smallest fluctuation distinguishable in quarterly data is one cycle every two periods, which is also called the Nyquist frequency.
35 To obtain the results in Table 2.4 we use the generalised instrumental variables estimator proposed by Corbae, Ouliaris and Phillips (1994).
36 Since inflation and money growth are nonstationary, the coefficient on money growth follows a Dickey-Fuller distribution. The coefficients on the other variables are distributed normally. As the Wald test assumes asymptotic normality of the coefficients, it is not strictly valid.
37 This follows from the fact that trigonometric functions underlying the Fourier transformation of the data are orthogonal for different frequencies.

References

Ashley, R. and J.R. Verbrugge (2005) 'Frequency Dependence in Regression Model Coefficients: An Alternative Approach for Modeling Nonlinear Dynamic Relationships in Time Series', mimeo, *Virginia Polytechnic Institute and State University*.

Assenmacher-Wesche, K. and S. Gerlach (2005) 'State-Space Estimates of a Two-Pillar Phillips Curve for the Euro Area', incomplete draft of working paper, *Swiss National Bank*.

Assenmacher-Wesche, K. and S. Gerlach (2006) 'Interpreting Euro Area Inflation at High and Low Frequencies', *Bank for International Settlements Working Paper* no. 195.

Baxter, M. and R.G. King (1999) 'Measuring Business Cycles: Approximate Band-Pass Filters for Economic Time Series', *Review of Economics and Statistics*, 81: 575–93.

Benati, L. (2005) 'Long-Run Evidence on Money Growth and Inflation', *Bank of England Quarterly Bulletin*, 45: 349–55.

Breitung, J. and B. Candelon (2005) 'Testing for Short- and Long-Run Causality: A Frequency-Domain Approach', *Journal of Econometrics*, 132: 363–78.

Bruggeman, A., G. Camba-Méndez, B. Fischer and J. Sousa (2005) 'Structural Filters for Monetary Analysis: The Inflationary Movements of Money in the Euro Area', *European Central Bank Working Paper* no. 470.

Cogley, T. (2002) 'A Simple Adaptive Measure of Core Inflation', *Journal of Money Credit and Banking*, 34: 94–113.

Corbae, D., S. Ouliaris and P.C.B. Phillips (1994) 'A Reexamination of the Consumption Function Using Frequency Domain Regressions', *Empirical Economics*, 19: 595–609.

Crowley, P.M. (2005) 'An Intuitive Guide to Wavelets for Economists', *Bank of Finland Discussion Papers* no. 1

Deutsche Bundesbank (2005) 'The Relationship Between Money and Prices', *Monthly Report*, January: 13–24.

Engle, R. F. (1974) 'Band Spectrum Regression', *International Economic Review*, 15: 1–11.

European Central Bank (2003) 'The Outcome of the ECB's Evaluation of Its Monetary Policy Strategy', *ECB Monthly Bulletin*, June: 79–92.

European Central Bank (2001) *The Monetary Policy of the ECB*. Frankfurt am Main: European Central Bank.

European Navigator (2004) 'The Creation of the ECU: Evolution of Currencies within the ECU Basket (1975–1987)', *http://www.ena.lu/mce.cfm*.

Fagan, G., J. Henry and R. Mestre (2005) 'An Area-Wide Model for the Euro Area', *Economic Modelling*, 22, 39–59.

Fitzgerald, T.J. (1999) 'Money and Inflation: How Long Is the Long Run?', *Economic Commentary*, Federal Reserve Bank of Cleveland, August.

Gerlach, S. (2003) 'The ECB's Two Pillars', *Centre for Economic Policy Research Discussion Paper* no. 3689.

Gerlach, S. (2004) 'The Two Pillars of the European Central Bank', *Economic Policy*, 40: 389–439.

Geweke, J. (1982) 'Measurement of Linear Dependence and Feedback between Multiple Time Series', *Journal of the American Statistical Association*, 77: 304–24.

Granger, C.W.J. (1969) 'Investigating Causal Relations by Econometric Models and Cross-Spectral Methods', *Econometrica*, 37: 424–38.

Granger, C.W.J. and J.-L. Lin (1995) 'Causality in the Long Run', *Econometric Theory*, 11: 530–36.

Haug, A.A. and W.G. Dewald (2004) 'Longer-Term Effects of Monetary Growth on Real and Nominal Variables, Major Industrial Countries, 1880–2001', *European Central Bank Working Paper* no. 382.

Hosoya, Y. (1991) 'The Decomposition and Measurement of the Interdependency between Second-Order Stationary Processes', *Probability Theory and Related Fields*, 88: 429–44.

Hosoya, Y. (2000) 'Elimination of Third-Series Effect and Defining Partial Measures of Causality', *Journal of Time Series Analysis*, 22: 537–54.

Ireland, P.N. (2005) 'Changes in the Federal Reserve's Inflation Target: Causes and Consequences', *Federal Reserve Bank of Boston Working Paper* no. 05–13.

Jaeger, A. (2003) 'The ECB's Money Pillar: An Assessment', *International Monetary Fund Working Paper* no. 82.

Jordan, T.J., M. Peytrignet and G. Rich (2001) 'The Role of M3 in the Policy Analysis of the Swiss National Bank', in H.-J. Klöckers and C. Willecke (eds), *Monetary Analysis: Tools and Applications*, Frankfurt: European Central Bank.

Kaiser, R. and A. Maravall (2001) *Measuring Business Cycles in Economic Time Series*, New York: Springer.

Lucas, R.E. (1980) 'Two Illustrations of the Quantity Theory of Money', *American Economic Review*, 70: 1005–14.

Maddala, G.S. and I.-M. Kim (1998) *Unit Roots, Cointegration, and Structural Change*. Cambridge: Cambridge University Press.

Neumann, M.J.M. (2003) 'The European Central Bank's First Pillar Reassessed', University of Bonn unpublished working paper.

Neumann, M.J.M. and C. Greiber (2004) 'Inflation and Core Money Growth in the Euro Area', *Economic Research Centre of the Deutsche Bundesbank Discussion Paper* no. 36.

Newey, W., and K. West (1987) 'A Simple, Positive Semi-Definite, Heteroskedasticity and Autocorrelation Consistent Covariance Matrix', *Econometrica*, 55, 703–8.

Phillips, P.C.B. (1991) 'Spectral Regression for Cointegrated Time Series', in W. A. Barnett, J. Powell and G.E. Tauchen (eds), *Nonparametric and Semiparametric Methods in Economics and Statistics*. Cambridge: Cambridge University Press.

Reynard, S. (2005) 'Money and the Great Disinflation', mimeo, Swiss National Bank.

Discussion

Michael Sumner

The authors helpfully review the previous literature, much of it produced by them, and utilise best-practice econometrics to estimate and test a simple but solid theoretical model. The chapter is very clearly and carefully written, as exemplified by the warning to the hasty reader not to confuse π, the inflation rate, with π, the ratio of the circumference of a circle to its diameter. In consequence there is little scope for criticism or complaint.

Some reassurance on the question of temporal homogeneity would however be a welcome addition. The estimation period spans the 1970s, with synthetic data using fixed (1975) weights, the ERM and the euro area, when area-wide inflation became a policy objective for the first time and euro M3 acquired real meaning and target status. Goodhart's law is not the only reason for hesitating to accept the results without question.

The extension of the previous literature by the introduction of cost-push shocks might be taken further in future work. Separating the foreign currency price and the exchange-rate components of euro oil and import prices might clarify the results reported in this chapter. Other issues for possible investigation include asymmetries in the magnitude or timing of cost-push impacts, and the influence of the changes in labour-market institutions documented by Nickell *et al.* (2004).

Applied papers typically conclude with a discussion of the policy implications of the analysis, but this chapter is atypical. The ECB's two-pillar framework is introduced in the first paragraph but does not reappear until the last one. In a softening of the criticisms made by one of the authors (Gerlach 2004), judgement on the utility of this framework for analysis and for the communication of policy decisions is ruled beyond the scope of the chapter, perhaps echoing their previous dismissal of this 'semantic question' (AWG, 2006). But the question provokes two further questions which are not semantic. First, why did the Bundesbank's two-pillar framework escape the charges of inconsistency and lack of clarity levelled at the ECB? Ten years ago several papers, for example Bernanke and Mihov (1997) and Clarida and Gertler (1997), explored the conduct of German monetary policy and concluded that the monetary targets were of very slight importance (a view not universally shared: Dornbusch (1997) is a major exception); but that did not lead them or others to question the framework itself. What has changed the psychology of economists or the sociology of economics in the last decade? Secondly, if the question had not been asked, would the decomposition of inflation into a long-run monetarily determined trend and deviations from it caused by the output gap and high-frequency cost-push factors have been executed? The policy implications of the analysis may be debatable, but the analytical implications of the policy constitute a valuable addition to economic understanding.

References

Assenmacher-Wesche K. and Gerlach S. (2006) 'Interpreting Euro Area Inflation at High and Low Frequencies', Bank for International Settlements Working Paper no. 195.

Bernanke B. and Mihov I. (1997) 'What Does the Bundesbank Target?', *European Economic Review*, 41: 1025–52.

Clarida R. and Gertler M. (1997) 'How the Bundesbank Conducts Monetary Policy', with Comment by R. Dornbusch, in C.D. Romer and D.H. Romer (eds), *Reducing Inflation*. Chicago and London: University of Chicago Press.

Gerlach, S. (2004) 'The Two Pillars of the European Central Bank', *Economic Policy*, 40: 389–439.

Nickell, S., L. Nunziata and W. Ochel (2004) 'Unemployment in the OECD since the 1960s: What Do We Know?', *Economic Journal*, 115: 1–27.

3
Monetary Policy Shifts and Inflation Dynamics

*Paolo Surico**

Introduction

The New Keynesian Phillips Curve (NKPC) has recently become the building block of many monetary policy models. This relation plays a central role in understanding aggregate fluctuations and quantifying the transmission mechanism of monetary policy. Most of the success of the NKPC hinges on the fact that it is derived from first principles, thereby implying that its estimates survive the Lucas (1976) critique.

As shown many times in the literature, a log-linearised version of the New Keynesian model gives rise to self-fulfilling expectations if the central bank does not raise the nominal interest rate sufficiently in response to a deviation of inflation from the target. This implies that sunspot fluctuations can influence the properties of the inflation process even if the 'true' NKPC is a structurally invariant relation.

Using Monte Carlo simulations from a monetary sticky price model, this chapter shows that the estimates of a hybrid NKPC are severely biased downward when two conditions are met. First, the data are generated under indeterminacy. Second, the empirical analysis implicitly and arbitrarily limits the solution of the model to the determinacy region. Specifically, the null hypothesis of no backward-looking component is strongly rejected in spite of the fact that the data-generating process does not exhibit any

*I wish to thank Peter Andrews, Luca Benati, Efrem Castelnuovo, David Cobham, Tim Cogley, Charlotta Groth, Jarkko Jääskelä, Ed Nelson, Gabriel Sterne, Ulf Söderström and Jonathan Thomas for very helpful conversations. Comments by seminar participants at the annual meeting of the Computing in Economics and Finance 2005, the MMF conference 'The Travails of the Eurozone' and the discussant at the latter conference, Fabrizio Mattesini, are gratefully acknowledged. The views expressed in this chapter are those of the author, and do not necessarily reflect those of the Bank of England. Address for correspondence: Monetary Assessment and Strategy Division, Bank of England, Threadneedle Street, London EC2R 8AH, United Kingdom. E-mail: paolo.surico@bankofengland.co.uk

exogenous or endogenous persistence. The slope of the Phillips curve takes a value that is not statistically different from zero. Moreover, the sum of autoregressive coefficients in the reduced-form process of inflation is close to one and, most importantly, is significantly different from the value of zero that would emerge in the unique rational expectations equilibrium. As under determinacy the estimates match the 'true' coefficients used to simulate the data, we refer to the difference between the generating process parameters and the relative estimates as 'neglected indeterminacy bias'.

This chapter cuts across two bodies of research. The first body is the literature on interest rate rules, inspired by the work of Taylor (1993) and Clarida, Galí and Gertler (2000), which documents a shift in the conduct of monetary policy around the beginning of the 1980s for several industrialized economies. The second strand of work includes Galí and Gertler (1999), Sbordone (2003), Eichenbaum and Fisher (2004), Lindé (2005) and Rudd and Whelan (2005) among many others, and reports conflicting estimates of the NKPC using a number of econometric techniques over various postwar *full samples*.

The results presented here suggest some caution is needed when interpreting the estimates of the structural NKPC obtained using a pool of observations that mixes different monetary policy regimes. The reason is that neglected indeterminacy can distort inference in an important dimension. In particular, it can introduce additional elements of persistence that are not present in the data generating process of inflation and thus are not an intrinsic, structural feature of the economy.

This chapter also contributes to the literature on inflation persistence. Several authors including Cogley and Sargent (2005) and Benati (2006) show that inflation inertia has been an historically limited phenomenon in the US and the UK. In particular, inflation can be characterised as highly persistent only during those periods that, in the empirical literature on monetary policy rules, are typically associated with a weak central bank response to inflation. Our simulations reveal that a *passive* monetary policy, in the form of a *less-than-proportional* response of the nominal interest rate to inflation, actually produces inflation persistence. This result can thus provide a rationale for the empirical regularity in Cogley and Sargent (2005) and Benati (2006).

The chapter is organised as follows. The next section presents the model that will serve as the data-generating process. A set of Monte Carlo experiments are then performed and the estimates of the structural process and the reduced-form process of inflation based on the simulated data presented. Sub-sample evidence on the UK, US and euro area is then presented to show that the data are consistent with the 'neglected indeterminacy bias' hypothesis. Conclusions are discussed in the last part while the Appendix describes a method to obtain a solution of the linear rational expectations model under indeterminacy and determinacy.

The model

This section describes a log-linearised New Keynesian sticky-price model of the business cycle. This model consists of the following three aggregate equations which King (2000) and Woodford (2003) derive from first principles:

$$\pi_t = \beta E_t \pi_{t+1} + k\,(x_t - z_t) \tag{3.1}$$

$$x_t = E_t x_{t+1} - \tau\,(i_t - E_t \pi_{t+1}) + g_t \tag{3.2}$$

$$i_t = \psi_\pi \pi_t + \psi_x\,(x_t - z_t) + u_t \tag{3.3}$$

where x_t is defined as the deviation of output from a long-run trend, π_t represents inflation, and i_t is the nominal interest rate. Inflation and the interest rate are expressed in percentage deviations from their steady state values.

Equation (3.1) captures the staggered feature of a Calvo-type world in which each firm adjusts its price with a constant probability in any given period, and independently from the time elapsed from the last adjustment. The discrete nature of price-setting creates an incentive to adjust prices more the higher is the future inflation expected at time *t*. The parameter $0 < \beta < 1$ is the agents' discount factor and k is the slope of the Phillips curve. The shock z_t is identically and independently distributed (*iid*) with standard deviation σ_z and it is meant to capture exogenous shifts in the marginal costs of production.

As there is no capital in the model, the second equation is a standard Euler equation for consumption combined with the relevant market clearing condition. It brings the notion of consumption smoothing into an aggregate demand formulation by making x_t a positive function of its future value and a negative function of the *ex ante* real interest rate, $i_t - E_t\pi_{t+1}$. The parameter $\tau > 0$ can be interpreted as the intertemporal elasticity of substitution. Preference shifts and government spending shocks are embodied in the *iid* process g_t which has standard deviation σ_g.

Equation (3.3) characterises the behaviour of the monetary authorities. As in Lubik and Schorfheide (2004), this is an interest-rate rule according to which the central bank sets the policy rate in response to deviations of inflation and output from their respective targets.[1] Without loss of generality, the target for inflation is normalised to zero. The shock u_t represents an *iid* monetary policy disturbance with standard deviation σ_u. There is no correlation between innovations.

The specification (3.1) to (3.3) with *iid* shocks and no interest rate smoothing has been deliberately designed to maximise the power of the tests on the (in)significance of the backward-looking components of the Phillips curve. As the data-generating process exhibits no persistence, a rejection of the null hypothesis $(1 - \beta) = 0$ on the simulated data can only be interpreted as a spurious result from neglecting indeterminacy in the estimation procedure.

The linear rational expectations model described by equations (3.1) to (3.3) can be represented in the following canonical form:

$$\Gamma_0 (\theta)\, s_t = \Gamma_1 (\theta)\, s_{t-1} + \Psi (\theta)\, \varepsilon_t + \Pi (\theta)\, \eta_t \tag{3.4}$$

where

$$\theta = [\psi_\pi, \psi_x, \beta, k, \tau]$$

$$s_t = [x_t, \pi_t, i_t, E_t x_{t+1}, E_t \pi_{t+1}]'$$

$$\varepsilon_t = [u_t, g_t, z_t]'$$

$$\eta_t = [x_t - E_{t-1} x_t, \pi_t - E_{t-1} \pi_t]'$$

The matrices Γ_0, Γ_1, Ψ and Π are given by the following expressions:

$$\Gamma 0 = \begin{bmatrix} 1 & 0 & 0 & 0 & 0 \\ 0 & 1 & 0 & 0 & 0 \\ 0 & 0 & 1 & 0 & 0 \\ 0 & 0 & -\tau & 1 & \tau \\ 0 & 0 & 0 & 0 & \beta \end{bmatrix}, \Gamma_1 = \begin{bmatrix} 0 & 0 & 0 & 1 & 0 \\ 0 & 0 & 0 & 0 & 1 \\ 0 & 0 & 0 & \psi_2 & \psi_1 \\ 0 & 0 & 0 & 1 & 0 \\ 0 & 0 & 0 & -k & 1 \end{bmatrix}, \Psi \begin{bmatrix} 0 & 0 & 0 \\ 0 & 0 & 0 \\ 1 & 0 & -\psi_2 \\ 0 & 1 & 0 \\ 0 & 0 & 1 \end{bmatrix}, \Pi = \begin{bmatrix} 1 & 0 \\ 0 & 1 \\ \psi_2 & \psi_1 \\ 1 & 0 \\ -k & 1 \end{bmatrix}$$

and they are conformable to the vectors of state variables s_t and s_{t-1}, to the vector of structural disturbances ε_t and to the vector of endogenous forecast errors η_t.

This log-linearised system gives rise to self-fulfilling expectations if the central bank does not raise the nominal interest rate enough in response to a deviation of inflation from the target. For the model used in this chapter, Woodford (2003) shows that the following condition must hold for the existence of a unique stable solution:

$$\psi_\pi \geq 1 - \frac{(1 - \beta)\, \psi_x}{k} \tag{3.5}$$

In all other cases, a sunspot shock ζ_t will affect the dynamics of output and inflation through the endogenous forecast errors, thereby causing the existence of multiple stable solutions.

A Monte Carlo experiment

The main experiment of the chapter is now ready to be run. We apply the solution method outlined in the Appendix to the New Keynesian model (3.1) to (3.3) and we generate artificial data under both determinacy and indeterminacy. To compute a solution under indeterminacy we follow

Lubik and Schorfheide (2004) and present results for two different identifying assumptions. Under the first assumption, the sunspot shocks are orthogonal to the structural shocks and the solution is referred to as 'orthogonality'. Under the second scenario, we assume that the impulse responses $\frac{\partial s_t}{\partial \varepsilon_t'}$ associated with the system (3.4) are continuous at the boundary between the determinacy and the indeterminacy regions, and the solution is labelled 'continuity'.

It is worth emphasising that in the data-generating process, inflation and output are purely forward-looking, errors are *iid* and there is no interest rate smoothing. In other words, the model deliberately lacks any source of either endogenous or exogenous persistence. We then use the simulated data to estimate the following hybrid version of the Phillips curve relation:

$$\pi_t = \omega\pi_{t+1} + (1 - \omega)\ \pi_{t-1} + kx_t + e_t \tag{3.6}$$

where $e_t \equiv -kz_t - \omega\ (\pi_{t+1} - E_t\pi_{t+1})$ and $\beta = 0.99$. Using the alternative parameterisation $\pi_t = \beta\ [\omega E_t\pi_{t+1} + (1 - \omega)\ \pi_{t-1}] + kx_t + v_t$ does not affect the results.

Table 3.1 shows the value of the parameters in the data-generating process under indeterminacy and determinacy. These values are borrowed from Lubik and Schorfheide (2004) who use Bayesian techniques to estimate a version of the model (3.1) to (3.3), augmented with autoregressive error terms and interest-rate smoothing, on US data. To make the indeterminacy bias transparent, we eliminate the persistence in the shocks and in the nominal interest rate by setting the autoregressive coefficients of the processes for g_t, z_t and i_t to zero across all simulations.

Table 3.1 Model parameters

Parameters	*Indeterminacy*	*Determinacy*
ψ_π	0.77	2.19
ψ_y	0.17	0.30
β	0.99	0.99
κ	0.77	0.77
τ^{-1}	1.45	1.45
σ^R	0.23	0.23
σ_g	0.27	0.27
σ_z	1.13	1.13
σ_ζ	0.20	–

Note: The parameterisation of the data-generating process under indeterminacy corresponds to the estimates in Lubik and Schorfheide (2004) over the pre-Volcker period. The solutions of the model under indeterminacy use the estimates in the second column. The solution of the model under determinacy uses the estimates in the third column.

The second column corresponds to the pre-Volcker period estimates. The interest rate response to inflation is below unity and therefore violates the Taylor principle (3.5). We use these estimates to generate artificial series of inflation, output and interest rate under the orthogonality and continuity identifications. The third column reports the values that parameterise the model under determinacy. For the sake of comparison, these coefficients are set to the same values used under indeterminacy, but with two important exceptions: both coefficients of the monetary policy rule now generate a unique rational expectations solution and they correspond to the estimates in Lubik and Schorfheide (2004) over the post-Volcker sample.

We consider three sample lengths. The baseline case consists of 200 observations, which at quarterly frequencies corresponds to fifty years. To explore the extent to which the estimates are sensitive to the sample length we also present results for periods of 80 and 400 observations. The former roughly matches the number of data points available to an econometrician from the beginning of the 1960s to the end of the 1970s.

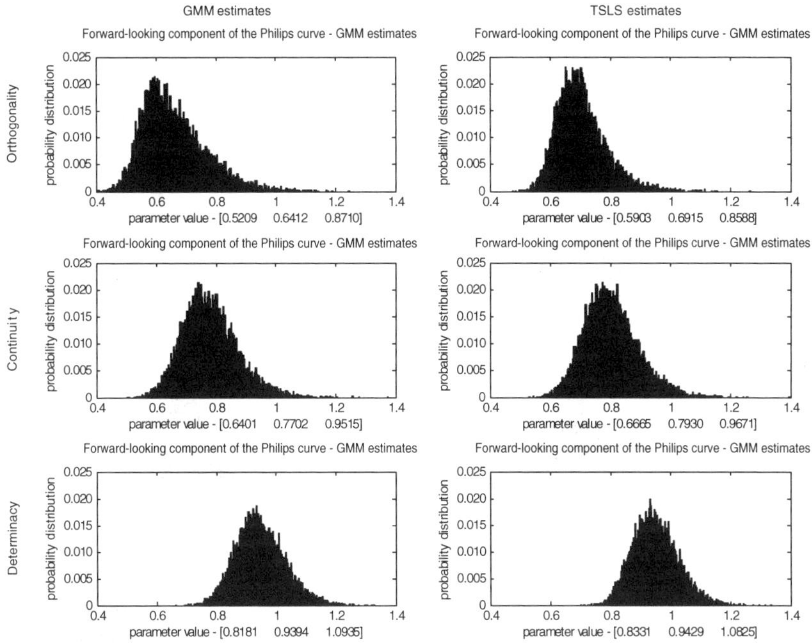

Figure 3.1 Forward-looking component in the Phillips curve

Note: The data-generating process is a purely forward-looking model. The parameters are set to the values in Table 3.1. Estimates are based upon 10,000 repetitions of a sample of 200 observations. Each simulated sample is initiated with 100 extra observations to get a stochastic initial state, and these are then discarded. Numbers in squared brackets represent the 5th, the 50th and the 95th percentiles of the confidence interval, respectively.

Results

Figures 3.1 and 3.2 present the results based on 10,000 repetitions. The hybrid New Keynesian Phillips curve (3.6) is estimated by generalised method of moments (GMM) and two-stage least-squares (TSLS) under the hypothesis of rational expectations. Starting from period $t - 1$ the instrument set includes past values of inflation, output and the nominal interest rate. The selection of the number of lags is based on the Schwartz lag-length criterion from an unrestricted vector auto regression (VAR) in the three simulated series.

Figure 3.1 shows the probability distributions of the estimates of the forward-looking component of the Phillips curve. The first two rows reveal that using the data generated under indeterminacy the estimates of ω from a conventional hybrid specification are significantly biased, with the median of the distribution around 0.64 (0.77) under orthogonality (continuity) in the GMM case. The bias is slightly less pronounced in the TSLS case. Hence, when indeterminacy is neglected the null hypothesis of no backward-looking component in the Phillips curve is strongly rejected even if the data-generating process is purely forward-looking.

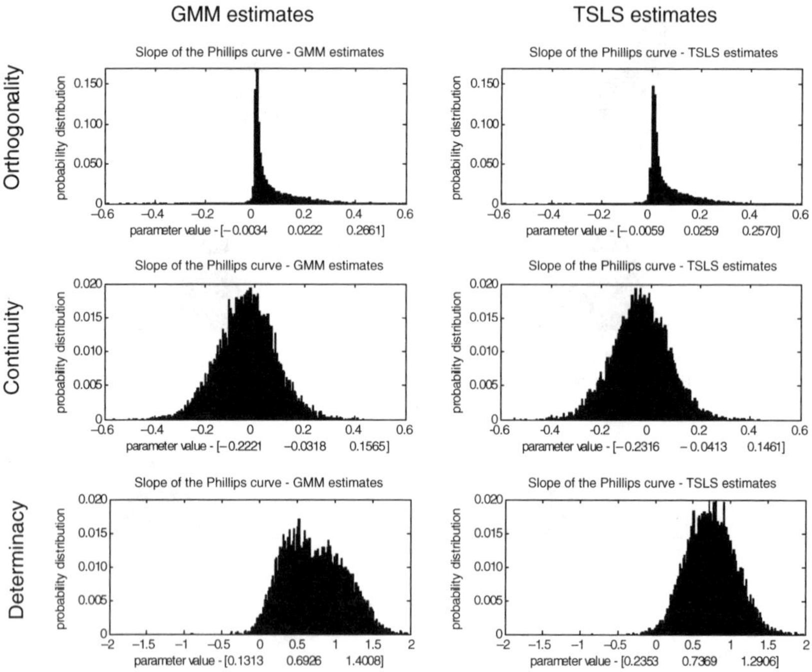

Figure 3.2 Slope of the Phillips curve
See notes to Figure 3.1.

An intuitive explanation for this result can be found in the self-fulfilling nature of inflation expectations under indeterminacy. The private sector anticipates that in response to a positive shock to inflation the monetary authorities will not raise sufficiently the nominal interest rate, and therefore anticipates a negative real rate. The fall in the *ex ante* real interest rate fuels a boom in real activity, and the boom in turn fuels further inflation. This implies not only that the expectations of high inflation are indeed confirmed but also that inflation remains persistently above target.

An aggressive monetary policy stance towards deviations of inflation from target implies, in contrast, that the real interest rate is implicitly set so as to outweigh a rise in expected inflation. This means that a pick-up in actual inflation is promptly followed by a reversal towards the target, and in the case of a perfectly credible inflation-targeting regime and a purely forward-looking model inflation is white noise.

The technical reason for the bias is that the solution of a linear rational expectations model requires that all unstable roots in the matrix of autoregressive coefficients Γ_1^* be suppressed. The New Keynesian model is characterised by two roots, λ_j with $j = 1, 2$. When monetary policy conforms to the Taylor Principle the two roots are unstable, that is the system is determinate, and the solution generates no 'extra' persistence relative to the specification of the model. This means that if the data-generating process is purely forward-looking, as it is here, the backward-looking term of the Phillips curve $(1 - \omega)$ should be zero statistically.

In contrast, indeterminacy is characterised by only one *unstable* root, thereby implying that the solution now generates 'extra' persistence through the *stable* root λ_1 – see equation (3.14) in the Appendix. This is confirmed by the third row of Figure 3.1. Under determinacy, the median estimates of ω are not statistically different from the true value of 0.99 at the 1 per cent significance level, though they are somewhat smaller numerically. As shown below using simulations from a longer sample, this is likely to reflect a small sample problem.

Figure 3.2 shows the results for the slope of the Phillips curve. The data are generated under the assumption that the true parameter is 0.77 but only the estimates on the series simulated under determinacy are consistent with this value. In contrast, using the orthogonality or the continuity assumption the estimates of k are severely biased towards zero and largely below the 'true' value.

Indeterminacy may also have important implications for the reduced-form properties of the (simulated) data. To explore this possibility we estimate with OLS the following process for inflation:

$$\pi_t = \mu + \phi_1 \pi_{t-1} + \phi_2 \pi_{t-2} + \ldots + \phi_p \pi_{t-p} + \xi_t \tag{3.7}$$

with $3 < p < 8$. Figure 3.3 reports the probability distributions of the sum of the autoregressive coefficients in equation (3.7). Indeterminacy generates a

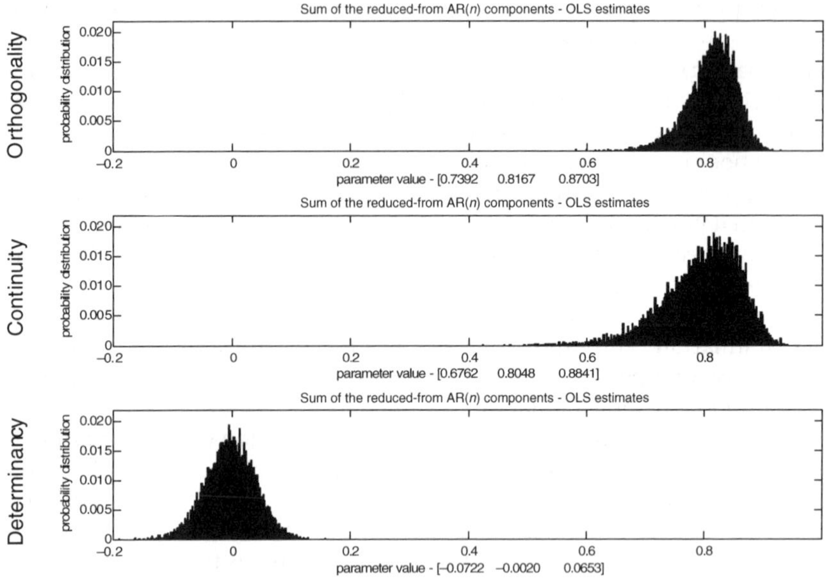

Figure 3.3 Sum of the reduced-form AR(n) components – OLS estimates
See notes to Figure 3.1.

sizable persistence, though the reduced-form persistence of a purely forward-looking model solved for the unique rational expectations equilibrium is zero. In contrast, the estimates on the inflation series are centred on zero under determinacy.

This finding also suggests that weak instruments are unlikely to be a concern under indeterminacy where inflation is quite a persistent process. Furthermore, while in principle it seems more reasonable to question the relevance of the instruments under determinacy, the third rows of Figures 3.1 and 3.2 show that in practice the GMM estimates match the 'true' values of parameters under determinacy.

The results so far reveal the extent to which the estimates of the New Keynesian Phillips curve are sensitive to a different monetary policy response to inflation. Figure 3.4 presents the estimates and the confidence intervals of the parameters of the inflation process as a function of ψ_π. The estimates are computed for a grid of 20 points over the interval [0, 2]. The interesting result from this experiment is that – with the exception of the slope of the Phillips curve – the size of the bias is a negative function of the distance of ψ_π from the border between the indeterminacy and the determinacy region. As far as the forward-looking component of the Phillips curve is concerned, only a central bank response to inflation close to zero would deliver an unbiased estimate of ω within the indeterminacy region.

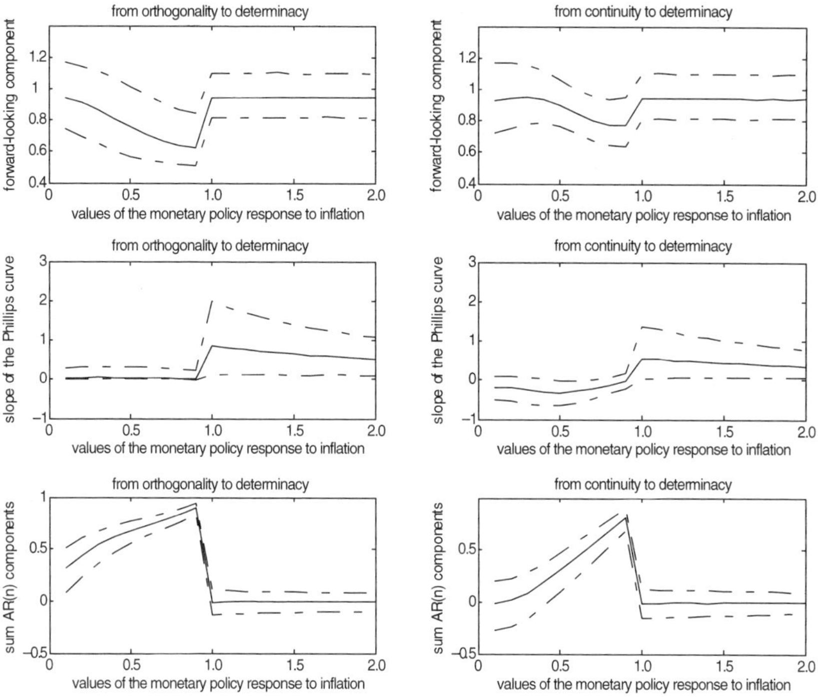

Figure 3.4 GMM estimates as a function of the monetary policy response to inflation – from indeterminacy to determinacy
See notes to Figure 3.1.

Robustness analysis

To investigate the relevance of sample length for our findings we repeat the experiment described above using 80 and 400 observations. As the previous results were robust to running 1,000 simulations, we set the number of repetitions to the latter value in an effort to make the computational burden lighter. Results in this section are available upon request.

The bias is still sizable in both experiments, though the estimates over a longer period are, not surprisingly, more accurate and precise. Moreover, the median estimate of the forward-looking component of the Phillips curve in the large sample is also now close to 0.99 numerically. This suggests not only that the 'neglected indeterminacy bias' is more than simply a small sample bias, but also that it is not likely to be merely a peculiarity of the instrumental variable estimators.

The results are also robust to using a 'mixed' sample of 160 observations in which the monetary policy rule switches from passive to active midway through the period. Specifically, the first 80 observations are generated under indeterminacy while the second half of the observations are generated under determinacy. The estimate of the forward-looking component of the NKPC is 0.81 (0.84) using the orthogonality (continuity) identification, the slope takes a value of 0.06 (0.12) and the sum of the autoregressive coefficients of the reduced-form process is 0.56 (0.72).

In another robustness check, we vary the standard deviation of the sunspot shocks, σ_ζ. The bias of the estimates of the forward-looking component increases with σ_ζ for empirically plausible values of this standard deviation. For values larger than 0.3, which exceeds the estimates in Lubik and Schorfheide (2004), the bias of the forward-looking term appears stable.

The estimates of the slope of the Phillips curve seem virtually unchanged by the size of the standard deviation. As indeterminacy can influence aggregate fluctuations both by affecting directly the equilibrium dynamics through the sunspot shock and by affecting indirectly the transmission of the structural shocks to the endogenous variables, this result suggests that the bias in the slope is mostly due to the indirect effect. The sum of the autoregressive coefficients of the reduced-form process of inflation is a decreasing function of σ_ζ. This is probably due to the fact that a larger variance of the sunspot shocks translates into a larger variance of the endogenous state variables without implying a higher covariance between inflation and its own lags. The overall effect is therefore a reduction in the OLS estimates.

Empirical evidence

The previous section showed that pooling observations from different monetary policy regimes can be highly misleading for the inference based on the full sample estimates of the NKPC. In this section, we present some evidence on UK, US and euro area quarterly data that is consistent with the 'neglected indeterminacy bias' hypothesis.

As a preview of the results, the policy regimes that the empirical literature on monetary policy rules typically associates with a weak interest rate response to inflation are characterised by a higher degree of inertia in the structural process of inflation.

For the purpose of estimation, the NKPC is specified in the following hybrid version:

$$\pi_t = \omega_f \pi_{t+1} + \omega_b \pi_{t-1} + kx_t + v_t \tag{3.8}$$

where $v_t \equiv -\omega_f\,(\pi_{t+1} - E_t\pi_{t+1})$. Inflation is measured as the annualised quarterly change in the GDP deflator. As far as excess demand is concerned, we present results using two alternative measures of the business cycle. The first measure is the output gap. For the US this corresponds to the deviation of real GDP from the official estimates of real potential output provided by the Congressional Budget Office (CBO), whereas for the UK it is the residuals from a regression of real GDP on a quadratic trend. The second measure is the labour share calculated as the ratio of nominal compensation to employees to nominal GDP. The data were obtained in January 2005 from the Bank of England and the Federal Reserve Bank of St Louis.

For the UK, we consider the period 1979:02 to 2003:04. The starting point corresponds to the date the Conservative government moved towards a more explicit counter-inflationary monetary policy. Moreover, data on the UK labour market, including unit labour costs, began to be systematically collected and published only in 1979 with the establishment of the Labour Force Survey. The full sample is divided around the fourth quarter of 1992 when the Bank of England announced for the first time an explicit target for inflation. Given the short length of the later period, we compare the estimates of the pre-1992 regime with the full sample estimates. Nelson (2003) shows that the pre- and post-1992 periods are characterised by a marked difference in the monetary policy stance in that the nominal interest rate was raised more than proportionally in response to inflation movements only after 1992.[2]

For the USA, we consider the period 1966:01 to 1997:04. The beginning of the sample corresponds to the date the Federal funds rate was first traded consistently above the discount rate. The first sub-sample ends in 1979:02 when Paul Volcker was appointed Chairman of the Fed and fighting inflation became a clear policy objective. The later sub-sample begins in 1982: 3 and therefore excludes the period in which Bernanke and Mihov (1998) document that the operating procedure of the Fed temporarily switched from federal funds rate to non-borrowed reserves targeting. The end of the sample is chosen so as to make our results comparable to the available literature, which typically uses observations until 1997:04 (see Galí and Gertler, 1999, and Lubik and Schorfheide, 2004). The results are not affected, however, by expanding the sample until 2003:04. Clarida, Galí and Gertler (2000) pioneered a large empirical literature which has found that the monetary policy stance of the Fed can be described as *passive* during the Pre-Volcker regime and *active* during the post-Volcker regime.

Estimates

Under rational expectations, the forecast error v_t is orthogonal to the current information set and equation (3.8) can be estimated with GMM using an optimal weighting matrix that accounts for possible heteroscedasticity and serial correlation in the error terms. In practice, we employ a three-lag Newey–West estimate of the covariance matrix where the number of lags is selected according to standard lag length criteria on a four-variate VAR in inflation, output gap, unit labour cost and nominal interest rate. Starting from date $t-1$, three lags of these four variables are included as instruments corresponding to 9 overidentifying restrictions that can be tested for. The null hypothesis of valid overidentifying restrictions is never rejected.

Table 3.2 GMM estimates of the NKPC, United Kingdom

Sample	*1979:02–1992:04*		*1979:02–2003:04*	
Specification	*Labour share*	*Output gap*	*Labour share*	*Output gap*
ω_f	0.594***	0.633***	1.002***	1.063***
	(0.126)	(0.137)	(0.134)	(0.124)
ω_b	0.396***	0.354***	0.016	–0.073
	(0.119)	(0.132)	(0.128)	(0.126)
κ	0.009	–0.023	0.037	–0.079*
	(0.072)	(0.043)	(0.046)	(0.042)
J-stat *p*-value	0.333	0.346	0.767	0.929
Analog F-stat	21.567#	17.858#	23.552#	25.472#

Notes: Standard errors using a three-lag Newey–West estimate of the covariance matrix are reported in brackets. If not specified otherwise, the instrument set includes three lags of inflation, output gap, labour share and nominal interest rate. *J* refers to the statistics of Hansen's test for *m* over-identifying restrictions which is distributed as a $\chi^2(m)$ under the null hypothesis of valid over-identifying restrictions. *Analog F* refers to the minimum eigenvalue of the matrix analog of the first-stage *F*-statistics. The test rejects the null hypothesis of weak instruments in favour of the alternative of strong instruments if *Analog F* exceeds the critical value. The critical value is computed at the 5% significance level. The superscript ***, ** and * denote the rejection of the null hypothesis that the true coefficient is zero at the 1 per cent, 5 per cent and 10 per cent significance levels, respectively. The superscript # denotes the rejection of the null hypothesis of weak instruments.

Table 3.2 reports the results for the UK. Regardless of the measure of excess demand, the pre-1992 estimates of the forward-looking component of the Phillips curve are statistically smaller than its full sample counterpart, consistently with the prediction of 'neglected indeterminacy bias'. In particular, the hypothesis of no backward looking in the NKPC can only be rejected in the earlier period. The estimates of the slope display a positive sign only when the labour share measure is used and they are larger in the full sample, though they are not statistically different from zero.

Restricting $\omega_b = (1 - \omega_f)$ does not alter our conclusions. Furthermore, letting the later sub-sample begin in the first quarter of 1993 produces results, not reported but available upon request, which are very similar to the full sample estimates. Given the limited number of observations available since the introduction of the inflation targeting regime however we prefer not to give much weight to the finding on the later sub-sample. Interestingly, these results are consistent with and complement the reduced-form evidence in Kuttner and Posen (1999), Batini and Nelson (2001) and Benati (2006) who shows that the persistence of inflation in the UK has dramatically declined since the announcement of an explicit target for inflation, moving from a value between 0.79 and 0.96 before 1992 to a value not statistically different from zero afterward.

Table 3.3 GMM estimates of the NKPC, United States

Sample	*1966:01–1979:02*		*1982:03–1997:04*	
Specification	*Labour share*	*Output gap*	*Labour share*	*Output gap*
ω_f	0.605***	0.721***	0.815***	0.802***
	(0.075)	(0.080)	(0.093)	(0.068)
ω_b	0.376***	0.274***	0.185**	0.188***
	(0.075)	(0.083)	(0.084)	(0.063)
κ	0.120	–0.072	0.194**	–0.034
	(0.096)	(0.062)	(0.089)	(0.046)
J-stat p-value	0.606	0.471	0.515	0.325
Analog F-stat	21.661#	27.218#	33.143#	18.103#

See notes to Table 3.2 for details.

The findings for the US are displayed in Table 3.3 and appear to bear out the evidence for the UK. The estimates of the forward-looking component are larger over the most recent monetary policy regime and they are significantly so using the labour share measure. Unlike the UK, the later sample seems characterised by a significant, albeit smaller, backward-looking term. The slope of the Phillips curve takes a positive sign only when unit labour costs are used and, consistently with the simulations in the previous section, it is statistically different from zero only in the

Table 3.4 GMM estimates of the NKPC in selected euro area countries

Countries	ω_f	ω_b	κ	*J-stat p-value*
Germany	0.702***	0.089	0.096***	
	(0.073)	(0.055)	(0.028)	0.731
France	0.653***	0.300***	0.040	
	(0.041)	(0.043)	(0.030)	0.859
Italy	0.409***	0.516***	0.059**	
	(0.047)	(0.032)	(0.023)	0.613
Spain	0.477***	0.495***	0.020	
	(0.052)	(0.019)	(0.018)	0.860
Netherlands	0.629***	0.368***	0.083***	
	(0.048)	(0.041)	(0.029)	0.898

Notes: Estimates are based on the unit labour costs specification of the Phillips curve. The instrument set includes three lags of inflation, output gap, unit labor costs and wage inflation. The superscript ***, ** and * denote the rejection of the null hypothesis that the true coefficient is zero at the 1 per cent, 5 per cent and 10 per cent significance levels, respectively.

Source: Benigno and Lopez-Salido (2006, table 1). Sample: 1970: 1–1998: 4.

post-Volcker period. The full sample estimates based on the labour share measure, not reported but available upon request, have a slope coefficient of 0.02 which is not statistically different from zero. The reduced-form analyses in Cogley and Sargent (2005 and 2002) reveal that the persistence of US inflation increased during the second half of the 1960s and during the 1970s and then fell in the 1980s and 1990s. Our results are compatible with the notion of a fall in inflation inertia.

Table 3.4 reports estimates of the NKPC based on unit labour costs for selected euro area countries. The sample is 1970–98. Forward-looking components are dominant in Germany, France and the Netherlands, whereas the process of inflation for Italy and Spain is significantly more backward-looking. For Germany, it is not possible to reject the null that lagged inflation is unimportant, whereas the forward-looking weight for Italy is significantly smaller than the backward-looking weight. The most striking result in Table 3.4 is that the countries with the strongest reputation for rigorous monetary policy are systematically associated with the largest estimates of the forward-looking term.

Results for the euro area are presented in Table 3.5. The sample is 1999: 01–2005:03 and the frequency is quarterly. As a meaningful analysis on the euro area constrains the length of the time period to be small, one should resist reading too much into those estimates. The forward-looking term is significantly larger than the backward-looking component and unit labour costs do have explanatory power. These estimates are similar to those obtained by Galí, Gertler and Lopez-Salido (2001) over the sample 1970–98. A comparison with Table 3.4 reveals that, through the lens of the NKPC, euro area and German inflation dynamics appear close. Whether the similarity is driven by the structure of the economy or by monetary policy, however, remains to be addressed.

The results in this section are of course only suggestive, and it is beyond the scope of this chapter to discriminate whether the observed decline in inflation inertia represents a genuine structural break, which is an intrinsic feature of the economy, or rather the effect of indeterminacy over the earlier samples. Nevertheless, it is intriguing to observe that the structural

Table 3.5 GMM estimate of the NKPC for the euro area, 1999:01 to 2005:03

	ω_f	ω_b	κ	*J-stat p-value*
Euro-area	0.769***	0.169*	0.052***	
	(0.061)	(0.095)	(0.013)	0.748

Notes: Estimates are based on the unit labour costs specification of the Phillips curve. The instrument set includes three lags of inflation, output gap, labor share and nominal interest rate. The superscript ***, ** and * denote the rejection of the null hypothesis that the true coefficient is zero at the 1 per cent, 5 per cent and 10 per cent significance levels, respectively.

and the reduced-form inertia of the inflation process appear a peculiarity of the periods associated with a passive monetary policy reaction function. And large estimates of the Phillips curve forward-looking component coincide with periods of activist monetary policy in euro area countries. Interestingly, Cogley and Sbordone (2005) show that a constant-parameter version of the NKPC can be consistent with a drifting-parameter VAR, thereby suggesting that a structural break in the Phillips curve does not seem to account for the changing persistence of US inflation.

Weak instruments

Instrument weakness is an important issue we must address in order to validate our estimates. Stock and Yogo (2003) tabulate critical values for the multiple endogenous regressor analog of the first-stage F-statistics and define weak instruments in terms of bias and in terms of size of the test. In particular, a set of instruments can be deemed strong if the analog of the F-statistics is sufficiently large that either the instrumental variable bias is no more than x per cent of the inconsistency of OLS or a 5 per cent hypothesis test rejects no more than y per cent of the time. The first definition is useful for inference purposes whereas the second seems appropriate for hypothesis testing. Unfortunately, there is no particular guidance for the selection of x and y other than the researcher's tolerance.

In general, we find that our set of instruments can be deemed strong using $x = 10$ and $y = 15$ – even more ambitious tolerance levels can be met in some cases – with two exceptions. Both of them correspond to the pre-1992 regime in the UK. We then expand the list of instrumental variables in these two cases to include wage inflation, according to the reasoning that important reforms in the labour market took place during the 1980s and it seems plausible to think they also had an impact on inflation. Moreover, in this estimation we reduce the number of lags of the instrumental variables from three to two in an effort to minimise the potential small-sample bias that may arise when too many over-identifying restrictions are imposed. The second and the third columns of Table 3.2 show that the expanded set of instruments can now be deemed strong over the the pre-1992 period as well, and the estimates reported in these columns refer to the expanded instrument set.

Conclusions

This chapter begins to bridge the gap between two bodies of research on inflation dynamics. The first body uses a microfounded NKPC to estimate the structural relation between inflation and marginal costs. On the promise of identifying truly structural parameters, this literature mainly focuses on the full postwar period with a typical sample starting in 1960. The second body uses the New Keynesian model to demonstrate that bad monetary policy in the form of a weak interest rate reaction to inflation generates sunspot fluctuations which can sizably influence the macroeconomic dynamics.

Using a purely forward-looking New Keynesian model as the data-generating process, we have computed the solutions of the rational expectations model for two classes of parameterisations of the interest rate rule. These parameterisations roughly correspond to the shift in the conduct of monetary policy that occurred in a number of industrialised countries around the beginning of the 1980s. Specifically, one class of coefficients represents a passive monetary policy stance according to which the central bank can generate indeterminacy by moving the nominal interest rate insufficiently in response to inflation pressures. The second class of parameterisations describes an activist conduct that conforms to the Taylor principle and therefore produces a unique stable solution.

Monte Carlo simulations demonstrate that the estimates of the forward-looking component and the slope of the NKPC can be severely biased downward whenever two conditions hold. First, the data are generated under a passive monetary policy rule. Second, the estimation procedure arbitrarily rules out the possibility of indeterminacy. Furthermore, this chapter shows that the bias becomes larger the more closely the interest rate response to inflation approaches the boundary between indeterminacy and determinacy. These results are robust to the number of observations in the simulated sample and to the selection of the instrumental variable estimator. Finally, when the above two conditions are met the sum of autoregressive coefficients in the reduced-form representation of the inflation process is close to one, even though the data-generating process exhibits no intrinsic persistence.

Empirical evidence on the NKPC using data for the UK, the US and the euro area shows that inflation inertia is far more pronounced during periods characterised by a less-than-proportional response of the nominal interest rate to inflation. This result holds independently of whether the measure of excess demand is labour share or output gap, and is in line with the prediction of the 'neglected indeterminacy bias' hypothesis. Moreover, our structural estimates are consistent with and complement the reduced-form evidence in Benati (2006) for the UK and in Cogley and Sargent (2005) for the US that the change in inflation persistence is concomitant with a policy regime shift.

Shifts in the monetary policy rule therefore have serious implications for inference based on the NKPC. This finding indicates some caution is needed to interpret the results from full sample analyses which pool observations from different monetary policy regimes. And the neglected indeterminacy bias can arise even if the Phillips curve is a structurally invariant relation.

An interesting avenue for future research is to estimate a time-varying structural model that at each point in time contemplates the possibility of a switch between the indeterminacy and the determinacy solution. Furthermore, a richer model of the business cycle may relax the tight link between the degree of activism in the policy rule and indeterminacy, with consequences for the 'neglected indeterminacy bias' that are worth exploring.

Appendix: solution of the LRE model

In order to transform the canonical form and solve the model, we follow Sims (2001) and exploit the *QZ* decomposition of the matrices Γ_0 and Γ_1. This corresponds to computing the matrices Q, Z, Λ and Ξ such that $QQ' = ZZ' = I_n$, Λ and Ξ are upper triangular, $\Gamma_0 = Q'\Lambda Z$ and $\Gamma_1 = Q'\Xi Z$. Moler and Stewart (1973) prove that the *QZ* decomposition always exists. Defining $\omega_t = Z's_t$ and pre-multiplying (4) by Q, we obtain:

$$\begin{bmatrix} \Lambda_{11} & \Lambda_{12} \\ 0 & \Lambda_{22} \end{bmatrix} \begin{bmatrix} \omega_{1,t} \\ \omega_{2,t} \end{bmatrix} = \begin{bmatrix} \Xi_{11} & \Xi_{12} \\ 0 & \Xi_{22} \end{bmatrix} \begin{bmatrix} \omega_{1,t-1} \\ \omega_{2,t-1} \end{bmatrix} + \begin{bmatrix} Q_{1.} \\ Q_{2.} \end{bmatrix} (\Psi\varepsilon_t + \Pi\eta_t) \tag{3.9}$$

where the vector of generalised eigenvalues λ, which is the ratio between the diagonal elements of Ξ and Λ, has been partitioned such that the lower block collects all the explosive eigenvalues. The matrices Ξ, Λ and Q have been partitioned accordingly, and therefore $Q_{j.}$ collects the blocks of rows that correspond to the stable ($j = 1$) and unstable ($j = 2$) eigenvalues respectively.

The explosive block of (3.9) can be rewritten as:

$$\omega_{2,t} = \Lambda_{22}^{-1}\,\Xi_{22}\omega_{2,t-1} + \Lambda_{22}^{-1}\,Q_{2.}\,(\Psi\varepsilon_t + \Pi\eta_t)$$

A non-explosive solution of the linear rational expectations model (3.4) for s_t requires $\omega_{2,t} = 0\ \forall t \geq 0$. This can be obtained by setting $\omega_{2,0} = 0$ and choosing for every vector ε_t the endogenous forecast error η_t that satisfies the following condition:

$$\Psi^*\varepsilon_t + \Pi^*\eta_t = 0 \tag{3.10}$$

where $\Psi^* = Q_2.\Psi$ and $\Pi^* = Q_2.\Pi$.

In general, we have to consider three different cases. If the number of endogenous forecast errors is equal to the number of unstable eigenvalues, the system is determined and the stability condition (3.10) uniquely determines η_t. If the number of endogenous forecast errors does exceed the number of unstable eigenvalues, the system is undetermined and sunspot fluctuations can arise. If the number of endogenous forecast errors is smaller than the number of unstable eigenvalues, the system has no solutions. This condition generalises Blanchard and Kahn's (1980) procedure of counting the number of unstable roots and predetermined variables.[3]

A general solution for the endogenous forecast error can be computed through a singular value decomposition of $\Pi^* = UDV'$. Lubik and Schorfheide (2003) show that this solution takes the following form:

$$\eta_t = (-V_{.1}D_{11}^{-1}U'_{.1}\Psi^* + V_{.2}M_1)\ \varepsilon_t + V_{.2}M_2\zeta_t \tag{3.11}$$

where D_{11} is the upper-left diagonal block of D, U and V are orthonormal matrices, and M_s with $s = 1, 2$ are the matrices that govern the influence of the sunspot shock on the model dynamics.

Solution (3.11) can be combined with (3.4) to yield the following law of motion for the state vector:

$$s_t = \Gamma_1^* s_{t-1} + [\Psi^* - \Pi^* V_{.1}D_{11}^{-1}U'_{.1}\Psi^*]\ \varepsilon_t + \Pi^* V_{.2}\ (M_1\varepsilon_t + M_2\zeta_t) \tag{3.12}$$

where for expositional convenience the notation (θ) is suppressed whenever we refer to a single vector of parameters equation-wide.

Equation (3.12) shows that indeterminacy has two consequences. First, sunspot fluctuations ζ_t can influence equilibrium dynamics as long as M_2 is a non-zero matrix. Second, the transmission of fundamental shocks ε_t to the endogenous variables is no longer uniquely identified as the elements of M_1 are not pinned down by the structure of the linear rational expectations model. Under determinacy $V_{.2} = 0$ and therefore the sunspot shock has no effect on aggregate fluctuations.

In order to compute the solutions of the model under indeterminacy, it is necessary to impose some additional restrictions on the endogenous forecast errors. In practice, we normalise $M_2 = 1$ such that ζ_t can be reinterpreted as a reduced-form sunspot shock. Moreover, we follow Lubik and Schorfheide (2003) and focus on two alternative identification schemes for M_1 which are labelled orthogonality and continuity. The first auxiliary assumption is that the effects of fundamental and sunspot shocks on the forecast error are *orthogonal* to each other. This corresponds to assuming $M_1 = 0$.

The second identifying scheme corresponds to choosing M_1 such that the impulse responses $\partial s_t/\partial \varepsilon_t'$ are *continuous* at the boundary between the determinacy and indeterminacy regions. Let Θ^I and Θ^D be the sets of all possible vectors of parameters, θ's, in the indeterminacy and determinacy region respectively. For every vector $\theta \in \Theta^I$ we identify a corresponding vector $\tilde{\theta} \in \Theta^D$ that lies on the boundary of the two regions and choose M_1 such that the response of s_t to ε_t conditional on θ mimics the response conditional on $\tilde{\theta}$. In practice, we minimise the least squares deviations of the two impulse responses such that:

$$M_1 = [B'_2(\theta)B_2(\theta)]^{-1}\ B'_2(\theta)\ [B_1(\tilde{\theta}) - B_1(\theta)] \tag{3.13}$$

where

$$B_1(\tilde{\theta}) = \frac{\partial s_t}{\partial \varepsilon_t'}(\tilde{\theta})$$

and

$$B_1(\theta) + B_2(\theta)M_1 = [\Psi^*(\theta) - \Pi^*(\theta)V_{.1}(\theta)D_{11}^{-1}(\theta)U'_{.1}(\theta)\Psi^*(\theta)] + \Pi^*(\theta)V_{.2}(\theta)M_1 = \frac{\partial s_t}{\partial \varepsilon_t'}(\theta, M_1)$$

The new vector $\tilde{\theta}$ is obtained from θ by replacing ψ_1 with condition (3.5), which marks the boundary between the determinacy and indeterminacy region in the system (3.1) to (3.3).[4]

The solution of (3.9) is now fully characterised and for any given vector of parameters of the model it is possible to compute the evolution of the state variables under both determinacy and indeterminacy. In particular, the forecast error η_t and the law of motion for the latent state:

$$\omega_{1,t} = \Lambda_{11}^{-1}\Xi_{11}\omega_{1,t-1} + \Lambda_{11}^{-1}Q_{1.}(\Psi\varepsilon_t + \Pi\eta_t) \qquad (3.14)$$

can be used to obtain $s_t = Z\omega_t$. The ratio $\Lambda_{11}^{-1}\Xi_{11} = \lambda_1(\theta)$ in (3.14) represents the generalised *stable* eigenvalue of $\Gamma_1^*(\theta)$ in the system (3.12) and it is the source of 'extra' persistence in the solution of the model (3.1–3) under indeterminacy.

Notes

1 The results below are not affected by excluding z_t from the policy rule.

2 As the chapter focuses on monetary policy, we abstract from fiscal policy considerations which may also have contributed to the inflation outcome of the 1980s.

3 Sims' solution method has the advantage that it does not require the separation of predetermined variables from 'jump' variables. Rather, it recognizes that in equilibrium models expectational residuals are attached to equations and that the structure of the coefficient matrices in the canonical form implicitly selects the linear combination of variables that needs to be predetermined for a solution to exist.

4 Lubik and Schorfheide (2004) note that this way of computing the vector M_1 relates to the search for the minimal-state-variable solution advocated by McCallum (1983), i.e. the most meaningful solution from an economic perspective among the n-possible ones under indeterminacy.

References

Batini, N. and E. Nelson (2001) 'The Lag from Monetary Policy Actions to Inflation: Friedman Revisited', *International Finance*, 4: 381–400.

Benati, L. (2006) 'U.K. Monetary Regimes and Macroeconomic Stylised Facts', Bank of England Working Paper no. 290.

Benigno, P. and J.D. Lopez-Salido (2006) 'Inflation persistence and Optimal Monetary Policy in the Euro Area', *Journal of Money, Credit & Banking*, 38: 587–614.

Bernanke, B. and I. Mihov (1998) 'Measuring Monetary Policy', *Quarterly Journal of Economics*, 63: 869–902.

Blanchard, O. and C.M. Kahn (1980) 'The Solution of Linear Difference Models under Rational Expectations', *Econometrica*, 48: 1305–13.

Clarida, R., J. Galí and M. Gertler (2000) 'Monetary Policy Rules and Macroeconomic Stability: Evidence and Some Theory', *Quarterly Journal of Economics*, 115: 147–80.

Cogley, T. and T.J. Sargent (2005) 'Drift and Volatilities: Monetary Policies and Outcomes in the Post WWII U.S.', *Review of Economic Dynamics*, 8: 262–302.

Cogley, T. and T.J. Sargent (2002) 'Evolving Post World War II U.S. Inflation Dynamics', *NBER Macroeconomics Annual*.

Cogley, T. and A. Sbordone (2005) 'A Search for a Structural Phillips Curve', mimeo, University of California, Davis.

Eichenbaum, M. and J. Fisher (2004) 'Evaluating the Calvo Model of Sticky Prices' mimeo, Northwestern University.

Galí, J. and M. Gertler (1999) 'Inflation Dynamics: A Structural Econometric Analysis', *Journal of Monetary Economics*, 44: 195–222.

Galí, J., M. Gertler and J.D. Lopez-Salido (2001) 'European Inflation Dynamics', *European Economic Review*, 45: 1237–70.

King, R. (2000) 'The New IS-LM Model: Language, Logic and Limits', *Federal Reserve Bank of Richmond Economic Quarterly*, 86: 45–103.

Kuttner, K. and A. Posen (1999) 'Does Talk Matter After All? Inflation Targeting and Central Bank Behavior', Institute for International Economics Working Paper no. 99–10.

Lindé, J. (2005) 'Estimating New Keynesian Phillips Curves: A Full Information Maximum Likelihood Approach', *Journal of Monetary Economics*, 52: 1135–49.

Lubik, T. and F. Schorfheide (2003) 'Computing Sunspot Equilibria in Linear Rational Expectations Models', *Journal of Economic Dynamics and Control*, 28: 273–85.

Lubik, T. and F. Schorfheide (2004) 'Testing for Indeterminacy: An Application to U.S. Monetary Policy', *American Economic Review*, 94: 190–217.

Lucas, R.E. (1976) 'Econometric Policy Evaluation: A Critique', *Carnegie-Rochester Conference Series on Public Policy*, 1: 19–46.

McCallum, B.T. (1983) 'On Non-uniqueness in Linear Rational Expectations Models: An Attempt at Perspective', *Journal of Monetary Economics*, 11(2): 139–68.

Moler, C. and G. Stewart (1973) 'An Algorithm for Generalised Matrix Eigenvalue Problems', *SIAM Journal of Numerical Analysis*, 10: 241–56.

Nelson, E. (2003) 'U.K. Monetary Policy 1972–1997: A Guide using Taylor Rules', in P. Mizen (ed.), *Central Banking, Monetary Theory and Practice: Essays in Honour of Charles Goodhart*. Cheltenham: Edward Elgar.

Rudd, J. and K. Whelan (2005) 'New Tests of the New-Keynesian Phillips Curve', *Journal of Monetary Economics*, 52: 1167–81.

Sbordone, A.M. (2002) 'Prices and Unit Labor Costs: A New Test of Price Stickiness', *Journal of Monetary Economics*, 49: 265–92.

Sims, C.A. (2001) 'Solving Rational Expectations Models', *Computational Economics*, 20: 1–21.

Stock, J. and M. Yogo (2003) 'Testing for Weak Instruments in Linear IV Regression', mimeo, Harvard University.

Taylor, J.B. (1993) 'Discretion versus Policy Rules in Practice', *Carnegie-Rochester Conference Series on Public Policy*, 39: 195–214.

Woodford, M. (2003) *Interest and Prices: Foundations of a Theory of Monetary Policy* Princeton, NJ: Princeton University Press.

Discussion

Fabrizio Mattesini

One of the most interesting advances in recent macroeconomic theory is the revival of the Phillips curve derived on the basis of monopolistic competition and sticky prices. Estimating the New Keynesian Phillips curve (NKPC), however, is quite problematic. One problem is the fact that the most common measures of the output gap enter the regression with the wrong sign; that is, they exhibit a negative relationship with inflation. The other problem is that, according to the NKPC, current inflation depends only on future expected inflation and past inflation does not play any role while, in contrast, empirical evidence finds a lot of persistence in inflation.

The first problem has been explained by Galí *et al.* (2001) by the fact that detrended GDP may be a very poor proxy of the output gap which, in turn, is used as a measure of current marginal costs. These authors have shown that if the labour share is used as a proxy for marginal cost in place of the commonly used measures of the output gap, then empirical estimates of the NKPC become consistent with the theory.

The second problem, however, still creates some embarrassment to the 'standard' Dynamic New Keynesian model. One way to solve the problem is to accept the fact that inflation is highly persistent and to propose a (indeed not fully convincing) theoretical modification of the standard model, such as the inclusion of 'rule of thumbers', that is agents who do not optimize intertemporally and base their consumption only on the past level of income.

In his interesting chapter, Paolo Surico proposes an alternative perspective on the issue, claiming that the empirical evidence on inflation persistence may not be correct because of the existence of a bias in the estimates that comes from neglecting the problem of indeterminacy. His analysis builds on an important strand of literature that aims at testing for indeterminacy and, especially, on the results obtained by Lubik and Schorfheide (2004), who try to assess empirically the consequences of the fact that the Dynamic New Keynesian model, like all linear rational expectations (LRE) models, can have multiple equilibria. If this occurs and indeterminacy arises, the propagation of fundamental shocks is not uniquely determined and sunspot shocks can induce business fluctuations. These authors propose a likelihood-based approach to test for indeterminacy and propose some estimates on postwar US data, finding that the Fed's policy is consistent with determinacy only after 1982. In the pre-Volcker period indeterminacy altered the propagation of the shocks.

Using this approach, Surico claims that the failure to account for indeterminacy might account for the persistence of inflation, and shows that if the data come from an indeterminacy regime, then the forward-looking component of inflation might be underestimated. Standard tests tend to reject the null hypothesis of no backward-looking component in the Phillips curve which implies that inflation persistence might not be an intrinsic feature of the economy but 'endogenous' to the policy regime.

Surico's contribution is extremely interesting. Cutting across two important and recent strands of literature, it provides a rigorous analysis of the consequences of multiple equilibria in dynamic LRE environments, and shows that persistence may be introduced by the existence of a stable root in the solution of the model. Since indeterminacy is a problem usually neglected in the empirical evaluation of macroeconomic models, its possible relevance for explaining important phenomena like the persistence of inflation is, without doubt, a fascinating hypothesis.

Like any interesting hypotheses, obviously, it is not devoid of problems. First, determinacy and indeterminacy regions are very model-dependent. The model considered is the 'standard' DNK model with a Taylor rule, a very successful and popular model. The Taylor principle, however, is often not robust to changes in the model. If, for example, money is also included in the policy function, then the determinacy conditions may change significantly.

Second, Surico's approach derives directly from the Lubik–Schorfheide (2004) analysis which, in turn, identifies a dramatic change in the way monetary policy was implemented during the Volcker–Greenspan years. The chapter, therefore, is part of a line of thought where we find, among others, Romer and Romer (2002) and Clarida, Galí and Gertler (2000), which views the great inflation of the 1970s as the result of 'bad policy' rather than 'bad luck'. There is no consensus, however, on the existence of a drastic policy shift in the behaviour of the Fed in the last forty years. Primiceri (2005) estimates learning models where the rise and fall of inflation is due to the interaction between incorrect beliefs and economic shocks. Sims and Zha (2006) estimate a multivariate regime switching model and identify three policy regimes but they argue that, with high probability, the monetary policy responses to inflation were strong enough to guarantee determinacy. Bernanke and Mihov (1998) and Leeper and Zha (2003) find no strong evidence against the stability of coefficients and, finally, Cogley and Sargent (2005) and Primiceri (2005) find little evidence of a dramatic change in the monetary policy rules.

A third observation concerns the empirical relevance of the indeterminacy hypothesis. Suppose then that we accept the view that indeterminacy may be the cause of observed inflation persistence in the data. How much of it should be attributed to the 'neglected indeterminacy bias'? Surico's chapter shows evidence of a significant reduction in inflation persistence especially in more recent periods, but persistence seems to characterize the Phillips curve also in periods where the response to inflation is strong like, for example, the period 1982–97 in the US. It is likely, therefore, that inflation persistence is a complex phenomenon that cannot be fully explained by the existence of an 'indeterminacy bias'.

Nevertheless, the chapter raises a subtle issue which is very important from the theoretical point of view, but could also be extremely relevant for the practical implementation of monetary policy in the eurozone. Traditionally, inflation in Europe is more persistent than in other countries like the US. This persistence is often attributed to institutional factors, such as rigidities in labour markets and the regulatory framework that governs product markets and financial markets. Surico's analysis suggests instead that what really matters is the adoption of a monetary policy rule that ensures equilibrium determinacy, such as a Taylor rule where interest rates overreact to inflationary shocks. Indeed the fact that the NKPC estimated by Galí *et al.* (2001) for Germany, a country traditionally highly averse to inflation, seems to be entirely forward-looking is strongly suggestive. Since the ECB has been quite successful, from its inception, in keeping inflation under control in the eurozone, can we infer from Surico's results that the framework used by the ECB is appropriate to achieve determinacy? The estimates of the NKPC for the ECB seem to point in that direction, but more work is necessary on individual countries and this certainly represents an important avenue for future research.

References

Bernanke, B. and I. Mihov (1998) 'Measuring Monetary Policy', *Quarterly Journal of Economics*, 63: 869–902.

Clarida, R., J. Galí and M. Gertler (2000) 'Monetary Policy Rules and Macroeconomic Stability: Evidence and Some Theory', *Quarterly Journal of Economics*, 115: 147–80.

Cogley, T. and T.J. Sargent (2005) 'Drift and Volatilities: Monetary Policies and Outcomes in the post WWII US', *Review of Economic Dynamics*, 8: 262–302.

Galí, J., M. Gertler and J.D. Lopez-Salido (2001) 'European Inflation Dynamics', *European Economic Review*, 45: 1237–70.

Leeper, E. and T. Zha (2003) 'Modest Policy Interventions', *Journal of Monetary Economics*, 50: 1673–700.

Lubik, T. and F. Schorfeide (2004) 'Testing for Indeterminacy: An Application to US Monetary Policy', *American Economic Review*, 94: 190–217.

Primiceri, G. (2005) 'Why Inflation Rose and Fell: Policymakers' Beliefs and US Postwar Stabilisation Policy', *Quarterly Journal of Economics*, forthcoming.

Primiceri, G. (2005) 'Time Varying Structural Vector Autoregressions and Monetary Policy', *Review of Economic Studies*, 72: 821–52.
Romer, C. and D. Romer (2002) 'The Evolution of Economic Understanding and Postwar Stabilisation Policy', in *Rethinking Stabilisation Policy*. Kansas City: Federal Reserve Bank of Kansas City.
Sims, C. and T. Zha (2006) 'Were There Regime Switches in US Monetary Policy?, *American Economic Review*, 96: 54–81.

4

Is European Monetary Policy Appropriate for the EMU Member Countries? A Counterfactual Analysis

*Bernd Hayo**

Introduction

The creation of the European Monetary Union (EMU) is the most important event in monetary economics in the last decade. It led to at least two potentially important changes with respect to the setting of short-term interest rates in the EMU member countries. First, the European Central Bank (ECB) bases its monetary policy decisions on aggregate developments in the euro area, which may conceal diverse developments at the national level. Second, the weights on inflation and output in the ECB Taylor rule may deviate from those that were a good description of national interest rates in the pre-EMU phase. The core question of this chapter is how appropriate the actual ECB interest rate setting is for each of the member countries compared to a (hypothetical) situation where national central banks are still responsible for monetary policy. This analysis may also yield some insights into the question of whether monetary policy can be blamed for the low GDP growth rate in a number of EMU member countries, e.g. Germany or Italy.

In this study we interpret short-term interest rates as the prime indicators of monetary policy. Estimated monetary policy reaction functions in the form of Taylor rules are often used as concise descriptions of the monetary policy stance. They explain how deviations of output from potential output and inflation from target affect the level of interest rates. To answer the above research question, we compare the actual short-term interest rate path in the euro area with simulated interest rate paths for the member countries in a counterfactual scenario.

The analysis should enable us to better understand how appropriate the centrally conducted monetary policy is for the respective member coun-

*The author would like to thank the participants of the accompanying workshop and in particular David Cobham, Carlo Favero, and Jacques Mélitz for helpful comments.

tries. If it turned out that the counterfactual national interest rate paths were relatively similar to the actual interest rate paths resulting from European monetary policy decisions, the cost of EMU from centralising monetary policy would be rather small. It would also be difficult to blame the ECB for contributing to the poor growth performance. On the other hand, if we found noteworthy deviations in the interest rate paths for at least some economies, this might raise concerns about the net benefits these countries can expect from EMU membership.

The plan of the chapter is as follows. The next section discusses the empirical approach and some specification issues. I then present and discuss the empirical results of the Taylor rule estimations, before comparing the money market rate in the euro area with counterfactual target rates based on the Taylor rule estimates from the previous section. A final section summarises the main points and concludes.

Empirical setup and econometric methodology

It has become common to operationalise monetary policy actions by a short-term interest rate. This variable is easy to obtain, and setting interest rates is perceived as the common practice of central banks (Borio, 1997). John Taylor's (1993) attempt to describe interest rate setting in terms of a monetary policy reaction function has been widely adopted. In such a so-called 'Taylor rule', the short-term nominal interest rate, representing the central bank's monetary policy instrument, responds to deviations of inflation and output from their target levels.

In order to address the questions raised above we estimate Taylor rules for most of the member countries of EMU using monthly data from the formation of the European Monetary System (EMS) onwards (April 1979 to December 1998). The central bank's target level for short-term nominal interest rates is modelled as a function of the deviation of current output from its trend and of the expected deviation of one-year-ahead inflation from its (constant) target:

$$i^T_t = r^* + \pi^* + \beta\,(\pi_{t+12} - \pi^*) + \gamma y_t \qquad (4.1)$$

where i^T = target nominal interest rate, r^* = long-run real interest rate, y = output gap, π = inflation rate, π^* = target inflation rate, β = inflation weight in the target interest rate, and γ = output weight in the target interest rate.

The long-run level of the nominal interest rate when inflation is equal to its long-run target level and the output gap is zero is given by $r^* + \pi^*$. The constant of the target interest rate is given by:

$$\alpha = r^* + (1-\beta)\,\pi^* \qquad (4.2)$$

where α = constant of the target interest rate.

Finally, we allow for interest rate smoothing by including a lagged interest rate term in the Taylor rule specification. Castelnuovo (2003) argues that the explicit modelling of a lagged interest rate term is preferable to an autoregressive errors specification. In the empirical estimations of the Taylor rules, we adopt the forward-looking specification first proposed by Clarida *et al.* (1998), which leads to the following equation:

$$i_t = \rho\, i_{t-1} + (1-\rho)\, \alpha + (1-\rho)\, \beta\, \pi_{t+12} + (1-\rho)\, \gamma y_t + \varepsilon_t \qquad (4.3)$$

where i = nominal short-term interest rate, ρ = degree of interest rate smoothing and ε = error term.

The presence of interest rate smoothing implies that there is partial adjustment of nominal interest rates to their target level, with a fraction of $1-\rho$ of the difference between the target rate and last period's rate being eliminated each period.

A major problem when working with forward-looking and contemporaneous variables is that they may be correlated with the error term, leading to biased estimates of the coefficients of interest. Therefore, these variables must be instrumented. In addition, the error term may experience non-normality, autocorrelation and heteroscedasticity, causing problems with respect to statistical estimation and inference. It is now common to use the general method of moments (GMM) estimator, as it accounts for endogeneity biases as well as non-spherical errors. However, while the GMM estimator possesses excellent asymptotic properties, it may perform poorly in small samples (see the special issue of the *Journal of Economics and Business Statistics*, 1996).

A potentially important general estimation problem in this context is the choice of instruments. Good instruments are variables that are uncorrelated with the error term and highly correlated with the variable that needs to be instrumented. Thus, good instruments should on the one hand fulfil the orthogonality conditions between regressors and error term. Typically, this assumption is investigated using a test of the validity of over-identifying restrictions when there are more instruments than estimated coefficients (Davidson and MacKinnon, 1993). However, it should be noted that the test of over-identifying restrictions in fact tests the joint hypotheses that the instruments are orthogonal to the error term *and* that the estimated model is correctly specified. Moreover, working with time-series data, it is easy to find instruments that pass this test. On the other hand, good instruments should be highly correlated with the instrumented variable. This aspect is almost never reported or even checked in applied empirical work, in spite of the fact that recent research shows that the use of weak instruments, that is instruments that do not contribute much to explaining the instrumented variable, can lead to substantial biases in both estimators and test statistics even in large samples (Hahn and Hausman, 2003, Stock *et al.*, 2002). Stock and Yogo (2003) propose a test for weak instruments based on the *F*-test value of the first-stage regression in a two-stage least-squares procedure.

However, one still has to solve the practical problem of choosing among a large number of potential instruments the ones that should be included. This instrument selection problem follows Hayo and Hofmann (2006) by applying a recently developed automatic model selection algorithm called GETS (see Hendry and Krolzig, 1999). GETS starts from a general model and removes redundant instruments. While doing so, it searches all possible paths of the testing-down process and reports the most parsimonious model that does not violate a reduction test. Thus, the strongest instruments will be selected from a given choice of variables and their lags. This does not remove all arbitrariness, as, for instance, the researcher still needs to choose the potential instrumental variables and their maximum lag length, but it appears to be superior to the *ad hoc* methods typically employed in empirical research.

Empirical estimation of national monetary policy reaction functions

To prepare the ground for the counterfactual simulations, we need to estimate the national Taylor rules before the start of EMU. The data utilized in the analysis are: the money market rate for the interest rate, seasonally adjusted industrial production for output and the annualized rate of change in the seasonally adjusted CPI for inflation.[1] As instruments, we use up to six lagged values of the interest rate, the inflation rate, the output gap, the growth rate of the effective real exchange rate, the growth rate of the oil price index in the local currency, and the monthly growth rate of narrow money. Following Clarida *et al.* (1998) the output gap has been constructed by taking the residuals of a regression of the industrial production series on a constant, a linear trend and a quadratic trend. Table 4.1 summarises the estimation results using the general method of moments (GMM). First, we should analyse the adequacy of the chosen instruments. As was expected, none of the instrument sets fails the *J*-test, the *p*-values of which are given in the last columns of Tables 4.1 and 4.2. Applying the weak instrument test by Stock and Yogo (2003) indicates that in almost all cases we can reject at a 5 per cent significance level the hypothesis that the instrumental variable estimator experiences a 5 per cent bias relative to the OLS estimator.

Exceptions are inflation in Ireland (only rejection of a 20 per cent bias) and the output gap in the Netherlands (only rejection of a 10 per cent bias). Testing the bias in the size of the instrumental variable tests at a 5 per cent level, we can reject the hypothesis of a 10 per cent bias in most cases. Again there are some problems, this time with inflation and the output gap in Belgium (only rejection of a 15 per cent bias), inflation in Ireland (not

Table 4.1 GMM estimates of national monetary policy reaction functions

	i_{t-1} (ρ)	π_{t+12} (β)	y_t (γ)	Constant (α)	No. of obs.	SE of regression	*J*-test (*p*-value)
Austria	0.89**	1.26**	0.31**	2.50**	237	0.46	0.15
Belgium	0.93**	1.23**	0.21	2.76**	237	1.01	0.51
Finland	0.97**	1.28*	0.39	3.01	237	0.68	0.90
France	0.93**	0.60**	0.45**	5.46**	234	0.64	0.81
France (sample 1987)	0.89**	1.61**	0.31**	3.04*	144	0.59	0.85
Germany	0.92**	1.25**	0.32**	2.56**	101	0.15	0.83
Ireland	1.08**	1.11**	0.28**	6.30**	234	3.77	0.99
Italy (sample 1987)	0.93**	1.87**	0.25	0.27	144	0.58	0.56
Netherlands	0.93**	2.99**	0.85*	–0.82	228	0.67	0.76
Portugal	0.97**	1.45	2.18	–1.67	191	2.23	0.96
Portugal (sample 1987)	Lag(1): 1.35** Lag(2): –0.39*	1.97(*)	2.39	–2.63	144	2.20	0.97
Spain	0.97**	0.96**	0.19	5.23**	235	1.61	0.93
ECB	0.85**	1.48(*)	0.60**	0.32	53	0.16	0.06

Notes: (*), * and ** indicate significance at a 10%, 5% and 1% level, respectively. Standard errors for coefficient estimates are computed using the procedure by Newey and West (1987). The estimates for the ECB and Germany are taken from Hayo and Hofmann (2006).

even rejection of a 25 per cent bias), and the output gap in the Netherlands (rejection of a 20 per cent bias). All in all, we should consider the instruments to be appropriate for our purposes but have to be aware of potential bias problems in instrumental variable estimates of the countries mentioned.

For some countries, plausible estimates over the full sample period could not be found. Alternatively, Taylor rules were estimated from January 1987 onwards, omitting the first phase of the EMS. In addition, there were missing values for some series, which also led to differences in the respective sample sizes. Lagged interest rates turn out to be highly significant, indicating that interest rate smoothing is important in all cases of our sample. For most countries coefficients on expected inflation greater than unity can be found. The reaction function in France estimated over the full sample period is the only instance where we have to reject the hypothesis that the coefficient is greater than unity, that is the so-called Taylor principle is

Table 4.2 GMM estimates of national monetary policy reaction functions (with German interest rate or start of sample in 1987:1)

	i_{t-1} (ρ)	δ_{t+12} (β)	y_t (γ)	German interest rate	Constant (α)	No. of obs.	SE of regression	*J*-test (*p*-value)
Austria	0.63**	1.08*	0.50**	0.28**	3.61*	237	0.43	0.37
Belgium	0.70**	2.24**	0.11	0.22**	2.56*	236	0.97	0.80
France	0.93**	0.54**	0.43**	–0.02	5.17**	234	0.65	0.88
Ireland	0.66**	1.29(*)	1.21(*)	0.29**	24.8*	222	2.02	0.99
Italy (sample 1987)	0.93**	1.48**	0.07	–0.05	0.81	144	0.61	0.63
Netherlands	0.93**	3.89**	–1.03*	0.02	–2.59	228	0.67	0.74
Spain	0.88**	1.89(*)	0.44	0.07	6.9	234	1.61	0.92

Notes: (*), * and ** indicate significance at a 10%, 5% and 1% level, respectively. Standard errors for coefficient estimates are computed using the procedure by Newey and West (1987).

not fulfilled. This principle ensures that real interest rates rise in response to increases in inflation. In Portugal the coefficient is not significantly different from zero when using the longer sample period. The point estimates of the output gap coefficients are generally larger than zero and lower than unity. In half of the cases, however, they are statistically not significantly different from zero (Belgium, Finland, Italy, Portugal, Spain). For robustness purposes, the Taylor rules were re-estimated after imposing zero restrictions on the output gaps where appropriate. It turned out that the resulting paths for the long-term target rates were similar to ones based on the unrestricted estimates and thus could be omitted. The constant term varies greatly between the countries and it can even take on negative values. Note, however, that in a number of cases it is not precisely estimated.

A number of EMU countries were formerly members of the EMS. Germany was typically perceived as performing the role of a nominal anchor and dominating the system (Wyplosz, 1989; von Hagen and Fratianni, 1990). To account for such an influence, we re-estimate the Taylor rules allowing for the German interest rate to enter as an additional exogenous regressor. The long-run coefficients are then computed based on the equilibrium condition: $i_t = i_{t-1} = i_t^{\text{Germany}}$. It turns out that for some countries it is not possible to derive sensible monetary policy reaction functions within such a specification. The cases that yield reasonable estimates are summarised in Table 4.2.

It should be noted that the German interest rate is significant in very few countries only, namely Austria, Belgium and Ireland.[2] However, the result in Ireland is very much a reflection of the interest rate convergence occurring in the period preceding EMU.[3] Interestingly, the German rate is not significant in the Taylor rule of the Netherlands, which kept a fixed rate to the DM since the breakdown of the Bretton-Woods system. Note that this is not an issue of collinearity with the lagged interest rate, as the estimated coefficient of this variable is virtually the same in the regression with and without the German interest rate.

In the counterfactual analysis below, the long-run coefficients β, γ and α will be used to derive target interest rates that are interpreted as indicators of how national monetary policy would have been pursued if EMU had not come about. However, there is a substantial problem related to the constant term in this analysis. The national Taylor rules contain constant terms that deviate substantially from the α estimated for the ECB Taylor rule. We can derive the implied long-run real interest rate by re-arranging equation (4.2):

$$r^* = \alpha - (1-\beta)\, \pi^* \tag{4.4}$$

If we assume an inflation goal of 2 per cent, the implied long-run real interest rate recovered from the Austrian Taylor rule in Table 4.1 is about 2 per cent. Assuming the same inflation goal for the ECB, we get a lower implied long-run real interest rate of 1.28 per cent. This difference in implied real interest rates between the two regimes may reflect lower real interest rates under the EMU regime due to the process of fiscal consolidation in the 1990s, but probably also due to lower levels of potential real growth in a number of EMU countries. Hence, the constant α may also have been lower under a counterfactual national monetary policy regime after 1999. For instance, in the case of Austria we get as an adjusted constant term:

$$\alpha^{adj} = r^*_{ECB} + (1 - \beta_i)\pi^* = 1.28 + (1 - 1.26)2 = 0.76 \quad (4.5)$$

Note that due to the large standard error of α in the ECB Taylor rule, the implied real interest rate is also very imprecisely measured. Furthermore, since there is (almost) a zero probability of observing a nominal interest rate very close to the real rate, r^* is not on the support of the probability distribution. For these reasons it seems advisable to look at the target rates based on both the originally estimated constant terms and the adjusted constant terms. It turns out, however, that in all cases the target rates based on the non-adjusted constant terms are way above the interest rate prevailing in EMU. It is very unlikely that the monetary policy of the ECB is too loose for every member of EMU. Therefore, in the following graphical comparisons, we show the target rates based on the adjusted constant terms only.

Finally, it should be pointed out that there is likely to be a difference between long-run target rates and actual interest rates. For example, Figure 4.1 shows the target rates for the ECB together with the actual money market rate.

Apparently, the actual interest rates deviate from the estimated Taylor rule, particularly during the last part of the sample, where the monetary policy reaction function would recommend raising interest rates while the ECB kept rates constant.[4] Hence, the comparison of counterfactual interest rate paths and actual EMU interest rates shown in the following section should be interpreted with caution.

Comparing counterfactual interest rate paths

This section compares in a counterfactual simulation analysis target rates based on national Taylor rules and national variables with the actual

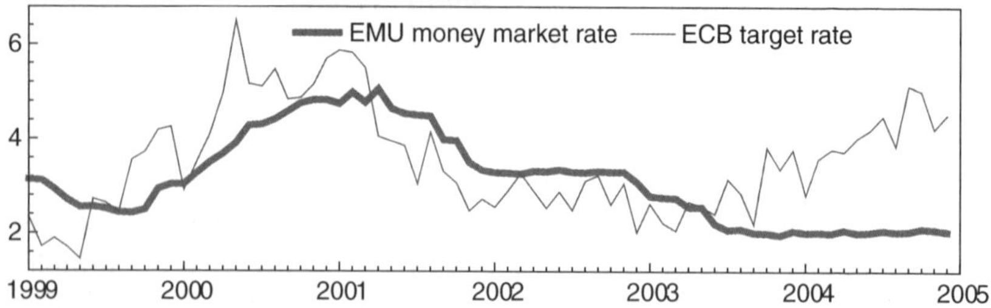

Figure 4.1 ECB target rates and EMU money market rates

money market interest rates in the euro area. Actual interest rate paths appear to be more useful for this comparison than ECB target rates for two reasons. First, they describe an actual development and not a counterfactual scenario. Second, it can be seen from Figure 4.1 that at the end of the sample period actual rates and target rates deviate substantially, which undermines the usefulness of ECB target rates in this context. An alternative approach would be to compare dynamic simulations based on the national estimated Taylor rules with actual interest rates (see, for example, Hayo and Hofmann, 2006). However, simulated interest rate paths tend to become rather implausible after only a few interactions. Moreover, a serious dynamic simulation study would need to take into account the data generating mechanism of the other variables in the model, in particular the output gap and the inflation rate. Finally, there is the issue of comparing the significance of target rates using confidence bands. As has been shown in, for example, Clausen and Hayo (2004), these tend to be extremely wide and interest-rate setting would need to be of an extreme nature to violate the 95 per cent bands. Thus, we concentrate on the estimated coefficients bearing in mind that these are estimated with considerable uncertainty.

Figure 4.2 presents the static simulations for Austria based on the estimated target rates. The graph suggests that for most of the time in 1999 and 2000, interest rates would have been substantially higher under a continuation of the national monetary policy regime. With the exception of

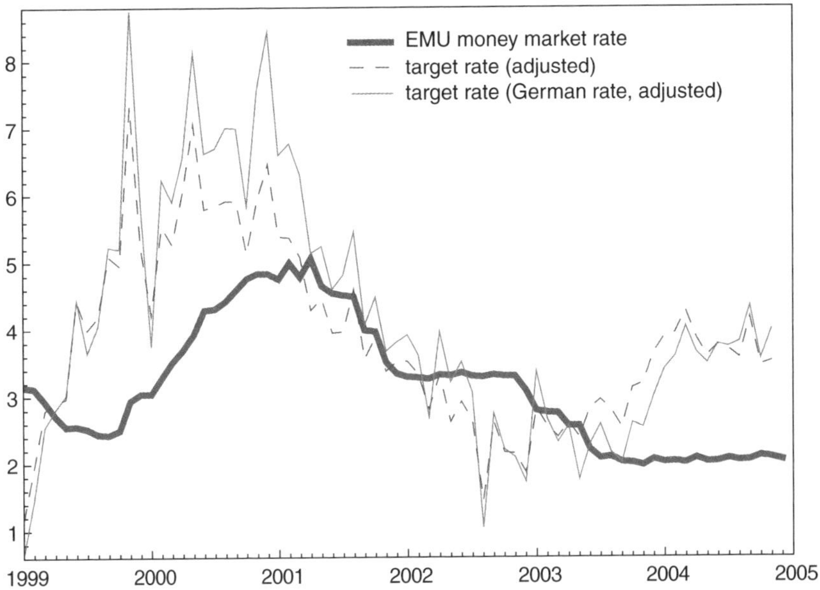

Figure 4.2 Austria: target rates and euro area money market rate (in %)

the second half of 2002, actual interest rates were very close to the target rates for Austria until the end of 2003. From 2004 onwards, interest rates in Austria would have risen under the hypothetical monetary policy regime. It is interesting to note that these conclusions are quite robust with respect to estimating the Taylor rule with or without the German interest rate.

In Figure 4.3, the simulations for Belgium are presented. The counterfactual target rates indicate that the ECB-controlled interest rates were too low for Belgium during the course of 1999 but were relatively adequate in 2000. Interest rates should have been lowered much faster during 2001 than they were by the ECB. In 2002 and the first half of 2003, actual and target rates are pretty close together. From mid-2003 onwards, the counterfactual Belgian central bank would have raised interest rates continuously, leading to a considerable gap between actual rates and target rates at the end of the sample period. Again, target rates estimated with and without a German interest rate are relatively close together most of the time.

Figure 4.4 shows the counterfactual scenario for Finland. Here only the Taylor rule without the German interest rate yielded reasonable estimates. The counterfactual target rates indicate that over the period from the start of 1999 to the end of 2000 nationally determined interest rates would have been much higher than those prevailing in the euro area. In 2001 and 2002, target and actual rates are very close, while in 2003 a continuation of the Finnish monetary policy rule would have led to lower rates. For 2004,

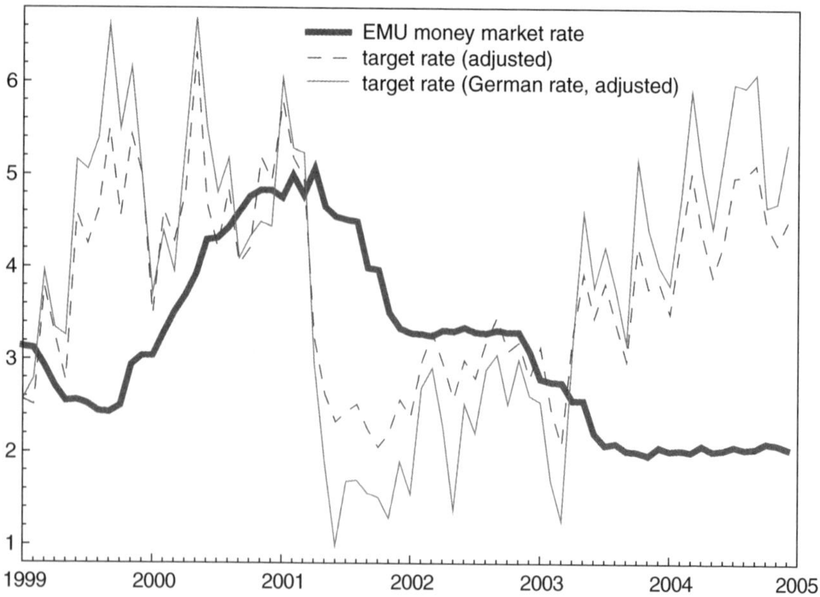

Figure 4.3 Belgium: target rates and euro area money market rate (in %)

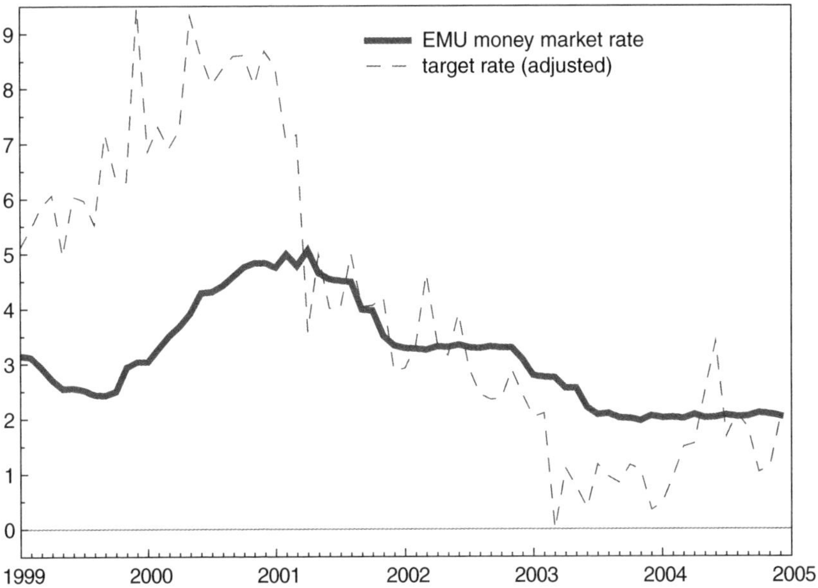

Figure 4.4 Finland: target rates and euro area money market rate (in %)

the simulations suggest that the euro area interest rate is relatively adequate for Finland.

The situation in France is described in Figure 4.5 using three alternative long-run target rates. The target rate estimated over the shorter sample period suggests that a somewhat lower rate would have come about in 2000 and 2001 but otherwise it is quite close to the other two rates that move almost synchronously. The French central bank would have set lower interest rates during the first part of 1999 but otherwise would have followed a course similar to that pursued by the ECB. However, while interest rates fell in the euro area over the course of 2003, in the counterfactual national regime target rates would have remained stable at the level reached at the end of 2002.

Analysing the results for the simulations in the case of Germany given in Figure 4.6, we find that the Bundesbank would have kept interest rates somewhat higher during 1999 and clearly higher over the first half of 2000. The downswing of interest rates in 2001 would have come half a year earlier and been much more pronounced in the counterfactual German monetary policy regime. Over the second half of 2002 and the first half of 2003 we see a convergence of rates, with actual euro area rates falling and German target rates rising. During the course of 2004 it is apparent that our counterfactual Bundesbank would have raised rates further, while the ECB held rates constant.

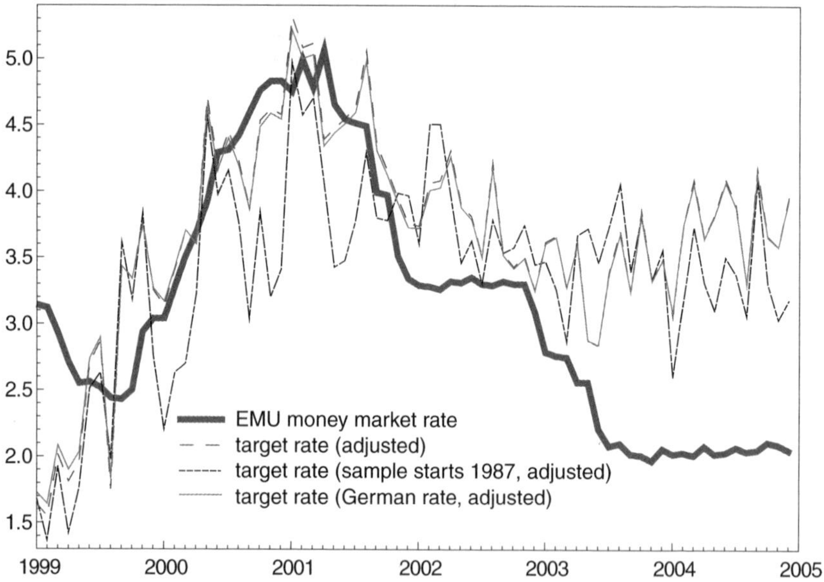

Figure 4.5 France: target rates and euro area money market rate (in %)

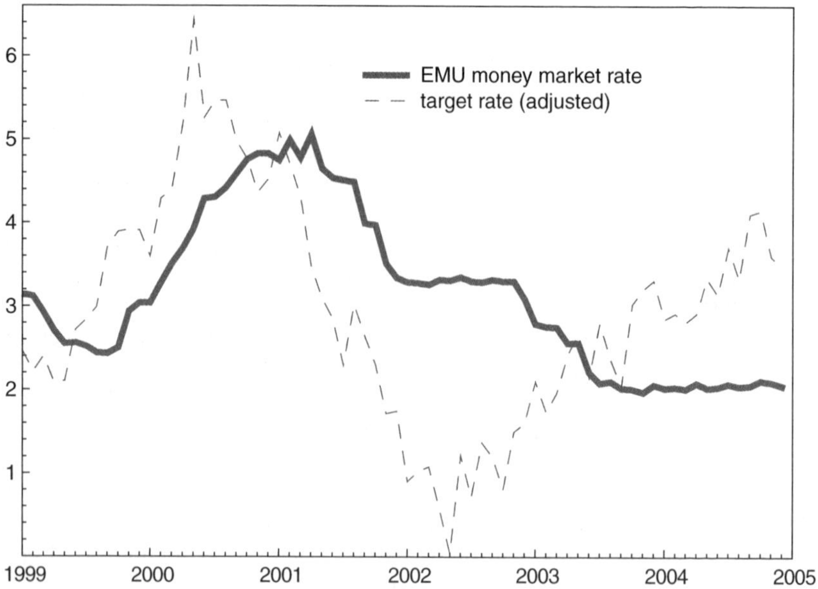

Figure 4.6 Germany: target rates and euro area money market rate (in %)

As can be seen in Figure 4.7, there is a lot of volatility in the target rates for Ireland. This may be due to the fact that the relatively more volatile producer prices are used instead of consumer prices. Moreover, in the second half of 2002 target rates become negative, which is clearly not plausible. The target rates based on the estimates without the German rate indicate that in the counterfactual situation the Irish central bank would have set interest rates much higher than euro area rates in 1999. There is some convergence over the course of 2000, where on average the euro area rate is only slightly below the target rate. However, euro area rates appear to be too high in most of 2001, 2002 and 2003 for Ireland, which seems unlikely. The target rates for Ireland based on the estimates including the German interest rate are far above the actual money market rates in the euro area over the first two years. In 2001, the target rates move closer to the actual euro area rates. In the second half of 2002, the rates even become negative for a few months. This counterfactual scenario suggests that on average the euro area rates were quite appropriate for Ireland until the autumn of 2003. At the end of the present sample (which stops at the end of 2003 due to limited data availability), the target rates are already above the EMU money market rates. All in all it appears to be the case that actual rates were below the ones that would have been set under a national monetary policy regime in Ireland.

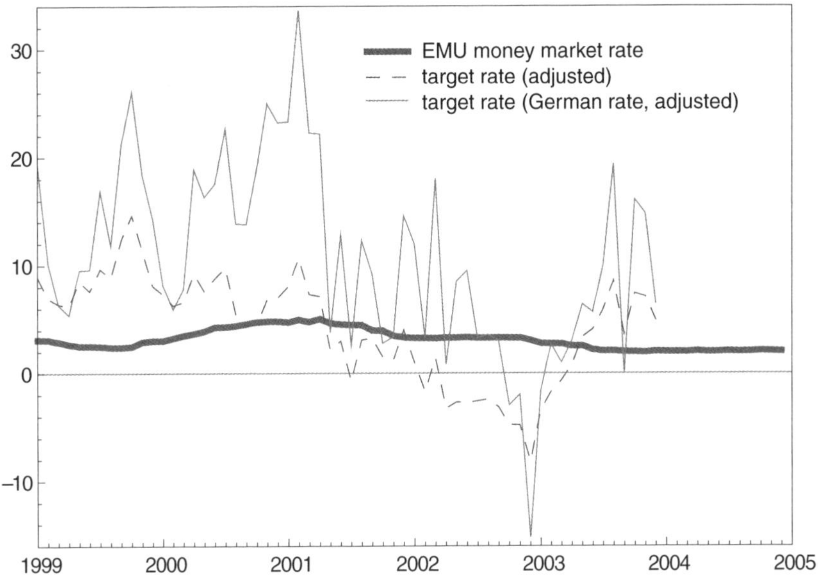

Figure 4.7 Ireland: target rates and euro area money market rate (in %)
Notes: The inflation rate is based on the producer price index.

A similar conclusion but based on more plausible interest rate paths is found for Italy. Figure 4.8 shows that under both scenarios the target rates are above the euro area interest rates in the first two years. This conclusion changes in 2001, where at least for the interest rate path based on the estimates with the German rate the EMU rates tend to be above what a counterfactual Italian central bank would have set. For the target rate derived from the estimations without the German rate, the euro area rates appear to be slightly too high in 2001. For the remaining years, however, both interest rate scenarios suggest that national rates would have been higher, with some convergence on actual money market rates occurring at the end of the sample period. The general shape of the EMU interest rate path on the other hand is very similar to what is suggested by the target rates.

The situation is relatively straightforward in the case of the Netherlands, as can be inferred from Figure 4.9. For the simulations which include the German interest rate, most of the time the euro area rate is quite close to the target rates. The exception is 2001, where a counterfactual Dutch central bank would have set a substantially higher interest rate. Since the target rate based on estimates without the German interest rate is more volatile and often becomes negative in 2003 and 2004 it does not appear to be very plausible.

The simulations for Portugal in Figure 4.10 do not appear to be very plausible, especially in the later part of the sample. The rates are systematically

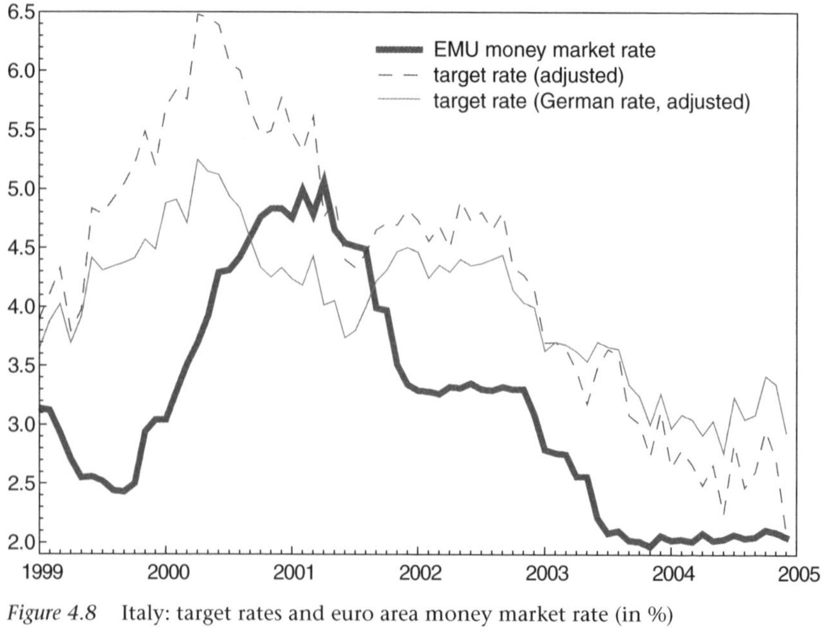

Figure 4.8 Italy: target rates and euro area money market rate (in %)

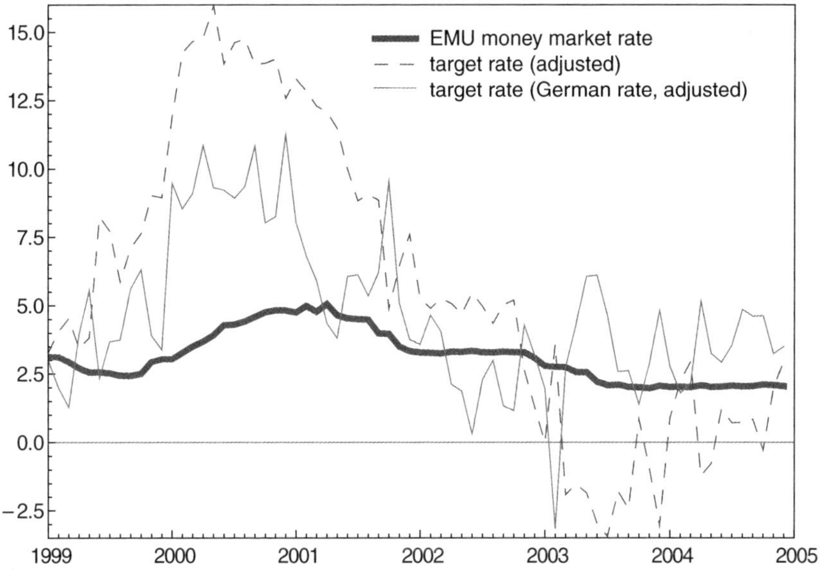

Figure 4.9 Netherlands: target rates and euro area money market rate (in %)

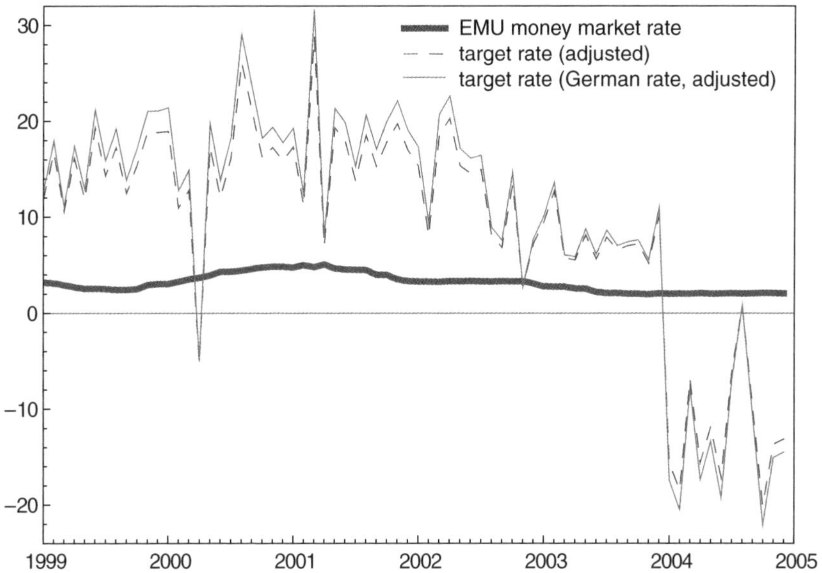

Figure 4.10 Portugal: target rates and euro area money market rate (in %)

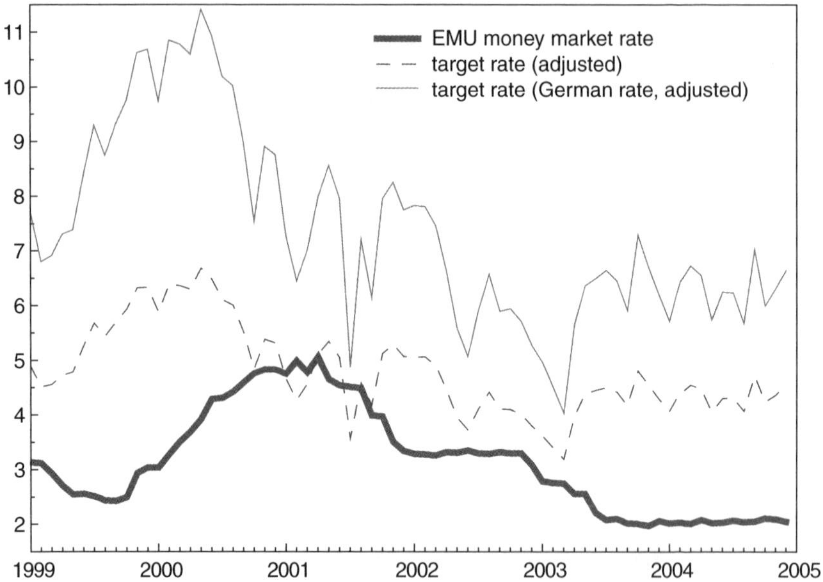

Figure 4.11 Spain: target rates and euro area money market rate (in %)

above the euro area rate until they become negative from 2004 onwards. A look at the data indicates that the substantial drop of industrial production in combination with the excessively large coefficient on the output gap is responsible for this outcome.

Finally, Figure 4.11 displays the simulated interest rate paths for Spain. The target rates based on the estimates without the German interest rate are consistently above the euro area rate over the full sample. The alternative target rate indicates that euro area rates are below counterfactual Spanish rates in 1999 and the first half of 2000. In the following period until the end of 2001, actual interest rates appear to be extremely close to the target rates. In 2002 the target rates are somewhat higher and the fall in actual rates from 2003 onwards stands in contrast to an increase in the target rates, resulting in a notable gap at the end of 2004.

Summarising these findings in a more quantitative manner, Table 4.3 shows the difference between the euro area interest rate and the respective target rates over countries and years for the target rate based on Taylor rule estimates without the German interest rate. Concentrating first on the country averages in the last column of the table, we find that in almost all countries actual euro area rates are below counterfactual target rates. There is one case where interest rates under the ECB regime are higher than under a continuation of its national monetary policy regime, namely Germany. This result is particularly affected by the year 2002, where counterfactual

Table 4.3 Difference between EMU money market rate and adjusted target rates (in percentage points)

	1999	*2000*	*2001*	*2002*	*2003*	*2004*	*Sum*
Austria	–1.2	–1.6	0.1	0.7	–0.5	–1.7	–4.3
Belgium	–1.3	–0.5	1.2	0.3	–1.0	–2.4	–3.8
Finland	–3.5	–3.9	–0.6	0.2	1.3	0.4	–6.0
France	0.2	0.0	–0.2	–0.5	–1.1	–1.7	–3.2
Germany	–0.2	–0.8	1.3	2.3	–0.2	–1.3	1.1
Ireland	–6.4	–2.9	0.2	6.1	–1.0	n.a.	–4.0
Italy	–1.9	–1.8	–0.5	–1.3	–1.0	–0.5	–7.0
Netherlands	–3.4	–10.0	–5.4	–1.2	3.6	1.0	–15.4
Portugal	–12.6	–10.8	–12.6	–8.8	–5.3	14.3	–35.7
Spain	–2.6	–1.8	–0.4	–1.0	–1.8	–2.3	–9.9
Sum	–32.8	–34.1	–16.9	–3.3	–7.0	5.7	
Sum (without Ireland and Portugal)	–13.9	–20.4	–4.5	–0.5	–0.7	–8.5	

Note: This compares the simulated interest rate functions *without* the German rate only.

German target rates are more than 2 percentage points above the euro area rates. The biggest deviations in absolute values are computed for Portugal, followed by the Netherlands and Spain. Note that particularly in the case of the Netherlands, using the estimates including the German interest rate would result in lower deviations. Second, analysing the results across years, we give the sum of these deviations over countries in a particular year in the second line from the bottom of the table. It becomes apparent that the largest deviations occur in the first two years, where euro area interest rates were particularly low compared to our estimates of the counterfactual national monetary policy regimes. In 2001 the average deviations across countries are smaller, in absolute terms, and they are close to zero in 2002. In 2004, the deviations turn positive but this is only due to the value for Portugal which has already been characterised as not particularly plausible. As indicated above, at least in 2003 the estimates for Ireland are also a bit dubious. The sum for every year without Ireland and Portugal, given in the last line of the table, yields a similar conclusion for the first two years of EMU: euro area rates are lower than what would have been set by national central banks on average. The average difference is only slightly negative in 2001, 2002 and 2003. For 2004, however, we can see that in a number of countries the target rates suggest that a tighter monetary policy would have been appropriate. This re-iterates the message from comparing ECB target rates and actual money market rates in Figure 4.1.

To get a better understanding of how the differences between the EMU money market rate and national target rates are related across time and countries, we make use of a statistical clustering method. Using the nearest

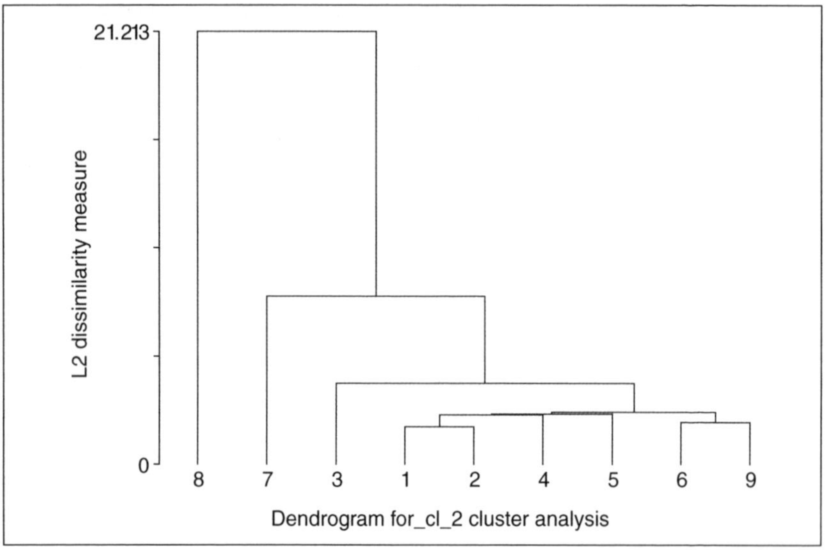

Figure 4.12 Dendrogram of country clusters
Notes: Country codes are: Austria, 1; Belgium, 2; Finland, 3; France, 4; Germany, 5; Italy, 6; Netherlands, 7; Portugal, 8; Spain, 9. This compares the simulated interest rate functions *without* the German rate only.

neighbour technique we perform a hierarchical cluster analysis. In a first step, we look for particular clusters among countries over the time period (we drop Ireland due to missing observations in 2004). The resulting dendrogram is given in Figure 4.12.

The deviations of target rates from actual interest rates in Austria, Belgium, France and Germany are particularly similar over the time period. Italy and Spain form a relatively close cluster. The Netherlands, Finland, and particularly Portugal are the outliers.

Looking for particular clusters with regard to the deviations of adjusted target rates from the EMU money market rate among the various years of our sample period, we get the dendrogram in Figure 4.13. The years 1999 and 2001 form a cluster, and 2002 is still quite close. 2003 and 2000 are different. The deviations of the adjusted target rates from the EMU money market rate are particularly different in 2004 compared to the other years. This is due to the fact that in this year the target rates of many countries tend to be well above the actual EMU money market rate.

Conclusions

In this chapter, we ask the question whether interest rate paths in most of the current member countries of EMU would have been different if the pre-

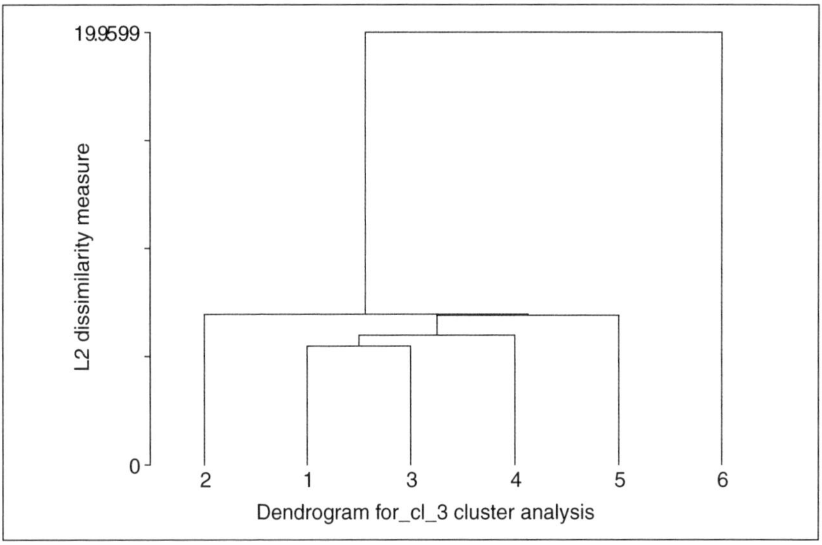

Figure 4.13 Dendrogram of year clusters
Notes: Year codes are: 1999: 1, 2000: 2, 2001: 3, 2002: 4, 2003: 5, 2004: 6. This compares the simulated interest rate functions *without* the German rate only.

vious national central banks had not given up control over monetary policy. Using estimates of monetary policy reaction functions over the last 20 years before the formation of EMU, we derive long-run Taylor rules for interest rate setting conditional on the expected one-year ahead inflation rate and the current output gap. These Taylor rules are employed in the simulation of counterfactual interest rate paths over the time period January 1999 to December 2004, which are then compared to actual short-term interest rates in the euro area. This study does not address the question of whether the deviations from the *optimal* interest rate paths are higher under EMU than they were during the respective national regimes.

The estimation of monetary reaction functions follows Clarida *et al.* (1998), where a single equation is estimated using GMM. In contrast to their approach, the present study applies a novel way of selecting instruments that avoids weak instrument biases and removes some arbitrariness in the selection process. In an alternative specification, the German short-term interest rate is also included in the analysis to account for the membership of some countries in the EMS. It turns out that the estimations of reaction functions are sometimes not robust or even plausible; for instance, the results for Ireland and Portugal raise some questions.

With respect to the core research question, we can summarise the results as follows. Perhaps not surprisingly, most countries would have set interest rates differently to what the ECB did over sometimes prolonged periods of time. More specifically, ECB interest rates tend to be below the national target interest rate even after explicitly accounting for a lower real interest rate in the EMU period. This is particularly true for the years 1999 and 2000, while the actual euro area rates were more appropriate for most countries in 2001 and 2004, and on average very close to the target rates in 2002 and 2003. However, for Germany the sum of actual money-market interest rates over this five year period is higher than the sum of the counterfactual national target rates. Under a counterfactual Bundesbank regime, the interest rates would have been below euro area rates in 2001 and especially in 2002. There is a cluster of countries that experience relatively similar deviations of national counterfactual target rates from actual interest rates, consisting of Austria, Belgium, France and Germany. Portugal and to a lesser extent the Netherlands tend to show a strikingly different pattern in this respect. Clustering over years indicates that 2004 is the main outlier, particularly due to a number of national target rates suggesting an increase in interest rates, while euro area rates remain unchanged.

To conclude, almost all countries in our counterfactual simulation realise lower nominal interest rates by being members of EMU when compared to a continuation of the previous national monetary regime. In other words, if EMU had not come about, the respective countries would have experienced more restrictive monetary policies than under the ECB regime. This gain in terms of lower interest rates is a result of the high credibility imported by becoming a member of the ECB. Thus, it seems implausible to explain the rather disappointing average GDP growth rates by pointing to excessively high euro area interest rates. On the other hand, these results do not answer the question of whether the deviations from an optimal interest rate path are now lower than they were under the national regimes.

The only exception is Germany, which may have had to cope with a somewhat higher interest rate under the ECB regime compared to a continuation of the former Bundesbank regime. The explanation of this outcome is straightforward: German interest rates were already low before the creation of EMU, but due to a substantial negative output gap in some years it found the ECB rates relatively too high. So while it is difficult to argue that the common monetary policy was the cause of the dismal growth performance of the German economy, as it benefited from relatively lower rates in 1999 and 2000, it may be the case that in some years EMU exacerbated the situation to a certain extent. It is important to note that this does not prove that Germany is relatively worse off as a member of EMU, as the other countries' interest rate levels would have been higher under a continuation of the former national monetary policy regimes. The interest rate impulse generated by joining EMU is likely to have affected economic growth positively in these countries. The export-oriented economy of Germany would have participated from this relative expansion of the other European economies, which would have helped to stabilise German output. However, within the current framework, we cannot analyse the net result of these two diverging effects. Finally, it is interesting to note that in 2004 German target rates would have been about one percentage point higher than the actual euro area rates. Even given the increase in the euro area money market interest rate at the end of 2005 to about 2.5 per cent, this suggests that for the last two years the ECB regime has provided an additional stimulus for Germany too.

Notes

1 The data source is *International Financial Statistics* (online access) published by the International Monetary Fund. In the case of Ireland, due to data availability producer prices were used instead of consumer prices. Interest rates were missing in the case of France from March to June 1986. Values were added based on a linear adjustment between these dates.

2 Clausen and Hayo (2006) estimate a small-scale macroeconomic model of Germany, France and Italy based on quarterly data that allows for a simultaneous influence of the German interest rate on the monetary policy reaction functions in the other countries. They find a significant impact at the 10 per cent level of the German rate on the dynamic French reaction function but no significant effect in Italy.

3 It may also be the case that the exchange rate plays a much larger role for monetary policy in the smaller countries of our sample and thus using a standard Taylor rule is not appropriate.

4 Note that the estimates for the ECB are taken from Hayo and Hofmann (2006), who use a sample from January 1999 to May 2004.

References

Borio, C.E.V. (1997) 'The Implementation of Monetary Policy in Industrial Countries: A Survey', *BIS Economic Papers*, no. 47, July.

Castelnuovo, E. (2003) 'Taylor Rules, Omitted Variables, and Interest Rate Smoothing in the US', *Economics Letters*, 81: 55–9.

Clarida, R., J. Gali and M. Gertler (1998) 'Monetary Policy Rules in Practice: Some International Evidence', *European Economic Review*, 42: 1033–67.

Clausen, V. and B. Hayo (2004) 'Monetary Policy in the Euro Area', *International Economics and Economic Policy*, 1: 349–64.

Clausen, V. and B. Hayo (2006) 'Asymmetric Monetary Policy Effects in EMU', *Applied Economics*, 38: 1123–34.

Davidson, R. and J.G. MacKinnon (1993) *Estimation and Inference in Econometrics*. New York: Oxford University Press.

Hahn, J. and J. Hausman (2003) 'Weak Instruments: Diagnosis and Cures in Empirical Econometrics', *American Economic Review*, 93: 118–25.

Hendry, D.F. and H.-M. Krolzig (1999) 'Improving on "Data mining reconsidered" by K.D. Hoover and S.J. Perez', *Econometrics Journal*, 2: 202–19.

Hayo, B. and B. Hofmann (2006) 'Comparing Monetary Policy Reaction Functions: ECB versus Bundesbank', *Empirical Economics*, forthcoming.

Newey, W.K. and K.D. West (1987) 'A Simple, Positive Semi-Definite, Heteroscedasticity and Autocorrelation Consistent Covariance Matrix', *Econometrica*, 55: 703–8.

Stock, J.H. and M. Yogo (2003) 'Testing for Weak Instruments in Linear IV Regression', mimeo, Department of Economics, Harvard University.

Stock, J.H., J.H. Wright and M. Yogo (2002) 'A Survey of Weak Instruments and Weak Identification in Generalized Method of Moments', *Journal of Business and Economic Statistics*, 20: 518–29.

Taylor, J. (1993) 'Discretion versus Policy Rules in Practice', *Carnegie-Rochester Conference Series on Public Policy*, 39: 195–214.

Von Hagen, J. and M. Fratianni (1990) 'German Dominance in the EMS: Evidence from Interest Rates', *Journal of International Money and Finance*, 9: 358–75.

Wyplosz, C.A. (1989) 'Asymmetry in the EMS: Intentional or Systemic?', *European Economic Review*, 33: 310–20.

Discussion

Carlo A. Favero

This chapter analyses whether interest rate paths in the EMU member countries would have been different if national central banks were still in charge of monetary policy by:

(a) estimating dynamic Taylor rules for national central banks on pre-EMU data to derive the equilibrium interest rate for each central bank:

$$i_t = \rho i_{t-1} + (1 - \rho)\, i_t^* + u_t \tag{4D.1}$$

$$i_t^* = A + B\,(\pi_{t+1}^e - \pi^*) + Cx_t \tag{4D.2}$$

where i_t^* are steady state equilibrium rates, that are postulated to be linear functions of the deviation of future expected inflation from target and the output-gap, and a partial adjustment scheme is assumed so that actual policy rates converge only gradually to equilibrium.

(b) comparing the time series of ***counterfactual*** pre-EMU ***equilibrium rates*** with ***actual*** monetary policy rates in the Euro-area over the sample 1999–2005

The main empirical conclusion of the analysis is that euro area interest rates tend to be below national target interest rates.

I shall discuss the estimation and simulation strategy of this chapter by making a general theory-related point and several specific points on the estimation and simulation exercise.

A general, theory-related, point

My general, theory-related, observation is the following: partial equilibrium analysis of the monetary policy reaction function does not lead to identification of the preferences of the monetary policy-maker.

A simple example, borrowed from Svensson (1987) and discussed more extensively in Favero-Rovelli (2004) will illustrate my claim.

Consider a situation in which the monetary policy-maker faces the following problem:

$$\min_{r_{t+i}} E_t \sum_{i=0}^{\infty} \delta^i L_{t+i}$$
$$L = \frac{1}{2}\left[(\pi_t - \pi^*)^2 + \lambda x_t^2\right] \tag{4D.3}$$

where r_t is the monetary policy instrument, and the loss function of the central banks depends on deviations of inflation from target and the output gap with a relative weight λ.

The optimization is constrained by aggregate demand and supply functions that take the following, very simple, backward looking specification:

$$x_{t+1} = \beta_x x_t - \beta_r (i_t - E_t \pi_{t+1} - \bar{r}) + u_{t+1}^d \tag{4D.4}$$

$$\pi_{t+1} = \pi_t + \alpha_x x_t + u_{t+1}^s \tag{4D.5}$$

The first-order conditions for optimality can be written as follows:

$$\frac{dL}{di_t} = (E_t \pi_{t+2} - \pi^*) = -\frac{\lambda}{\delta \alpha_x k} E_t x_{t+1} \tag{4D.6}$$

$$k = 1 + \frac{\delta \lambda k}{\lambda + \delta \alpha_x^2 k} \tag{4D.7}$$

An interest rate rule can be then derived by substituting the constraints in the optimality conditions (4D.6):

$$i_t^* = \bar{r} + \pi^* + \left(\frac{1 + \alpha_x \beta_r}{\alpha_x \beta_r}\right)(E_t \pi_{t+1} - \pi^*) +$$
$$+ \frac{\beta_x}{\beta_r} x_t + \frac{\lambda}{\beta \alpha_x k} \frac{1}{\alpha_x \beta_r} E_t x_{t+1}$$

The optimal reaction function looks remarkably similar to the steady-state solution of the specification for the Taylor rule adopted in this paper, but the parameters in the monetary policy reaction function are convolutions of the parameters describing the preferences of the monetary policy maker, λ and δ, and the parameters describing the structure of the economy, α_x, β_r, β_x. Therefore it seems unwise to infer preferences of the central banker from the estimated parameters in a Taylor rule.

Specific points on the empirics

I have three main observations on the empirics.

1 The simulation exercise is based on rules estimated on a sample mixing different regimes: pre-EMU and post-EMU. I find it very hard to believe that the reaction function of European central banks is the same across these two different regimes. The author attempts to correct for this problem by including the German interest rates in the reaction function of non-German countries in the EMS era. However this variable is then excluded on the evidence of its small contribution to the explanation of the dynamics of non-German policy rates, and on the basis that the hypothesis of policy rates equalisation between German and non-German countries in the steady state is uniformly rejected. I think that this evidence points towards mis-specification of the Taylor rules for the EMS regime. Adding the German policy rate to a reaction function depending only on domestic variables does not seem to be sufficient to model monetary policy for non-German countries in the EMS era. EMS requires that inflation targets are the same across participating countries but such restriction is not satisfied by the adopted specifications. In my experience (Favero *et al.*, 2000) respecifying the non-German countries' reaction functions with German inflation as a target helps in finding evidence for the equalisation between German and non-German rates in the steady-state.

2 In the simulation counterfactual equilibrium rates are compared with actual policy rates in the euro area. This is problematic if actual rates are different from steady state equilibrium rates for the ECB. In fact, Figure 4D.1 illustrates that this is exactly the case from 2003 onwards. Such evidence weakens considerably the main conclusion of the empirical analysis suggested in this chapter.

3 There is considerable uncertainty around the constant in the Taylor rule, and the constant is a crucial parameter in determining the outcome of the simulation exercise. Moreover no confidence intervals are reported around the simulated rates and without confidence intervals it is impossible to tell if the differences between actual and simulated policy rates are significant and therefore interesting. To illustrate this point, I have reconsidered the case of Italy. I have taken the estimated Taylor rule by the author over the sample January 1987 to December 1998 and dynamically simulated from 1999 onwards:

$$i_t = \underset{0.04}{0.93} i_{t-1} + (1 - 0.93)\, i_t^* + u_t$$

$$i_t^* = \underset{1.87}{4.00} + \underset{0.39}{1.87}\,(\pi_{t+12}^e - \pi^*) + \underset{0.20}{0.25} x_t \qquad (4D.9)$$

$$\pi_{t+12}^e = f(i_{t-1}, i_{t-2}, \pi_{t-1}, \pi_{t-2}, x_{t-1}, x_{t-2}, \Delta e_{t-1}, \Delta oil_{t-k})$$

$$x_t = f(i_{t-1}, i_{t-2}, \pi_{t-1}, \pi_{t-2}, x_{t-1}, x_{t-2}, \Delta e_{t-1}, \Delta oil_{t-k})$$

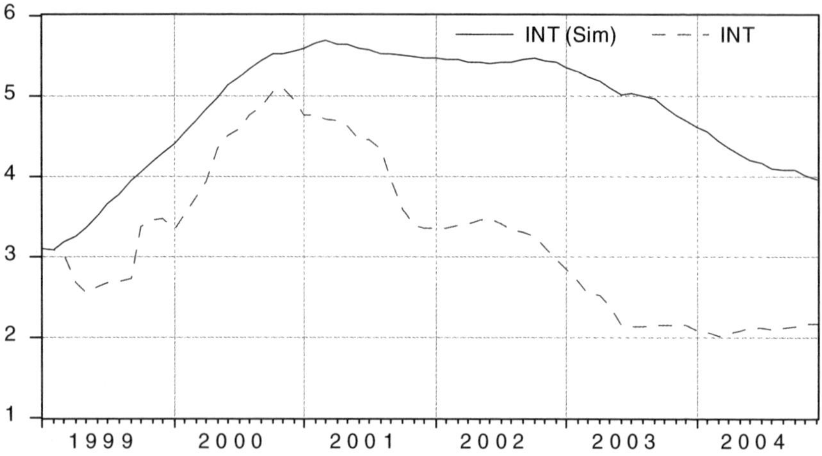

Figure 4D.1 Actually and dynamically simulated (for exogenous *e*, *oil*) Italian policy rates

The implied reduced form has been used to project inflation and the output gap taking exchange rates and oil prices as exogenous. Importantly, dynamic simulation generates interest rates that are directly comparable with actual policy rates. I report in Figure 4D.1 simulated rates based on the

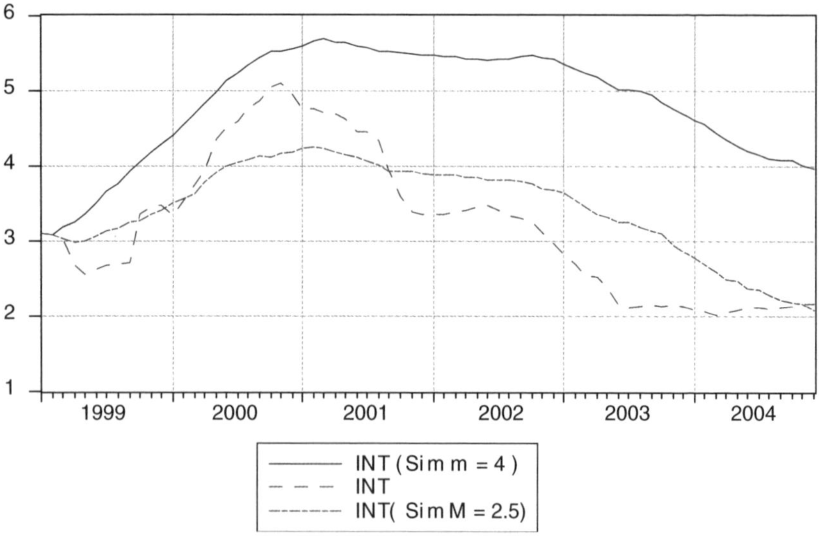

Figure 4D.2 Actually and dynamically simulated (for exogenous *e*, *oil*) Italian policy rates with alternative (but not statistically different) long-run means

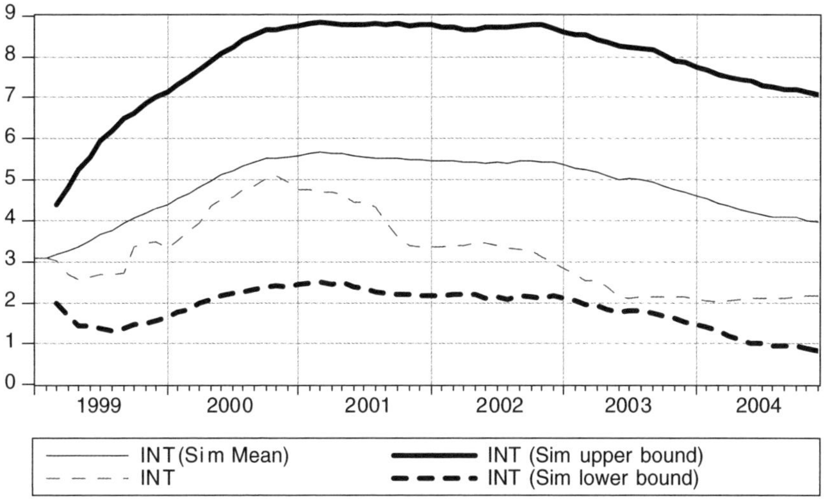

Figure 4D.3 Dynamically simulated Italian policy rates with upper and lower bounds

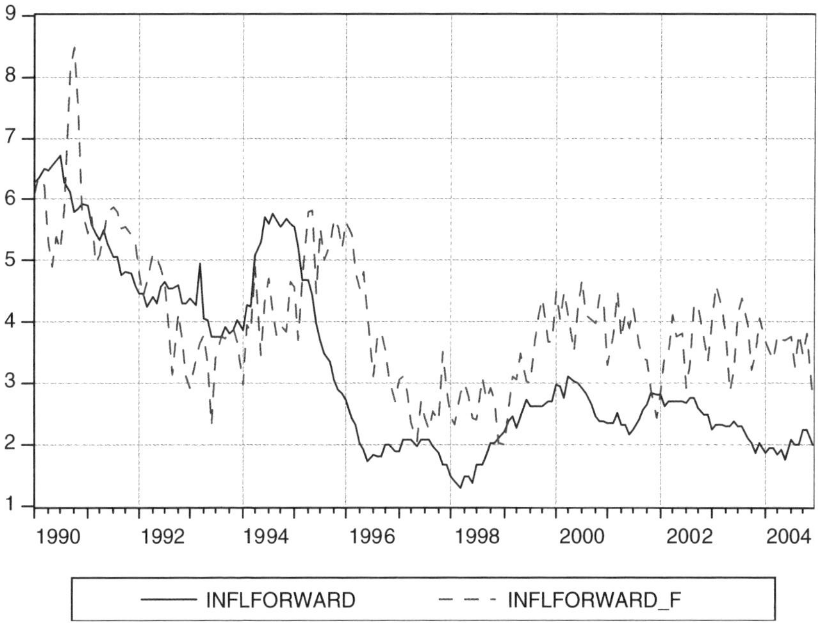

Figure 4D.4 Forecasting Italian inflation using the implicit reduced form

point estimates reported above, in Figure 4D.2 simulated rates based on a version of the Taylor rule where the intercept is fixed at 2.5 (a value not statistically different from 4 on the basis of the standard error in the GMM estimation), in Figure 4D.3 the results of a stochastic simulation where simulated policy rates are plotted with their 95 per cent confidence interval (in fact, uncertainty is underestimated here because of the assumption of exogeneity of oil prices and exchange rates and because coefficient uncertainty is ignored in the simulation). Figure 4D.1 confirms the evidence based on equilibrium policy rates proposed in the paper, Figure 4D.2 contradicts it. Figure 4D.3 explains the different messages of the two proceeding figures. Finally Figure 4D.4, which is a byproduct of the simulation exercise, shows another point of possible concern: model-based expected inflation is consistently biased upwards over the ECB period. Model-based policy rates are therefore higher as a consequence of such mis-prediction. ECB rates could have been lower just because the ECB had better inflation forecasts than those generated by the implied reduced form in the GMM estimation adopted here.

References

Favero, C.A., F. Giavazzi, F. Iacone and G. Tabellini (2000) 'Extracting Information from Asset Prices: The Methodology of EMU Calculators', *European Economic Review*, 44: 1607–32.

Favero, C.A. and R. Rovelli (2003) 'Macroeconomic Stability and the Preferences of the Fed. A Formal Analysis', *Journal of Money, Credit and Banking*, 35 (4): 545–56.

Svensson, Lars E.O. (1997) 'Inflation Forecast Targeting: Implementing and Monitoring Inflation Targets', *European Economic Review*, 41: 1111–46.

5

Fiscal Policy, Labour Markets and the Difficulties of Inter-Country Adjustment within EMU

*Christopher Allsopp and David Vines**

Introduction

This chapter examines the macroeconomic performance of the euro area. It is widely agreed that this performance has been poor; low growth and poor productivity performance have been combined with high and rising unemployment and, especially in the 'core' countries, with budget deficits and increasing government debt. This poor performance on the real side has not, however, been matched by undershooting on inflation. It thus appears that the 'trade-off' between growth and inflationary pressure has become highly adverse within the euro area. The Lisbon 'agenda' of reforms to the European macro-economy – which was intended to improve the potential for non-inflationary growth – appears to be in tatters.

Of course, the macroeconomic issues facing Europe are complex, but one thing stands out. Within EMU, there is a single centralised monetary policy carried out by a constitutionally independent European Central Bank. It has long been known that adjustment to asymmetric, or country-specific, shocks, will be difficult in these circumstances.

The aim of this chapter is to show that this process of adjustment to asymmetric shocks is much more difficult than has been realised, because of the interaction of the single European monetary policy with 12 *different and politically independent* fiscal authorities, and with 12 *different* labour markets. We demonstrate that, in a country which experiences an asymmetric shock, the wage-setting decisions of that country, and its fiscal policy stance, must *together* manage *both* its rate of inflation relative to the euro area average, *and* its price level relative to the euro area average. We show how difficult this is.

We argue that the Stability and Growth Pact (SGP) makes this process of adjustment to asymmetric shocks much more difficult. We demonstrate

*We are grateful to Michael Cheng, Tatiana Kirsanova, Peter Westaway and Simon Wren-Lewis for helpful discussions.

that the orthodox approaches to fiscal policy, drawn from the 'new macroeconomic consensus', which have inspired the revisions to the Stability and Growth Pact (SGP) point in the wrong direction. We show that that the enforcement of tight targets for deficits and debt, of the kind still found in the revised SGP, is likely to *severely* destabilise this adjustment process.

The overall purpose of this chapter is to argue that difficulties in this process of inter-country adjustment within EMU can help to explain why European macroeconomic performance has been so poor. Indeed, we suggest that difficulties in this process may have become the Achilles' heel of the whole EMU project.

The chapter is set out as follows. In the next section we discuss whether the problems in Europe-wide macroeconomic performance can be found at the aggregate level – in the conduct of monetary policy, or in the operation of fiscal policy, at the Europe-wide level. We conclude that the answer is no. We then present the argument of the paper, which focuses on the process of inter-country adjustment within EMU. We argue that the conduct of fiscal policy in the euro area will need to be reformed if European macroeconomic performance is to be improved, and we discuss the regime of 'constrained fiscal discretion' which might be necessary. A final section concludes.

Existing explanations of poor performance

Most observers believe that the poor macroeconomic performance in the euro area reflects deep structural problems, but there are sharp divergences of view about what these deep problems are. In this section we identify two existing views, and argue that they are both inadequate.

The incompleteness of a supply-side explanation

The first, and most familiar, kind of explanation is that the problems arise on the *supply* side. On this view potential output growth is low and structural unemployment is high, in countries such as Germany, Italy and France, because of adverse supply-side developments. An influential Report – *EMU after 5 Years* – published in 2004 took this line (European Commission, 2004). We do not wish to dispute the importance of this supply-side explanation; no sensible person would want to do that, given what has been happening in the euro area in the past few years.

What we do wish to dispute is the view that, since this supply-side explanation for Europe's problems is already at hand, there is no point in seeking any further explanation. This is essentially the argument presented in *EMU after 5 Years*. Instead we seek to argue that a poor macroeconomic policy framework might *also* be important in explaining the poor outcomes in the euro area.

The inadequacy of an explanation which blames the aggregate macroeconomic framework

Of course, if one wants to explain poor economic performance by means of a poor macroeconomic framework, one starts at the aggregate, Europe-wide level. Here, there are three main areas of policy concern: (1) price stability, (2) fiscal stability, and (3) supply-side developments. It is helpful to identify who, within the euro area, is meant to be responsible for which area of concern, in what we can call the 'Maastricht Assignment' (see Issing, 2000). First of all, the ECB is responsible for price stability. It is charged to pursue this objective by means of a single, euro-wide, monetary policy. By contrast, the pursuit of fiscal stability is decentralised; it is the responsibility of the 12 national governments. But these governments will be subject to the provisions of the Stability and Growth Pact (SGP), which are designed to reinforce pressures that push towards fiscal discipline. Finally, supply-side developments (including the implementation of reforms under the 'Lisbon agenda') are also decentralised to national governments. In particular, wage developments in relation to productivity are the responsibility of individual governments and of bargaining between the 'social partners', at the national level.

A comparison of this macroeconomic policy framework with that in, say, the UK and the US can throw light on our question – whether this framework, at the euro area level as a whole, can account for the poor performance of the euro area. The aim of the next two sections is to show that it cannot do this. First, some theory is helpful.

The theory of inflation-targeting systems

The ECB lies at the centre of the macroeconomic policy framework of the euro area, with its responsibility for price stability. It pursues this by means of an inflation-targeting regime, similar in kind to the flexible inflation-targeting regimes operated in the UK and the US. The UK is clearly a version of such a regime, which we can call an 'inflation-forecast targeting' regime (see, for example, Woodford, 2003). The USA approximates to such a description (though there is no formal inflation target in that country). The system in the euro area can also be described like this (see Alesina *et al.*, 2001), especially since the so-called 'monetary pillar' in the EU's description of what it does has recently been downgraded.

The nature of a flexible-inflation-targeting regime

The monetary policy-oriented systems in the UK and the US are generally regarded as working well[1] and are seldom blamed for poor overall economic performance there. The reason for this is that a flexible inflation targeting system allows the monetary policy-makers to deliver not just inflation control in the medium term (price stability), but also (in the short term) as much stabilisation against common shocks as is compatible with this primary objective. We can think of this as a regime of 'constrained discretion'.

In such a setup, the 'constraint' works as follows. If inflation were to rise above its target level, then monetary policy would be able to contain it by means of a rise in the interest rate which is only temporary. This is possible due to the existence of a natural rate of output (see Allsopp and Vines, 2005). In such a setup, if inflation were to rise above its target level then monetary policy would increase the interest rate, which would depress output below its natural rate. That would cause inflation to fall. It would go on falling until it had returned to its target level. At that point the interest rate could be lowered again, back to the level at which output is equal to its natural level. From then on output would be able to continue to grow at its potential level. How quickly this disinflation should be done is a matter of choice for the monetary policy-maker.[2] But the fact that it can be done in this way means that inflation can be kept permanently on target in such a system by means of a deviation of output from its natural level which is temporary and not permanent. This 'two for one' property of flexible inflation targeting systems has allowed Alesina *et al.* (2001, pp. 2–4) to describe inflation targeting as 'simply a good idea' and as 'employment friendly'.

The 'discretion' in this system works as follows. If the demand for output were to fall below the natural level of output, then a remedy would be available even more quickly than that just described. Interest rates could be immediately lowered to bring output back to its natural level, as quickly as possible, without endangering inflation (since an inflation risk would only emerge if output had risen *above* its natural level). Again, in the face of a demand disturbance, the two-for-one property would be evident.

What all this means is that to see whether the ECB does provide a best-practice contribution to the macroeconomic policy framework in the euro area, we should ask whether it has, in fact, operated a regime of 'constrained discretion'. Has it ensured price stability, and, *without prejudice to that*, ensured stabilisation (of output and inflation) in the face of common, area-wide shocks?

The role of fiscal policy within a monetary-policy-oriented inflation-targeting regime

In an inflation-targeting regime of this kind the monetary authority will need to take into account other influences, such as changes in private-sector demand, or changes in oil prices, when working out how to get as close as possible to its objectives. Similarly it will need to take account of the effects of fiscal policy on the economy. In a properly-working version of such an inflation-targeting regime, the central bank's policy responses will take into account, or *internalise*, what is happening elsewhere, including what is happening to fiscal policy.

Of course this has important implications for how fiscal policy needs to be conducted. If monetary policy needs to take account of fiscal policy, then a sensible outcome for monetary policy will only be possible if fiscal policy is itself sensible.

It is widely – and correctly – agreed that a necessary condition for fiscal policy to be sensible is that it should be sustainable. If it was not, and – say – taxes lay perpetually below government expenditure, then an explosive track for public debt would emerge. But that would go on stimulating expenditure and so would go on requiring perpetually rising interest rates. Indeed it would eventually mean that the system as whole was unstable. It is thus necessary for the good functioning of an inflation-targeting regime that fiscal policy-makers behave in such as way as to prevent this happening.

The simplest way to induce such sustainability is to introduce negative feedback from the level of public debt to the fiscal instruments; that is to say, some kind of a *fiscal policy reaction function*. This would involve having a target for public debt, deviations from which are meant to prompt tax increases.

It turns out that this feedback can be gradual; the feedback from public debt to taxes – or to government expenditure – does not have to be large and indeed needs to be just a bit bigger than the growth-adjusted real interest rate. The reason that this is sufficient is obvious. Any excess of current government expenditure over current taxes, that is any primary deficit, necessarily causes debt to rise. If there were a debt-target system operating in such circumstances, then the tax rate would (gradually) rise until taxes equalled government expenditure. Furthermore, if the feedback were bigger than the appropriate real interest rate, then any increases in public debt which happened during the adjustment process would be prevented from causing increases in debt interest which themselves caused the ratio of debt to income to rise.[3]

But not much more than this is necessary for a well-functioning system. That is because, providing there is solvency, the expansionary effects of any increase in the fiscal deficit, or of any increase in public debt, can be 'internalised' by the monetary authority (and vice versa). This is simply a case of the more general point that, providing that solvency is ensured, the monetary authority, in setting the interest rate, will need to take account of *all* other things that are happening, including the stance of fiscal policy.

A few (practical) examples may be helpful here. First, if one considers US monetary policy in the early 1980s, during the 'Volcker disinflation', it is clear that interest-rate policy had to take into account ('internalise') the effects of the large budget deficits of the Reagan years. Interest rates were higher than they would have been without 'Reaganomics'. A second example is the large fiscal expansion in the UK around 2001/02. Without this offset to the downward demand shocks coming from the world economy, the UK's Monetary Policy Committee (MPC) would have had to set lower interest rates as it tried to meet its objective for inflation in the medium term.[4] The conclusion is that, providing that this internalisation of the effects of fiscal policy is done properly, the course of fiscal policy does *not* matter for the course of output and inflation. These outcomes can be treated *as if* they were controlled solely by the monetary authorities.

This means that if the *aggregate, euro area-wide,* macroeconomic policy framework is under consideration, then – providing that fiscal policy is sustainable – the focus of attention has to be on monetary policy and on the behaviour of the ECB. In this aggregate story, fiscal policy is of secondary importance. We have merely to ask whether the monetary authority did, in fact, appropriately internalise the effects of what happened on the fiscal policy front.

Application of this theory to the euro area

An analysis of the ECB's inflation-targeting system

We thus now consider whether the ECB has indeed provided a best-practice contribution to the macroeconomic policy framework in the euro area. Has the ECB ensured price stability, and, *without prejudice to that,* ensured the best possible stabilisation (of output and inflation) in the face of common, area-wide shocks?[5]

In fact, the ECB's interest-rate policy has been of the right type, compared with estimated reaction functions for the US and the UK (see European Commission, 2004). It has also been relatively 'active', more active than would be suggested by a commonly used standard of reference – the 'Taylor Rule'. In addition it appears the reaction function has been reasonably symmetric in operation despite a rather asymmetric specification of the meaning given by the ECB to 'price stability' – less than 2 per cent inflation over the medium term for the euro area HICP price index.[6]

Nevertheless criticisms have been made. Most of them amount to the proposition that the ECB's reaction function is not as good as it could be. The first kind of criticism is that whatever the formal comparisons may show, the ECB has nonetheless *failed* to offset the recent macroeconomic slowdown. This is sometimes backed up with the observation that, in the US, the Fed was prepared to drive real short-term interest rates down to substantially negative levels to generate recovery – whereas in the euro area nominal rates appear to have got stuck at 2 per cent – approximately zero in real terms.[7] Moreover, there are occasions on which the ECB has appeared to be relatively 'sluggish' with delayed responses to the developing slowdown (Begg *et al.*, 2002). The implicit claim is that a more proactive interest rate policy could have offset recession and promoted recovery – without causing inflation.

Rather similar implications come from some more technical criticisms. Thus it is suggested that a higher and more symmetric target for inflation would have allowed a more proactive monetary policy. Alternatively, a greater accent on 'core' inflation rather than the official index would also have allowed a more active policy (and core inflation, excluding oil price effects, indirect taxes and so on has recently been low). Finally, ECB forecasts for growth have tended to start off overoptimistic, with successive downward revisions occurring as the forecast date approaches. If the forecasts had been better, the argument goes, policy, which should react to expected future developments, would have been more stimulatory and offsetting.

There is some force in these criticisms. They all amount to calls for improvement in the ECB's policy reaction function. We believe the reaction function, and its policy process, could both be improved. Nevertheless these criticisms immediately come up against the difficulty that inflation has not been undershooting its implicit target. Indeed the official inflation rate in the euro area has typically been *above* 2 per cent, which is not consistent with the claim that the ECB's monetary policy has been too restrictive. This response even applies to the most telling criticism – about the ECB's failure to prevent the substantial slowdown in the early years of the decade. Despite that failure, inflation has not undershot significantly. There is thus no clear signal that more expansionary policies have been needed. Given this, it has been easy for the ECB to counter most of these criticisms, and it is correct that it should have done so.[8]

The unimportance of fiscal policy for Europe-wide outcomes

Consider the other important claim about the inadequacy of the aggregate macroeconomic framework of the euro area. This is the claim that the fiscally constraining effects of the SGP in the euro area are in part to blame for recession and low growth in the region.

It is immediately clear that this claim is suspect at the aggregate level of the euro area as a whole, precisely because the ECB has been operating an effective, flexible, inflation-targeting regime. In this framework, if fiscal policy had been more expansionary, then the ECB's interest-rate policy would have been adjusted accordingly and interest rates would have been higher. The only way of escaping from this conclusion would be if inflation within the euro area had been below target. Only then would a more expansionary policy have been desirable in the face of the constraining effects of the SGP. But this is not true. So we conclude that, at the aggregate level, the macroeconomic policy framework in the euro area cannot explain the poor macroeconomic performance in the euro area.

An explanation of poor performance based on the interaction between countries

We now seek to construct an explanation of the poor performance of the euro area by focusing on the international interactions *between* countries within EMU. Again some theory is helpful for this discussion, and we will present this by considering what would happen to a country within EMU if it were to experience a permanent loss of international competitiveness. We will consider other shocks below.

In carrying out our analysis, it is useful to compare what would happen inside EMU with the international interactions which would happen if this country were a (well-run) country outside EMU. One way of doing this comparison is to thus to examine the behaviour of a country contemplating EMU entry (both the UK and Sweden are good examples). We compare what would happen in this country, subject to the permanent external shock, if it were not a member of the euro system with what would happen if it were in EMU. That enables the comparison of macroeconomic policy issues outside EMU with macroeconomic policy issues for the same country within EMU.[9]

The theory of inter-country adjustment outside EMU

For the purposes of the thought-experiment we may assume that, outside EMU, the fiscal and monetary arrangements are working 'well'. Monetary policy is responsible for stabilising output and inflation within a regime of constrained discretion. Fiscal policy is sustainable – committed, say, to a sustainable path for national debt in the medium and longer term. Monetary policy internalises alternative fiscal policy outcomes in the way discussed above.

Suppose, for example, that our country were to experience a permanent loss of international competitiveness. By this we mean a permanent increase in its demand for imports, or a permanent reduction in the world's demand for its exports, caused, say, by 'globalisation'. (The difficulties affecting the tradable sector in Italy at present, caused by competition from China, come to mind.) How will monetary policy deal with this?

We have a clear way of understanding what will happen, provided by Rudi Dornbusch (1976), long before inflation-targeting systems were invented. According to his model, members of the MPC in our country are meant to go on TV, on the morning that international competitiveness falls – which just happens to be the morning of their meeting – and say 'the loss in demand means that, ceteris paribus, inflation will fall. This means that we will have to put down the interest rate when we all meet at lunch time.' But, by the time that lunchtime comes, financial markets will have depreciated the exchange rate so much, and thereby have increased exports so much, that the demand shock will already have been controlled. The MPC will not actually need to lower the interest rate to keep inflation and output on track. Their appearance on TV, and the consequential movement in the real exchange rate, will be enough to ensure this.

All of us think that this Dornbusch story oversimplifies, and that the MPC will have to reduce the interest rate at lunchtime because of lags in the adjustment of net exports to the exchange rate, and because of difficulties for the private sector in learning the point to which the exchange rate will need to move, and so on. The depreciation of the exchange rate will probably overshoot.[10] But, nevertheless, the depreciated real exchange rate will gradually stimulate output, and so the interest rate can gradually return to the world rate, and any overshoot of the real exchange rate will gradually be undone. Inflation will remain under control in response to this shock.

The theory of inter-country adjustment within EMU

For the purposes of our thought-experiment we will also assume that, inside EMU, the fiscal and monetary arrangements are working 'well'. Monetary policy will be responsible for stabilising both output and inflation for the euro area *as a whole*, within a regime of constrained discretion. Fiscal policy in each country will be sustainable – committed, say, to a sustainable path for national debt in that country in the longer term. Monetary policy will 'internalise' whatever fiscal policy outcomes emerge *at the Europe-wide level*.

Suppose that our particular country within EMU were to experience a permanent loss of international competitiveness. How would the euro area macroeconomic policy system deal with this?[11] Because of the common monetary policy within EMU, our individual country within EMU will have to take the interest rate as given from outside (by the ECB) and will also have to cope with an irrevocably fixed *nominal* exchange rate. Thus this asymmetric shock can not be dealt with by means of monetary policy. Membership of EMU means the loss of the 'stabilisation function' of monetary policy in dealing with such a shock. What happens then?

The need to get the real exchange rate right: implications for fiscal policy

After the initial, but permanent, loss of competitiveness our economy would tend to suffer recession, and output would tend to fall below its productive potential trend. There would be rising unemployment.

It is possible to imagine a policy response which tried, permanently, to use fiscal deficits to counter this permanent shock. But doing that would lead to perpetually rising debt levels, and so would eventually lead to the violation of fiscal sustainability, something which we have assumed to be holding. The only way for adjustment to this shock to happen is for there to be an improvement of international competitiveness so as to make good the initial reduction in competitiveness which the country has suffered. Given the level of productivity, that will require a fall in the wage level and the price level relative to other countries in EMU. Only then would our country be able to return to a full utililisation of its resources without requiring fiscal policy to be permanently expansionary to make this happen. That is to say, the *real* exchange rate must adjust appropriately if adjustment to the shock is to happen and, at the same time, fiscal policy is to remain sustainable. This requirement for the real exchange rate to adjust greatly complicates what fiscal policy needs to do during the adjustment process.

What we have just said implies that a fully offsetting fiscal strategy – maintaining full employment growth – would be dangerous. This means that, for example, a simple fiscal rule seeking merely to stabilise the output gap would actually be dangerous in the EMU setting which we are examining.

At the other extreme, a rigorous insistence on, say, meeting tight fiscal targets throughout the adjustment process would cause something very different to happen. Such fiscal tightness would cause output to fall, and unemployment to rise, possibly by a large amount. As a result of this the domestic Phillips curve would then lead to a rapid fall in relative prices and wages. A process would begin which – if it worked – might lead to a very quick adjustment in the relative real exchange rate.

There will be other responses possible which are, in some sense, 'in the middle' between these two extremes. That is to say, policy might be neither – on the one hand – endlessly accommodating, nor – on the other hand – very tight. Instead it might seek to – in some sense – stabilise the economy during the adjustment process.

It thus appears that the fiscal authority can *choose* how quickly the adjustment of the real exchange rate happens. We will argue below that – in all likelihood – the fiscal authority *must* make this choice. That is to say, we will argue that fiscal policy-makers probably cannot just sit on their hands and let the adjustment process look after itself. If our argument is correct, then this will mean that the details of fiscal policy arrangements turn out to be really important for the good functioning of EMU. They will be *much more important* than they are outside EMU. The difference arises because – as we have argued at length above – such arrangements are not very important at all for the stabilisation of such non-EMU economies. We will also argue that the fiscal policy arrangements need to be much more subtle than the arbitrary rules expressed in the Stability and Growth Pact.

The need for a fiscal regime of constrained discretion

Of course, if fiscal policy is to be directed in this way towards stabilising the adjustment process, it must continue to be *sustainable*. The task for the national fiscal authorities within EMU thus appears to be a complicated one. Stabilisation needs to be combined with sustainability, and it is immediately clear that there is a timing issue here. Stabilisation is a shorter term requirement, whilst by contrast the need for sustainability is a longer-term requirement.

Not surprisingly, many interesting recent studies of fiscal policy design within EMU attempt to draw lessons about this timing issue from best-practice monetary policy. Thus, Wyplosz (2002) suggests that, given the complexity just described, fiscal policy should be delegated to independent fiscal policy committees (FPCs), analogous to Monetary Policy Committees (MPCs), and that these FPCs should be responsible for both stabilisation and sustainability.[12] A central reason for this suggestion by Wyplosz, based by him on an analogy with best-practice monetary policy, is that the latter also involves the solution to such a timing issue. As discussed earlier such monetary-policy regimes aim to ensure price stability over the longer term and, *without prejudice to that,* aim to stabilise output in the shorter term. The phrase 'regime of constrained discretion' used to describe such setups captures the fact that they are designed to deal with this problem of timing.

Similarly, we have argued that the aim for fiscal policy in the euro area should be to institute a fiscal regime which ensures sustainability over the longer term and, *without prejudice to that,* also helps to ensure the stabilisation of the economy in the shorter term. To solve this timing problem for fiscal policy, we also need, in effect, to set fiscal policy-making within a framework of 'constrained discretion'.

But what we require in such a regime of constrained discretion for fiscal policy is *more* complicated than finding the appropriate point on a single trade-off between the maintenance of sustainability in the long run and assistance with stabilisation of the economy in the shorter term. This is because, even if sustainability is maintained, the country faces *two* kinds of stabilisation tasks, not just one:

1 The country *may* wish to stabilise its level of output and inflation during the adjustment process. As already described the country will certainly need to avoid too slow a fall in output, and too slow an adjustment of inflation, relative to the rest of Europe, since that would be coupled with such an expansionary fiscal outcome that fiscal solvency would be endangered. But, as already described above, it may also wish to avoid too large a fall in output, and so to avoid a very rapid adjustment of the rate of inflation, relative to that in the rest of Europe. We will argue below that because of what we will call the 'Walters critique', some such stabilisation of the level of output, and inflation, during the adjustment process may not just be a matter of choice; it may be something that the country *must* do.
2 As already discussed above, the country *must* also ensure that it ends up with the appropriate level of the *real* exchange rate, and so with an appropriate level of competitiveness. But this will mean that the country will need to ensure that its *nominal level of prices* ends up in a particular position, namely at a level which is consistent with the level of prices in the EMU area as a whole. That is, in turn, because the level of prices for the euro area as a whole is controlled by the ECB. Thus – obviously – it is

> not enough to ensure that inflation is under control in our economy. Membership of EMU will require that that any deflationary process – caused, say, as the country adjusts in response to the reduction in competitiveness that we are studying – comes to an end *at the right place*. If the deflation of the price level were – say – to go too far then that overshooting of the price level would need to be undone. We will argue below that there is a real risk of this.

In understanding the regime of constrained discretion which we seek, it is helpful to make three comparisons with the kind of regime of constrained discretion in which inflation-targeting monetary policy systems operate, the regime which was discussed earlier in the chapter.

First, there is an important similarity between what we are studying here and the setup in an inflation-targeting system. If, in such a system, the rate of inflation were to rise above its target level, then it would be brought back down again through monetary policy actions by means of a *temporary* rise in the interest rate. This policy action could be temporary, for a reason which we have already pointed out, namely because of the existence of a natural rate of output. In this EMU system a (relative) loss of competitiveness by one country means that its relative price level is too high, and that the price level must be brought down again. That will require a *temporary* reduction in output. The fact that this reduction in output can be temporary is again due to the existence of a natural rate of output. This 'two for one' property of adjustment with the EMU system might allow us to describe this process – if it works properly – as 'simply a good idea' and as 'employment friendly', the words that Alesina *et al.* (2001, pp. 2–4) used to describe inflation-targeting systems. But before we can say that, the EMU system of adjustment has got to actually work properly.

Second, there is another important similarity with such an inflation-control system. If, in such a system, the rate of inflation were to rise above its target level, then the monetary authority could *choose* the speed at which inflation is brought down by choosing the extent to which the real interest rate was raised in response to the inflationary problem (see Bean, 1998; Cechetti, 2000; and Henry, Satchi and Vines, 2006). In this EMU system a (relative) loss of competitiveness by one country means that its relative price level is too high, and must be brought down again. The fiscal authority can, by its behaviour, *choose* the speed at which this improvement in competitiveness happens.

Third, there is also an important *contrast* with the regime of constrained discretion in which inflation-targeting systems operate. In such systems, if inflation were to rise above its target level, and then be brought down again in the way which we have just described, the price level will slip away from the level which it would have had if, instead, it had risen at a steady rate without the shock. Such slippages are not normally corrected in inflation-targeting regimes. In this EMU regime, however, such a slippage of the price level is not possible. In this system an initial loss of competitiveness means that the relative price level is too high. It must be brought down, not just to any old level, but to the right level at which full employment of resources could be regained, without having to rely on fiscal irresponsibility.

A spectrum of possible regimes of constrained discretion

We are studying the effects of a loss of competitiveness by a country and how it can be corrected by a reduction in its price level, relative to that of other countries in EMU. We have argued that the fiscal authority can, by its behaviour, *choose* the speed at which this improvement in competitiveness happens.

At one extreme the authorities could, as already noted, seek to delay the deflationary forces by expanding fiscally so as to prevent the loss in competitiveness leading to a large increase in unemployment. This would mean that the fall in relative inflation in our country would be very slow. But as wage developments were eventually moderated and the required adjustment took place, the fiscal deficits would need to fall as the real exchange rate became more competitive and net exports rose. Eventually, as correction was fully achieved, the fiscal deficit would need to be removed.

Alternatively, the authorities could accept the initial deflationary forces, which would lead to a rapid rise in unemployment, and could let that high level of unemployment lead to a process of rapidly falling relative inflation. They could do this by, say, just allowing the automatic stabilisers to operate, being content with a reduction in tax revenues as a result of the lower level of output.

In between these two possibilities, the fiscal authorities might choose to moderate the rate of disinflation by engaging in some additional tax cuts or increases in deficit spending. At the other extreme they could rigidly target deficits and debt, *raising* taxes as output was reduced and tax revenues fell, so as to keep actual tax takings more or less constant. This is what an extreme version of the SGP would require.

The need for careful design of the regime of constrained discretion within which fiscal policy operates

The critical point, to which we have been remorselessly building, is that this choice of speed might need to be made with some care by the fiscal authorities. If not, we argue, the adjustment process might not work properly. It might even become unstable. There are two problems.

The 'Walters critique'

One central problem is that, with interest rates given by the centralised monetary policy, the process just described can become unstable because of the behaviour of the real interest rate. As inflation falls relative to the rest of Europe, and even becomes negative, the real interest rate would rise. This in turn this would lead to lower and lower demand, intensifying the downward movement of wage inflation and price inflation; that movement might turn into a downward spiral. A well-known condition for a sensible monetary policy is that nominal interest rates need to rise more than inflation as inflation rises – so that *real* interest rates rise with any rise in inflation. This condition, which is known as the 'Taylor principle', also suggests, of course, that real interest rates need to fall as inflation falls. However, our discussion above suggests that this requirement is in danger of being violated within EMU. The difficulty has become known as the 'Walters critique', stemming from the argument of Sir Alan Walters against British membership of the ERM when he was advisor to Margaret Thatcher. It is, potentially, a seriously destabilising mechanism.

In more detail, the possibility of instability arises for the following reason. The low domestic demand during the adjustment process comes not just from the initial worsening of competitiveness, but also from reductions in domestic consumption caused by the relatively high real interest rates which arise within the country during the course of adjustment.[13] As disinflation occurs, relative to the other countries in the euro area, the country's price level will fall and so its real exchange rate will fall. Of course this will cause an improvement in net exports, that is in the balance of payments, and that will cause an increase in the demand for output. Furthermore the balance of payments improvement will increase domestic liquidity and wealth, which has further positive effects on spending. These are the forces that make for a gradual recovery of demand, as the *price level* falls. But the reductions in domestic demand, caused by the rise in real interest rates as the rate of *inflation* falls, could actually overrule these forces. The process could even become unstable[14] (see Kirsanova, Vines and Wren-Lewis, 2006a).[15] Even if it were not actually unstable such an adjustment process might be an unattractive one for policymakers.

The only way for fiscal policy-makers to prevent this difficulty would be by introducing a sufficiently strong fiscal feedback from inflation. This would mean that, as the price level falls, the system as a whole does actually lead to increases in overall spending, so that the output gap closes. This requirement is an analogue of the Taylor principle in inflation-targeting systems.[16] The need to implement such a strong fiscal reaction function might be a very demanding one for policy. In particular, the automatic stabilisers might not be strong enough to provide an adequate degree of fiscal stabilisation. Taxes might actually need to be *cut*, at least in the early stages of the adjustment process, just to avoid instability (again, see Kirsanova, Vines, and Wren-Lewis, 2006a).

Some modern macroeconomists might criticise this argument, and advise policy-makers not to listen to it. They might – correctly – argue that forward-looking wage and price-setters would see through this problem, would know that wages and prices would need to be lower, and would bring about an outcome in which wages and prices fell more easily and quickly than we have supposed here. Westaway (2003), in the study he prepared for the UK Treasury in the run-up to the UK's decision not to join the euro, in fact assumed that wages and prices were sufficiently forward-looking to prevent this instability, without having to rely on any fiscal feedback at all. These economists might also – correctly – argue that forward-looking consumers and investors would see through this problem, would know that wages and prices would not need to fall below their final lower level, and would thus know that if wages and prices had begun to do this they would need to rise again, which would in due course cause real interest rates to fall again. That would lead them to increase their expenditures. Such consumers and investors would thus, of themselves, prevent the instability from getting out of hand. Kirsanova, Satchi, Vines and Wren-Lewis (2006) show that this is indeed true. However, Kirsanova, Vines and Wren-Lewis (2006b) also show that either a proportion of liquidity-constrained consumers, or a proportion of backward-looking behaviour in the Phillips curve, can easily lead to a re-emergence of these 'Walters critique' problems. They thus suggest that it might be over optimistic to rely on such forward-lookingness.

If policy-makers are not prepared to rely on forward-lookingness, then along the adjustment path fiscal policy would need to cancel out at least some of the demand-lowering effects of higher real interest rates – the consequence of relative disinflation – so that the demand–increasing effects of improved competitiveness could take hold. If this happened the adjustment process could become reasonably smooth and benign. In practice this might mean that there was a need to actively use fiscal policy to support demand during the adjustment process, so that it becomes more stimulatory when inflation falls too much. Cheng and Vines (2006) and Kirsanova, Satchi, Wren-Lewis and Vines (2006), which are the two most thorough studies of this issue available, show that such a policy could significantly improve performance within EMU, in response to the kind of shock that we are studying here.

Cycles due to the 'price level problem'

The second difficulty – which we have already noted – is that for a country in EMU, the targeting of *inflation* is not enough. With a fixed nominal exchange rate, the *price level* matters for the real exchange rate and competitiveness, and, as a result, movements in the price level are crucial for the adjustment process. This means that it is not sufficient for the inflation rate to home in on the Europe-wide rate of inflation. In addition the economy needs to home in on the appropriate price level. In other words, for the adjustment process to come to an end, it is not sufficient that any shortfall of inflation below the EMU average be corrected. It is also necessary that this happens in just such a way that any overshooting of the price level is avoided or corrected.

It will, in fact, be quite difficult to ensure this. The reason is as follows. The initial reduction in competitiveness (the shock that we are studying) must increase unemployment so as to make the price level start falling. That is to say, the inflation rate will initially go below the Europe-wide level. As this happens, the level of competitiveness will gradually improve. Let us suppose that the Walters-critique problems, discussed above, are avoided by a sufficiently active fiscal policy. Then, providing that this is true, after an initial fall output will begin to rise back up again, and unemployment will begin to fall as the economy becomes more competitive again. That will mean that the pressures that are making inflation fall further will weaken. There will come a time when the price level has fallen enough to remove the reduction in demand which was caused by the initial fall in competitiveness. But, at that point, the *level of inflation* will still be lower than it is in the euro area as a whole. This obviously means that the *price level* will overshoot. As that happens, demand will increase further, causing the rate of inflation – relative to the euro area average – to rise back to zero. But at this point the level of prices is low, demand will be higher than equilibrium, and the inflation rate will be increasing. Such behaviour is cyclical in nature.

Analytically, the point being made here relates to ideas about simple harmonic motion that come from physics. Suppose – for simplicity – that the Phillips curve is entirely backward-looking. Then this Phillips curve says that the *rate of change* of inflation depends negatively on output. Output will, in turn, depend negatively on the level of prices, p, through the effect of the real exchange rate on net exports. But the rate of change of inflation is just d^2p/dt^2. Hence, in a very simple description of what is going on, we have an adjustment equation for prices that can be written:

$$d^2p/dt^2 = -kp$$

for some constant k. This is the form of equation that is used to describe the simple harmonic motion displayed by a pendulum.[17] Of course this story exaggerates. For one thing there will be damping effects on any such oscillatory forces (which act like friction in a pendulum). And for another, forward-looking wage and price-setters will see through this oscillatory process; their resulting behaviour will also tend to damp the tendency towards oscillation. Nevertheless what we have just shown, both verbally and analytically, is that there is a tendency for the price level to overshoot and thus for the system to cycle. Westaway (2003) confirmed this, and showed that, as a consequence, shocks within EMU are likely to lead to substantially greater fluctuations as compared with what would happen to a country outside EMU. That suggests that an active fiscal policy – deployed so as to smooth down these cycles – might be helpful. This strengthens the case for relatively active fiscal stabilisation which we advanced when discussing the Walters critique. We here have a second, additional, reason for such an active fiscal policy.

This suggests that, *even if there is quite a considerable degree of forward-lookingness in the economy*, active fiscal policy might be needed if we are to avoid the adjustment process to the new equilibrium being oscillatory, with an overshoot of the price level.[18] Kirsanova, Satchi, Vines and Wren-Lewis (2006) show that this is indeed true. And they show that a very great improvement in performance can be achieved if fiscal policy feeds back, not only on inflation (so as to avoid Walters-critique problems), but also on the extent to which the real exchange rate differs from its long-run equilibrium level. Their analysis was conducted on a state-of-the-art, microfounded, new Keynesian model of EMU, and has been confirmed in a parallel study by Cheng and Vines (2006). Their findings agree with the earlier study by Westaway (2003).

Alternatives to the Stability and Growth Pact

Why the SGP is disastrous – even in its revised form

We have described a *spectrum* of possible regimes of constrained discretion for fiscal policy. But we have also presented a compelling argument that, for a good outcome, the choice that is made along this spectrum would need to involve:

(a) active fiscal policy feedback which becomes more stimulatory if inflation goes too low; and
(b) active feedback from the equilibrium real exchange rate to fiscal policy, so that it becomes more expansionary as the real exchange rate falls towards its equilibrium level, in order to prevent the real exchange rate overshooting.

This immediately suggests that arbitrary fiscal rules, of the kind which appear innocuous in a monetary policy-oriented system, could well be disastrous in EMU. Such a suggestion is bad news for the Stability and Growth Pact. This is because it is clear that the fiscal authorities cannot *both* tightly target fiscal sustainability (aiming, say, for a constant debt ratio) as in the SGP, and at the same time target the inflation rate and the real exchange rate, as suggested above. They have to choose one or the other (or a consistent combination).

An alternative is that, instead of following SGP-type rules, the fiscal authorities instead:

(i) ensure that the fiscal position is sustainable in the longer term; and
(ii) actively target the inflation rate and the real exchange rate in the shorter term.

That is what we recommend. The Stability and Growth Pact forbids it.

It is clear from the above analysis that if our country were to follow the Stability and Growth Pact, when adjusting to a downturn in competitiveness this would have two effects. First, the fiscal authorities would be unable to prevent the Taylor principle being violated. As a result, the fall in inflation would, quite possibly, be undesirably rapid, as suggested by the Walters critique. Secondly the price level would be likely to overshoot. It would fall too far and have to come back again.

All this leads us to the conclusion that there is serious interference between the fiscal arrangements of the SGP, and the need to adjust real exchange rates between countries within EMU. We believe that the rigidities of the SGP – which apply particularly and asymmetrically to countries facing competitiveness problems and/or persistent low domestic demand trends – seriously interfere with the fiscal policy responses which are desirable. Because of this, such countries experience unnecessary and costly deflation or instability, to no benefit. The general prescription is that there should be a much greater delegation of fiscal freedom to those countries which are suffering from negative external shocks.

A corollary is that greater devolution of fiscal freedom to such countries will enable better policies to be adopted. Importantly, such policies, if adopted, will not lead to higher inflation or to the postponement of necessary adjustments of the relative real exchange rate. Specifically, the additional fiscal freedom will allow the adjustment path desired by the authorities to be achieved without unnecessary unemployment and it will allow these countries to avoid the dynamic instabilities (such as overshooting) that at present arise during adjustment.

Our overall conclusion is that such additional policy freedom, enabling a more intelligent fiscal policy, is likely to improve the trade-offs in the country concerned, resulting in higher levels of activity without additional inflation. In itself this would tend to improve overall euro area performance. As discussed in the Conclusion, this might lead, further, to higher investment and so to increased growth in the euro area. There could be some consequence for euro area wide interest rates, due to the positive spillover of demand effects on *other* countries. There are few who would not regard that as a price worth paying.

A regime of constrained discretion that would be better than the SGP

We have argued that, instead of the SGP, the fiscal authorities should:

(i) ensure that the fiscal position is sustainable in the longer term; and
(ii) actively target the inflation rate and the real exchange rate in the shorter term.

We can put what we are suggesting in another way. Effectively we are suggesting that the fiscal authorities target the longer-term fiscal position – but only in such a way that they ensure that in moving towards it they also steer the real exchange rate towards its right position. Alternatively, we suggest they might target (that is introduce feedback from) an appropriate *future* real exchange rate, where that target is chosen to be consistent with longer-term fiscal sustainability.

There appear to be two good reasons in favour of this latter course. The first is that the debt ratio *per se* does not normally, of itself, have much weight in the authorities' objective function. The fiscal position needs to be sustainable, as we have seen, but otherwise debt can act as a shock absorber. More than this, debt *should* act as a shock absorber in this way.[19]

But there is a second, stronger, political-economy reason. A fiscal objective for debt – in the sense of feedback onto a targeted debt ratio like that in the SGP – risks producing the interpretation, as in the SGP, that this feedback needs to be quick. Such a *tight* fiscal feedback for debt would rule out the kinds of targeting of inflation and the real exchange rate that we have said may be essential. A fiscal feedback on debt, because it risks being turned into a *tight* fiscal feedback on debt, is dangerous. It risks *causing* the kinds of instability and cycles discussed in this chapter.

It is clear that what we are suggesting for fiscal policy involves a regime of 'constrained discretion'. The longer-term objective for fiscal policy, or the 'constraint', can remain that of 'sustainability'. This would be an objective just like that in the SGP, specified in accordance with a framework of 'sustainability pacts' (see Coeuré and Pisani-Ferry, 2006). But the difference of our approach from that in the SGP lies in the way in which 'discretion' would operate. The policy action which we suggest, in response to indications of 'unsustainability', would be very different from what is now meant to happen within the SGP. At present, within the SGP, the required response to this problem is a programme of budgetary cuts, *even if* the problem is caused by a loss of competitiveness, as in the thought-experiment that we have been carrying out. We suggest that this risks causing instability and cycles. What we are suggesting instead would be a policy directed towards achieving gradual changes in the real exchange rate over time, towards a long run target. *That target would be the one which was consistent with the sustainability objective.* The required move of the economy towards this position would be assisted by fiscal restraint. But that restraint would be devised so as to achieve adjustment at a satisfactory, and ideally optimal, rate over time.

No one would suggest that the policy framework which we are outlining is a simple one. But adjustment of the real exchange rate in a way consistent with fiscal sustainability in the longer term is, as we have argued, not a simple problem. Since fiscal policy is difficult, the suggestion that delegation of fiscal policy to fiscal policy committees, charged to act in a way which is to some degree comparable to monetary policy committees, as suggested by Wyplosz (2002), is attractive.

Most of the time, with real exchange rates at their appropriate levels, the fiscal authorities would simply get on with their job of stabilising prices, and the output gap, as far as possible. The real difficulties will appear when fiscal sustainability is threatened and adjustment is needed. This fits in well with a framework of 'constrained discretion' for fiscal policy. In 'normal times' with the real exchange rate appropriate for longer term fiscal sustainability, fiscal policy could concentrate on stabilising inflation and offsetting demand shocks. But the framework would need to recognise that real exchange rates (and the balance of payments position) would need to be adjusted from time to time, to be consistent with the longer-term internal objectives. Without this 'override' there is a clear danger that fiscal policy will prevent the needed adjustments from taking place. The override would ensure that the policy of the 'good times' – that of stabilising prices and the output gap – does *not* continue unamended, when what is needed is careful adjustment. But the override would *also* ensure that over-strict rules, as tight as those in the SGP, were not imposed either. As we have argued in this paper, those rules would probably mess up the adjustment process, by causing instability and overshooting.

Clearly, if policies other than fiscal policy were available to help with adjusting the real exchange rate in appropriate ways, the task of the fiscal authorities in EMU would be vastly easier. Supply side policies, to tackle relative competitiveness directly, would be one such instrument. But under the Lisbon agenda, such policies are recommended for all countries. They would not be much use for changing *relative* competitiveness, unless they happened disproportionately fast in the country which was subject to the most competitive pressure. This is at least possible, but it should hardly be relied upon.

The other policy that would appear extremely helpful, given the difficulties, would be some form of incomes policy – which took into account the need for relative competitiveness adjustments. With this additional – and very European – instrument of policy in place, the fiscal authorities could concentrate on stabilising output, subject to a sustainability constraint.

Conclusions

Europe has been underperforming, most obviously in terms of productivity performance, but perhaps more seriously in terms of an apparently unfavourable trade-off between growth and inflation. As we have seen, the 'official' diagnosis of this problem has given macroeconomic policy a relatively clean bill of health, and has pointed instead to supply-side issues and the need for supply-side reform.

At the macro (area wide) level, the euro system is comparable to that in the US or in the UK. Studies suggest that the ECB's behaviour has been comparable to that of other central banks in other inflation-targeting countries: that it has been relatively active, and that despite low growth, headline inflation has, for most of the time since the start of EMU, overshot the ECB's target.

This poses a challenge for those who want to argue that macroeconomic policy is at fault. On the face of it, there appears to have been little room for a more expansionary monetary policy. If this is the case, there has been little room for a fiscally-induced expansion either, since, in a monetary policy-oriented system, this would just be offset by higher interest rates.

In this chapter we have presented an alternative argument about faulty macro policy-making. This argument focuses on the process of inter-country adjustment, and on the connections between this adjustment process and fiscal policies and labour markets within the euro area. For an individual country within EMU, fiscal policy is much more important than it is at the aggregate level of the euro area as a whole. We argue that fiscal policy and adjustment issues have, within EMU, interacted in unfavourable and possibly destabilising ways. Our analysis suggests that these problems arise for countries facing particular circumstances. We have focused on those countries which are needing to improve their relative international competitiveness, and which are also suffering from downturns in investment and increases in savings resulting from this poor international competitiveness. It is in countries in these circumstances that the fiscal rules of the SGP bind most strongly. They constrain macroeconomic policy in the most damaging ways in such countries.

In broad terms, this combination of adjustment problems and binding fiscal constraints can be seen as characterising the 'German problem'. We believe that poor performance in Germany and some other large countries has been caused by the problems described in this chapter. We think that this could explain a large part of the euro area's poor performance in aggregate, and we intend to describe this specific empirical claim in some detail in a later paper.

Our argument is that a 'sensible' use of fiscal policy during adjustment would violate the existing fiscal rules. This means that those rules should be changed. Restoring greater fiscal sovereignty to national governments could enable better performance to be achieved in countries such as Germany without engendering inflation. There is no reason why such policies should be inconsistent with the requirement that fiscal policy be sustainable in the longer run.

Our arguments suggest that the ECB's well-known opposition to any relaxation of the rules of the SGP is distinctly unhelpful – and arguably damaging to its own reputation for competence. Our arguments also suggest that a somewhat higher inflation target would be helpful in allowing easier (and quicker) relative adjustment between countries.[20] None of this means that supply-side problems are not important or that they should not be addressed. It is widely argued, however, that important supply-side reforms and adjustments would be easier to introduce with a better macroeconomic framework and greater confidence that the euro area's growth potential will be realised.[21]

If this claim is true, then we have provided support for a compelling explanation of poor European macroeconomic performance. It is our belief that this claim is true and thus that we have indeed provided such an explanation. Our belief is that a better macroeconomic policy framework would, itself, have been conducive to improvements on the supply side in the euro area, including the kind of supply-side improvements advanced under the 'Lisbon agenda'. It is also our view that the overrestrictive and otherwise badly designed macroeconomic policies which we have described in this paper have hindered reforms, and have thereby worsened inflationary pressure, and the supply side, within the euro area. We therefore suggest that a better-designed macroeconomic framework would indeed improve the potential for non-inflationary growth within the euro area.

Notes

1 In the UK, the reputation for successful macroeconomic policy has developed alongside relatively poor supply-side (productivity) performance. In the US, the reputation for good macroeconomic policy developed in tandem with exceptionally good productivity performance. Since the large recent expansion in the US budget deficit, questions have developed over the sustainability of macroeconomic policy there.

2 This choice is discussed in Bean (1988), Cechetti (2000) and Henry, Satchi and Vines (2006).

3 For a full discussion of the stability conditions for a system like this see Kirsanova, Stehn and Vines (2005).

4 The UK Treasury argues that fiscal policy has supported the 'stability oriented monetary policy' in the UK. But although the fiscal expansion in the UK was well-timed, it was in fact carried out for reasons which had little to do with such stabilisation objectives.

5 Note that this question puts the emphasis on the way in which the ECB has in fact behaved, rather than putting emphasis on what the ECB has said it does. In its statements, the ECB has typically downplayed the secondary aspects of its mandate, insisting instead that medium-term control of inflation (its primary mandate) is the best basis for growth and full employment. But we are interested in the outcomes, not in the ECB's words.

6 This is how the objective was originally expressed. The more recent specification is 'The ECB aims at inflation rates of below, but close to, 2 per cent over the medium term' (ECB website 2005).

7 Moreover, the Fed, as nominal interest rates approached the 'lower bound' of zero, welcomed the additional stimulus of fiscal policy. The ECB's rhetoric has been very different – favouring fiscal consolidation and the rigorous application of the SGP, despite the developing slowdown and historically low interest rates.

8 As already noted, the ECB's own rhetoric has been misplaced. It has argued that what it was 'really' doing was medium-term control of inflation because that is what is important for full employment and growth. But the critical point is that short term control of inflation would not have allowed the ECB to have been

any more expansionary. Indeed it would, if anything, have suggested the opposite.

9 Important studies of these issues have been made by the Swedish government (2002) and by the UK Treasury (HM Treasury, 2003), in two countries that have been contemplating the implications of joining the currency area.

10 See Carlin and Soskice (2006) for a formal discussion of exchange-rate overshooting in response to an IS shock, as a consequence of lags in the adjustment of net exports to the real exchange rate.

11 To the extent that a reduction in the competitiveness of an individual country causes a reduction in competitiveness of the euro area as a whole, it will be dealt with by Europe-wide monetary policy. This means that a change in the competitiveness of a large country will influence the Europe-wide interest rate. For expositional simplicity, this complication is neglected here. To allow for this complication, we should think of our shock as a permanent loss of competitiveness in our country, *relative to that of the euro area as a whole.*

12 The Swedish Government Report (2002) indeed flirts with that idea – but rejects it in favour of an independent committee with an advisory and 'naming and shaming' role. The UK Treasury (drawing analogies with the mandates of the ECB and the Bank of England) has suggested a hierarchical ordering of objectives for fiscal policy, with the primary mandate being to ensure 'sustainability' with, 'subject to that', an important role in stabilisation. They too rule out an independent fiscal policy committee on grounds of incompatibility with the sovereignty of parliament.

13 The inherent instability of the processes involved has in fact probably been attenuated by a limit on the rate at which prices and wages in Germany can fall relative to other countries. It is often suggested that there is a 'floor' to the rate of wage inflation in Germany (Hanke and Soskice, 2003) and, given the ECB's target for inflation, a limit to the rate at which the real exchange rate can adjust.

14 Unstable in the sense of an ever increasing rate of deflation, or cyclically unstable, with the cycles increasing through time.

15 It is actually this kind of difficulty which can arise in an inflation-targeting system when the Taylor principle does not hold.

16 Technically, this is a fiscal-policy add-on to the 'Taylor principle'. It suggests that the joint effects of the lower price level and of fiscal policy must together dominate the effects of falling consumption and investment, coming from the rise in the real interest rate caused by the fall in inflation, so that the level of demand actually increases as the price level falls. This means that the rate of fall of inflation would diminish as the price level fell. That would prevent the fall in inflation from getting out of hand.

17 It is possible to understand why this is so without understanding much mathematics. Suppose that a system does display simple harmonic motion. Then a plot of its displacement x, relative to the origin, will look something like a sin curve. So let us suppose that $x = \sin t$. Now we know that $d \sin t/\mathrm{d}t = \cos t$. But we also know that $d \cos t/\mathrm{d}t = -\sin t$. Therefore we can see that $\mathrm{d}^2\sin t/\mathrm{d}t^2 = -\sin t$, or that $\mathrm{d}^2x/\mathrm{d}t^2 = -x$, which is an equation of the required kind. This suggests that the equation shown in the text, namely $\mathrm{d}^2p/\mathrm{d}t^2 = -kp$ does indeed have a solution which displays simple harmonic motion.

18 As noted above, Westaway adopted a partly forward-looking Phillips curve in his study. Nevertheless his EMU system oscillated markedly without fiscal intervention. That is also true in the systems described in Kirsanova, Satchi, Vines and Wren-Lewis (2006).

19 This point is discussed in detail in Kirsanova, Stehn and Vines (2006) and Kirsanova, Satchi, Vines and Wren-Lewis (2006)
20 This claim is a controversial one and we have not argued it here in detail.
21 This too is a big claim which we do not attempt to substantiate here.

References

Alesina, A., O. Blanchard, J. Gali, F. Giavazzi and H. Uhlig (2001) *Defining a Macroeconomic Framework for the Euro Area,* Monitoring the European Central Bank 3. London: CEPR.

Allsopp, C.J. and M. Artis (2003) 'EMU Four Years On', *Oxford Review of Economic Policy*, 19: 1–29.

Allsopp, C.J. and D. Vines (1996) 'Fiscal Policy and EMU', *National Institute Economic Review*, no. 158: 91–107.

Allsopp, C.J., and D. Vines (1998) 'Macroeconomic Policy after EMU', *Oxford Review of Economic Policy*, 14(3): 1–23.

Allsopp, C.J. and D. Vines (2000) 'Macroeconomic Policy', *Oxford Review of Economic Policy,'* 16(4): 1–32.

Allsopp, C.J. and D. Vines (2005) 'The Macroeconomic Role of Fiscal Policy', *Oxford Review of Economic Policy*, 21(4): 585–08.

Bean, C.R. (1998a) 'The New UK Monetary Arrangements: A View from the Literature', *Economic Journal*, 108: 1795.

Bean, C.R. (1998b) 'Monetary Policy under EMU', *Oxford Review of Economic Policy*, 14(3): 41–53.

Begg, D.F. Canova, F.P. De Grauwe, A. Fatas and P.R. Lane (2002) *Surviving the Slowdown*, Monitoring the European Central Bank 4. London: CEPR.

Carlin, W. and D. Soskice (2005) *Macroeconomics: Imperfections, Institutions and Policies*. Oxford: Oxford University Press.

Cecchetti, S. (2000) 'Making Monetary Policy: Objectives and Rules', *Oxford Review of Economic Policy*, 16 (4): 43–59.

Cheng, M and D. Vines (forthcoming) 'Inflation Persistence: Implications for Fiscal Policy in EMU', Discussion Paper from Centre for Economic Policy Research, London.

Coeuré, B. and J. Pisani-Ferry (2005) 'Fiscal Policy in Emu: Towards a Sustainability and Growth Pact?', *Oxford Review of Economic Policy*, 21, 598–617.

Dornbusch, R. (1976) 'Expectations and Exchange Rate Dynamics', *Journal of Political Economy*, 84: 1161–76.

European Commission (2004) 'EMU after 5 Years': *European Economy,* Special Report, available at http://europa.eu.int/comm/economy_finance/publications/european_economy/2004/eesp104en.pdf

Hancke, B. and D. Soskice (2003) 'Wage Setting and Inflation Targets in EMU' *Oxford Review of Economic Policy,* 19: 149 – 160.

HM Treasury (2003) *Fiscal Stabilisation and EMU*. London: HM Treasury.

Henry, B., M. Satchi and D. Vines (2006) 'The Effect of Discounting on Policy Choices in Inflation Targeting Regimes', *Economic Journal,* 116: 266–82.

Issing, O. (2002) 'On Macroeconomic Policy Coordination in EMU', *Journal of Common Market Studies,* 40: 345–58.

King, M. (1997) 'The Inflation Target Five Years On', *Bank of England Quarterly Bulletin*, 37: 434–42.

Kirsanova, T., M. Satchi, D. Vines and S. Wren-Lewis (2006) 'Optimal Fiscal Policy Rules in a Monetary Union', Discussion Paper no. 5533. Centre for Economic Policy Research, London.

Kirsanova, T., J. Stehn and D. Vines (2006) 'The Interaction of Fiscal Policy and Monetary Policy' *Oxford Review of Economic Policy,* 21: 532–64; also available as CEPR Discussion Paper no 5464.

Kirsanova, S., D. Vines, and S. Wren-Lewis (2006a) 'Fiscal Policy and Macroeconomic Stability within a Monetary Union', Discussion Paper no. 5584. Centre for Economic Policy Research, London.

Kirsanova, T., D. Vines, and S. Wren-Lewis (2006b) 'Credit Constrained Consumers, Inflation Inertia, and Instability under Fixed Exchange Rates', Discussion Paper, Economics Department, University of Exeter.

Swedish Government (2002) 'Stabilisation Policy in the Monetary Union: Summary of the Report', *The Commission on Stabilisation Policy for Full Employment in the Event of Sweden Joining the Monetary Union,* Swedish Government Official Reports SOU 2002:16, Stockholm.

Westaway, P. (2003) *Modelling Shocks and Adjustment Mechanisms in EMU,* London: HM Treasury.

Woodford, M. (2003) *Interest and Prices,* Princeton: Princeton University Press.

Wyplosz, C (2002) 'Fiscal Policy: Institutions versus Rules', Discussion, Paper no. 3238, Centre for Economic Policy Research, London

Discussion

*Charles Nolan**

This is an interesting and thought-provoking chapter, as one would expect from Christopher Allsopp and David Vines (A&V, hereafter). Their basic argument appears familiar: In a monetary union it may be difficult for countries to adjust to asymmetric shocks as monetary policy cannot respond. As a result, fiscal policy becomes more important as a stabilisation tool. It follows that the SGP is potentially flawed.

Fiscal policy straightjackets and asymmetric shocks

A&V provide an example of the kind of scenarios that may arise. Consider a country in monetary union that experiences a permanent negative demand shock. As the nominal exchange rate cannot respond, and in the absence of price and wage flexibility, fiscal policy ought to take up the slack in the transition. Ultimately, they argue, the real exchange rate needs to change. However, if the SGP is constraining countries from employing fiscal policy along the adjustment path, then a painful recession may be unavoidable. There is an added twist of the knife, however, since the lack of response of short-term nominal interest rates means that real interest rates will rise, exacerbating the original contraction in demand.

They argue that unless we have a robust response from fiscal policy to offset this negative demand shock and the Walters critique-type follow-on effect, and/or an incomes policy, and/or a real exchange rate target, then the fault lines running through the euro area's macroeconomic framework are potentially hugely damaging.

How worried should we be?

It seems to me that the analysis in this chapter may be way too pessimistic on these issues. There is an obvious solution to the particular dilemma that

*I would like to thank, without implicating, David Cobham for helpful comments.

A&V are worried about, and it is embodied in the Lisbon agenda and in other purely national policy reforms. The idea behind these reforms is to make economies more responsive to competitive pressures. Of course, we know that attempts to free-up product and, especially, labour markets are far from politically/economically costless. But the authors even deny that the Lisbon agenda is a solution to the ills they seek to avoid:

> under the Lisbon agenda, such policies are recommended for all countries. They would not be much use for changing relative competitiveness unless they happened disproportionately fast in the country which is subject to the most competitive pressure, which is possible, but which could hardly be relied upon.

But, as a key aim of the Lisbon agenda is to make prices and wages more flexible, isn't the success of the Lisbon agenda *all* we need? If all countries are more flexible as the result of Lisbon-type reforms then the competitiveness of each one will respond more readily to shocks to competitiveness, so that real exchange rates will adjust more quickly. If countries succeed in making prices and wages more flexible, then output will remain at (or, closer to) its natural rate. Isn't the success of the Lisbon agenda *exactly* the right policy to be pursuing?

Next, how worried should we be about 'asymmetric shocks'? These mythical beasts may, for all I know, strike terror into the heart of policy-makers in EMU (so long as price and wage flexibility – another couple of mythical European beasts? – are absent). I am not so sure these are a problem, however. As James Tobin argued some time ago:

> When the export–import balance becomes the strategic component of aggregate demand, one country's expansionary shock is another country's deflationary shock.

So the ECB may well want to 'rescue' a country from an asymmetric shock, since a big asymmetric shock, especially to a 'big' country, may well end up looking a lot like a symmetric shock. But then, what about small countries? Well, small countries are often found to benefit most from a monetary union and in the run up to EMU such countries often demonstrated a track record of being able to walk in lock-step with a larger neighbour.

But I agree that fiscal policy *may* be unnecessarily tethered under the current set-up in the euro area, if any of the participating countries take the fiscal rules seriously. And that is, perhaps, the problem. The reason that the rules were introduced in the first place was to counter a perceived political pressure to run excessive deficits and debts. Hence, for me the real questions are: Should we design more robust stabilisers? What is the optimal design of the stabilisers? Are they better suited to demand or supply shocks? These are the real issues, I believe, but they are seldom raised or discussed in any detail. A&V of course mention the existence and relevance of the automatic fiscal stabilisers (the systematic component of fiscal policy), but it seems to be taken as read that they are insufficient for the job A&V have in mind for fiscal policy. But how do we know that? I know of no study that addresses these issues in an optimising theoretical framework. And until we know the answers to these questions, it may be premature to recommend possibly radical ways to change the way fiscal policy operates.

Reference

Tobin, J. (1978) 'A Proposal for International Monetary Reform', *Eastern Economic Journal*, 4, July/October: 153–9.

6

The Economic Importance of Fiscal Rules

*Michael J. Artis and Luca Onorante**

Introduction

The European Council of 22–23 March 2005 agreed on some long-awaited reforms of the Stability and Growth Pact (SGP). The Pact includes two Council regulations: Regulation 1466/97 on the strengthening of budgetary surveillance and coordination of economic policies (the so-called 'preventive arm'), and Regulation 1467/97 on the excessive deficit procedure (the co-called 'corrective arm'). In applying to both arms of the Pact the reforms are in principle quite comprehensive and they appear also to be quite detailed and complex. The objective of this chapter is to provide an assessment of these reforms, using an empirically based model to do so. The background to the reforms and analysis of the economic rationale for a fiscal pact of the type represented by the SGP can be found in, for example, Calmfors (2005) and Beetsma and Debrun (2006). The working paper versions of this chapter (Artis and Onorante, 2006a, 2006b) also contain a review of these important issues. However the main business of the current chapter is to lay out and estimate an empirical model which can be used to simulate the effects of alternative fiscal rules, including both the reformed and the pre-reform versions of the SGP. We begin by identifying the agreed amendments to the two 'arms' of the old Pact that constitute the reforms agreed upon.

The principal constituents of the reform package

The amendments to the so-called 'preventive' arm of the Pact include the following:

*The authors would like to thank Roberto Perotti, Jürgen von Hagen, Carlo Favero, Olivier Blanchard, Ludger Schuknecht, Jean-Pierre Vidal and Paolo Paesani for very useful discussions and insights. All mistakes are ours. The views expressed in this paper do not necessarily reflect those of the European Central Bank.

- In the old version of the Pact member countries were enjoined to treat as a 'medium-term objective' a budgetary position of 'close to balance or in surplus' (CTBOIS). This was (and still is) to be seen as providing a safety margin with respect to the 3 per cent government deficit ratio, violation of which – with exceptions to be mentioned below – generally can be taken as triggering the 'excessive deficit procedure'. In the new formulation the medium-term objective (MTO) should be differentiated for individual member states, to take into account the diversity of economic and budgetary positions and developments as well as of fiscal risk to the sustainability of public finances. The medium-term budgetary objectives may diverge from CTBOIS for individual member states. The adoption of new, looser medium-term targets implicitly recognises the lack of rationale of the close to balance or in-surplus requirement which, if continuously respected, would drive debt ratios to zero or even to negative values. For euro area and ERM2 member states, budgetary objectives shall be specified within a defined range between – 1 per cent of GDP and balance or surplus, in cyclically adjusted terms,[1] net of one-off and temporary measures.
- The adjustment effort towards the medium-term objective should consist of an annual adjustment in cyclically adjusted terms, net of one-off and temporary measures, of 0.5 per cent of GDP as a benchmark. The Commission should issue policy advice to encourage member states to stick to their adjustment path.
- When defining the adjustment path towards the MTO major structural reforms which have direct long-term cost-saving effects, including by raising potential growth, will be taken into account. A safety margin with respect to the 3 per cent reference value must, however, be maintained at all times.

Changes in the corrective arm include:

- A change in the growth threshold for an appeal to the 'exceptional circumstances' by virtue of which the excessive deficit procedure may be held in abeyance. In the new formulation of the Pact, a deficit over the reference value may be considered exceptional if it results from a negative growth rate or from an accumulated loss of output during a protracted period of very low growth relative to potential.[2]
- In its recommendations, the Council shall request that a member state in excessive deficit achieves a minimum annual improvement of at least 0.5 per cent of GDP as a benchmark, in its cyclically adjusted balance net of one-off and temporary measures, in order to ensure the correction of the excessive deficit within the deadline set in the recommendation.
- Other relevant factors to be taken into account in Commission reports under Article 104(3) of the Treaty are to include developments in the

medium-term economic position, and in the medium-term budgetary position. Consideration will also be given to any other factors that the member state concerned deems relevant. Special consideration will be given to any excess over the reference value that reflects the implementation of pension reforms.

- The political commitment to reduce government debt would be reaffirmed. The debt-surveillance framework would be strengthened by clarifying in qualitative terms the concept of a rate of debt ratio decline 'sufficiently diminishing and approaching the reference value at a satisfactory pace'. It is unclear, however, whether a commitment in qualitative terms can be considered a reinforcement of the debt criterion.[3]
- The deadline for the correction of an excessive deficit should in theory remain the year after its identification. In practice, the initial deadline could be set one year later in case of special circumstances, based on the other relevant factors mentioned above. Moreover, the initial deadline could be revised at a later stage if unexpected adverse economic events with major unfavourable budgetary effects occur.

The reform of the Pact attempts to strike a balance between flexibility and sustainability.[4] The automatic stabilisers could work during the period of consolidation. The process of convergence would be smoothed over time; furthermore, a fixed speed of convergence is indicated, allowing those countries that are more distant from a balanced budget a longer time period. The sanctions of the SGP remain unaltered, but it seems clear that the changes in the corrective arm make them less likely to be invoked.

Since the purpose of this chapter is to estimate an empirical model which can be used to investigate the principal features of these reforms, in the next section we briefly review the existing empirical literature on fiscal policy.

Modelling fiscal policy: the empirical literature

The investigation of the interaction between fiscal policy and macroeconomic developments requires, as a first step, the identification of the contribution of fiscal policy to the economic cycle.

Structural regressions have been widely used in this context. Van den Noord (2002) groups the structural methods into three categories. A first approach runs regressions of fiscal variables on different sets of explanatory variables; for instance, Galí and Perotti (2003) estimate fiscal rules for the discretionary budget deficit, using data on EMU countries for a sample period very similar to the one used in this chapter. This approach gives reliable results only if the set of explanatory variables is sufficiently large, but may suffer from misspecification if the correct lags are not included. A second approach uses macroeconometric models, whose equations are calibrated. Macro models have the advantage of allowing the identification of different kinds of shocks, but suffer from the same problems as those just described because the equations need first to be estimated in order to calibrate the elasticities in the model. The third approach is used by the OECD, and consists of a mix of different methodologies. The elasticities of the cyclical components of taxes and expenditure are computed relative to a measure of the output gap independently estimated.

A different approach tries to overcome the difficulties of correctly specifying a model by using structural vector autoregression models (SVARs), which require only minimal identifying assumptions. SVAR models are widely used in empirical studies of monetary policy, but their use in the analysis of fiscal policy is fairly recent.

The lack of high frequency fiscal data or of long annual data series is partially responsible for this lack of interest. However, a number of important contributions have shown that the approach can give useful results. Blanchard and Perotti (1999) use an SVAR with taxes, government spending and GDP, all expressed in real terms, to investigate the dynamic effects of shocks in government spending and taxes in the US. A similar approach, with different specification of the model, can be found in Fatás and Mihov (1999). De Arcangelis and Lamartina (2001) use different identifying restrictions to explore the existence of different fiscal policy regimes. Perotti (2002) studies the effects of fiscal policy on GDP, prices and interest rates in five OECD countries. Favero (2003) and others have shown that fiscal and monetary policy cannot be estimated separately, because the interaction effects would bias the estimates.

Following Blanchard and Quah (1989), some authors use long-run restrictions, which are relatively easy to reconcile with economic theory. This is the case of Bayoumi and Eichengreen (1992), who apply long-run restrictions to distinguish supply from demand shocks, and more recently of Dalsgaards and de Serres (2000), who estimate an SVAR for the 11 EMU countries.[5] Garcia and Verdelhan (2001) use a specification scheme which includes both short and long-run restrictions. They apply it to synthetic euro area data, including yearly GDP, inflation, real short-term interest rates and budget balances, and manage to identify four types of shocks: supply, demand, monetary and fiscal. They also estimate cyclically adjusted budget balances and a synthetic indicator of the policy mix.

An SVAR has some properties that make it particularly suitable for the present study. First, it can incorporate a measure of the cycle that is completely consistent with the model itself, without requiring additional information as input. It also avoids the need to identify specific and possibly restrictive fiscal and monetary policy rules. The presence of a sufficient number of lags can also embrace forward-looking behaviour on the part of policy-makers, to the extent that VAR models can be interpreted as reduced forms of forward-looking models (see for example Favero, 2003). A specific advantage of SVAR models is that at least some identifying restrictions can be specified in the form of behavioural rules. This is the case, for example, of the Blanchard and Quah long-run restrictions. Behavioural restrictions can normally be reconciled with a large variety of economic models, and are therefore easier to accept. Our restrictions are of this nature.

Building on the SVAR approach, we estimate a simultaneous equation model, identifying fiscal shocks on the basis of long-run restrictions.[6]

The model

The structure of the reduced-form model used for estimation is the following:

$$Y = \sum_{L=1}^{p} C(L)Y + \sum_{L=1}^{q} D(L)X + e \tag{6.1}$$

where $C(L)$ and $D(L)$ are polynomials in the lag operator and the matrices are defined as follows:

$$Y = \begin{pmatrix} \gamma \\ d \\ \pi \end{pmatrix};\ X = \begin{pmatrix} r \\ oil \\ b \end{pmatrix};\ e = \begin{pmatrix} e_\gamma \\ e_d \\ e_\pi \end{pmatrix} \tag{6.2}$$

The model expresses the deficit/GDP ratio d_t the growth rate γ_t and the inflation rate π_t as linear functions of their own lagged values and of the debt/GDP ratio b_t, the real interest rate on debt r_t (or, in a robustness check, the long-run interest rate on debt) and the oil price index oil_t The reduced form residuals e are assumed to be identically and independently distributed with mean zero and variance-covariance matrix $\Sigma = E(ee')$

Our structural model contains three structural shocks: an aggregate supply shock ε_t^S, an aggregate demand (non-fiscal) shock $\varepsilon_t^D$and a fiscal shock ε_t^F. In order to identify these shocks we can rewrite the model in moving average (MA) form. Omitting the exogenous component we have:

$$Y = \sum_{L=0}^{\infty} A(L)e \tag{6.3}$$

where $A(L) = [I - C_1 - \ldots - C_p]^{-1}$ and $A(0) = I$ are known.

The structural form residuals ε_t are assumed to have a normalised covariance matrix: $E(\varepsilon\varepsilon') = I$. They are linked to the reduced-form residuals e by the linear transformation S:

$$\varepsilon_t = \begin{bmatrix} \varepsilon_t^S \\ \varepsilon_t^F \\ \varepsilon_t^D \end{bmatrix} = S^{-1}e_t\ \forall t \tag{6.4}$$

Since $\varepsilon = S^{-1}e$ or $S\varepsilon = e$ then:

$$E(ee') = E(S\varepsilon\varepsilon'S') = SS' = \Sigma \tag{6.5}$$

Taking into account that $SS^{-1} = I$, equation (6.3) may be rewritten:

$$Y = \sum_{L=0}^{\infty} A(L)SS^{-1}e = \sum_{L=0}^{\infty} B(L)\varepsilon \tag{6.6}$$

where

$$B(L) = A(L)S \ \forall L \tag{6.7}$$

$$B(1) \equiv \sum_{L=1}^{\infty} B(L) = \sum_{L=0}^{\infty} A(L)S \equiv A(1)S$$

Equations (6.6) and (6.7) imply:

$$E(ee') = SS' = \Sigma$$

$$A(1)^{-1} B(1)B(1)'(A(1)^{-1}) = \Sigma \tag{6.8}$$

$$B(1)B(1)' = A(1)\Sigma A(1)'$$

where the right-hand side matrixes are known, since they are estimated from the reduced-form VAR.

Three identifying restrictions are required to just-identify the long-run matrix $B(1)$ from the reduced-form VAR. Following a solidly established tradition, we identify the supply shocks ε_t^S as the only shocks to have a permanent long-run effect on growth. This is equivalent to restricting to zero the (1,2) and (1,3) elements of matrix $B(1)$. Moreover, the aggregate (temporary) demand shock ε_t^D is assumed to have no long-run impact on the deficit/GDP ratio. This is equivalent to restricting to zero the (2,3) element of matrix $B(1)$. The fiscal shock ε_t^F is left free. After imposing these restrictions, the long-run matrix $B(1)$ looks like:

$$B(1) = \begin{bmatrix} b_{11} & 0 & 0 \\ b_{21} & b_{22} & 0 \\ b_{31} & b_{32} & b_{33} \end{bmatrix} \tag{6.9}$$

The restrictions on the B matrix and the normalisation of the residuals of the structural form are sufficient to solve for $B(1)$. Finally, the matrix S is found as:

$$S = A(1)^{-1} B(1) \tag{6.10}$$

and the restricted model is thus identified.

After imposing these restrictions, the signs of some of the elements of the S matrix need to be normalised.[7] We choose a normalisation such that the structural disturbances correspond to what are normally considered positive shocks.

The variables

Our dataset contains 25 annual observations of six variables for each of the EMU countries, with the exception of Luxembourg, over the years

1980–2004. The beginning of the sample in 1980 is chosen in order to concentrate on monetary regimes that stabilise inflation around a target value and to avoid modelling the impact of the two oil shocks.

The endogenous variables are: the rate of inflation (GDP-deflator based) π_t, the real GDP growth rate y_t and the deficit/GDP ratio d_t. A negative value of d_t indicates a deficit, a positive value a surplus. The exogenous variables include a measure of the real interest rate on debt (the implicit interest rate, calculated as general government interest as percent of gross public debt of preceding year) r_t, the oil price index expressed in national currency oil_t and the debt/GDP ratio b_t. The use of annual data when working with a dataset containing fiscal variables is in line with the literature and due to the absence of non-interpolated data at higher frequencies. The real interest rate on debt is introduced to take into account the relationship between financial and monetary developments and the interaction between fiscal variables, inflation and real GDP. A robustness check using long-term bond yields leads to similar results. Oil prices are used to capture the world economic cycle and exchange rate movements. The lagged value of government debt is introduced on the basis of the arguments contained in Favero and Monacelli (2003) and OECD (2003), according to which sustainability problems associated with indebtedness seem to be an important determinant of whether the fiscal stance is pro-cyclical. In the interests of saving space a full presentation of the estimation results and associated unit root tests is bypassed here (they may be consulted in the working paper versions of this chapter, Artis and Onorante 2006a,b). We can pass immediately to a consideration of what the model has to say about the impact of fiscal policy in the past. (The hypothesis that EMU might bring about a structural change which would invalidate our system is tested and rejected in the working paper versions of this chapter; see Artis and Onorante, 2006a,b.)

The historical effect of European fiscal policy

This section assesses whether, in the past, discretionary fiscal policy has been effective in smoothing the economic cycle, or whether a procyclical component has prevailed, thus increasing the amplitude of the cycle. By the term 'discretionary fiscal policy' we mean here those changes in fiscal variables that do not respond automatically to changes in economic conditions, as opposed to the so-called automatic stabilisers. Indeed, several recent works (for example Fatás and Mihov, 2003) have questioned the conventional wisdom that fiscal policy is necessarily counter-cyclical by showing that in many countries discretionary fiscal policy has been procyclical. Other authors (such as Mélitz, 2000) have claimed that in Europe the conduct of discretionary fiscal policy also reduced the effectiveness of the automatic stabilisers. A study by the OECD (2003) finds evidence of procyclical easing in upturns and suggests that a high level of automatic stabilisation associated with large public sectors may easily lead to more pro-cyclical discretionary fiscal policy. Galí and Perotti (2003) conclude that discretionary fiscal policy has become more counter-cyclical over time in EMU countries; but they find the same trend in other industrialised countries.

The evaluation of the past effect of fiscal policies is carried out here by comparing the variance of synthetic economic cycles, each constructed under different assumptions about fiscal policy. How a cycle can be constructed in the context of our estimated model is quite straightforward: only one of the identified shocks has a permanent effect on growth, the two other shocks (demand and fiscal) measure the temporary component, that is the cycle as actually observed. By further eliminating the fiscal shocks (that is setting them to zero) a 'no-policy' cycle can be isolated.

Different assumptions on the fiscal shocks produce counterfactual economic cycles, whose variance can easily be compared. By assumptions about fiscal policy we simply mean a sequence of fiscal shocks, which can be for example the sequence of residuals estimated from the deficit equation (we refer to this case as observed fiscal policy) or some other completely different sequence. The only limit imposed on these alternative sequences is that the probability distribution from which each shock is drawn is the same as the distribution of the observed residuals. This bootstrapping technique allows us to derive different fiscal policies but keeps them reasonable. It has to be noted that every different sequence of shocks defines a different *discretionary* fiscal policy; the systematic component of fiscal policy, the so called automatic stabilisers, is always operating, as it is embedded in the structural parameters of the model.

The 'pure'cycle, demonstrating simply the demand shocks, is our baseline scenario and is compared with counterfactual cycles derived from dif-

Table 6.1 The variability of growth, 1993–2004

Country	*The cycle, 'no policy'*	*The cycle, actual policy*	*The cycle, optimal policy*
Belgium	100	139.2	93.5
Germany	100	107.6	90.8
Spain	100	109.0	91.0
France	100	100.8	95.5
Ireland	100	100.2	97.6
Italy	100	109.9	90.7
The Netherlands	100	106.5	90.7
Austria	100	101.1	94.7
Portugal	100	101.7	93.9
Finland	100	120.2	90.8

ferent fiscal shocks. Its variability (measured by the variance of growth) is normalised to 100 in column 1 of Table 6.1 for comparability purposes. The results are reported here for the whole sample.

The second column shows what happens when the discretionary part of fiscal policy is allowed in. Then actual fiscal shocks complement the operation of the automatic stabilisers. Thus the cycle in this 'actual policy' column is derived by shutting down (putting to zero) the permanent shocks, thus constructing a cycle purely driven by the (demand) shock and the actual fiscal shocks.

The third column represents an attempt to see whether a better use of discretion in fiscal policy could not have improved matters. In column 3, whilst the permanent shock remains shut down, the demand shock is joined by an 'optimal' discretionary policy shock. Lower figures in column 3 than are found in column 1 then demonstrate a *potential* stabilising effect of discretionary fiscal policy even if the figures shown in column 2 demonstrate that actual discretionary policy in practice has had no stabilising effect and has been significantly destabilising in at least two cases.

The figures shown in column 3 are derived in the following way. Our simulation proceeds in two steps: in the first, we simulate the effect of quasi-random sequences of fiscal shocks, where the definition of quasi-random refers to the fact that the sequences of fiscal shocks are bootstrapped from the observed ones in order to have the same *a priori* distribution.[8] Among the simulations, we then choose as the optimal fiscal policies those that best succeed in minimising the variance of the cycle. However, the implementation of such optimal fiscal policies would require an amount of resources and information which is equivalent to perfect foresight and is way beyond the possibilities of any government. We take this objection into account and at the same time increase the robustness of the analysis by considering, among the possible fiscal policies, the 5th to the 10th percentile of best-scoring fiscal policies, and by averaging the corresponding variability of the cycle. On this basis it appears that fiscal policies could have been better used for countercyclical purposes in many countries. However, the only really big effects are to be found in Belgium and Finland, where the variability of growth is reduced by more than 25 per cent. Germany, Italy and Spain present potential reductions close to 20 per cent – that is when, columns 2 and 3 are compared. It can be seen, though, that relative to the 'no policy' scenario the gains are of a smaller – and often much smaller – order of magnitude. Thus it appears that in practice the best policy can be to some extent approximated by not using discretionary fiscal policy and simply letting the automatic stabilisers work freely. This latter solution also requires a comparatively minimal amount of information.

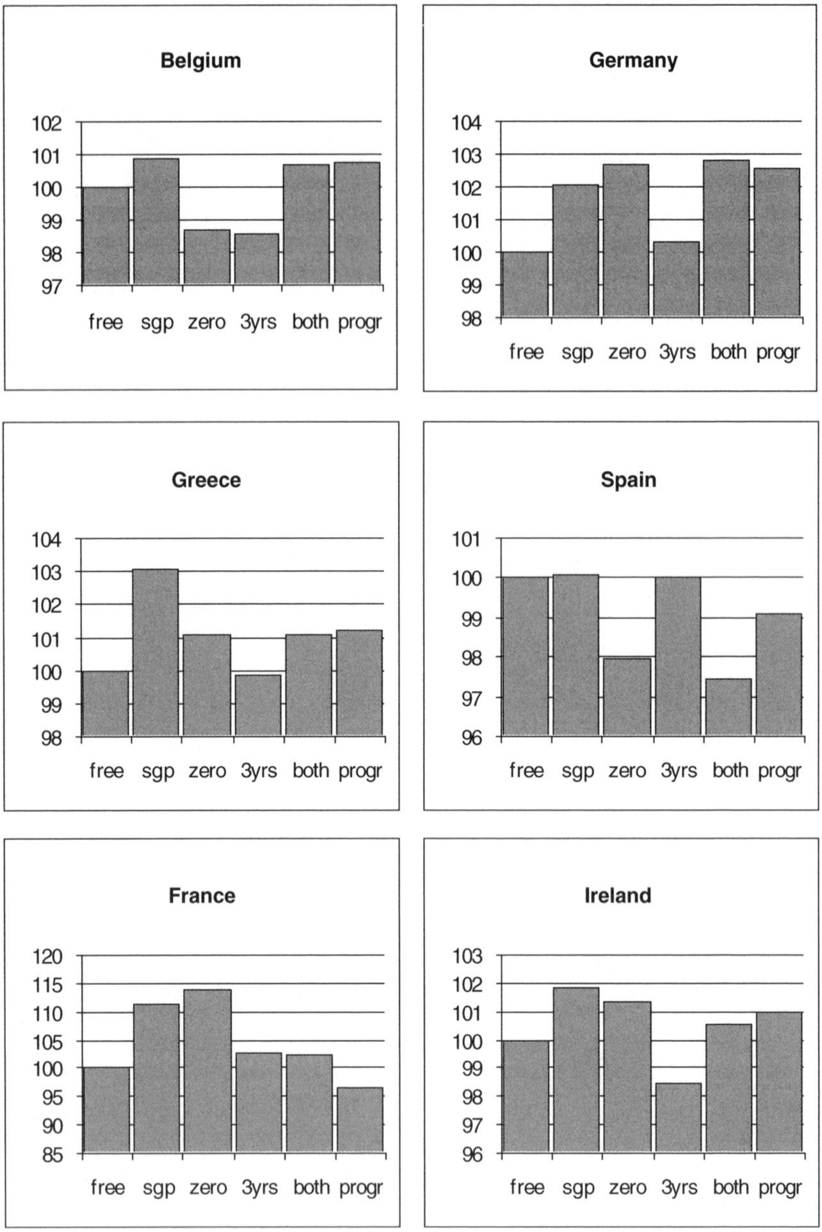

Figure 6.1 The variability of output under simulated fiscal policy variants

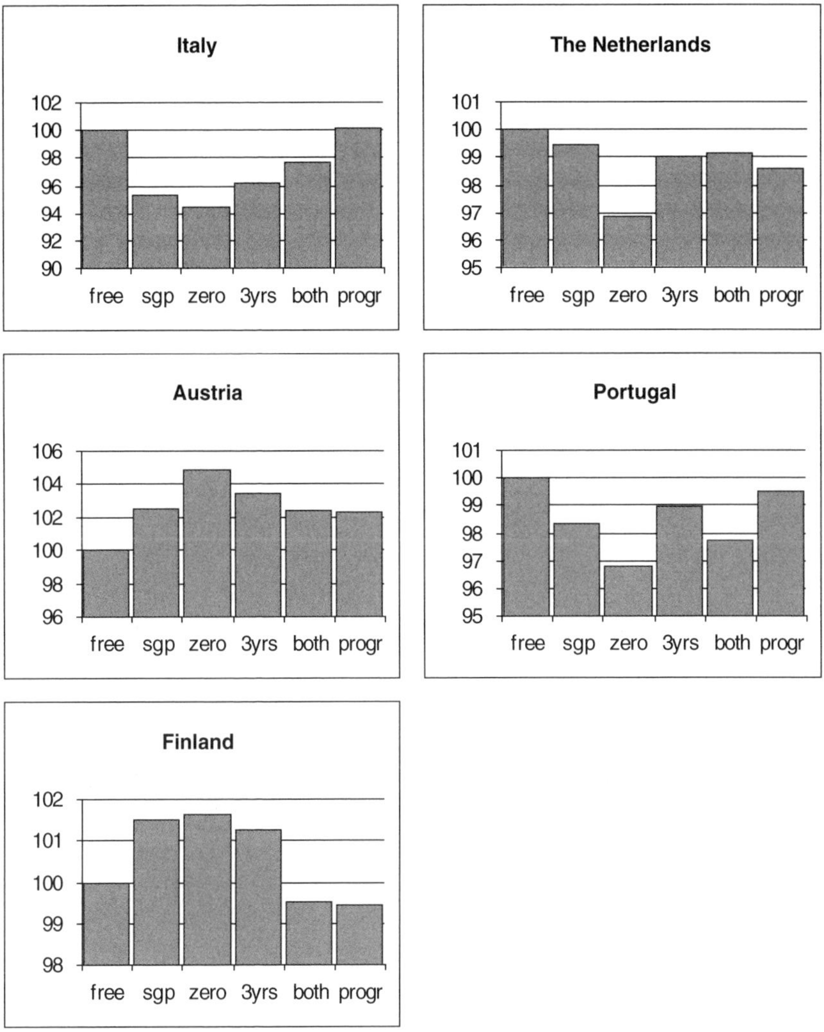

Figure 6.1 *Continued...*

Simulating reforms to the corrective arm

The model allows us to comment on a number of aspects of the reforms. In this section we concentrate on simulating the effects of changes in the corrective arm of the Pact. (We bypass here the interesting task of calculating the new MTOs, where a comparison with the results obtained by Artis and Buti, 2000, for the pre-reform version of the Pact could be instructive.)

In order to perform statistical analysis, we resort to dynamic stochastic simulation (DSS). As a statistical methodology, DSS is based on two assumptions. First, that the estimated model provides an adequate description of the economic phenomenon under consideration over the simulation period. Second, that the original distribution of estimated residuals is an adequate empirical measure of economic shocks, embracing a sufficiently ample spectrum of possibilities to form an adequate basis for the bootstrapping exercise.[9] For any period in the simulation, DSS requires the following steps:

1 A shock is randomly chosen among the residuals of the estimated model (bootstrapping).
2 A new (simulated) data point is obtained by applying this shock to the estimated model.
3 This new corrected data point is added to the data.
4 For every period over the simulation horizon, points 1 to 3 are repeated. At every step, statistics of interest are collected.

Replicating the simulation described in steps 1–4 a congruous number of times (10,000 in our case for each country), each time with a new set of shocks randomly chosen from the original distribution, it is possible to construct an ample set of alternative paths the economy might follow on the basis of the structure of the model and of the original distribution of residuals. These replications are the basis for our subsequent analysis.

A 'no Pact' scenario is the first benchmark. In this case, the simulation is simply run on the estimated model without any constraint on fiscal variables.

For the corrective arm of the Pact the effect of different sets of rules is simulated: in the SGP scenario the simulation is conducted in accordance with a stylised version of the old rules. In practice, as the operation of the corrective arm in the previous formulation of the SGP required that an excessive deficit must be corrected in the year following its identification, up to two years above 3 per cent are allowed in the simulation before the deficit is forced to fall below the reference value again. The imposed correction, when it happens, is instantaneous. This rule is not applied in the presence of exceptional circumstances, defined for this simulation as a negative growth rate of –0.75 per cent of GDP.

The three following simulations assess the effect of different individual reforms of the Pact. The current SGP is modified in the third scenario to allow for the modification of the growth threshold at which the excessive deficit procedure may be held in abeyance to one of zero growth. The fourth scenario allows for a longer time period (three years) above the reference value, whilst the fifth scenario brings into play both of the previous two conditions (the modification of the growth threshold and the lengthening of the corrective period) at the same time. The final scenario allows a country to revert below the 3 per cent threshold progressively and taking into account the cycle, that is by imposing a 0.5 per cent structural consolidation per year.

The simulations aim at evaluating the systematic effect of different fiscal rules on the amplitude of the economic cycle and on the level of deficits which are obtained under normal economic fluctuations. The six scenarios described at the beginning of the section are simulated and the resulting variability of growth is compared.

According to the chosen scenario, suitable shocks are fed into the simulation. The working of fiscal rules which act *ex post* is imposed on the simulated data: if a simulation violates the rules imposed by the scenario (for example a simulated deficit/GDP ratio higher than 3 per cent in scenario 2), a correction is applied. Dynamic stochastic simulation allows us to determine the distributions and probabilities of the real growth rate and of the deficit/GDP ratio, and to calculate means and variances.

The results for the variability of growth are summarised in Figure 6.1. Each graph shows the effect on the variance of output growth of the fiscal policy variant under consideration, country by country. The variability of output corresponding to the benchmark scenario (free fiscal policy, without any constraint from the pact) has been normalised to 100 for comparability purposes. Then the result for each of the scenarios described is shown in the graph in the order in which they were discussed above (the abbreviations used for the name of the scenario should make the relevant simulation easy to identify).

The figures provide somewhat surprising results. First, the variability of growth increases under the effect of the SGP rules only for about a half of the countries considered. Among those we find some of the countries that have been struggling to respect the rules, or that have failed to do so, such as Germany, Greece and France, but not Italy and Portugal, which on the contrary seem to have benefited from the higher discipline that the Pact imposed on a naturally pro-cyclical fiscal policy. Even for these countries, however, the effect is limited. A possible interpretation of this result could be that for many countries the Stability and Growth Pact has been little more than a formalisation on paper of policies which were already in place.

This conclusion is supported by comparing the *sgp* column with the following columns in each graph. Column *zero*, corresponding to the new 0 per cent growth threshold for applying the exceptional circumstances clause, is at least 2 per cent lower than the SGP column in Belgium, Spain and the Netherlands, and at least 2 per cent higher in France only. A longer time span given to correct a situation of excessive deficit (*3yrs*) seems to moderately reduce the variability of the cycle in several countries, namely Belgium, Germany, Greece, France, Ireland and the Netherlands. This change in the Pact seems as a matter of fact to improve economic stabilisation by avoiding an immediate correction of the deficit below the 3 per cent. On the other hand, the progressive correction of excessive deficit, in column *progr*, does not seem to have similar effects. This may be due to the fact that even in our 'free from policy' simulations (*free*) the countries are never willing to go from one year to the other to such high deficits that an instantaneous correction is much different from a progressive one.

Finally, the interaction of the different modifications (*both*) has some effect only in Italy, Spain and France, which are affected by at least one of the single provisions anyway. The hypothesis that the effects of different aspects of the reform may reinforce each other does not seem to be confirmed.

Overall, the impact of different rules on the variability of growth is relatively modest. From this result it follows that the modifications of the Pact are likely to give the governments only a limited extra leeway to reduce the variability of the cycle. This evidence is consistent with previous findings, for example by Galí and Perotti (2003) or OECD (2003), according to which the constraints of the Maastricht treaty and the SGP do not seem to have created a pro-cyclical bias in the conduct of fiscal policies. The explanation of such a limited impact of different rules is easily found in the following Figure 6.2, which reports on the average deficit that the model simulates under each set of rules.

Greece, France and Italy appear to be the only countries whose deficit would naturally be higher without the SGP rules. For these countries, our simulations indicate that the change of threshold that now defines 'exceptional circumstances' as zero growth does not make any difference. On the other hand, having one more year to correct the excessive deficit increases the average deficit, and the introduction of a progressive approach from excessive deficit also weakens fiscal discipline for all three of these countries. For most other countries the current set of rules, if used to the maximum extent, would have resulted in a very small change compared to the no-Pact scenario.

Following these considerations, it can be expected that changes in the rules of the Pact are likely to have very little impact on fiscal policies, as the previous rules already guaranteed ample margins of discretion.

The previous analysis was conducted over more than one economic cycle, and it therefore took into consideration the variability of growth. However, in the current stagnating economic environment many of the proposals for reforms of the Pact are aiming at short run increases in economic growth. An evaluation of the different scenarios in relative terms in the short run has been implemented via simulations covering a period of five years after the end of the sample (2004–08). The evaluation of the short-run effects of the different rules is in this case based on mean variables. The analysis (for which the full results are not presented here) confirms the long-run conclusions: the extra leeway in the conduct of fiscal policies is extremely limited, and the effect on growth is absolutely negligible (less than 0.1 per cent extra growth per year for all the countries).

Conclusions

This chapter provides an assessment of the effect of the reform of the Stability and Growth Pact on the European economy. A set of structural

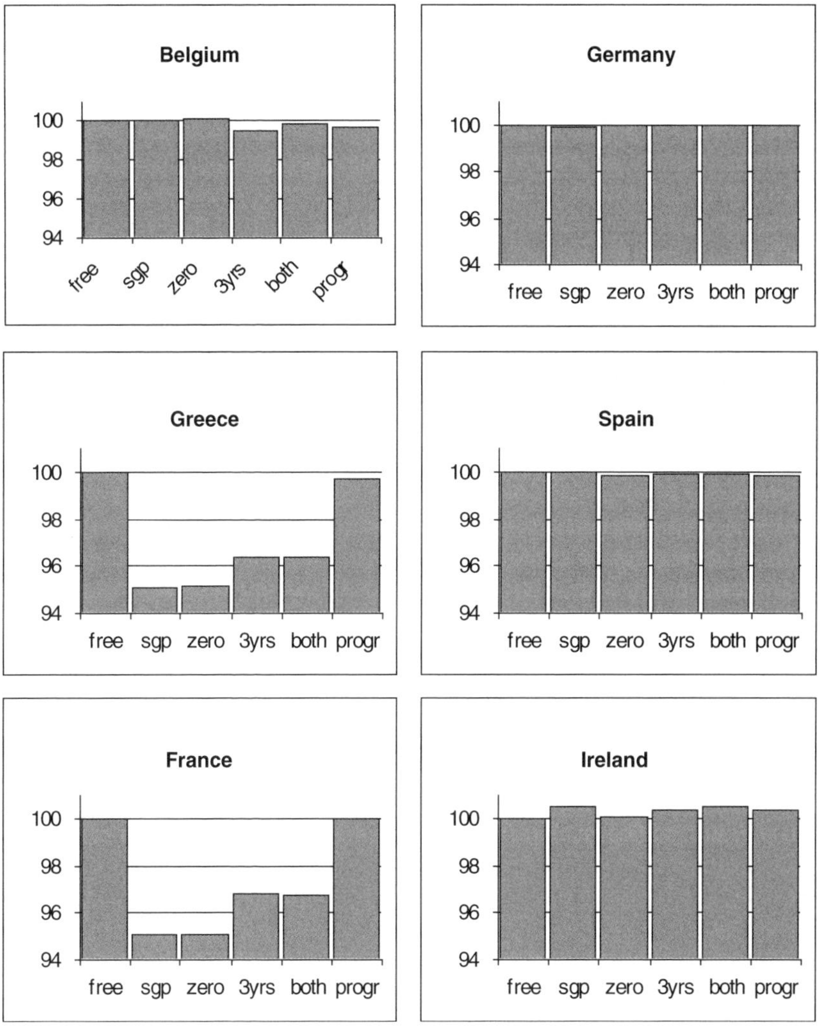

Figure 6.2 The level of the budget deficit ratio under the simulated fiscal policy variants

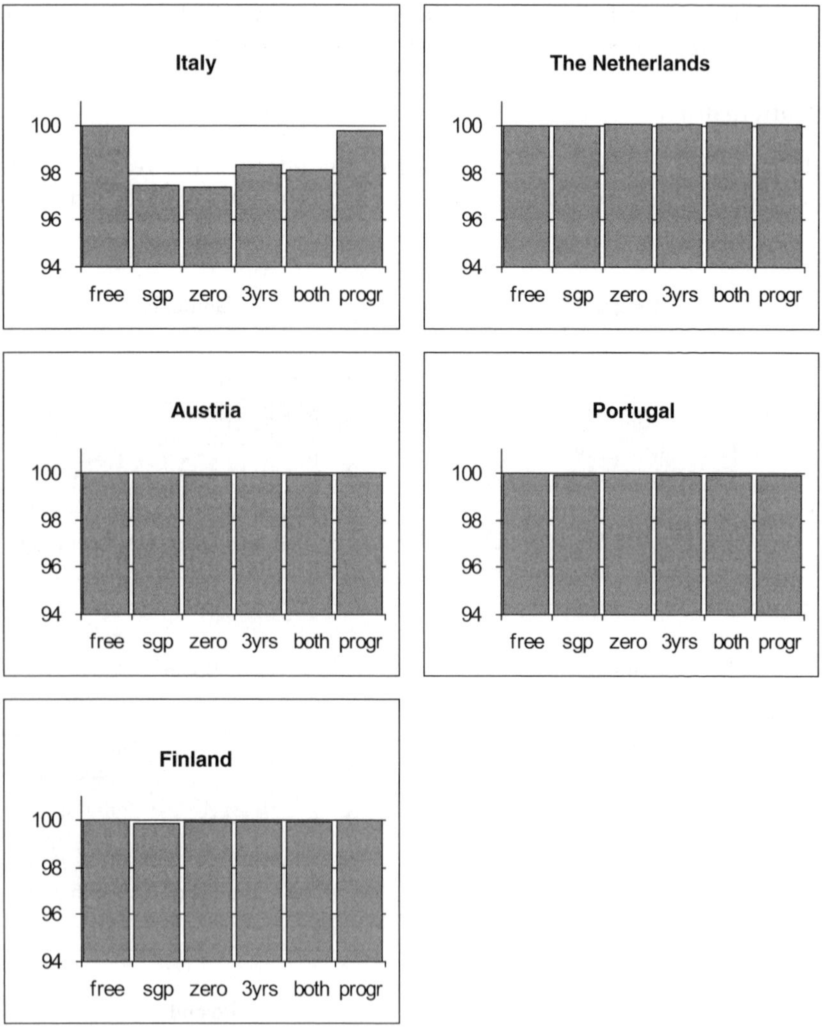

Figure 6.2 *Continued ...*

VARs, one for each eurozone country, has been estimated, and the estimated models used to assess the possible effect of alternative sets of fiscal rules, with particular reference to the Stability and Growth Pact in its old and reformed versions.

The investigation highlights a number of facts:

- Fiscal policy has not been effectively used as a counter-cyclical macroeconomic tool, nor it has had strong pro-cyclical characteristics; simply, the discretionary component of fiscal policy seems to have been mainly assigned to objectives other than stabilisation. The overall evidence suggests that, in general, fiscal policy in the 1990s has had a limited (if any) smoothing effect on the cycle and may have exacerbated cyclical instability in some cases.

- The restricted impulse response functions confirm that fiscal policy generally has a limited and ambiguous effect on output.
- The results of a best stabilising fiscal policy are difficult to obtain even for a benevolent government, due to informational constraints. However, the best policy can be approximated by not using discretionary fiscal policy and simply letting the automatic stabilisers work freely. This latter solution requires a comparatively minimal amount of information and is less prone to abuse by politicians.

Dynamic stochastic simulation is used to assess the effect of the fiscal rules of the old and the reformed SGP.

- Overall, the cost in terms of stabilisation of the old rules in the corrective arm of the Pact was limited. A possible interpretation of this result could be that for many countries the Stability and Growth Pact has formalised on paper policies which were already in place. Furthermore, while the variability of the cycle increased under the SGP rules for some countries, others seem to have benefited from the greater discipline that the Pact imposed on naturally pro-cyclical fiscal policies.
- The simulations of the modifications of the corrective arm of the Pact suggest that they are likely to give the national governments only a limited additional fiscal freedom. The more lenient threshold for appealing to exceptional circumstances and the progressive rules for correcting excessive deficits are of little quantitative importance, while a longer time span given to correct a situation of excessive deficit only moderately affects fiscal policy and reduces the variability of the cycle in only a few countries. The findings also suggest that the scenarios with the assumed interpretation of the new Pact would raise deficits only in some of the high debt countries. This evidence is consistent with previous findings in the literature.

The results of this study should be interpreted with caution. First, the estimation of the model assumes that government behaviour over the 1980–2004 period can be conveniently represented by a unique model with some dummies. Second, it is assumed that governments do not change behavioural preferences in the EMU and that they strictly comply with the assumed interpretation of the fiscal rules under any given scenario. In reality a more lenient Pact may incline governments towards a more relaxed attitude on deficits. Third, trend growth may in the future be lower than in the past 25 years so that instances with negative or even significantly negative growth may become more frequent than expected according to the estimated models.

Notes

1 The production function approach of the European Commission provides a common framework for calculating cyclically adjusted budget balances. For a description of the Commission's production function approach, see Denis, McMorrow and Röger (2002).

2 On the figures for the eurozone countries in the whole period 1980–2004, real output growth was below –2 per cent in 1.45 per cent of the cases and below –0.75 per cent in 6.91 per cent of the cases. Where these thresholds of –2 per cent and –0.75 per cent appeared in the old version of the SGP, the new dispensation would allow for a more extensive application of the exceptional circumstances: for example, in the period 1980–2004, growth was below 0 per cent in 9.82 per cent of cases.

3 Initial proposals were inspired by the work of some economists (Calmfors and Corsetti, 2003, and EEAG, 2003) and favoured a solution linking the deficit threshold to the level of the debt/GDP ratio. The final solution is a weakening of the original proposals: the deficit threshold in the corrective part of the pact remains at 3 per cent, while the Medium Term Objective in the preventive arm of the pact is country-specific and related to the debt ratio and the level of structural growth.

4 Beetsma and Debrun (2005) provide an interesting theoretical model in which the trade-off between enforcement of the new rules and flexibility is taken into account. Their model also considers the effect of different degrees of transparency in the national budgets.

5 Their restrictions are that only supply shocks have a permanent effect on output, and that nominal shocks have a permanent impact on prices only.

6 For a careful description of the properties of simultaneous equation models see Lütkepohl (1993, ch. 10). For a model with variables similar to ours see Canova and Pappa (2003).

7 See Christiano, Eichenbaum and Evans (1999) for a discussion of this issue.

8 The simulation is conducted on the shocks over the whole sample and on two subsamples representing the 1980s and the 1990s, in order to check robustness. The model is always the one estimated over the whole sample.

9 In this context, DSS assumes that the cyclical behaviour of the economies has not changed with the advent of EMU. This hypothesis is unlikely to hold in the long run. Artis and Buti point out that as the cyclical behavior of the euro-area economy adapts to the new EMU environment, the medium-term targets will need to be re-assessed.

References

Artis, M.J. and M. Buti (2000) 'Close to Balance or in Surplus: A Policy Maker's Guide to the Implementation of the Stability and Growth Pact', CEPR Discussion Papers no. 2515.

Artis, M.J. and L. Onorante (2006a) 'The Economic Importance of Fiscal Rules', CEPR Discussion Papers, no. 5684.

Artis, M.J. and L. Onorante (2006b) 'The Economic Importance of Fiscal Rules', European Central Bank Working papers, forthcoming.

Bayoumi, T. and B. Eichengreen (1992) 'Shocking Aspects of European Monetary Integration', in F. Torres and F. Giavazzi (eds), *Adjustment and Growth in the European Monetary Union*. Cambridge: Cambridge University Press.

Beetsma, R. and X. Debrun (2006) 'The New Stability and Growth Pact: a First Assessment', *European Economic Review*, forthcoming.

Blanchard, O. and D. Quah (1989) 'The Dynamic Effects of Aggregate Demand and Aggregate Supply Shocks', *American Economic Review*, 79: 655–73.

Blanchard, O. and R. Perotti (1999) 'An Empirical Characterisation of the Dynamic Effects of Changes in Government Spending and Taxes on Output', NBER Working Paper no. 7269.

Calmfors, L. (2005) 'What Remains of the Stability Pact and What Next?', Swedish Institute for European Policy Studies, Report no. 8.

Calmfors, L. and G. Corsetti (2003) 'How to Reform Europe's Fiscal Policy Framework', *World Economics*, 4(1), January–March.

Canova, F. and E. Pappa (2003) 'Price Dispersions in Monetary Unions: the Role of Fiscal Shocks', CEPR Discussion Papers no. 3746.

Christiano, L., Eichenbaum, M. and C. Evans. (1999) 'Monetary Policy Shocks: What Have we Learned and to What End?', in J. Taylor and M. Woodford (eds), *Handbook of Macroeconomics*, Vol. 1. New York: North Holland.

Dalsgaard, T. and A. de Serres (2000) 'Estimating Prudent Budgetary Margins for EU Countries: a Simulated SVAR Model Approach', *OECD Economic Studies*, 30(1): 115–147

De Arcangelis, G. and S. Lamartina (2004) 'Fiscal and Policy Regimes in Some OECD Countries', in R. Beetsma, C. Favero, A. Missale, A. Muscatelli, P. Natale, and P. Tirelli (eds), *Monetary Policy, Fiscal Policies and Labour Markets: Macroeconomic Policy Making in the EMU*, Cambridge: Cambridge University Press.

Denis, C., K. McMorrow and W. Röger (2002) 'Production Function Approach to Calculating Potential Growth and Output Gaps. Estimates for the EU Member States and the US', European Commission Economic Papers no. 176.

EEAG European Economic Advisory Group (2003) *Report on the European Economy*, CESifo, Munich.

Fatás, A. and I. Mihov (2003) 'The Case for Restricting Fiscal Policy Discretion', *Quarterly Journal of Economics*, 118: 1419–47.

Fatás, A. and I. Mihov (1999) 'Government Size and Automatic Stabilisers: International and Intranational Evidence', CEPR Discussion Papers no. 2259.

Favero, C.A. and Monacelli, T. (2003) 'Monetary-fiscal Mix and Inflation Performance: Evidence from the US', CEPR Discussion Papers no. 3887.

Favero, C.A. (2003) 'How do European Monetary and Fiscal Authorities Behave?' in M. Buti (ed.), *Monetary and Fiscal Policies in EMU*, Cambridge: Cambridge University Press.

Galí, J. and R. Perotti (2003) 'Fiscal Policy and Monetary Integration in Europe', *Economic Policy*, 37: 533–72

Garcia S. et A. Verdelhan (2001) 'Le Policy-mix de la Zone Euro: une Évaluation de l'Impact des Chocs Monétaires et Budgétaires', *Economie et Prévision*, 148, 40.

Lütkepohl, H. (1993) *Introduction to Multiple Time Series Econometrics*, 2nd edn. Berlin: Springer-Verlag.

Mélitz, J. (2000) 'Some Cross-country Evidence about Fiscal Policy Behaviour and Consequences for EMU, *European Economy*, 2: 3–21.

OECD (2003) *OECD Economic Outlook* 74.

Perotti, R. (2002) 'Estimating the Effects of Fiscal Policy in OECD countries', Working Paper series no. 168, European Central Bank.

P. van den Noord (2000) 'The Size and Role of Automatic Fiscal Stabilisers in the 1990s and Beyond', OECD Economics Department Working Paper no. 230, OECD Economics Department.

Discussion

Campbell Leith

Introduction

The chapter uses structural VARs to assess the implications of recent reforms to the Stability and Growth Pact on European economies' abilities to use fiscal policies to stabilise their economic cycles. Comparing the implied volatility of output in the case of 'observed' fiscal policy with that under a random draw of policy suggests that for most countries fiscal policy has not played a significant role in smoothing the business cycle. Furthermore, fiscal policy does not even appear to have the potential to offset the business cycle, and not operating a discretionary fiscal policy (that is leaving automatic stabilisers to operate unfettered) is often just as effective.

In light of these results it is not surprising that the authors also find little impact on the stabilising properties of fiscal policy when the new fiscal rules of the reformed SGP are applied.

These are striking results. However, there are some reasons why the chapter may underestimate the potential for discretionary fiscal policy to have significant welfare-improving impacts on the business cycle. We shall consider each of these in turn.

Measuring the benefits of business cycle stabilisation

The chapter uses as its metric of business cycle stabilisation the ability of fiscal policy to reduce volatility in output growth. Following Rotemberg and Woodford (1998), recent analysis of the welfare costs of business cycles in the presence of sticky prices has focused on a measure of the output gap which is defined as output relative to its level in the absence of nominal frictions. Accordingly, it is fluctuations in this measure of the output gap that are important for welfare, not fluctuations in output itself. Additionally, this analysis suggests that inflation has costs because it increases the dispersion of prices across firms, and that the weight given to such costs in quadratic approximations to welfare is typically much larger than the importance attached to the output gap. Therefore the chapter may not be capturing the full benefits of fiscal stabilisation.

Choice of fiscal policy instrument

Another key aspect of the chapter which may affect the results is that fiscal policy is modelled as a shock to the deficit equation. In other words there is no distinction made between shocks to revenues or expenditures. One of the main advantages of fiscal policy is that it offers a wide range of instruments which could potentially have a role to play in stabilising the economy. For example, in the monetary policy literature a role for policy is typically introduced by assuming the existence of Calvo contracts in prices, and sometimes wages. Leith and Wren-Lewis (2006) show that variations in income taxes and sales taxes can influence the forcing variables in such wage and price inflation equations, so that fiscal policy can potentially be used to offset wage and price cost-push shocks in a way which monetary policy cannot. However, the effectiveness of fiscal policy in this context depends crucially on the nature of the shocks hitting the economy and the particular fiscal instruments policy makers have access to.

Furthermore, in the case of a country participating in EMU fiscal policy can have a role to play in compensating for the loss of the monetary policy instrument when either economies are asymmetric or shocks are idiosyncratic. In a stylised model of monetary union, Leith and Wren-Lewis show that government spending, provided it has a bias towards domestically produced goods, can act as a very effective substitute for monetary policy, more than halving the costs of shocks to the economy. Of course it can be objected that government spending cannot be varied in this way, although in this stylised model government spending essentially represents a fiscal instrument that has a direct demand effect. Therefore what that analysis suggests is that the ability of fiscal policy to stabilise the economy depends crucially on the nature of the shocks, the instrument used and the policy context in which this takes place, that is inside or outside of EMU. The current analysis, on the other hand, does not identify which fiscal instrument is employed and does not take into account that the efficacy of that instrument will change post-EMU.

Sustainability

The chapter assesses the sustainability of the public finances using an off-model description of debt dynamics. This is what Bohn (2005) would refer to as '*ad hoc* sustainability' since it implicitly uses an exogenous path for the discount factor used to discount future government surpluses. In order to correctly assess the sustainability of public finances Bohn argues the need to have a fully specified pricing kernel with which to discount the future surpluses. Effectively, it is necessary to model risk premia. Polito and Wickens (2005) construct VAR models of fiscal policy which include debt and interest rates as endogenous variables. This goes some way towards addressing the critique of Bohn since debt levels can influence the rate of return payable on debt. The authors also note the need to account for changes in the structural equations of the VAR when considering alternative policy scenarios and this allows the assessment of fiscal sustainability under alternative fiscal policy rules.

Conclusions

The current chapter is a very interesting attempt both to assess the ability of fiscal policy to stabilise economies and to infer the impact of recent SGP reforms on that ability. However, it may underestimate the potential to utilise fiscal policy by using an inappropriate welfare metric and failing to distinguish between alternative fiscal instruments in different policy settings.

References

Bohn, H. (2005) 'The Sustainability of Fiscal Policy in the United States', CESifo Working Paper no. 1446.

Leith, C. and S. Wren-Lewis (2006) 'The Costs of Fiscal Inflexibility', mimeo, University of Glasgow.

Polito, V. and M. Wickens (2005) 'Measuring Fiscal Sustainability', University of St Andrews, Conference Paper no. CO503.

Rotemberg, J. and M. Woodford (1998) 'An Optimisation-Based Econometric Framework for the Evaluation of Monetary Policy: Expanded Version', NBER Technical Working Paper no. 233.

7
Has EMU Had Any Impact on the Degree of Wage Restraint?

*Adam S. Posen and Daniel Popov Gould**

Introduction

The Lucas Critique notwithstanding, applied economic research has paid a great deal of attention in recent decades to the potential for changes in monetary regimes to induce lasting changes in economic structures and behaviour. In particular, given the key role of inflation expectations in wage setting, and the presumed endogeneity of such practices as indexation to the price environment, theorists have developed increasingly sophisticated models of the interaction between central banking and labour market institutions.[1] The creation of the euro presents a natural opportunity for the investigation of these models' predictions. Economies that varied substantially in wage bargaining institutions and practices suddenly underwent a simultaneous shift in monetary regime.

The shift in monetary regime to the Eurosystem would not necessarily have had the same effect on all eurozone member countries' economies – the preexisting extent of unionisation, degree of centralisation and coordination in wage bargaining, the relative size of the economy in the monetary union, and so on, could condition a given economy's response.[2] In this conditionality, the theorists were generally building upon the insights of Calmfors and Driffill's (1988) seminal paper on the interaction between centralisation of wage bargaining and macroeconomic performance.[3] Interestingly, there was little agreement between the predictions of European theorists and policy-makers. Labour economists and political scientists whose

*Posen's work on this project was supported by a Houblon-Norman Fellowship at the Bank of England. We benefited from comments from our discussant John Driffill and from other participants in the Money, Macro and Finance Research Group and University Association for Contemporary European Studies Conference on 'The Travails of the Eurozone', Edinburgh, 24 March 2006. The views expressed here and any errors are solely those of the authors, and not those of the Houblon-Norman Fund, the Bank of England, or IIE. Contact: aposen@iie.com.

approach worked from wage-bargaining institutions upwards to macroeconomic outcomes tended to emphasise the risks to macroeconomic performance from EMU causing a mismatch between institutions which might result in sub-optimal coordination. On the other hand, almost all eurozone macroeconomists and central bankers felt that short-run inflation and output volatility would generally improve with the monetary regime shift, and many went further, suggesting that more credible policy would emanate downwards and induce structural reform in labour markets.[4]

Two difficulties have limited the success of empirical inquiries into this issue. The first, well-recognised, difficulty is that there are a limited number of country observations available to investigators, and so limited degrees of freedom for distinguishing robustly among competing hypotheses.[5] The second difficulty is the tendency for the vast majority of empirical studies to focus on aggregate macroeconomic outcomes – normally inflation and/or unemployment – even though the underlying theory will usually be generating hypotheses about real wage determination.[6] The first is largely unavoidable, though there is hope that with the passage of time and with different cuts at the problem some clarity might be achieved. The second difficulty, however, is unnecessary, and may in fact exacerbate the first problem. If the competing theories have differing implications for real wages or functions thereof, it may be possible to distinguish between them by looking directly at predictions for those variables, and thus not to have to burn degrees of freedom (and simply confuse the matter) by trying to control for shocks to inflation or unemployment or country-specific effects with respect to those variables.

This chapter investigates the empirical implications of the various theories for EMU's effect on *wage restraint*, the degree to which wage increases do or do not exceed productivity growth. In so doing, we attempt to avoid the second of the above noted difficulties. Wage restraint in some sense automatically controls for country-specific effects and shocks, beyond those directly accounted for in the observable labour and monetary institutions, because it is defined as a response to a given country's productivity performance, not a function of the level. It is also explicitly and frequently cited as a primary conscious concern of labour leadership, employers, and central bankers, who are presumed to be the actors at work in these models – and in the reality of wage bargaining and monetary policy-making. We also hope to partially alleviate the first difficulty, of inherently limited observations, by focusing on this dependent variable rather than the perhaps too difficult to pin down inflation or unemployment. To our knowledge, no prior paper in this context has made wage restraint itself the focus of its empirical work.[7] In addition, taking advantage of the time that has passed since the launch of the euro, we accompany our cross-sectional work with a comparison of time-series behaviour in two critical countries, Germany and Italy, that differ markedly in what the theories predict would be the effect of EMU on wage restraint.

To preview our results, we find that wage restraint is either unchanged or increased following EMU in the vast majority of countries, with no instances of significant declines in restraint. This contradicts the predictions of a widely-cited family of models which rest on labour's representatives in wage bargaining taking into account the external effect of their demands on aggregate inflation. In particular, Germany would have been expected to display the greatest decline in wage restraint under these models, given that the relative importance of its major unions in the central bank's calculus of inflationary pressures declined most both with respect to size and to weighting by the central bank (given the shift from Bundesbank to the ECB), and we find no indication of such a decline. If anything, wage restraint in Germany increased post-EMU.

The overall shift in the countries examined towards greater wage restraint is consistent with the models that emphasise the gains to macroeconomic stability from monetary credibility, downplaying the coordination or labour centralisation issues. The time-series evidence on Italy, which shows a significant increase in wage restraint after eurozone entry, is also supportive of this view, given that the restraint is mostly determined by the degree of monetary credibility (proxied by the Italian interest rate differential vs. the lowest government bond rate in the eurozone). That said, the increase in wage restraint associated with increased monetary credibility in the eurozone is matched by that shown to be associated with the increase in credibility seen in the UK and Sweden after adopting inflation targeting post-1992. This result emphasises that the effect being seen is one due to monetary regime changes and perhaps global pressures on labour bargaining power, and not one of EMU *per se*, or of the political coordination issues or international integration that accompanied EMU.

The next section further elaborates on our definition of wage restraint, its operationalisation, and the distribution of outcomes in our sample. We then discuss the implications of five major theories about the determinants of wage restraint for what should happen after EMU, and whether or not non-eurozone advanced economies should see a similar effect. Our cross-sectional analysis is then presented, looking at the extent of wage restraint before and after EMU in a sample of 19 economies (11 EMU members, 8 not) and its determinants. Our time-series analysis of the movements in wage restraint is set out, controlling for the business cycle in Germany and Italy, and of whether those dynamics changed after convergence in interest rates (our operationalisation of monetary credibility) and the shift in monetary decision-making from the Bundesbank to the ECB. The implications for two major theoretical approaches to the determinants of wage restraint and for policy are considered, given what seems to be clear evidence in support of one and in apparent rejection of the other.

The role and measurement of wage restraint

Central bankers and financial market observers often refer to the degree of 'wage restraint' in a country, or in a given wage negotiation. By this they mean the degree to which increases in real wages are commensurate with increases in (labour) productivity. As argued by Bruno and Sachs (1985), the existence of a real wage gap – a persistent rise in real wages unmatched by productivity – can be used to explain stagflation in the 1970s. In a more recent example, the extensive and persistent high unemployment in the former East Germany is usually attributed to a lasting wage bargain that overpriced Eastern labour relative to its productivity.[8] Others (for example Ball and Moffitt, 2001; Blanchard and Philippon, 2004) attribute part of the rise and in some countries fall of the NAIRU to the lags with which wage-setters recognised shifts in productivity growth. This is of course loosely analogous to 'classical' views of unemployment, where labour is overpriced relative to its returns, as opposed to more 'Keynesian' views where nominal rigidities and insufficient demand are the root cause.[9]

Assessment of wage restraint continues to play a significant role in the determination of monetary policy now that all central banks in advanced economies, including the ECB, are committed to forward-looking strategies for the stabilisation of low inflation. The belief that wage increases 'out of line with productivity' are potentially inflationary is widespread. In the mental background is the stylised picture of the German economy and of Bundesbank behaviour in the 1950–70 period, where economic growth was accompanied by union wage restraint, with real wages rising but less than the rate of growth in productivity – and the Bundesbank explicitly threatening to raise interest rates should wage demands be 'excessive'.[10] The decline in the US unemployment rate in the 1990s is widely attributed in large measure to interaction between the outpacing of wage growth by productivity growth and the readiness of the Federal Reserve partly as a result to maintain low interest rates even as past benchmarks for growth and unemployment were surpassed.[11]

It must be noted that wage restraint is not an entirely neutral concept distributionally. An increase in wages above the rate of productivity growth will embody some combination of pass-through of inflationary expectations, of (mis)perception of the rate of productivity growth, *and* of an increase in labour's share of income relative to capital.[12] Since ultimately factors of production would be expected over the longer-term to earn their marginal products, this is less of an issue for multi-year averages than for any specific year's wage settlement, but after some years of wage restraint, it could well be reasonable for labour's share to catch-up by growing above productivity temporarily.[13] As pointed out by Caballero and Hammour (1996) and by Blanchard and Philippon (2004), on average capital's share of income has been rising along with unemployment in Europe since the mid-1980s, suggesting that in recent years wage restraint has been ample and that the real wage gap is therefore not the source of current unemployment.[14] The relevant point for our analysis is that we focus on year-to-year wage restraint because it is of declared and demonstrated importance to monetary policy decisions, not because it is necessarily an optimal intermediate target for central banks or because it is welfare enhancing in and of itself.

Operationally, we define wage restraint as the difference between the rate of real wage growth and productivity growth for a given country in a given year. A negative (positive) observation indicates below (above) productivity wage growth. We use two different measures of productivity from the OECD. One is multi-factor productivity [MFP] growth resulting as the residual from the OECD's growth accounting exercises; the other is growth in GDP per hour worked, calculated from Gröningen national accounts data. The two measures are highly though not precisely correlated for multi-year averages, so we report all results below for both measures (where data is available). For consistency, we also rely on the OECD's *Economic Outlook* as the source for our wage data, using their total compensation per employee measure. While we also work with the OECD's more narrowly defined 'wage rate, business sector' series, we prefer total compensation because the data coverage is more complete and because the anecdotal evidence is that central banks pay more attention to changes in total compensation than in wages per se. Also, arguably there are wage negotiations where wage increases are kept low, but additional benefits with regard to pensions or the like are part of the package. To get real wage growth, we deflate each observation by the country specific deflator (productivity growth is of course automatically in real terms).

Table 7.1 presents the basic data on wage restraint for our full sample of 21 countries, comprised of the 12 Eurozone members, the three EU members outside of the Eurozone (Denmark, Sweden, and UK), and six other advanced economies (Australia, Canada, Japan, Norway, Switzerland and the USA). For three (Luxembourg, Norway and Switzerland), only GDP per hour growth data is available, not data on MFP growth. Since the focus of the chapter is on the impact of EMU on wage restraint, we compute annual averages for the pre- (1991–98) and post- (1999–2003 or 2004) euro periods, subject to data availability. The mean and median change in wage restraint in the sample is negative, meaning greater restraint in the post-euro period, for both measures of productivity. On productivity measured by MFP, the mean change is just short of being significantly different from zero at the 5 per cent significance level (it is at the 7 per cent significance level) and on the order of one percentage point (of the gap between productivity and wage growth) per year. Two countries, Greece and Sweden, show a significant increase in wage restraint under both measures, and two, Australia and the Netherlands, show a significant decrease in restraint under both

Table 7.1 Changes in average wage restraint between 1991–98 and 1999–2004

	Real Comp-MFP	*Real Comp-GDP p/h*
Australia[b]	0.010*	0.012*
Austria[a]	–0.006	0.004*
Belgium	0.004*	0.003
Canada	–0.007	–0.002
Denmark	0.007*	0.003
Finland	–0.007	0.002
France[b]	–0.009	–0.006
Germany[c]	–0.003	0.004*
Greece	–0.093*	–0.096*
Ireland	–0.001	–0.001
Italy	–0.007	–0.006
Japan[b]	–0.015	–0.015
Luxembourg	n.a.	0.004*
Netherlands	0.011*	0.010*
Norway	n.a.	0.003*
Portugal[a]	–0.006	0.002
Spain[b]	–0.012	–0.010
Sweden	–0.025*	–0.021*
Switzerland	n.a.	–0.017*
United Kingdom	–0.022*	–0.015
United States	–0.004	–0.008
Average of EU12	–0.0117	–0.0086
Average of non-EU12	–0.0079	–0.0065
Mean	–0.0102	–0.0068
Standard error	0.0054	0.0046
Median	–0.0065	–0.0013
Confid, lvl. 95.0%	0.0113	0.0096

Notes: Differences between 1991–98 and 99–2004 averages of productivity growth and compensation growth are subtracted from each other.
[a]MFP growth 1996–99 average; [b]MFP growth 1999–2002 average; [c]1992–1998 average;
* signifies significantly different from the mean, at 5%.

measures, as can be seen more clearly in Figure 7.1. Overall most EMU members showed no significant change in wage restraint post-EMU.[15]

Five theories of the determinants of wage restraint

At any given moment, both unions and individual workers are conducting wage negotiations with employers. Much of the negotiations' results are determined by idiosyncratic factors, having to do with the particular results and conditions for specific sectors, firms, or individuals. Other negotiations are largely determined by automatic factors like cost-of-living allowances (COLAs), albeit of diminished significance since the 1970s. The overall macro-

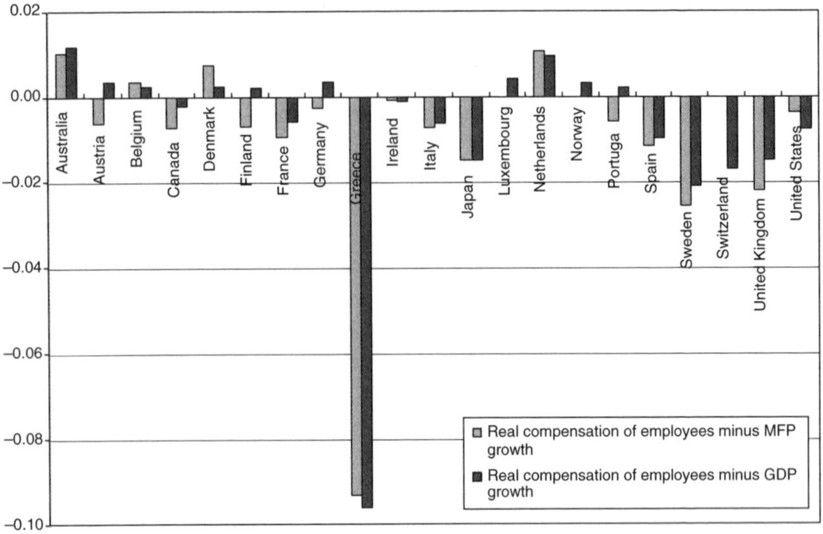

Figure 7.1 Change in average wage restraint between 1991–98 and 1999–2004
Source: OECD and author's calculations.

economic environment, including productivity growth, however, also plays a role in wage negotiations, particularly since individual or industry productivity is often difficult to verify in real time. As bargaining becomes more collective and centralised, and especially when it takes place at a national level, such aggregate measures take on an even greater importance. Similarly, as central banks become more focused on maintaining low inflation (rather than reducing high inflation or pursuing other medium-term goals), the extent of wage pressures relative to productivity growth across the economy becomes a more salient issue. From these rather innocuous observations arise a number of theories about how labour and monetary institutions should influence wage restraint. These are summarised with their empirical implication for restraint and whether they apply solely to eurozone members in Table 7.2.

The first set of theories builds directly on Calmfors and Driffill (1988) and concerns the extent to which unions take into account the inflationary impact of their wage bargains as a function of their membership. The more encompassing the membership, that is the greater the share of workers represented by the union, the more the union internalises the cost of inflation induced by wage pressures, and thus the more likely it is to exercise wage restraint.[16] In particular, Cukierman and Lippi (1999, 2001) and Iversen and Soskice (1998, 2000) develop models of games between the ECB and unions as compared to the form of wage bargaining within countries before EMU. Both sets of papers predict that after EMU there will be a coordination

Table 7.2 Summary of hypotheses on the effect of EMU on wage restraint

Channel of transmission	*Effect on wage restraint*	*Conditionality of effects*	*Eurozone only?*
Relative size of external effects	Decreases	Larger on larger countries or those with independent monetary policy	Yes
Openness to international competition	Increases	Larger on those countries with high intra-EMU trade	Yes
Unions' political bargaining power (not vs. firms)	Increases	Larger for those countries with more centralisation	Yes
Decreased union density	Increase	Larger for large countries where unions had more security from competition	No
Counter-inflationary credibility of central bank	Increases	Larger for those countries who gain more credibility	No

problem. Unions that used to be large relative to their respective country's total labour force, and whose bargaining had to be taken into account by their respective country's central bank as a result when the latter was focused on national inflation rates, will after EMU become small(er) relative to the Eurozone-wide labour market and will not have to be taken into account by a European Central Bank focused on eurozone-wide inflation.

As a result, these models predict that wage restraint will decline after EMU. Unions' incentives for wage restraint are reduced in two ways: one, 'excessive' wage demands will have less effect on overall inflation so the cost to the unions' members will be lower; two, and probably more importantly, wage restraint from unions within one country will be less likely to induce monetary ease – and therefore growth and employment increases – from the ECB that benefit their members because the impact on eurozone-wide inflation will be smaller (countries where unions were already small or decentralised or absent would simply move further towards irrelevance for ECB monetary policy-making). So economies of large size before EMU where the central bank pursued an independent (nationally-oriented as opposed to exchange-pegged) monetary policy should exhibit a significant decrease in wage restraint post-EMU – and this should be most marked in Germany where not only was the economy the largest, while the Bundesbank most clearly took into account domestic wage developments when setting policy, but the unions were large and there was (is) nationwide wage bargaining. There is no reason to think that non-Eurozone member countries should be affected by this shift.

The second set of theories relates to the degree of international competition in product markets, and was formalised by Demaine and Hunt (1994). In this framework, unions have some concern for the employment of their membership, and recognise that employment will in part depend upon the price-competitiveness of their home country's firms on world markets.[17] If wage increases outstrip productivity while other countries' producers benefit from wage restraint, the home-country producers could lose market share, and the union members could lose jobs. As a result, the greater the exposure to international competition, the greater the wage restraint (Danthine and Hunt, 1994, portray this as a shift in the Calmfors–Driffill curve). In the context of EMU, we can derive the prediction that to the extent that the introduction of the euro increased intra-Eurozone trade, whether through increased transparency, lower transaction costs or whatever means, there should be greater wage restraint within the eurozone.[18]

A third set of theories comes more directly out of the political science tradition, though it is sometimes supported by economists on the left in Europe. In this approach the models of games between the ECB and labour unions become matters of outright bargaining between interest groups – where the ECB (like most central banks) is characterised as emphasising inflation versus growth and employment objectives, while the labour representatives pursue the reverse (Garrett, 1998; Hibbs, 1987). The greater the political pull of the unions *vis-à-vis* the central bank, whether through threat of direct action because of union density and centralisation or via the influence of elected representatives favourable to union objectives, the lower the wage restraint because the central bank would be less willing (politically able) to 'cut-off' growth in the economy. Absent the threat to tighten policy, the central bank would be unable to prevent a rise in labour share which would mean real wage growth outpacing productivity. This approach would predict that after EMU wage restraint would increase because the ECB would be less accountable to democratic control (given its insulation from national politicians) and there is no comparable Europe-wide labour institution to bargain on workers' behalf. In particular, the countries where unions were more centralised and thus had greater political influence at home should see the greatest declines in wage restraint post-EMU.

A fourth set of theories has more to do with globalisation worldwide, and its impact on the industrial democracies in general, than with EMU *per se*. Given the effective rise in labour supply from emerging markets to compete with workers employed in production in the advanced economies, and the increase in international capital mobility and supporting institutions making shifting of production to lower-cost sites easier, there is increasing pressure on first-world workers to remain competitive, if not decrease their unit labour costs. Add to this the more general trend towards deunionisation in the major economies, or at least their private sectors, and the pressure for wage restraint should increase (Dumont, Rayp, and Willeme, 2006).[19] This is in many ways parallel to the second set of theories regarding openness to competition, but rather than emphasising the change in incentives for given union structures and densities, this framework suggests a decline in those union densities. Thus the empirical prediction of this approach is that wage restraint should increase – both in and outside the eurozone – but primarily for the larger countries where labour had been less subject to international competitive pressure in the past than in those small countries which are already open.

The final set of theories of the determinants of wage restraint we will consider are those proposed by the monetary economists and central bankers suggesting positive structural effects from EMU (for example, Bundesbank, 1998). In this framework, in economies where the commitment to price stability of the central bank was less than credible unions and workers had less incentive to take into account the costs of their own pursuit of inflationary wage settlements. On the one hand, their real wages were more likely to be eroded by increases in inflation, which would arise out of others' wage and price expectations (and negotiations), so any union negotiators would feel they had more at risk from wage restraint; on the other hand, the likelihood that there would be short-term costs to employment from 'excessive' wage settlements would be lower because the central bank would be less credible in its threats to tighten policy should wage pressures rise.[20] This is the converse of the Bundesbank story behind the first set of theories discussed, and as such is usually thought of as applying to Italy, for example, in the postwar period through the 1970s (or later). A rise in the credibility of central banks' commitment to price stability should therefore induce greater wage restraint by reducing the fear that restraint will be self-defeating and increasing the fear that the central bank will not accommodate wage increases. The empirical prediction of this theory is that wage restraint should increase most for those countries which have the greatest increases in monetary credibility, whether through membership in EMU or through other means (such as the adoption of an inflation target).

Cross-sectional analysis of post-EMU changes in wage restraint

As discussed above, the limited number of observations available when considering these issues among the industrialised democracies encourages prudence in the use and interpretation of econometric analysis. Accordingly, when trying to sort out the impact of EMU on wage restraint, and the various theories of the determinants of wage restraint discussed in the preceding section, we stick to a simple approach. For those countries for which we have pre- and post-EMU average wage restraint observations (a total of 18)[21], we estimate ordinary-least-squares regressions (OLS) of the form:

$$\Delta WR = \beta_0 + \beta_1\text{*eurodum} + \beta_2\text{*(union variable)} + \beta_3\text{*(union variable*eurodum)} + \beta_4\text{*(}\Delta\text{monetary credibility)} + \beta_5\text{*(}\Delta\text{monetary credibility*eurodum)} + \varepsilon \quad (7.1)$$

where 'eurodum' denotes membership in the eurozone, 'union variable' is a measure of union density or centralisation or coordination (taken from the literature), and 'Δmonetary credibility' is a measure of the change in the credibility of the central bank's commitment to price stability between the two periods. A full list of variables and data sources used in the cross-sectional analysis is given in the Appendix.

We use different trade union variables as a robustness check of our results. The first indicator is 'Trade Union Density', obtained from the OECD *Employment Outlook* 2004, which utilised survey results to calculate this variable. We use the data on density in 1990 and 2000, labelling the variable 'TUdense' in the estimation output. As a separate variable to control for trade union influence we also use collective bargaining coverage. This is expressed as the fraction of the total labour force that is covered by collective bargaining. Collective bargaining coverage rates were compiled by the OECD, which in turn took or estimated these from several sources. Wherever possible, coverage rates were adjusted for employees (particularly in the public sector) who do not have the right to bargain.[22] Once again, we take values for 1990 and 2000 as pre- and post-EMU variables. Centralisation of wage bargaining and coordination of wage bargaining are the final two measures of trade union sway. These are constructed using survey data, also by the OECD, and are presented in the form of a cardinal scale from 1 to 5, increasing in half-point increments to indicate greater centralisation/coordination.

We proxy the change in monetary credibility by the difference between monthly long-term (10 year) government bond yields averaged for 1995m1–1997m12 and 1998m1–2000m12.[23] A bigger difference indicates a larger decline in government bond rates, and thus in inflation expectations and in doubts about the central bank's commitment to price stability. As shown in Figure 7.2, there is a wide range of changes, with almost all economies in the sample seeing a minimum drop in bond rates of 150 basis points between the two periods considered, due presumably to global changes in inflation, the business cycle, and international arbitrage as the US and Japanese rates sank. Within Europe, as one might expect, Italy had the largest gain in credibility from EMU (nearly 300 bps above average), with Portugal and Spain gaining next most, and then Greece.[24] Notably, however, Sweden and the UK also had substantial drops in long bond rates over the period despite staying out of the eurozone.

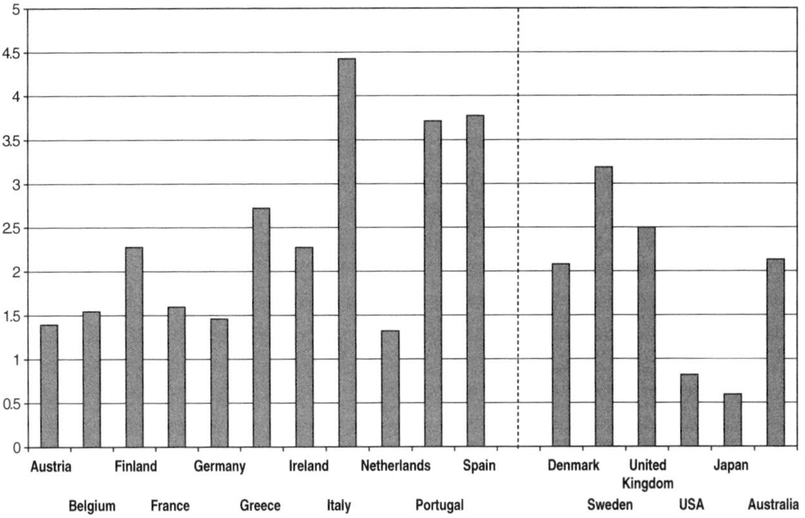

Figure 7.2 Credibility proxy – difference between pre- and post-euro LT bond rates (3 year period averages)

Note: Proxy calculated by taking the difference between long-term govt bond yields averages for 1995m 1–1997m 12 and 1998m 1–2000m 12 period averages. Data are from IMF's IFS and Eurostat.

Given the predictions of the various theories as outlined in Table 7.1, the effects of wage bargaining structure and density, conditional (or not) on eurozone membership, and of monetary credibility should allow us to distinguish between them (if the data is willing). Table 7.3 presents our results from these cross-sectional (not panel) estimates. The three sets of estimates present a consistent set of results. An increase in monetary credibility has a significant increasing effect (at the 5 per cent significance level) on wage restraint, and this result is not dependent on eurozone membership (the (b) estimations), but is associated with all variation in monetary credibility in the sample.[25] The effect is economically meaningful as well with a 100 bps drop in long bond rates associated with a 0.42 per cent increase in wage restraint (the differential between productivity growth and real wage growth in terms of percent). Given an average for the sample of change (increase) in wage restraint of 0.68 per cent, this is a substantial effect. Such a large effect associated with decreased long-term interest rates is consistent with the last of the theories discussed in the preceding section, that greater central bank credibility would induce greater wage restraint. Given the imprecise estimates of the constant terms and of most of the coefficients on the other explanatory variables, changes in monetary credibility alone appear to explain 40 per cent of the cross-national variation in changes in wage restraint.[26]

Table 7.3 Cross section wage restraint analysis, regression results

	1		1(b)		2		2(b)		3		3(b)	
	Coeff.	*Std. Err.*	*Coeff.*	*Std. Err.*	*Coeff.*	*Std. Err.*	*Coeff.*	*Std. Err.*	*Coeff.*	*Std. Err.*	*Coeff.*	*Std. Err.*
EMUtrade2	0.0006	0.012	0.0059	0.015	–0.0032	0.013	0.0080	0.018	–0.0044	0.010	–0.0014	0.014
eurodum	0.0045	0.013	0.0026	0.017	0.0072	0.0169	–0.0052	0.027	–0.0186	0.015	–0.0114	0.019
constant	0.0042	0.006	–0.0028	0.007	–0.0051	0.009	–0.0141	0.011	0.0103	0.006	0.0012	0.007
Tudense	0.0000	0.000	0.0000	0.000					–0.0001	0.000	–0.0001	0.000
TUdense*gdp	–0.0000*	0.000	0.0000	0.000					–0.0000**	0.000	0.0000	0.000
collect1					0.0001	0.000	0.0001	0.000				
collect1*gdp					0.0000	0.000	0.0000	0.000				
central2*eurodum	0.0011	0.003	0.0020	0.004	0.0008	0.004	0.0029	0.004				
coordin2*eurodum									0.0068	0.003	0.0062	0.005
cred1	0.0042**	0.002			0.0045**	0.002			0.0038**	0.002		
cred1*eurodum			0.0026	0.003			0.0018	0.004			0.0032	0.003
Adj *R*-sq	0.32		–0.04		0.30		–0.04		0.51		0.07	
n	16		16		17		17		18		18	

Notes: 'Real Compensation Growth-GDP p/h growth' is the dependent variable; countries include EU15 members, Australia, Canada, Japan, United States; *X*(b) signifies the same model as model *X* but interacting the credibility variable with the euro membership dummy. For variables and sources see the Appendix. **, * signify 1% and 5% significance, respectively.

Trade union density interacted with economy size shows up as significant in the third regression, with a negative sign (it also has a negative coefficient significant at the 10 per cent level in the first column, the other place it appears). This would be weak evidence against the fourth of the theories discussed in the preceding section, since it implies that declining trade union density, conditional on being in a country large enough to have had some independence of labour supply, decreases wage restraint. It seems consistent with Calmfors-Driffill's underlying intuition that moving towards decentralisation in the mid-range of unionisation would reduce incentives to restraint. The average size of economy in our sample is US$1136.29 million (1999, WEO). This means that a fall in trade union density from the sample average of 40 per cent to 20 per cent would lead to a non-trivial decline in wage restraint of 0.16 percentage point. Yet for the hump-shape argument, it is a problem that the sample mean of the density is 40 per cent, since that would seem to put any declines in density to the right of the hump and therefore likely to lead to greater restraint.

Trade union density on its own, uninteracted with size of gdp, does not appear to be significant, just as the other measures of labour union organisation and wage bargaining centralisation do not, whether interacted with economic size or eurozone membership. This result is inconsistent with the third of the theories discussed earlier (p. 154*f*), that declining political power or centralisation of unions after EMU insulated monetary policy-making from dealing with labour would explain the observed increase in wage restraint. The extent of trade within the eurozone (EMUtrade2), presumably the exposure to international competition most directly affected by the launch of the euro, also does not show up as having a significant effect on wage restraint, as opposed to the hypothesised positive coefficient.[27] As with the monetary credibility hypothesis, the determinants of wage restraint in the advanced countries appear on this data to be global (or by country) rather than associated with eurozone membership.

Particularly striking is the apparent rejection of the best formally developed of the theories of determination of wage restraint: those hypothesising that a coordination problem would arise after EMU with the countries previously having unions which were large enough to internalise the costs of 'excessive' wage demands showing a decline in wage restraint. As suggested in Table 7.1 with the sample averages, the cross-sectional analysis confirms that there is no association between the centralisation or coordination of wage bargaining, whether conditional on size or not, and wage restraint for eurozone members – or for any countries in the sample. Since two distinct sets of models (Cukierman and Lippi, 1999, 2001; Iversen and Soskice, 1998, 2000) both make the strong prediction that wage restraint should have gone down after EMU, in contrast to the other theories predicting conditional increases in restraint, and the change went the other way on average and specifically when controlling for the institutional structures underlying these models, it seems time to reconsider those models. Before doing so, however, we turn to time-series data to examine from another angle the empirical validity of the clear and contrasting predictions of the first (wage restraint down conditional on EMU and wage bargaining structure) and last (wage restraint up conditional on change in monetary credibility but not on EMU) theories from Table 7.1.

Time-series analysis of wage restraint in Germany and Italy

We are now into the seventh year since the launch of the euro, it begins to be feasible to undertake time-series analysis of even low-frequency data that span the periods before and after EMU in order to look for EMU's impact. With regards to wage restraint, the question is whether the adoption of the euro made any difference to year-by-year wage negotiations given expected central bank reactions, or non-reactions according to some theories. In the previous section, we analysed differences in multi-year averages for a set of 18 countries – here we turn to cyclical variation (or not) in wage restraint as a function of interest rates and structural factors for a pair of countries from 1980–2003. While estimating the interaction between directly estimated central bank reaction functions and wage equations is left for future research, we hope to distinguish between factors affecting wage restraint by careful choice of cases to consider.

Comparing the time-series behaviour and determinants of wage restraint in Germany and Italy should allow us to see which effects of the euro are and are not evident. Germany was the economy with the *de facto* anchor currency of the pre-euro EMS, and had some of the largest unions with some of the most centralised and coordinated wage-bargaining institutions in Europe. This combination of central bank independence (legally and in interest-rate setting) with centralised wage bargaining should have produced great incentives for wage restraint in Germany pre-EMU, according to the theories which emphasised incentives for union internalisation of inflation costs. By the same token, the entry of Germany into the eurozone should have produced a marked drop in wage restraint – the German unions became notably smaller relative to the economic zone relevant for monetary policy-making, and monetary policy-making shifted away most clearly from a focus on German domestic inflation. In short, if the Cukierman–Lippi/Iversen–Soskice story in the spirit of Calmfors and Driffill should show up anywhere, it should be in a decline in wage restraint in Germany post-EMU. For fans of the monetary credibility story, there should either be no effect (assuming, as bond markets indeed seem to, that the ECB has just as credible a commitment to price stability as the Bundesbank did) or a slight decline in wage restraint (to the degree that the ECB either through lesser credibility or broader eurozone focus allows more inflation in Germany at the margin).

For Italy, a different set of expectations are generated. As shown in Figure 7.2, Italy enjoyed the largest credibility gain for its monetary policy commitment to low inflation upon admission to the eurozone. Prior to this credibility gain, Italy should have exhibited low wage restraint according to the theories emphasising monetary credibility. In an economy where indexing was rife and inflation expectations were high and unanchored, there should have been little incentive for unions to exercise wage restraint – and little reason to think that the central bank would tighten policy in response to excessive wage growth.[28] After EMU, with a large gain in counter-inflationary credibility for Italian monetary policy (set by the ECB), Italian unions and wage bargainers should have shown a significant increase in wage restraint. Even if the ECB was not setting policy on the basis of Italian wage developments, the eurozone more generally would be following a policy consistent with price stability, while the Italian economy would no longer be able to devalue or inflate at (political) will. If the monetary credibility story in the spirit of the postwar Bundesbank beliefs should show up anywhere, it should be in an increase in wage restraint in Italy post-EMU. Of course, according to the wage-bargaining coordination problem theories, Italy as a large economy should be subject to a lesser version of the same phenomenon besetting Germany with the move into the Eurozone, and so should show no effect on wage restraint post-EMU or a slight decrease.

To examine the determinants of wage restraint in these two critical country case studies, we look at annual data from 1980 to 2003 for compensation and for productivity growth. In contrast to the cross-sectional data on multi-year averages, here we utilise annual *nominal* compensation growth (from OECD) along with contemporaneous GDP per hour growth (from Gröningen data as discussed in the previous section) to construct wage restraint. The switch from nominal to real wages is to take into account the money illusion, and more broadly the difficulty for workers and unions in discerning real productivity growth in real time. The actual computations of real GDP per hour or of the residual from growth regressions that economists produce and we use above only appear with a lag usually of several months to actual events, whereas often wage negotiations are on an annual or 2–3 year basis and are conducted in nominal terms.

To examine the competing hypotheses, we estimate on German and Italian data separately regressions of the form:

$$WR = \beta_0 + \beta_1\text{*Output Gap} + \beta_2\text{*inflation expectations} + \beta_3\text{*EMU dummy} + \beta_4\text{*nominal central bank interest rate} + \beta_5\text{*additional variables} + \varepsilon \qquad (7.2)$$

where the additional variables include trade within the EU, trade union density, and the spread between the country's and Swiss long-term bond rates as a proxy for the nation's central bank credibility. (A list of variables and data sources used in the time-series analysis is given in the Appendix.)

In the absence of time-series data on trade union density we use the share of private-sector employment in the economy. Inflation expectations were obtained by following Chinn and Frankel (2003) – they take the average of month-to-month annual CPI growth at 12-month leads and use this as an inflation expectation proxy. Our main interest is to see whether the EMU dummy is significant and negative, particularly for Germany, which would be consistent with the wage coordination story, or significant and positive, particularly for Italy, which would be consistent with the monetary credibility story.

Tables 7.4 and 7.5 present the results for Germany and for Italy respectively. All regressions have 24 observations except for those in column II on each table, where data limitations on the trade union density variable limit us to 13 observations. For Germany (Table 7.4), we find the only factor significantly affecting wage restraint is the central bank instrument rate (which is consistent with the Bundesbank wage restraint and deterrence story), with rises in that rate increasing restraint. Interestingly, this does not change after EMU, seemingly implying that German wage bargainers continue to keep their eye on the ECB response to their negotiations much as they did on the Bundesbank's response. Surprisingly, even the German output gap and inflation expectations have no significant direct effects on wage restraint in Germany. There is no evidence that a structural break occurred around German economic unification in 1990–91 in any of the estimates, so we do not report separate results. Given the separation out of the eastern German labour market, and its small share in overall German employment, this is not entirely surprising. Finally, there is evidence of a statistically significant (but not economically large) effect of the public budget deficit on wage bargaining (model VI), where a larger deficit increases wage restraint, perhaps in anticipation of either budget cutbacks or monetary response. Still, despite the sole explanatory power of the central bank interest rate, year to year variation in wage restraint is reasonably well-accounted for in Germany by this factor.

For Italy (Table 7.5), unemployment turns out to be a better measure than the output gap of the importance of the business cycle, and has a consistently significant effect, in the intuitive direction: an increase in unemployment increases wage restraint. Meanwhile EMU membership per se does not come in significantly for Italy, nor does the central bank interest rate itself – perhaps reflecting the *de facto* lack of independence of Italian monetary policy over the period. A direct measure of inflation expectations, however, is estimated to have a significant (5 or 10 per cent level) and positive coefficient across most specifications, including ones where the EMU dummy is included, meaning that when there is a decrease in inflation expectations wage restraint increases. In a similar spirit, the spread between the Italian and Swiss long-term government bond rates has a significant positive coefficient; when the spread increases, consistent with a

Table 7.4 Time-series analysis: German wage restraint, 1980–2003

	Model I		Model II		Model III		Model IV		Model V		Model VI		Model VII	
Variable	*Coef.*	*Std. Err.*	*Coef.*	*Std. Err.*	*Coef.*	*Std. Err.*	*Coef.*	*Std. Err.*	*Coef.*	*Std. Err.*	*Coef.*	*Std. Err.*	*Coef.*	*Std. Err.*
restr_c_n														
gap	–0.0006	*0.001*	–0.0028	*0.002*	–0.0006	*0.001*	–0.0012	*0.002*	–0.0012	*0.002*	–0.0009	*0.001*	*–0.001*	*0.002*
r	0.0054***	*0.002*	0.0076*	*0.004*	0.0057**	*0.002*	0.0062**	*0.002*	0.0064**	*0.003*	0.0054**	*0.002*	*0.0055***	*0.002*
inflexpect	0.3538	*0.353*	0.6476	*0.786*	0.3108	*0.374*	0.3063	*0.384*	0.3615	*0.410*	0.5218	*0.368*	*0.481*	*0.405*
EMU			0.0113	*0.013*	0.0089	*0.011*	0.0087	*0.011*	0.0041	*0.008*	0.0058	*0.008*	*0.016*	*0.022*
TUden			–0.0004	*0.003*										
nongovtempl					–0.1922	*0.330*							*–0.268*	*0.662*
trade_eu							0.0049	*0.109*					*–0.092*	*0.205*
trade_tot							–0.0623	*0.094*					*–0.019*	*0.098*
spread									–0.0019	*0.006*				
structdefc~g											–0.0004*	*0.000*	*0.000*	*0.000*
constant	–0.020***	*0.007*	–0.0285	*0.063*	0.1435	*0.288*	–0.0036	*0.040*	–0.0228**	*0.010*	–0.0260	*0.009*	*0.231*	*0.601*
Adj *R*-sq.	0.62		0.70		0.59		0.57		0.59		0.64		0.58	
n	24		13		24		24		24		24		24	

Notes: Dependent variable – wage restraint calculated using annual nominal compensation growth and contemporaneous GDP p/h growth.
Model II – Trade Union density time series only extends from 1990 to 2003 for Germany.
***, **, * signify 1%, 5% and 10% significance, respectively.

Table 7.5 Time-series analysis: Italian wage restraint, 1980–2003

	Model I		Model II		Model III		Model IV (1)		Model V		Model VI		Model VII		Model VIII	
Variable	*Coef.*	*Std. Err.*	*Coef.*	*Std. Err.*	*Coef.*	*Std. Err.*	*Coef.*	*Std. Err.*	*Coef.*	*Std. Err.*	*Coef.*	*Std. Err.*	*Coef.*	*Std. Err.*	*Coef.*	*Std. Err.*
restr_c_n																
gap	–0.0005	*0.003*														
unempl			–0.0122***	*0.003*	–0.023**	*0.009*	–0.010*	*0.005*	–0.013**	*0.006*	–0.013***	*0.004*	–0.015***	*0.004*	–0.0091	*0.006*
r	0.0016	*0.003*	0.0007	*0.002*	–0.0048	*0.007*	0.0017	*0.003*	0.0004	*0.003*	–0.0006	*0.002*	–0.0004	*0.002*	0.0030	*0.003*
inflexpect	1.1634***	*0.170*	0.781***	*0.167*	–0.6536	*0.891*	0.4501	*0.261*	0.700***	*0.206*	0.476**	*0.197*	0.683***	*0.193*	0.4276	*0.336*
EMU					–0.0011	*0.022*	–0.0205	*0.013*	–0.0154	*0.020*	0.0023	*0.013*	–0.0125	*0.013*	–0.0265	*0.022*
TUden					0.0117	*0.010*										
nongovtempl							1.7866	*1.416*							1.8887	*1.835*
trade_eu									–0.0563	*0.452*					0.1778	*0.494*
trade_tot									0.0718	*0.100*					0.0589	*0.134*
spread											0.004**	*0.002*				
structdefc~g													–0.0035	*0.014*	–0.0143	*0.017*
constant	–0.0128	*0.011*	0.128***	*0.039*	–0.1256	*0.296*	–1.3656	*1.217*	0.1174	*0.108*	0.129**	*0.052*	0.167***	*0.054*	–1.5261	*1.550*
Adj *R*-sq.	0.82		0.89		0.46		0.89		0.88		0.91		0.89		0.88	
n	24		24		13		24		24		24		24		24	

Notes: Dependent variable – wage restraint calculated using annual nominal compensation growth and contemporaneous GDP p/h growth.
Model II – Trade Union density time series only extends from 1990 to 2003 for Italy.
***, **, * signify 1%, 5% and 10% significance, respectively
(1)–Model IV estimated with wage restrained calculated with 1-period lagged GDP p/h growth yields a significant result for inflation expectations

decline in Italian monetary credibility, wage restraint diminishes. It is consistent with the predictions of the monetary credibility theory of wage restraint that this should show up strongly in Italy. Unlike in Germany, there is no evidence that budget deficits have any effect on wage restraint, but like in Germany the various measures of trade union structure and trade have no discernable impact.[29]

Implications for future research

Enhanced monetary credibility, as proxied by the decrease in the long government bond rate after the launch of the euro, can explain a significant portion of the cross-sectional variation in the observed increase in wage restraint seen in European countries since 1999. The effect of monetary credibility on wage restraint is not limited to eurozone members, though; such countries as Sweden and the United Kingdom which had a similarly measured gain in central bank commitment to price stability also saw similarly significant increases in wage restraint. This effect occurred completely independently of the wage-bargaining institutions in the countries involved. In fact, in contradiction of those theories that suggested a coordination problem would emerge post-EMU between labour representatives and the ECB in those large economies where before EMU bargaining was centralised and directly with their national central banks, there is no evidence of a decline in wage restraint in those countries. Looking more closely at time-series evidence for Germany, where that hypothesised effect was supposed to be strongest, offers no support for the theories; time-series evidence for Italy on the variation of interest rate spreads over time, on the other hand, strongly supports the view that monetary credibility matters irrespective of wage-bargaining arrangements.

As always in this literature, given the limited sample of countries involved and the limited data (both cross-sectional and time-series) available on institutional change, these results cannot be taken as dispositive. Yet, neither are they fit for dismissal, as they do not differ in substance whether either of two measures of productivity growth or of wage/compensation growth are used, and using a variety of available controls. Given the strength of the predictions of the Cukierman–Lippi (1999, 2001) and Iversen–Soskice (1998, 2000) models that EMU should lead to a decline in wage restraint, particularly in large countries, the apparent rejection of those predictions should be taken seriously. Since the ECB has put lower weight on individual countries' cyclical and wage developments – particularly Germany's – than the pre-EMU Bundesbank did when setting monetary policy (Posen and Popov Gould, 2006; Hayo in this volume), the rejection is not because the ECB behaved contrary to expectations either in these models or more generally.

For future research, then, these results lead naturally to questions of what on the labour institution side was at work that coordination problems did not arise in wage bargaining post-EMU and wage restraint rose. When labour representatives appear on the basis of these results to be forward-looking and concerned enough with macroeconomic conditions to respond to changes in counter-inflationary credibility, it is somewhat surprising that the internalisation dynamic for the effect of wage bargaining on inflation pressures does not carry through as well. Perhaps the labour representatives' utility functions in the above models were simply misspecified, with too little regard for employment effects and too much for the costs of inflation. Although Shiller (1996) and survey work that followed established a healthy dislike for inflation among a wide range of the populace in many of the countries considered here, that is not equivalent to establishing such a dislike among labour leaders, where anecdotal, political science and historical evidence has tended to show labour as being far more concerned about output and employment than inflation (at least at low-to-moderate levels of inflation).

Another related possibility is that these labour and union institutions were themselves always overestimated in importance as determinants of wage-bargaining behaviour, with actual coordination or centralisation in practice fundamentally mis-measured by the available coded classifications. More moderately, it could be that while these institutions do have some sway, they allow for a great deal of variation in bargaining behaviour over time, and those variations are not picked up in the available measures and thus our analyses. While perhaps this seems on the face of it unlikely given the long emphasis on tripartite bargaining and corporatism in Europe, as well as the supposed recent successes of such mutual accommodation in Ireland, the Netherlands and Sweden, the result should not be used to impute the cause. It remains possible that the effect or effectiveness of these labour-market institutions is endogenous to the political and economic forces in civil society, and so produces the degree of wage restraint in keeping with the political pressures of the time, largely irrespective of apparent form.[30]

In any event, it may be necessary to go beyond investigating wage restraint (let alone unemployment or inflation outcomes) at the national level, and consider sectoral differences in both wage-bargaining structures and degree of wage restraint. This might not only better distinguish between these potential explanations for the absence of impact of wage-bargaining structures on changes in wage restraint in the OECD in the last 15 years; such an approach might also allow for more direct grappling with the alternative hypotheses advanced earlier in this chapter, particularly regarding the influence of globalisation and competition on wage-setting.[31]

For analysts of monetary policy, particularly in the eurozone, one message at least is clear: the ECB has delivered wage restraint on the Bundesbank deterrence model where adoption of the euro led to credible declines in inflation expectations. This could be taken to indicate that concerns about establishing monetary toughness or the emergence of wage-push inflation pressures are unnecessary, especially since the adoption of inflation targeting in Sweden and the UK led to similar effects without any suggestion that they went through a similar proving process.

Appendix

Table 7A.1 Variable list and data sources for cross-section analysis

Variable name	*Variable label*	*Data source*
cntry	country name	
MFPnom	wage restraint: nominal compensation growth minus MFP growth	OECD Economic Outlook (compensation) OECD Productivity DB (MFP, GDP p/h)
GDPnom	wage restraint: nominal compensation growth minus GDP p/h growth	
MFPreal	wage restraint: real compensation growth minus MFP growth	
GDPreal	wage restraint: real compensation growth minus GDP p/h growth	
EMUtrade1	country's trade with eurozone countries, avrg 1995–1998	IMF's DOTS database
EMUtrade2	country's trade with eurozone countries, avrg 1999–2004	
cred1	credibility gain from euro – pre-emptive convergence assumed	long-term govt bond yield data from IMF's IFS database
cred2	credibility gain from euro – NO pre-emptive convergence assumed	
central1	centralization of bargaining – 1990–1994	Driffill (2005)
central2	centralization of bargaining – 1995–2000	
coordin1	coordination index – 1990–1994	
coordin2	coordination index – 1995–2000	
collect1	collective bargaining coverage 1990	
collect2	collective bargaining coverage 2000	
TUdense	Trade union density, 2000	
gdp	1999 GDP, current prices, US$ billions, (WEO)	IMF, World Economic Outlook Database
tu90gdp	interacted term – TU density in 1990, GDP	
tu20gdp	interacted term – TU density in 2000, GDP	
eurodum	eurozone member dummy	
cred1euro	interacted credibility with euro dummy	
cred2euro	interacted credibility with euro dummy	
central1gdp	interacted centralisation with gdp	
central2gdp	interacted centralisation with gdp	
central1euro	interacted centralisation with euro d	
central2euro	interacted centralisation with euro d	
coordin1euro	interacted coordination with euro d	
coordin2euro	interacted coordination with euro d	
collect1gdp	interacted collective bargaining coverage	
collect2gdp	interacted collective bargaining coverage	

Table 7A.2 Variable list and data sources for time-series analysis: Germany, Italy

Variable name	*Variable label*	*Source of data*
year	time variable	
restr_c_r	wage restraint-contemporaneous, real compensation growth	– Total Compensation data from OECD, Economic Outlook #78. – GDP p/h from: The Conference Board and Gröningen Growth and Development Centre, Total Economy Database, January 2006
restr_l_r	wage restraint-1 period lag of productivity growth, real compensation growth	
restr_c_n	wage restraint-contemporaneous, nominal compensation growth	
restr_l_n	wage restraint-1 period lagged productivity growth, nominal compensation growth	
gap	output gap	OECD, Economic Outlook #78
nongovtempl	share of total empl not in public sector	
unempl	unemployment rate	
structdefchng	% change in structural deficit	
gdp	gdp, billions, US$	
TUden	TU density	Visser (2006)
inflexpect	inflation expectations	IMF, IFS database (12m average of m-to-m CPI growth, 12m lead)
r	Buba/ECB money market interest rate	IMF, International Financial Statistics
spread	Italian-Swiss LT govt bond spread	
trade_eu	Italian trade with eurozone countries-% GDP	IMF, Direction of Trade database
trade_tot	total Italian trade (X+M), % GDP	
EMU	start of EMUIII dummy	

Notes

1 See among others Bean (1998), Bayoumi and Sgherri (2004), Calmfors (1998), Cukierman and Lippi (1999, 2001), Duval and Elmeskov (2005), Gruener and Hefeker (1999), Hall and Franzese (1998), Iversen and Soskice (1998, 2000), Saint-Paul and Bentolila (2000) and Sibert and Sutherland (2000).

2 Calmfors (2001) and Cukierman and Lippi (2001) give useful albeit partial surveys of the factors involved.

3 These authors acknowledge their debt in turn to Olson (1982), who first outlined why the behaviour of interest groups depends upon how 'encompassing' their membership is.

4 Posen (1999) expressed an early American skepticism on both these counts. Duval and Elmeskov (2005) and Posen (2005) both give references to statements by euro proponents pre-EMU that the euro would strongly induce if not force structural change

5 Blanchard (2005) is particularly articulate on the challenge presented to such cross-national datasets by the existence of a multiplicity of shocks. Calmfors (1993) and Driffill (2005) also note these limitations.

6 Richard Freeman raised this concern in initial comments on Calmfors and Driffill (1988). This is not true of all empirical investigations (e.g., Layard *et al.*, 1991, estimate wage equations before turning to unemployment outcomes), but most focus on inflation or unemployment directly. Some of the models, such as those of Cukierman and Lippi (1999, 2001), map directly from real wages to aggregate outcomes.

7 Of course, the concept of wage restraint and its importance is well-established. Bruno and Sachs (1985) first brought in the modern concept of the wage gap and related it to institutions, and many of the papers cited in note 1 deal with real wage determination. Bean (1994, 2005), Blanchard (1991, 2000), Layard *et al.* (1991) and Nickell *et al.* (2005) all consider the role of real wage rigidities in determining unemployment. Yet, the empirical linkage between wage restraint and changes in monetary policy regimes to our knowledge remains uninvestigated.

8 See the summary and references in Posen (2006, ch. 6). The 'overpricing' in turn can be attributed to the incentives for union insiders in then West Germany to prevent low-wage competition for their membership.

9 As Caballero and Hammour (1996) and Blanchard (2005) point out, though, even if a wage-gap story can be used to explain much of the rise of European unemployment in the 1970s and early 1980s, it cannot be assigned a leading role in the persistence and, in some European countries, continued rise of unemployment in more recent years, precisely because there has been a period of relative wage restraint.

10 See Streeck (1994) or Siebert (2005, ch. 4).

11 Blinder and Yellen (2001) articulate this position very well from the point of view of Federal Reserve decision-makers.

12 As we are considering aggregate measures of wage restraint, we are abstracting from the bargaining over rents and quasi-rents between firms and unions, which are also a component of wage growth when considered at the sectoral or individual firm level.

13 In current monetary policy-making, the analogy would be made to a supply-shock that embodied a relative price shift. If the relative price of labour was going up due to structural reasons, and not simply as a response to broader price pressures, the central bank could accommodate the relative price shift by only gradually tightening in response to any inflationary effects, and largely withholding any interest-rate response unless/until there were 'second-round effects' of the wage increase on inflation expectations.

14 The outlier status of the US economy with regards to income and wealth inequality is not attributable to wage restraint either. As Dew-Becker and Gordon (2005) and Piketty and Saez (2006) recently demonstrated, the large increase in income going to the top 1 per cent and 0.1 per cent of earners in the USA over the

recent decade is largely due to the extraordinary rise in executive pay cumulated over several years.

15 Greece clearly has by far the largest change in wage restraint. Dropping Greece from our sample would of course drive down the average change observed, but also decrease the standard deviation of changes observed, so the number of (eurozone) countries showing a significant increase in wage restraint in fact rises in that subsample. Details available from the authors upon request.

16 In their famous U-shaped curve, Calmfors and Driffill (1988) suggest that extreme decentralisation of wage-bargaining will also lead to wage restraint because atomistic workers bargaining individually cannot drive up inflationary pressures. For purposes of considering the effects of EMU, the issue is whether economies on the 'right' side of the hump with more concentrated wage bargaining move towards the sub-optimal centre where less internalisation takes place, so we focus on that end here.

17 Katzenstein (1985) first suggested this feedback effect in his study of small states in world markets. Such internalisation of competitiveness concerns, however, is also a staple of policy discussions where there is tripartite bargaining. See for example Honohan and Lane's (2002) depiction of the role of negotiated wage restraint in providing the conditions for the recent Irish miracle.

18 The discussion of the size of the increase in intra-European trade due to the adoption of the euro remains lively, with some very large estimates (e.g., Rose, 2000) offered. See Baldwin (2005) and Frankel (2005) for a constructive debate over the accumulated empirical evidence.

19 Whether the trend to deunionisation is a result of these forces or is itself an independent cause, at least in part, is beyond the scope of this chapter to consider.

20 Obviously, we do not assume a stable trade-off between inflation and unemployment, or the absence of costs to inflation. Hence the mention of 'short-term costs to employment', since presumably central bank laxity would at some point induce real costs either from extra inflation and/or sharper tightening of policy.

21 As shown in Table 7.1, we are missing observations for Luxembourg, Norway and Switzerland.

22 OECD, *Employment Outlook* 2004, chapter 3

23 The data is taken from the IMF's *International Financial Statistics*. The first average ends in 1997m12 to allow for changes in bond yields in anticipation of EMU, and the horizons are shorter before and after than the wage-restraint horizons to focus on the credibility impact of monetary regime shifts at the time.

24 Greece itself did not join the eurozone until January 2001, so the change seen here is assumed to have only captured part of EMU's impact on the economy's inflation expectations, with markets discounting until membership was sure.

25 Note that wage restraint is defined to be negative (it is wage growth minus productivity growth), so the more negative the number, the greater the restraint. This is why there is a positive coefficient on the credibility variable: cred1 is also negative, representing a fall in long-term rates from pre-EMU period to post-EMU period.

26 It is worth pointing out that these results are not driven by the inclusion of Greece, an outlier in degree of increase in wage restraint (see Figure 7.1). Given missing data for Greece on all trade union variables other than density, and our inclusion of the centralisation variable in the baseline and other regressions, it is not in the sample for Table 7.3. Obviously, were Greece to be included the credibility-restraint correlation would only strengthen, given the observations on both of those variables.

27 Given the size of the increase in intra-eurozone trade often claimed, the clear difference in the impact inside and outside the eurozone assumed (even though we allow for a trade-with-eurozone increase for non-member countries in the sample as well), and the more direct measurement of this explanatory variable than of some of the labour-institutional variables, it seems to be a particularly clear rejection of this hypothesis.
28 Some commentators will insist that the Banca d'Italia did have significant counter-inflationary credibility from the time of its 'divorce' from the Italian Treasury, or with the advent of later reforms. This begs credulity given the revealed drop in long bond rates upon eurozone entry and the prior devaluations from the ERM – let alone the desire of Banca d'Italia senior officials to gain eurozone entry.
29 In both the German and Italian time-series, one might expect the trade-union coordination, centralisation and density variables to have limited explanatory power given their low variation over the period.
30 See Posen (1998b) for a general discussion of the endogeneity of institutional impact in political economy and macroeconomics.
31 We are grateful to Philip Lane for this latter suggestion regarding globalisation.

References

Baldwin, R. (2005) 'The Euro's Trade Effects', ECB Workshop, 'What Effects is EMU Having on the Euro Area and its Member Countries?,' Frankfurt, June.

Ball, L. and and R.A. Moffitt (2001) 'Productivity Growth and the Phillips Curve', NBER Working Paper no. W8421, in A. Krueger and R. Solow (eds), *The Roaring Nineties*. New York: Russell Sage Foundation.

Bayoumi, T. and S. Sgherri (2004) 'Monetary Magic? How the Fed Improved the Flexibility of the U.S. Economy', IMF Working Paper no. WP/04/24, February.

Bean, C. (1994) 'European Unemployment: A Retrospective', *European Economic Review*, 38: 523–34.

Bean, C. (1998) 'The Interaction of Aggregate Demand Policies and Labour Market Reform', *Swedish Economic Policy Review*, vol. 5(2).

Bean, C. (2005) 'Comments on Blanchard' (2005), *Economic Policy*, 21: 47–51.

Blanchard, O.J. (1991) 'Wage Bargaining and Unemployment Persistence', *Journal of Money, Credit, and Banking*, 23: 277–92.

Blanchard, O. (2000) 'The Economics of Unemployment: Shocks, Institutions, and Interactions', Lionel Robbins Lectures, London School of Economics, mimeo.

Blanchard, O. (2006) 'European Unemployment: The Evolution of Facts and Ideas,' *Economic Policy*, 21: 5–47.

Blanchard, O. and T. Philippou (2004) 'The Quality of Labour Relations and Unemployment', MIT Department of Economics Working Paper no. 04–25, June.

Blinder, A. and J. Yellen (2001) *The Fabulous Decade*. Washington: Century Foundation.

Bruno, M. and J. Sachs (1985) *The Economics of Worldwide Stagflation*. Oxford: Blackwell.

Caballero, R. and M. Hammour (1998) 'Jobless Growth: Appropriability, Factor Substitution, and Unemployment' *Carnegie-Rochester Conference Series on Public Policy*, 48: 51–94.

Calmfors, L. (1993) 'Centralisation of Wage Bargaining and Macroeconomic Performance – A Survey,' *OECD Economic Studies*, 21.

Calmfors, L. (1998) 'Macroeconomic Policy, Wage Setting, and Employment – What Difference Does the EMU Make?', *Oxford Review of Economic Policy*, 14.

Calmfors, L. (2001) 'Wages and Wage-bargaining Institutions in the EMU – A Survey of the Issues', Seminar Paper no. 690, Institute for International Economic Studies, University of Stockholm, May.

Calmfors, L. and J. Driffill (1988) 'Bargaining Structure, Corporatism, and Macroeconomic Performance', *Economic Policy*, 6:41–61.

Chinn, M. and J. Frankel (2003) 'The Euro Area and World Interest Rates', Santa Cruz Center for International Economics, Working Paper Series no. 1016, Center for International Economics, UC Santa Cruz.

Cukierman, A. and F. Lippi (1999) 'Central Bank Independence, Centralisation of Wage Bargaining, Inflation and Unemployment: Theory and Some Evidence', *European Economic Review*, 43: 1395–1434.

Cukierman, A. and F. Lippi (2001) 'Labour Markets and Monetary Union: A Strategic Analysis', *Economic Journal*, 111:541–565.

Danthine, J.-P. and J. Hunt (1994) 'Wage Bargaining Structure, Employment and Economic Integration', *Economic Journal*, 104, 528–541

Dew-Becker, I. and R. Gordon (2005) 'Where did the Productivity Growth Go?', National Bureau of Economic Research working paper 11842, December.

Driffill, J. (2005) 'The Centralisation of Wage Bargaining Revisited: What Have We Learned?', Mimeo, Birkbeck College, November.

Driffill, J. and M. Miller (2003) 'No Credit for Transition: European Institutions and German Unemployment', *Scottish Journal of Political Economy*, 50:41–60.

Dumont, M., G. Rayp and P. Willemé (2006) 'Does Internationalisation Affect Union Bargaining Power? An Empirical Study for Five EU Countries', *Oxford Economic Papers*, 58: 77–102.

Duval, R. and J. Elmeskov (2005) 'The Effects of EMU on Structural Reforms in Labour and Product Markets', OECD Economics Department Working Paper no. 438, July.

Frankel, J. (2005) 'Comments on Baldwin: The Euro's Trade Effects', ECB Workshop, 'What Effects is EMU Having on the Euro Area and its Member Countries?,' Frankfurt, June.

Garrett, G. (1998) *Partisan Politics in the Global Economy*, Cambridge, UK: Cambridge University Press.

Gruener, H.P. and C. Hefeker (1999) 'How Will EMU Affect Inflation and Unemployment in Europe?', *Scandinavian Journal of Economics*, 101, 33–47.

Hall, P. and R. Franzese (1998) 'Mixed Signals: Central Bank Independence, Coordinated Wage-Bargaining, and European Monetary Union', *International Organisation*, 52.

Hayo, B. (2006) 'Is European Monetary Policy Appropriate for the EMU Member Countries: a Counterfactual Analysis', this volume.

Hibbs, D. (1987) *The Political Economy of Industrial Democracies*, Cambridge, MA: Harvard University Press.

Iversen, T. and D. Soskice (1998) 'Multiple Wage-Bargaining Systems in the Single European Currency Area', *Oxford Review of Economic Policy*, 14.

Iversen, T. and D. Soskice (2000) 'The Nonneutrality of Monetary Policy with Large Price or Wage Setters', *Quarterly Journal of Economics*, February.

Katzenstein, P. (1985) *Small States in World Markets*, Ithaca: Cornell University Press.

Layard, R.S. Nickell, and R. Jackman (1991) *Unemployment, Macroeconomic Performance and the Labour Market*, Oxford: Oxford University Press.

Nickell, S., L. Nunziata and W. Ochel (2005) 'Unemployment in the OECD Since the 1960s: What do We Know?', *Economic Journal* 111, 1–27.

Nicoletti, G. *et al.*, (2001) 'European Integration, Liberalisation and Labour Market Performance', in G. Bertola, T. Boeri and G. Nicoletti (eds), *Welfare and Unemployment in a United Europe*. MIT Press.

Olson, M. (1982) *The Rise and Decline of Nations*, Yale University Press

Organization for Economic Cooperation and Development (1999) *Implementing the OECD Jobs Strategy: Member Countries' Experience*. Paris: OECD.

Organization for Economic Cooperation and Development (2004) *Employment Outlook*. Paris: OECD.

Piketty, T. and E. Saez (2006) 'The Evolution of Top Incomes', NBER working paper no. 11955, January.

Posen, A. (1998a) 'Central Bank Independence and Disinflationary Credibility: A Missing Link?,' *Oxford Economic Papers*, 50, 335–359.

Posen, A. (1998b) 'Do Better Institutions Make Better Policy? A Review Essay', *International Finance*, 1, 173–205.

Posen, A. (1999) 'Why EMU is Irrelevant for the German Economy,' Institute for International Economics Working Paper no. 99–05, May.

Posen, A. (ed.) (2005) *The Euro at Five: Ready for a Global Role?* Washington: Institute for International Economics

Posen, A. (2006) *Reform in a Rich Country: Germany*. Washington: Institute for International Economics, forthcoming

Posen, A. and D. Popov Gould (2006) 'Divergence Eurozone', mimeo, Institute for International Economics, April.

Rose, A. (2000) 'One Money, One Market: Estimating the Effect of Common Currencies on Trade', *Economic Policy*, 30, 09–45.

Saint-Paul, G. and S. Bentolila (2000) 'Will EMU Increase Euroclerosis?', Discussion Paper no. 2423, CEPR, April.

Shiller, R. (1996) 'Why do People Dislike Inflation?', NBER Working Paper no. W5539, April.

Sibert, A. and A. Sutherland (2000) 'Monetary Union and Labour Market Reform', *Journal of International Economics*, 51.

Siebert, H. (2005) *The German Economy: Beyond the Social Market*, Princeton, NJ. Princeton University Press.

Spielmann, C. (2005) 'Report: Recent Changes in the German Wage Bargaining Process,' Mimeo, Birkbeck College, Februrary.

Streeck, W. (1994) 'Pay Restraint Without Income Policy: Institutionalised Monetarism and Industrial Unionism in Germany', in R. Dore, R. Boyer and Z. Marn (eds), *The Return of Incomes Policy*, London: Pinter.

Visser, J. (2006) 'Union Member Statistics in 24 Countries', *Monthly Labor Review*, 129: 38–49.

Discussion

*John Driffill**

There has been a great deal of theorising about the effects of EMU on real wages and unemployment, as well as its effects on inflation, but little if any empirical analysis. Seven years after the inception of EMU, sufficient data is becoming available to begin econometric analysis. Therefore Adam Posen and Daniel Gould's examination of the data is both very timely and very welcome. They ask whether EMU has had any effects on wage restraint, and summarise five groups of theories that bear on the question. Identifying the effects of EMU on the behaviour of wage-setters is bound to be a tricky business, since there is still relatively little data, and real wage rates, employment and inflation depend on so many other factors. I admire and applaud the authors' choice of wage restraint as the key variable to be explained. I find their arguments compelling; firstly, that by taking in the growth of real wages it is a variable that is much closer to the direct predictions of many of the theories in this area, which extrapolate to implications for inflation and unemployment; and secondly, by netting out productivity growth it adjusts for many of the otherwise unobserved differences between countries and over time. I greatly value their careful summary of the five groups of theories of why EMU might have affected wage restraint, and how EMU would have affected countries differentially under each of group of theories.

A key element of this chapter is the definition of wage restraint. The authors define it as the change in real wage rates less the change of productivity. Productivity is measured in two alternative ways. One is multi-factor productivity growth, the residual from a growth-accounting exercise. The other is growth in GDP per hour worked, based on national accounts data. The hypothesis is that joining EMU may have changed the rate of wage restraint, and the extent of the change may depend on a number of factors – the change in monetary credibility in the country concerned, and a -

*School of Economics, Mathematics and Statistics, Birkbeck College, University of London, Malet Street, London WC1E 7HX. Phone 020 7631 6417, fax 020 7631 6416, e-mail j.driffill@bbk.ac.uk.

measure of the amount of influence that trade unions have. A number of different variables are used to capture this: density of trade union membership, degree of coverage of trade union bargains, degree of centralisation of union wage bargaining, and so on.

The use of wage restraint defined in this way as the variable to be explained is very appealing, as is the idea that wage growth in excess of productivity growth will push up labour costs and reduce employment. However, the potential response of employment to real wages and productivity leads me to be somewhat concerned about the informativeness of this measure. If productivity were completely independent of real wage rates, this would not be a concern. But, on the first measure of productivity used in the chapter, growth of real wages in excess of the growth of GDP per hour worked, if employment grows as real wages fall then output per hour worked may fall proportionately, and there will be no effect on measured wage restraint, even though real wages have indeed fallen.[1] In an extreme case there might be no effect at all on measured wage restraint, despite a fall in real wages (relative to what would have happened in the absence of EMU). In less extreme cases, the adjustment of employment (and output per hour worked) may partially offset the effect of slower real wage growth. This may be one of the reasons why the authors found relatively small changes in wage restraint after EMU for many countries, and why the cross-section estimates were able to identify only a few effects. This comment applies to the measure of wage restraint used in the estimates of Table 7.3. It does not apply to the alternative measure, real wage growth less the growth rate of multi-factor productivity, providing the estimates of this are able to capture the exogenous element in technical progress. However, it is notoriously difficult to extract, from data, estimates of MFP growth that are unaffected by changes in mark-ups, capital utilisation rates, overtime rates, and so on.

Allied to this observation, two more might be made, I think. One is that if there were a fall in real wage growth due to EMU, perhaps it would only be a temporary fall in the growth rate of real wages, so leading to a fall in the level of real wages and an increase in employment, relative to the counterfactual, as a result of EMU. This again would tend to make it difficult to identify changes using the cross-section regressions in Table 7.3. However, if there was a period of learning around the time of the introduction of EMU, with markets unsure of the policies the ECB would employ on interest rates and inflation, then this dip in real wage growth may have been spread out over a longer period, and appear as a sustained fall over the short sample period available for this study. The second point is that EMU may have caused an increase in competition in markets for products, and forced firms to have cut their mark-ups of prices over production costs. This would have had the effect of offsetting the effects on real wages of changes in unions' bargaining behaviour. This again suggests that there may have been changes of the kind the authors are looking for that the measured wage restraint has not captured.

Nevertheless, the authors have been able to find some clear results from their cross-section regressions. The result that greater credibility of the central bank has significantly increased wage restraint both inside and outside EMU is very striking, as is the result that lower trade union density in bigger economies has been associated with less wage restraint. The authors remark that, since the union density across the sample of countries is 40 percent and a fall from there to 20 percent reduces wage restraint non-trivially, the peak of the hump must occur at a low level of density. But in most OECD countries, coverage of bargains greatly exceeds density, and so this might imply a hump with its peak at a plausibly high level of coverage.

The authors comment that the results here give no support to the theory that in a large country like Germany, formerly operating an independent monetary policy, with large and powerful unions, a shift to EMU should have caused a fall in wage restraint. This is based on the first group of theories, associated with Cukierman and Lippi and Iversen and Soskice. The shift from the Bundesbank to the ECB, for whom German inflation has only a small influence on eurozone inflation, and whose response to wage moderation by German unions would be likely to be smaller than would the Bundesbank's, should have induced less wage restraint. The cross-section data show no sign of this effect. Is it possible that this is a reflection of the Bundesbank's having taken a hard line on inflation, and having been impossible for the unions to influence? If indeed inflation had been the Bundesbank's only target, then there would have been little scope for unions' interaction with it to induce more or less restraint. If the ECB follows a similarly inflation-only policy – if they take their mandate from the European Treaties literally – then the absence of change need not be inconsistent with the theories. This implication of the cross-section results in Table 7.4 seems to be consistent with the time-series results for Germany. The theories that predicted a fall in wage restraint after EMU may be correct in principle, but the size of their predicted effects may be too small to detect in this data.

The strong message that emerges from the chapter is that wage restraint has been affected primarily through increased credibility of central banks' commitment to low inflation, whether this appears through the long-term-interest differential in the cross-section study, the central bank's own interest rate in the German time-series results, or inflation expectations in the Italian case. There is only weak evidence that differences in union density or other measures of union influence, either across countries or over time, have had an influence. The changes that have occurred are not inherently caused by EMU. Non-EMU countries enjoyed similar effects of greater central bank credibility. The authors make the point that the effects of wage bargaining market institutions may differ over place and time in ways that their measured features do not capture. Their point that the effects of labour-market institutions may be 'endogenous to the political and economic forces in civil society' appears to be shared by David Soskice, who has argued that both unions and central banks may be endogenous institutions, rather than two exogenous influences.[2] These factors make it even harder to disentangle the contributions of each of them separately.

There is further evidence, that the move towards credible low-inflation policies in the hands of independent central banks has induced large changes in the way that economies operate, to be found in the recent experience of central banks themselves in meeting their inflation targets much more frequently than had been predicted in advance, and in the sustained falls in unemployment rates seen in several OECD countries, including the USA and the UK, in recent years, beyond forecast levels, with no increase in inflation. The unemployment-inflation trade-off seems to have improved markedly, and the natural rate of unemployment or NAIRU, if there is one, seems to have been falling. Charles Bean's scatter-plot of inflation versus unemployment for the UK (2006), and similar plots for other economies, makes this point. Such observations reinforce the view that the changes in the monetary policy regime have had far-reaching and partly unpredicted effects.

Nevertheless, the results of the chapter are striking, and suggest a need for further examination of theories of the strategic interactions between unions and central banks. The authors have, through meticulous analysis, teased some clear results from rather unpromising data. The results invite further analysis of the data, collection of more data, and use of more disaggregated data as the authors suggest. This is a bold and thought-provoking chapter, which will, I have no doubt, stimulate much further work on these important questions.

Notes

1 To take a very simple example, suppose the aggregate production were Cobb-Douglas: $Y = AL^{a}K^{1-a}$; and unions set wages in a right-to-manage framework, while employers determined employment. With prices set as a mark-up on marginal cost, employment would be set so that the marginal product of labour was a mark-up on the real wage. Then if the real wage w was proportional to $\partial Y/\partial L = \alpha Y/L$ there would be no change in the growth of real wages relative to production per labour-hour ($\Delta w/w - (\Delta Y/Y - \Delta L/L)$)) no matter what happened to the growth of real wages. Lower real wages would simply create more employment. This is a rather extreme example. Less clear-cut results would emerge if the production function were say CES rather than Cobb–Douglas.

2 The endogeneity of institutions is a theme that runs through much of the work of David Soskice and his co-authors on labour markets and macroeconomic policy. There is, for example, Soskice and Iversen (1998).

References

Bean, C. (2006) 'Comments on Olivier Blanchard', *Economic Policy*, 45: 50.

Cukierman, A. and F. Lippi (2001) 'Labour Markets and Monetary Union: A Strategic Analysis', *Economic Journal*, 111: 541–65.

Iversen, T. and D. Soskice (2000) 'The Nonneutrality of Monetary Policy with Large Price or Wage Setters', *Quarterly Journal of Economics*, February.

Soskice, D. and T. Iversen (1998) 'Multiple Wage-Bargaining Systems in the European Single Currency Area', *Oxford Review of Economic Policy*, 14: 110–24.

8

Structural Reforms and European Monetary Union: What Can a Panel Analysis for the World versus OECD Countries Tell Us?

*Ansgar Belke, Bernhard Herz and Lukas Vogel**

Introduction

Recently, the economics of structural reforms has attracted increasing attention in the academic literature (Abiad and Mody, 2005; Helbling *et al.*, 2004; for a survey see Heinemann, 2004, 2005). A more practical question is whether being part of European Monetary Union tends to help or hinder structural reform. This ongoing research is driven by the fact that, for a number of EU countries, the speed of structural changes lags behind what is necessary, given high structural unemployment and imminent demographic change. Policy fields where a striking contrast between needs and deeds of institutional change has been identified are, for instance, government size, labour market, product market, credit and business regulation.

Although the existing empirical literature has started to identify important drivers and obstacles of reforms with regard to different policy fields, the interplay of structural reforms and monetary policy autonomy has been neglected so far. While the theoretical literature has formulated some hypotheses on how monetary policy may act as a catalyst for reform processes, few thorough empirical studies based on the experience of a large number of industrial countries are available. This is even more true with respect to European Monetary Union, since any effort to estimate the impact of EMU on the degree of reforms empirically must suffer from a lack of degrees of freedom.

Nevertheless, our study intends to help to fill this gap in the literature by a clever trick. We are interested in the effect of EMU on structural reform

*We would like to thank Friedrich Heinemann, Eduard Hochreiter, and the participants of the 'Travails of the Eurozone' Conference, especially Gulzin Ozkan, David Cobham, John Driffill and Adam Posen, for helpful comments and suggestions. We gratefully acknowledge the hospitality of the Oesterreichische Nationalbank (OeNB) where the first author was a visiting researcher while parts of this chapter were written. For delivery of data we are grateful to Stefan Pitlik and Andreas Freytag.

but we investigate this by examining the relationship between fixed exchange rates and reform in two wider samples of countries, in order to avoid the problem of insufficient degrees of freedom. On the basis of these results, we try to infer the implications for EMU as a variant of irrevocably fixed exchange rates from the perspective of an individual EMU member country. Our guiding research question is whether and how monetary policy autonomy can help to increase the likelihood of reform and to safeguard the continuation and successful implementation of initial reform processes. Based on a model depicting the simultaneous determination of reform activity and monetary policy, the empirical part of the chapter will be devoted to scrutinising the role of monetary policy autonomy in the context of reform processes for a panel of OECD countries. Here, sophisticated measures of reform developments and monetary autonomy will be employed, distinguishing between reforms of labour markets, financial markets and product markets, and a reduction of government size.

A further important distinction concerns the exchange rate regime. Necessarily, the link between national reform processes and monetary policy must be relatively loose where, for instance, fixed exchange rate regimes restrict monetary policy (see Calmfors, 1998, 2001; Duval and Elmeskov, 2005). Hence, we start from the empirical puzzle laid out by Herz and Vogel (2005), that more open economies do not reform more than less open ones, and we focus on different exchange rate arrangements as one of the main determinants of monetary policy autonomy. The study's results will be of high relevance for the ongoing debate as to how Europe can overcome the obstacles to faster potential growth and what role monetary policy can (and cannot) play in this field.

The first-best solution to this problem is to *remove labour market rigidities*, the fundamental cause of high structural unemployment (Svensson, 1997, p. 104 and p. 109; Duval and Elmeskov, 2005, p. 5).[1] However, such a proposal could be regarded as rather naive from a public choice perspective which emphasises that labour market institutions, as an outcome of rational political choice, have to be *implemented in the loss function* of politicians.

Cross-country event studies are one approach to empirically examining the impact of monetary policy strategies on the degree of economic reform, but there are, however, severe limitations to this approach. The United States, for example, are a monetary union with labour market institutions that encourage a low natural rate of unemployment. The European Monetary System (EMS) commitment was extremely helpful in fostering the reform process in the Netherlands and Denmark, and the same holds for Austria under the DM peg (Hochreiter and Tavlas, 2005). In contrast, the UK and New Zealand experienced extensive labour market reforms without adhering to an international exchange rate arrangement. Hence, we choose an econometric analysis for a large sample of countries in order to include a variance between countries which would not be available if we concentrated entirely on the EMU irrevocably fixed exchange rate case. Thus we go beyond the EMU case studies by van Poeck and Borghijs (2001), Bertola and Boeri (2001), and IMF (2004) which are rare examples of empirical investigations in this field.[2]

The remainder of the chapter is structured as follows. The next section considers the question of whether EMU has fostered reform efforts in the countries of the euro area with strict reference to the more general relationship between monetary policy autonomy and structural reforms in open economies. We then consider the extension of monetary rules to the open economy case. In order to put the discussion on a more rational basis, we also obtain testable hypotheses concerning the impact of exchange rate flexibility on reforms. Panel estimates on the relationship between the exchange rate regime and the degree of reforms are then presented. The regressions also include a set of additional variables and extensive robustness checks, and the euro area countries are considered as a special case of irrevocably fixed exchange rates throughout the analysis. A final section summarises and draws some policy conclusions with respect to the case of EMU.

Theory: monetary policy autonomy and structural reforms, the case of European Monetary Union

The discussion of whether EMU has fostered reform efforts in the countries of the euro area, that is the relation between the degree of monetary policy autonomy and structural reforms, is characterised by a wide spectrum of conflicting views. We start with a sketch of the literature on monetary policy autonomy and reforms and throughout refer to a prominent example of the loss of monetary autonomy, the irrevocable fixing of exchange rates under European Monetary Union (EMU). In the run-up to EMU, a number of studies tried to assess the incentive effects of alternative monetary policy strategies on labour market reforms. According to the proponents of a liberal view, EMU, as a classical variant of a rule-based monetary policy, should have a disciplinary impact on national labour markets.[3] In the first place, EMU enhances the credibility of monetary policy and thereby lowers inflation expectations. Negative employment effects as a result of (too) high wage claims can no longer be accommodated by discretionary monetary policy. The responsibility of wage-setters for unemployment increases significantly, because they now negotiate not about nominal wages but about *real* wage growth. The responsibility for existing unemployment is more transparently assigned to the parties which negotiate the relative price of labour. In contrast, autonomous discretionary monetary policy makes it more difficult to remove market rigidities because there is still the option to solve or at least to shift the unemployment problem onto third parties, via an expansionary monetary policy.

Insofar as the single currency increases transparency, the costs of structural rigidities, as reflected in relative prices, become more evident. Lower trading costs and higher transparency jointly tend to foster competition in goods markets, which in turn reduces the available product market rents. If these rents are smaller, the incentive to resist reforms that prevent such rents from being captured is smaller as well.

Overall, the incentives for extensive reforms of goods, labour and capital markets increase under a regime of EMU, that is irrevocably fixed exchange rates.[4] If changes in monetary policy and the nominal exchange rate are not available, and if labour is immobile as is the case in most parts of the euro area, there is no option other than to undertake reforms in order to facilitate the market-based adjustment to shocks. Hence, credible currency pegging in general and EMU in particular has often been interpreted as a version of Mrs Thatcher's There-Is-No-Alternative (TINA) strategy.[5] In this chapter, we generalise this striking TINA argument empirically and extend it also to countries beyond the narrow focus of the euro area, which is what Duval and Elmeskov (2005), for instance, concentrate on.

However, there are also important arguments against a positive impact of monetary rules on economic reform which can be applied to EMU as a specific monetary rule as well. First, based on OECD macro-model simulations it was often argued with respect to EMU that the so-called up-front costs of structural reforms may be larger within a currency union. This holds especially for large and relatively closed countries for which changes in the real exchange rate by a period of low inflation are not so effective in alleviating the necessary 'crowding-in' effect. Removing restrictions in financial markets tends to stimulate demand more than labour market reforms and hence allows an easier and quicker 'crowding-in' of reforms (Bean, 1998; Duval and Elmeskov, 2005, pp. 10–12; Saint-Paul and Bentolila, 2000). Hence, the prior in this case would be that rule-based monetary policy regimes, like EMU, lead to more reforms in the financial market than in the labour market. This argument appears to have a special bearing for EMU, since there is clear evidence that France as a large country has experienced less reforms since the start of EMU than, for instance, the Netherlands as a small euro area member country.

Second, Calmfors (1997) and Sibert and Sutherland (1997) argue that one should not expect monetary policy with its mainly short-run real economy effects to diminish structural unemployment in the euro area significantly. Hence, rule-based monetary policy induced by EMU does not necessarily imply more reform pressure for a euro area member country. In the same line, empirical analysis indicates that the capability of exchange rates to absorb asymmetric shocks to labour and goods markets is rather low in the euro area. Hence, the flexibility of intra-European exchange rates does not seem to be a good substitute for reforms and so the degree of reforms is not necessarily higher under fixed intra-European exchange rates (Belke and Gros, 1999).

Third, some analysts support the view that rule-based monetary policy, at least if it takes effect through entry into an irrevocably fixed exchange rate regime like EMU, has no disciplinary effects on the wage-setting process, but leads to centralisation processes and strengthens the incentives to claim high wages on the part of unions. In a game-theoretic setting, Cukierman and Lippi (1998) assess the interaction between central bank independence and the degree of centralisation of wage negotiations and the effects on inflation and employment. In contrast to the traditional time-inconsistency literature it is assumed that, to an extent which depends on the degree of centralisation, unions tend to internalise the effects of their decisions on the decision process of central bankers with respect to inflation. A diminishing degree of centralisation as implied by the start of EMU reduces the extent to which unions take the strategic effects of their actions into consideration. That is why highly centralised wage-setting parties produce relatively low real wages and low natural unemployment if the central bank pursues a discretionary regime. The reason is that unions do not have to fear that high wage claims are compensated by high inflation rates.

Fourth, the limited evidence of price structure convergence, for instance among core-EMS or EMU countries as compared with other countries, speaks against any significant impact of credible exchange rate stabilisation on product-market competition. Hence, there are still product-market rents to be captured and there will still be resistance to reforms (Haffner *et al.*, 2000).

From these introductory remarks it should be clear that the implementation of specific monetary policy rules, for instance by EMU, significantly changes the conditions for and the efficiency of structural reforms. The usual result of this strand of literature is that under EMU, interpreted as a monetary rule from the perspective of the individual member countries, there will be a lower degree of reforms than under autonomous monetary policy outside EMU, where reforms reduce both unemployment and the inflation bias. In contrast, rule-based monetary policy inside EMU limits the benefits of reforms to a positive impact on employment (Calmfors, 1997, 1998; Gruener and Hefeker, 1996; and Ozkan, Sibert and Sutherland, 1997).

Hence, our central empirical question relates to the correlation between reform intensity and the degree of autonomy of monetary policy, which might be determined to a large degree by the exchange rate regime, at least if the country is small and open (Duval and Elmeskov, 2005 p. 9 and pp. 23 *ff.*). Again, we regard EMU as an important sub-case. We focus on the notion of monetary policy autonomy instead of discretion since we consider autonomy outside EMU as an important prerequisite of discretionary monetary policy. In this respect, our approach strictly follows Duval and Elmeskov (2005, p. 25) who measure the loss of autonomy of monetary policy by the degree of participation in any kind of fixed exchange rate agreement.

More specifically, we will test the following hypotheses:

1 The degree of reforms turns out to be higher in the case of monetary policy autonomy than under a monetary policy rule.
2 This should be valid not only for labour market reforms but also for complementary reforms in the goods and financial markets.
3 However, if the TINA view of exchange rate fixing as a hard constraint is valid, one should expect the contrary, namely a positive impact of a monetary policy rule on the extent of reforms.

The open economy case

Economic openness generally relates to the share of exports and imports in GDP. A stronger exposure of firms to international competition is often assumed to increase the pressure and the incentives for market-oriented reforms. In open economies, output and employment tend to be highly responsive to price competitiveness and, hence, incentives to undertake reforms are large (see for example, Katzenstein, 1985; and Nickell, 2005, pp. 2–3). However, empirical evidence is, surprisingly, not especially supportive of the view that open economies are more likely to liberalise. Although Pitlik and Wirth (2003) report a positive impact of economic openness on market-oriented reforms, Herz and Vogel (2005) and Pitlik (2004) do not find robust significant coefficients of economic openness for their summary indicator. Only the trade policy indicator points to a positive effect of economic openness on liberalisation. Similarly, the constitutional requirements of political decision-making influence the feasibility of policy changes. However, the previous section indicates a possible solution to this puzzle. The key insight is that more open economies are more likely to implement rule-based exchange rate stabilisation and, hence, generally implement less reforms. Table 8. 1 illustrates this empirical relation between economic openness and exchange rate policy. Exchange rate flexibility is measured on a scale from one (hard peg) to four (free float). The

Table 8.1 Economic openness and exchange rate regimes, 1970–2000

Degree of openness (trade/ GDP)	*Average*	*Median*	*Observations*
< 0.25	2.65	2.93	60
0.25–0.75	2.27	2	471
0.75–1.25	1.98	2	200
> 1.25	1.51	1	59

Sources: The data on exchange rate flexibility are taken from Reinhart and Rogoff (2002). We measure economic openness as the sum of exports plus imports relative to GDP). The data are extracted from the *World Development Indicators* database (World Bank, 2002).

average and median statistics indicate that less-open economies tend to have relatively flexible exchange rate regimes, whereas very open economies tend to favour currency fixes.

We continue to assume that the main aim of reforms is to lower structural unemployment, but use the term monetary policy rule in a more general fashion, as comprising both monetary and exchange rate policy. Following this notation, we equate the case of flexible exchange rates with the case of autonomous and discretionary monetary policy and use the notion of a fixed exchange rate system in cases which we originally addressed as rule-based monetary policy. But is it legitimate to generalise in this way, that is to interpret our model in terms of exchange rate regimes instead of monetary policy regimes?

As a stylised fact, the amount of money in an open economy with a non-flexible exchange rate is not determined autonomously by the central bank but is determined endogenously by the exchange rate regime (see for example Annett, 1993, p. 25; Krugman and Obstfeld, 2003, chapters 16 and 17). From early political business-cycle research it is well-known that especially in the case of small open economies there is little evidence of rational partisan cycles (rational partisan theory, RPT), that is high and increasing inflation rates under left-wing governments and low and diminishing inflation rates under right-wing regimes.[6] In the standard literature, the failure to establish partisan cycles is generally traced back to the fact that small open economies tend to have fixed exchange rates and, hence, the ability of these countries to exert an ideologically motivated impact on the inflation rate is limited.[7] If the limited degree of monetary policy autonomy under fixed exchange rates is raised by the adoption of a flexible exchange rate regime, there is more scope for partisan-oriented monetary policies. Wage negotiating parties tend to anticipate and account for different preferences of political parties only if exchange rates are flexible. It is only in this case that incumbent governments are able to manipulate the inflation rate by monetary and exchange rate policies. Hence, higher inflation rates under left-wing governments induced by a dynamic inconsistency problem can arise only if exchange rates are flexible.[8]

A second argument underpins this view. Assume the existence of an international business cycle. In more open economies partisan considerations that arise at the domestic level are more likely to affect policy-makers' incentives to engage in international cooperation. Left-wing governments cannot credibly commit themselves to international cooperation and prefer beggar-thy-neighbour policies so that the inflation bias of left-wing governments is stronger in open economies. International cooperation, for example by fixed exchange rate arrangements, tends to eliminate the inflation bias via the same mechanism (Lohmann, 1993, pp. 1374 *ff.*). The final argument in favour of our approach is that the hypothesis of a loss of monetary autonomy under fixed exchange rates rests on the assumption of perfect international capital mobility. This mobility has increased since the start of the 1970s, the beginning of the time period investigated in this chapter.

Empirical studies of the rational partisan theory clearly show that – assuming a monetary model of the exchange rate – party-specific trajectories of money growth and inflation rates go along with proportional movements of the exchange rate. For instance, left-wing governments are more likely to experience inflation, capital flight, current account deficits and currency devaluation.[9] Hence, we feel justified to equate a flexible exchange rate system with a regime of autonomous and discretionary monetary policy and a system of fixed exchange rates with a rule-based monetary policy regime. From this point of view, our previous arguments that have been elaborated for the concepts 'rule-based versus discretionary monetary policy' can be transferred to those of 'fixed versus flexible exchange rate systems' and can be tested empirically in a straightforward fashion.

Empirical analysis

Hypotheses

After developing the theoretical arguments we now turn to our empirical analysis. We investigate the existence of a significantly positive correlation between exchange rate flexibility and market liberalisation, and control for other potential determinants of economic reform such as the macroeconomic environment and political or institutional impediments. Hence, we test for a significant coefficient on our measure of exchange rate flexibility in regressions using reform indices as the dependent variable, and then check the robustness of the results. We suggest the following hypotheses:

1. If it is true that monetary policy autonomy encourages reform, the degree of reforms should be higher under more flexible exchange rates, net of other economic and political factors.
2. If the TINA view of exchange rate fixing as a structural constraint is valid, however, one should expect the contrary, namely a negative impact of exchange rate flexibility on the degree of economic reform, net of other factors.
3. If other factors, for example the initial need or pressure for reforms, dominate the relationship, the exchange rate regime should turn out to be less significant in our regressions.

Note that 1 to 3 should be valid not only for labour market reforms, but also for complementary structural reforms in goods and financial markets.

Data and definitions

We estimate and test the impact of the exchange rate regime on the degree of market-oriented reforms in a panel of 178 countries and a panel of

23 OECD economies.[10] Data are available for the period 1970 to 2000. However, the final years of the Bretton Woods system, which were characterised by significant capital controls and quite autonomous monetary policies, constitute a special experience that may bias our results. Therefore we only report and comment on estimates for the 1980–2000 interval.[11]

Our dependent variable (see Table 8.2) is the extent of economic liberalisation as measured by the Economic Freedom of the World (EFW) index and the sub-indices *money and banking system, government size, labour market, credit and business regulation* and *trade*, respectively (Gwartney and Lawson, 2003; Gwartney *et al.*, 2003). These indices range from one to ten, whereby a higher value corresponds to a higher level of economic freedom.[12] Positive changes therefore indicate market-oriented reforms. We thus focus on a wider, but also more aggregated reform database than Duval and Elmeskov (2005), who investigate data from five policy areas: unemployment benefit systems, labour taxes, employment protection legislation, product market regulation and retirement schemes.

Our discussion of the explanatory variables (see Table 8.2) focuses on the measure of exchange rate flexibility. Earlier we explained the linkage between monetary policy autonomy and participation in exchange rate agreements. Adopting the exchange-rate variable instead of any alternative monetary commitment indicator allows us to exploit a wider cross-country and time-series dataset than would be possible otherwise. Our analysis does not cover some of the idiosyncratic characteristics of currency unions compared to other fixed exchange-rate arrangements, however. The EMU exam-

Table 8.2 Data and variables

Variable	*Source*
Economic freedom summary indicator money and banking system government size market regulation trade liberalisation	Gwartney *et al.* (2003)
Exchange rate regime	Reinhart and Rogoff (2002)
Monetary commitment	Freytag (2005)
Inflation	OECD (2002), World Bank (2002)
Economic growth	OECD (2002), World Bank (2002)
Economic openness (trade/ GDP)	OECD (2002), World Bank (2002)
Political constraints (POLCON5)	Henisz (2000, 2002)
Number of government changes (GOVCHANGES)	Beck *et al.* (2001)

ple indicates that the adoption of a single currency makes the TINA argument emphasized earlier in the chapter more compelling than in the case of other, less irreversible exchange-rate regimes. With an eye on these arguments, we decided to employ the Reinhart and Rogoff (2002) index of *de facto* exchange rate arrangements.[13] Reinhart and Rogoff (2002) distinguish between exchange rate pegs (1), limited flexibility (2), managed floating (3), and freely floating (4).[14] Thus, the higher the index value the higher is the *de facto* flexibility of exchange rates. For our purpose and due to the time structure of the EFW data, we average the Reinhart and Rogoff (2002) index values over five-year intervals.

The additional control variables that we consider include inflation, economic growth and openness as proxies of the pressure to reform. Data are available from the *World Development Indicators* database (World Bank, 2002). Economic openness is defined as exports plus imports relative to GDP. To account for the potential endogeneity and in accordance with other contributions (for example Herz and Vogel, 2005; Lora, 2000; Pitlik, 2004; Pitlik and Wirth, 2003), we include these variables in first lags. A final set of controls accounts for political and institutional barriers to reforms of economic policy. Here we include POLCON5 and the number of government changes. POLCON5 (Henisz, 2000, 2002) measures the effective political restrictions on executive behavior. It accounts for the veto powers of the executive, two legislative chambers, the sub-national entities and an independent judiciary. The index ranges from zero to one, where a higher value indicates stronger political constraints on government. Given the dependent variable's time structure, we use POLCON5 average values for the respective five-year intervals. GOVCHANGES counts the number of government changes that entail a significant programmatic reorientation. The data are taken from Beck *et al.* (2001) and account for the idea that frequent government changes may reduce the credibility, the reliability and the long-term orientation of economic policy.

Empirical model

To investigate the impact of monetary commitment, economic crises and institutional characteristics on economic reform, we estimate the equation:

$$\Delta EFW_{it} = \alpha_0 + \alpha_1 EFW_{i,t-1} + \alpha_2 EXR_{i,t-1} + \alpha_3{}' X_{i,t-1} + \alpha_4{}' Y_{i,t-1} + \eta_i + \lambda_t + \varepsilon_{it}$$

where ΔEFW represents our index of reforms, that is the change in economic freedom. EXR is our measure of exchange rate flexibility, X is the vector of macroeconomic variables (growth, inflation, openness), Y captures the political and institutional determinants of the capacity to reform, and i is a country index. Most importantly, and according to the Calmfors view, we expect $\alpha_2 > 0$ to hold, if a high degree of exchange rate flexibility leads to more reforms (see our earlier discussion). However, we should obtain the contrary, namely $\alpha_2 < 0$, if the TINA view holds. We add country-specific (η_i) and time-specific effects

(λ_t) to account for unobserved heterogeneity across countries and across time and to capture the systematic impact of omitted variables on economic reforms. The short time dimension of our sample complicates the use of fixed effects, however. There are at most six observations per country. Consequently, any estimate of the individual effects would be very imprecise, while significantly reducing the degrees of freedom.

A common approach to circumvent this problem is to estimate a within-group transformation (see for example Pitlik, 2004; Pitlik and Wirth, 2003). The within transformation considers differences from the respective country average, and as a result country dummies and time-invariant indicators drop out (Baltagi, 1995; Hsiao, 2003). The flip side of the within-transformation is that it neglects the cross-sectional information in the data. It disregards the impact of time-invariant cross-sectional differences on the dependent variable. Therefore we also report pooled OLS estimates without country-specific effects. Pooled OLS exploits the cross-sectional information in our sample, but estimates may be subject to the omitted variable bias.

Results

In the following we present and comment on the regression results for the broad country sample and the sample of high-income OECD economies, respectively. We report the estimates for overall liberalisation, money and banking system, government size, market regulation and freedom to trade as the dependent variables. Tables 8.3 to 8.7 display the results from both OLS-within and pooled OLS without country fixed effects for the sample period 1980–2000.

The dominant and most robust result is the negative impact of the initial level of economic freedom on the extent of subsequent market-oriented reforms in all regressions. The higher the initial level of economic freedom the lower are the scope and the need for further liberalisation and the higher is conditional policy convergence (Duval and Elmeskov, 2005, p. 23 *ff*). We are mainly interested in the impact of the exchange rate system on market-oriented reforms, however. For our world sample, we find a robust negative impact of exchange rate flexibility on overall liberalisation, as measured by the chain-linked *EFW* index (Table 8.3). The pooled OLS estimates for money and banking sector reform in Table 8.4 partly confirm the robust negative link between exchange rate flexibility and overall economic reform in the broad dataset. For government size we obtain a significantly negative coefficient for the unconditional OLS-within specification in Table 8.5 (column 1), whereas exchange rate flexibility does not have any significant impact on world-wide market regulation reform (Table 8.6). Thus, the world sample estimates provide some evidence for the TINA view of a positive impact of exchange-rate fixity on structural reforms, and against the theoretical arguments earlier in the chapter which suggested a positive impact of exchange-rate flexibility on economic liberalisation.

Table 8.3 Panel estimates for overall liberalisation, 1980–2000

	World sample				*OECD*			
	OLS within		*OLS pooled*		*OLS within*		*OLS pooled*	
***EXR* flexibility**	**–0.20*****	**–0.08*****	**–0.07****	**–0.08*****	–0.09	–0.11	0.03	**0.04***
	(–2.72)	(–2.65)	(–2.21)	(–2.65)	(–1.14)	(–1.20)	(1.05)	(1.85)
EFW (*t*–1)	**–0.62*****	**–0.64*****	**–0.17*****	**–0.30*****	–0.53***	**–0.57*****	**–0.24*****	**–0.24*****
	(–10.3)	(–10.7)	(–7.96)	(–10.7)	(–6.05)	(–5.14)	(–7.45)	(–4.56)
Inflation (*t*–1)		0.01		0.01		–0.57		0.97**
		(0.47)		(0.25)		(–0.69)		(2.40)
Growth (*t*–1)		0.94		0.27		–4.52		–3.19
		(1.21)		(0.30)		(–1.30)		(–1.26)
Openness (*t*–1)		0.29		0.14		–0.32		0.10
		(0.64)		(1.35)		(–0.39)		(1.29)
POLCON5		**1.13*****		**0.84*****		**1.13****		0.38
		(4.89)		(6.42)		(2.34)		(0.77)
GOVCHANGES		**–0.13*****		**–0.07***		–0.01		–0.03
		(–2.59)		(–1.84)		(–0.19)		(–0.84)
Constant			1.08***	1.47***			1.60***	1.27***
			(7.39)	(8.01)			(7.29)	(3.35)
Time effects (χ^2)	111.4***	68.16***	73.04***	60.45***	26.79***	23.66***	37.59***	43.51***
R^2	0.40	0.47	0.24	0.33	0.41	0.45	0.33	0.39
Observations	397	370	400	375	90	90	90	90

Note: *t*-values in parentheses, significance levels: 10% *, 5% **, 1% ***.

The OECD sub-sample results differ from our world sample regressions, however. The coefficients for the exchange-rate regime are insignificant at conventional significance levels in most cases. For both overall and government sector reform we obtain one significantly positive coefficient on exchange-rate flexibility out of two pooled OLS specifications (Tables 8.3 and 8.5). As mentioned above, these results may suffer from an omitted variable bias. Additionally, the within and pooled coefficient estimates differ in sign. Only for market liberalisation (Table 8.6) does the OECD sample exhibit a positive coefficient on exchange rate flexibility in all regression specifications – in line with the Calmfors view. It is statistically significant at 10 per cent in two out of four specifications.

How can we reconcile the different findings for the overall index and the sub-indices as well as the differences in the estimates of the world sample and the OECD countries? One candidate explanation is that the positive impact of fixed exchange rates on market-oriented reforms is mainly driven by its positive impact on price stability and the credibility of monetary policy. The significantly negative estimate for exchange rate flexibility in the pooled OLS regressions for monetary and banking reform in the world sample (Table 8.4) lends some support to this hypothesis and to our prior discussion earlier in the chapter. The significantly negative impact of flexibility on trade liberalisation (Table 8.7) is another important driver of the overall result. From our OECD sub-sample we conclude that the exchange rate regime has no significant impact on the amount of economic liberalisation in high-income industrialised countries. Only the robustness and partial significance of the exchange-rate variable in the market-regulation regressions provide some evidence for a positive impact of exchange-rate flexibility on labour and product market reform in this group of countries.

Taken together, the insignificant or negative parameter estimates for the impact of exchange-rate flexibility on overall liberalisation and its sub-indicators contradict the hypothesis that the exchange-rate flexibility has a positive impact on structural reforms, that is contradict the TINA view, in our world sample. The evidence for the OECD economies, however, lends some support to the idea that exchange-rate flexibility positively affects the extent of market deregulation within this group of industrialised countries. With regard to the additional control variables we find a significantly negative impact of the initial levels of economic freedom on subsequent liberalisation. The results also suggest a positive impact of political constraints on liberalisation, and for the world sample we obtain a negative impact of frequent government changes on overall economic reforms and on money and banking sector liberalisation. Herz and Vogel (2005) and Pitlik (2004) provide a more detailed exposition and discussion of similar results within a different model context.

Table 8.4 Panel estimates for money and banking, 1980–2000

	World sample				*OECD*			
	OLS within		*OLS pooled*		*OLS within*		*OLS pooled*	
***EXR* flexibility**	–0.28	–0.11	**–0.31*****	**–0.35*****	–0.15	–0.28	0.01	–0.03
	(–1.45)	(–0.67)	(–4.03)	(–5.22)	(–0.68)	(–1.09)	(0.14)	(–0.45)
M (*t*–1)	**–0.75*****	**–0.67*****	**–0.29*****	**–0.34*****	–0.58***	**–0.81*****	**–0.43*****	**–0.66*****
	(–11.2)	(–10.9)	(–9.57)	(–9.25)	(–5.01)	(–6.36)	(–9.78)	(–6.73)
Inflation (*t*–1)		0.10***		0.06***		–7.75***		–5.09**
		(5.55)		(3.80)		(–3.30)		(–3.01)
Growth (*t*–1)		8.24***		8.53***		–3.50		–0.13
		(3.77)		(4.01)		(–0.30)		(–0.02)
Openness (*t*–1)		1.51		0.13		–0.69		0.05
		(1.60)		(0.57)		(–0.31)		(0.25)
POLCON5		**1.17***		**1.31*****		**3.57*****		2.74***
		(1.67)		(4.85)		(3.88)		(4.47)
GOVCHANGES		**–0.57*****		**–0.19***		–0.04		0.01
		(–3.83)		(–1.71)		(–0.16)		(0.08)
Constant			2.60***	2.48***			3.44***	3.65***
			(8.32)	(6.72)			(7.87)	(5.05)
Time effects (χ^2)	49.02***	34.60***	37.42***	26.29***	17.10***	8.725**	14.75***	11.13**
R^2	0.44	0.48	0.23	0.32	0.41	0.45	0.45	0.49
Observations	401	371	403	376	90	90	90	90

Note: *t*-values in parentheses, significance levels: 10% *, 5% **, 1% ***.

Table 8.5 Panel estimates for government size, 1980–2000

	World sample				*OECD*			
	OLS within		*OLS pooled*		*OLS within*		*OLS pooled*	
***EXR* flexibility**	–0.16*	–0.10	0.02	0.01	–0.10	–0.10	0.13*	0.11
	(–1.86)	(–1.31)	(0.46)	(0.21)	(–0.99)	(–1.08)	(1.69)	(1.48)
G (*t*–1)	–0.80***	–0.82***	–0.22***	–0.22***	–0.55***	–0.56***	–0.15**	–0.15***
	(–11.4)	(–11.1)	(–6.76)	(–5.64)	(–15.0)	(–9.20)	(–2.49)	(–2.87)
Inflation (*t*–1)		0.01		0.01		0.55		**2.10****
		(0.23)		(0.29)		(0.58)		(2.34)
Growth (*t*–1)		–2.88**		–2.25		–6.55		–7.49*
		(–2.14)		(–1.33)		(–1.17)		(–1.82)
Openness (*t*–1)		0.54		–0.08		–1.78		–0.07
		(1.21)		(–0.53)		(–1.00)		(–0.46)
POLCON5		**0.76****		0.11		**3.36*****		0.46
		(2.40)		(0.72)		(5.26)		(0.83)
GOVCHANGES		–0.09		–0.02		–0.09		–0.06
		(–1.26)		(–0.36)		(–1.02)		(–0.81)
Constant			1.03***	1.16***			0.33	0.12
			(4.59)	(3.98)			(1.28)	(0.24)
Time effects (χ^2)	45.77***	24.14***	21.66***	15.01***	11.12**	3.716	9.308**	9.220**
R^2	0.47	0.52	0.16	0.16	0.36	0.45	0.14	0.22
Observations	385	369	392	374	90	90	90	90

Note: *t*-values in parentheses, significance levels: 10% *, 5% **, 1% ***.

Robustness checks

Tables 8.3 to 8.7 report OLS-within and pooled OLS estimates for five different reform indices and the world and OECD country samples. Both the within and pooled OLS estimator do not account for the dynamic structure of the regression equation and the possible endogeneity of contemporary explanatory variables. The presence of a lagged dependent variable and the possible endogeneity of other explanatory variables violate the assumption of strict exogeneity in static panel regressions (see Baltagi, 1995; Hsiao, 2003, for a detailed discussion). The endogeneity of explanatory variables potentially applies to both the exchange-rate commitment and the political variables. The idea of reverse causation is most obvious for the macroeconomic indicators. That is the reason for which our analysis includes them at one lag. Economic crises affect economic policy, but economic policy also impacts on economic performance. Reverse causation may concern the stability of government and the number of effective veto players, however.

We therefore reran the regressions with the Arellano and Bond (1991) IV-GMM estimator. IV-GMM deals with individual fixed effects and endogeneity; it estimates the equation in first differences and with lagged values of the regressors as instruments (Baltagi, 1995; Hsiao, 2003). As in the OLS-within, the differencing disregards the cross-sectional information in the data. Secondly, the time dimension of our sample is rather short, which strongly limits the availability of lagged values to instrument the regressors. We used the IV-GMM as a robustness check for the world-wide sample. The results are similar to our OLS estimates, replicating the negative impact of exchange-rate flexibility on overall liberalisation and trade liberalisation and the insignificant estimates on the exchange-rate coefficient for the sub-areas' government size and market regulation. It is only the exchange-rate impact on money and banking sector reform that becomes insignificant at conventional levels.[15]

The empirical analysis equates the exchange-rate regime with monetary commitment or autonomy (discretion). Exchange-rate flexibility indicates autonomy and a discretionary monetary policy, while an exchange-rate fix represents the adoption of a monetary rule. Monetary commitment does not require a fixed exchange rate, however. We therefore check the robustness of our results with an alternative indicator of monetary commitment due to Freytag (2005). The latter combines different dimensions of central bank independence and monetary commitment, such as the personal and political independence of monetary policy, the price-level stabilisation objective, lending restrictions for the central bank and the submission to an exchange-rate target. It measures monetary commitment on a scale from zero to one. The higher the value the higher the degree of monetary commitment. The indicator is available only for a small number of countries that basically coincide with the 23 high-income OECD economies. As the indicator is available only at the frequency of decades, the sample shrinks to three observations per country.[16]

Table 8.6 Panel estimates for market regulation, 1980–2000

	World sample				*OECD*			
	OLS within		*OLS pooled*		*OLS within*		*OLS pooled*	
EXR flexibility	–0.06 (–0.68)	–0.02 (–0.27)	–0.02 (–0.56)	–0.00 (–0.02)	0.12* (1.92)	0.06 (0.74)	0.07 (1.52)	0.09* (1.73)
R (*t*–1)	–0.77*** (–11.7)	–0.72*** (–9.22)	–0.20*** (–5.99)	–0.27*** (–8.48)	–0.77*** (–7.62)	–0.84*** (–8.02)	–0.19*** (–3.63)	–0.21*** (–3.37)
Inflation (*t*–1)		0.03 (0.86)		0.05 (1.56)		–0.79 (–1.28)		0.31 (0.93)
Growth (*t*–1)		–0.11 (–0.10)		0.18 (0.23)		–5.65* (–1.92)		–7.33*** (–3.45)
Openness (*t*–1)		0.02 (0.04)		**0.21*** (1.81)		–1.13 (–0.96)		0.09 (1.07)
POLCON5		0.31 (1.11)		**0.71***** (6.64)		**–1.07**** (–2.20)		0.04 (0.10)
GOVCHANGES		–0.06 (–1.12)		–0.02 (–0.47)		0.09 (0.96)		–0.06 (–1.38)
Constant			1.06*** (5.06)	1.04*** (4.96)			1.03*** (3.89)	1.21** (2.58)
Time effects (χ^2)	109.1***	97.07***	124.0***	87.75***	201.8***	179.6***	130.1***	139.0**
R^2	0.51	0.51	0.29	0.38	0.73	0.76	0.57	0.60
Observations	376	351	381	357	90	90	90	90

Note: *t*-values in parentheses, significance levels: 10% *, 5% **, 1% ***.

Table 8.7 Panel estimates for trade liberalisation, 1980–2000

	World sample				*OECD*			
	OLS within		*OLS pooled*		*OLS within*		*OLS pooled*	
***EXR* flexibility**	–0.30*	–0.37***	–0.03	–0.07	–0.25	–0.27	–0.09***	–0.13***
	(–1.93)	(–3.07)	(–0.55)	(–1.53)	(–1.25)	(–1.30)	(–3.32)	(–3.67)
T (*t*–1)	–0.75***	–0.80***	–0.26***	–0.39***	–0.54***	–0.64***	–0.25***	–0.35***
	(–11.6)	(–10.6)	(–6.16)	(–8.79)	(–5.42)	(–6.85)	(–6.13)	(–8.26)
Inflation (*t*–1)		0.05		0.01		**–1.97***		**–1.20***
		(1.61)		(0.42)		(–1.95)		(–1.88)
Growth (*t*–1)		–3.22*		–2.37		–1.85		–1.92
		(–1.73)		(–1.58)		(–0.37)		(–0.61)
Openness (*t*–1)		–0.86		0.15		–1.30		–0.03
		(–1.46)		(1.04)		(–1.01)		(–0.38)
POLCON5		1.05***		1.13***		3.26***		1.42**
		(2.68)		(5.34)		(4.48)		(2.31)
GOVCHANGES		–0.06		–0.08		–0.10		–0.07
		(–0.65)		(–1.23)		(–1.21)		(–1.48)
Constant			1.53***	2.07***			2.31***	2.28***
			(5.73)	(6.68)			(6.70)	(4.98)
Time effects (χ^2)	61.53***	40.12***	30.10***	28.21***	17.81***	5.34	10.8**	6.30*
R^2	0.47	0.55	0.24	0.33	0.37	0.46	0.32	0.36
Observations	362	344	372	352	90	90	90	90

Note: *t*-values in parentheses, significance levels: 10% *, 5% **, 1% ***.

Table 8.8 displays the OLS-within estimates for this measure of monetary commitment. Monetary commitment is statistically insignificant in the regression for overall liberalisation. Conditional on the other variables, it has a negative impact on *government sector* reform, whereas the positive impact on *market regulation* becomes insignificant when we introduce additional control variables. The relation between monetary commitment and reforms in the *money and banking sector* is robust and significantly positive. The positive sign indicates that, on average, monetary commitment favours the implementation of structural reforms in banking and financial markets. The positive or insignificant coefficient for the impact of monetary commitment on *market regulation* contradicts the estimates for OECD economies in Table 8.6 that point to a positive impact of exchange-rate flexibility on market liberalisation.

We can now summarise the main results of our analysis about the impact of exchange rate commitment on economic reform: The adoption of an exchange rate rule is positively correlated with market-oriented reforms in general, and with trade policy as well as money and banking sector reforms in our broad country sample. We do not find a robust significant effect for government sector or market regulation reform, however. Presumably, it is the positive impact of exchange-rate commitment on trade liberalisation and on the money and banking sector that drives the positive impact on market-oriented reforms in general. The OECD sample does not indicate any significant relationship between the exchange-rate regime and overall structural reforms, money and banking-sector reform and the change in government size. It points to a positive impact of exchange-rate commitment on trade liberalisation and to a positive relationship between exchange-rate flexibility and product and labour-market reform. The latter result is not robust against the alternative monetary commitment indicator of Freytag (2005). This indicator gives a positive impact of commitment on market liberalisation for a similar country sample. Taken together our results do not show a robust and significantly positive impact of exchange-rate flexibility or monetary discretion on structural reforms. Hence, they do not confirm the theoretical implications of the Calmfors-type model presented earlier in the chapter.

Conclusions

In this chapter, we were interested in examining the effect of EMU on structural reform and we investigated this by an examination of the relationship between fixed exchange rates and reform in two wider samples of countries. Our results indicate that – in the context of OECD countries and with respect to reform beyond money and banking – EMU should not have been clearly expected to encourage structural reform.

We estimated and tested the relationship between exchange rate regimes and the degree of economic reforms by estimating panel regressions. As

Table 8.8 OLS-within estimates with monetary-commitment indicator

	EFW		*Money and banking*		*Government size*		*Market regulation*		*Trade policy*	
Monetary commitment	0.65 (1.26)	0.36 (1.07)	**2.69*** (1.81)	**2.54**** (2.32)	–1.17 (–1.31)	**–1.59*** (–1.95)	**0.73**** (2.16)	0.58 (1.56)	0.72 (0.60)	0.70 (0.65)
EFW, M, G, *R* (*t*–1)	**–0.70***** (–3.66)	**–0.51***** (–3.12)	**–0.97***** (–7.28)	**–0.65***** (–2.76)	**–0.71***** (–7.33)	**–0.61***** (–5.73)	**–0.84***** (–5.89)	**–0.91***** (–6.51)	**–1.15***** (–8.51)	**–1.21***** (–12.0)
Inflation (*t*–1)		**3.90***** (3.11)		**11.2**** (2.52)		**4.84*** (1.81)		0.23 (0.11)		0.79 (0.33)
Growth (*t*–1)		**7.41**** (2.42)		**20.0**** (2.28)		2.68 (0.42)		4.72 (1.25)		–3.16 (–0.53)
Openness (*t*–1)		–0.93 (–1.60)		**–4.04*** (–1.77)		–0.08 (–0.10)		0.56 (0.51)		–2.72 (–1.41)
POLCON5		0.87 (1.23)		0.73 (0.28)		**3.30**** (2.09)		–1.05 (–1.39)		**3.16*** (1.79)
GOVCHANGES		0.09 (1.24)		0.46 (1.57)		0.11 (0.49)		0.14 (1.23)		0.18 (0.84)
Time effects (χ^2)	39.07***	72.40***	18.59***	11.52***	22.88***	46.26***	94.97***	55.73***	18.88***	17.66***
R^2	0.81	0.90	0.61	0.76	0.82	0.88	0.87	0.89	0.66	0.72
Observations	59	58	59	58	59	58	58	57	59	58

dependent variable we used the degree of market-oriented reforms. As independent variables we included indicators of the flexibility of the exchange-rate system, the stability of monetary policy and further control variables including economic performance as a proxy for reform pressure and institutional impediments to further reform. The results of our empirical analysis suggest that the adoption of an exchange-rate rule like EMU is positively correlated only with market-oriented reforms in a broad world sample, and with reforms in the money and banking sector in particular. For the government sector and for market regulation, we do not find a robust significant effect, however. The impact of exchange-rate policy on economic reforms is not significant in the sample of OECD countries. The use of an alternative indicator of monetary policy commitment supports these findings.

Overall, these results do *not* confirm the implications of our Calmfors-type model, namely that one should observe a higher degree of reforms under monetary policy autonomy, that is outside EMU. However, our empirical results at least partly confirm the TINA argument that limiting monetary policy autonomy (like a common monetary policy under EMU from the perspective of a single EMU member) tends to raise the probability of the implementation of structural reforms/liberalisation steps. The seemingly irrevocable elimination of the exchange-rate option seems to extend the incentives for painful but long-term beneficial institutional adjustments on labour and product markets for developing countries and emerging markets, but not for OECD countries. If one subsumes euro area countries among the latter, it becomes immediately clear that the disappointing EMU reform experience is totally consistent with our estimates.

Finally, the exchange-rate regime often turned out to be insignificant when we applied it to reforms in areas other than the money and banking system. Instead, the usual suspects like the so-called problem pressure variable, as measured by the initial degree of freedom, dominate the regressions with coefficients roughly around values of –0.50 at the 1-per cent level. These results imply that a higher initial level of economic freedom leads to a lower scope for further liberalisation and a higher conditional policy convergence. If the exchange-rate regime is significant, these coefficients are around three times as high as the coefficients measuring exchange-rate flexibility. In a sense, one could even argue that a change in a nominal variable, like the exchange-rate regime, appears to have effects mainly on other nominal variables like the monetary and banking system, a view often condemned as too pessimistic in the discussions during the run-up to the euro.

Hence, the upshot of our study is that one should not exaggerate the impact of monetary policy autonomy and the exchange-rate regime on economic freedom, given the large status-quo bias and path-dependence of reform intensity. There is no empirical basis for the argument that discretionary monetary policy is preferable because it gives more incentives for structural reforms. This insight probably represents the most robust result of this contribution.

From this perspective, our estimation results are strikingly similar to the huge amount of non-results which Duval and Elmeskov (2005) found for their sample of euro area countries. Moreover, our results are compatible with the widely held prior view that EMU was not at all important for incentives to reforms in Europe. They can also explain why the euro proved to be neither a job machine, nor a job killer as claimed by politicians before the start of EMU.

Any policy consequences which may emerge from the empirical results for the case of EMU have thus to be carefully interpreted with regard to credibility and commitment issues on the side of both the European Central Bank and the euro area governments responsible for reforms. Only to the extent that euro area governments can credibly commit to future reforms can the ECB support reform processes in advance without putting the price stability objective at risk. If this commitment on the side of the euro area governments is not possible, it is problematic for European monetary policy to react to mere reform announcements. In addition, policy conclusions have to pay attention to the specific scenario in the context of EMU where rather independent national reform players face one monetary actor.

Notes

1 OECD (2005) applies a consistent procedure to derive the policy priorities required to foster growth across OECD countries and identifies labour-market reforms as being particularly important in, for example, the euro area. However, this does not imply that reforms in other areas are unimportant. Hence, we analyse a variety of different reform measures in the empirical part of the chapter.

2 Van Poeck and Borghijs (2001) argue that the prospect of qualifying for EMU should provide as big an incentive for labour-market reform as EMU membership itself. They conclude that EMU countries did not reform more than other countries and, unlike elsewhere, their progress on reform seemed unrelated to the initial level of unemployment. For a period from the early 1990s up to 1999, Bertola and Boeri (2001) focus on cash transfers to people of working age, for example unemployment benefits, and on job protection. They arrive at exactly opposite conclusions; that is, reforms accelerated more in the euro area than outside. The IMF (2004) looks at the impact of a range of factors including macroeconomic conditions, political institutions, reform design and variables aimed to capture attitudes towards structural reform in different policy areas across OECD countries from the mid-1970s up to the late 1990s. It finds that EU membership leads to faster moves towards liberalisation of product markets. However, it does not clarify whether this represents an effect of EMU and/or of policies to prepare for EMU. See also Duval and Elmeskov (2005, p. 10).

3 For recent surveys of the arguments see Duval and Elmeskov (2005) and Hochreiter and Tavlas (2005).

4 See Alogoskoufis (1994), Calmfors (1997), Duval and Elmeskov (2005, p. 6), Mélitz (1997) and Sibert and Sutherland (1997).
5 See Bean (1998), Calmfors (1998, p. 28), Duval and Elmeskov (2005, p. 5) and Saint-Paul and Bentolila (2000).
6 Early sources are Alesina (1992, pp. 13–14), Alesina and Roubini (1992, p. 680) and Annett (1993, pp. 25 and 42).
7 See Alogoskoufis, Lockwood and Philippopoulos (1992, p. 1384) and Ellis and Thoma (1990, pp. 17 and 24).
8 See Alesina and Roubini (1992, pp. 673–4), Alogoskoufis and Philippopoulos (1992, p. 397), Alogoskoufis, Lockwood and Philippopoulos (1992, pp. 1370–1) and Annett (1993, pp. 25 and 33).
9 See Simmons (1994, p. 59). Ellis and Thoma (1990) estimate rational partisan theory approaches for open economies. In their study, party-specific inflation rates lead to party specific differences in exchange rate movements.
10 These 23 OECD economies correspond to the category 'high-income industrialized countries' in the *World Development Indicators* database (World Bank, 2002) and cover Australia, Canada, the former EU15, Iceland, Japan, New Zealand, Norway, Switzerland and the United States. The complete list of countries included in the world sample is available from the Frazer Institute web site at http://www.freetheworld.com/release.html.
11 Estimates for the full 1970–2000 sample give very similar results. They are available from the authors upon request.
12 We use the chain-weighted EFW index (Gwartney *et al.*, 2003), which corrects for the limited availability of some components over time. This chain-linked index is only available for the summary indicator, however. For the sub-areas government size and market regulation we have to rely on uncorrected data.
13 The *de facto* measure improves on the *de jure* classification of IMF (2003) since it takes into account the fact that *de jure* exchange rate regimes are not necessarily applied in practice. This has especially been the case in developing countries, but also in industrialised countries. Austria, for example, had a *de facto* fixed exchange rate regime *vis-à-vis* Germany for a long time without being a formal member of the exchange rate mechanism of the EMS. See Hochreiter and Tavlas (2005).
14 Reinhart and Rogoff (2002) include freely falling rates as an additional category. We add the cases of freely falling rates to the free-float category, however.
15 The results are available on request.
16 The correlation between the Reinhart and Rogoff (2002) exchange-rate classification and the Freytag (2005) indicator of monetary commitment is rather weak (–0.02). The correlation coefficient between the change in exchange-rate flexibility and the change in monetary commitment amounts to –0.27. Moving towards a more fixed exchange-rate regime increases the degree of monetary commitment.

References

Abiad, A. and A. Mody (2005) 'Financial Reform: What Shakes It? What Shapes It?', *American Economic Review*, 95: 66–88.

Akerlof, G., W. Dickens and G. Perry (1996) 'The Macroeconomics of Low Inflation', *Brookings Papers on Economic Activity*: 1–59.

Alesina, A. (1992) 'Political Models of Macroeconomic Policy and Fiscal Reform', *Policy Research Working Papers*, WPS 970, The World Bank.

Alesina, A. and H. Rosenthal (1989) 'Partisan Cycles in Congressional Elections and the Macroeconomy', *American Political Science Review*, 83: 373–98.

Alesina, A. and N. Roubini (1992) 'Political Cycles in OECD Economies', *Review of Economic Studies*, 59: 663–88.

Alogoskoufis, G.S. (1994) 'On Inflation, Unemployment and the Optimal Exchange Rate Regime', in F. van der Ploeg (ed.), *The Handbook of International Macroeconomics*. Oxford: Blackwell.

Alogoskoufis, G.S. and A. Philippopoulos (1992) 'Inflationary Expectations, Electoral Uncertainty and the Exchange Rate Regime – Greece 1958–1989', *European Journal of Political Economy*, 8: 375–99.

Alogoskoufis, G.S., B. Lockwood and A. Philippopoulos (1992) 'Wage Inflation, Electoral Uncertainty and the Exchange Rate Regime – Theory and UK Evidence', *Economic Journal*, 102: 1370–94.

Annett, A.M. (1993) 'Elections and Macroeconomic Outcomes in Ireland – 1948–1991', *Economic and Social Review*, 25: 21–47.

Arellano, M. and S. Bond (1991) 'Some Tests of Specification for Panel Data: Monte Carlo Evidence and an Application to Employment Equations', *Review of Economic Studies*, 58: 277–97.

Baltagi, B. (1995) *Econometric Analysis of Panel Data*, Chichester: John Wiley & Sons.

Bean, C. (1998) 'The Interaction of Aggregate-demand Policies and Labour-market Reform', *Swedish Economic Policy Review*, 5(2).

Beck, T., G. Clarke, A. Groff, P. Keefer and P. Walsh (2001) 'New Tools in Comparative Political Economy: The Database of Political Institutions', *World Bank Economic Review*, 15: 165–76.

Beetsma, R. and L. Bovenberg (1998) 'The Optimality of a Monetary Union Without a Fiscal Union', *CEPR Discussion Paper* no. 1975.

Belke, A. and D. Gros (1999) 'Estimating the Costs and Benefits of EMU: The Impact of External Shocks on Labour Markets', *Weltwirtschaftliches Archiv*, 135: 1–48.

Belke, A. and D. Gros (2001) 'Real Impacts of Intra-European Exchange Rate Variability: A Case for EMU?', *Open Economies Review*, 12: 231–64.

Belke, A. and A. Kamp (1999) 'When Do Labour Market Reforms Achieve a Double Dividend under EMU? Discretionary versus Rule Based Monetary Policy Revisited', *Journal of Economic Integration*, 14: 572–605.

Bertola, G. and T. Boeri (2001) 'EMU Labour Markets Two Years On: Microeconomic Tensions and Institutional Evolution, paper presented at the Workshop 'The Functioning of EMU: Challenges of the Early Years' organised by the Directorate General for Economic and Financial Affairs, European Commission, Brussels, 21–22 March 2001, 27 April 2001.

Calmfors, L. (1997) 'Unemployment, Labour-Market Reform and EMU', *IIES Seminar Paper* no. 639, Institute for International Economic Studies, Stockholm.

Calmfors, L. (1998) 'Macroeconomic Policy, Wage Setting and Employment – What Difference Does the EMU Make?', *Oxford Economic Policy Review*, 14: 125–51.

Calmfors, L. (2001) 'Unemployment, Labor-Market Reform and Monetary Union', *Journal of Labor Economics*, 19: 265–89.

Castrén, O., T. Takalo and G. Wood (2004) 'Labour Market Reform and the Sustainability of Exchange Rate Pegs', *ECB Working Paper Series* no. 406, European Central Bank, Frankfurt.

Cukierman, A. and F. Lippi (1998) 'Central Bank Independence, Centralisation of Wage Bargaining, Inflation and Unemployment – Theory and Evidence', *CEPR Discussion Paper* no. 1847, London.

Dornbusch, R. and C.A. Favero (1998) 'A Red Letter Day?', *CEPR Discussion Paper* no. 1804.
Duval, R. and J. Elmeskov (2005) 'The Effects of EMU on Structural Reforms in Labour and Product Markets', mimeo, paper prepared for the Conference on 'What Effects is EMU Having on the Euro Area and its Member Countries?' organised by the European Central Bank in Frankfurt.
Ellis, C.J. and M.A. Thoma (1990) 'The Implications for an Open Economy of Partisan Political Business Cycles: Theory and Evidence', University of Oregon. *Department of Economics Working Paper* no. 90/2.
Freytag, A. (2001) 'Does Central Bank Independence Reflect Monetary Commitment Properly? Methodical Considerations', *BNL Quarterly Review*, 217: 181–208.
Freytag, A. (2005) 'The Credibility of Monetary Reform: New Evidence', *Public Choice*, 124: 391–409.
Gruener, H.S. and C. Hefeker (1996) 'Militant Labour and Inflation Aversion – The Impact of EMU on Labour Union Interaction', University Bonn, *SFB 303 Discussion Paper A-539*.
Gwartney, J. and R. Lawson (2003) 'The Concept and Measurement of Economic Freedom', *European Journal of Political Economy*, 19: 405–30.
Gwartney, J., R. Lawson, W. Park and C. Skipton (2003) 'Economic Freedom of the World: 2003 Annual Report', Fraser Institute, Vancouver.
Haffner, R.C.G., S. Nickell, G. Nicoletti, S. Scarpetta and G. Zoega (2000) *European Integration, Liberalisation and Labour Market Performance*: Report for the Fondazione Rodolfo DeBenedetti.
Heinemann, F. (2004) 'Explaining Reform Deadlocks', *Applied Economics Quarterly Supplement*, 55: 9–26.
Heinemann, F. (2005) 'How Distant is Lisbon from Maastricht? The Short-run Link Between Structural Reforms and Budgetary Performance', mimeo, prepared for the DG ECFIN workshop 'Budgetary implications of structural reforms', Brussels, 2 December 2005.
Helbling, T., D. Hakura and X. Debrun (2004) 'Fostering Structural Reforms in Industrial Countries', *World Economic Outlook*, 103–46.
Henisz, W. (2000) 'The Institutional Environment for Economic Growth', *Economics and Politics*, 12: 1–31.
Henisz, W. (2002) 'The Institutional Environment for Infrastructure Investment', *Industrial and Corporate Change*, 11: 355–89.
Herz, B. and L. Vogel (2005) 'Determinants of Market-Oriented Policy Reforms: An Empirical Analysis', mimeo.
Hochreiter, E. and G.S. Tavlas (2005) 'The Two Roads to the Euro: The Monetary Experiences of Austria and Greece', in S. Schadler (ed.) *Euro Adoption in Central and Eastern Europe – Opportunities and Challenges*, Washington, DC: International Monetary Fund.
Hsiao, C. (2003) *Analysis of Panel Data*, Cambridge: Cambridge University Press.
IMF (2003) *International Financial Statistics*, CD-ROM, International Monetary Fund, Washington DC.
IMF (2004) 'Fostering Structural Reforms in Industrial Countries', ch. III, in *World Economic Outlook, Advancing Structural Reforms*, Washington DC: International Monetary Fund.
Johansson, A. (1998) 'The Interaction between Labour Market Policy and Monetary Policy: An Analysis of Time Inconsistency', mimeo, paper presented at the Institute for International Economic Studies Seminar in Stockholm, (April 1998).

Jimeno, J. (2005) 'Comments on Duval, R., Elmeskov, J. "*The Effects of EMU on Structural Reforms in Labour and Product Markets*"', paper prepared for the Conference on 'What Effects is EMU Having on the Euro Area and its Member Countries?' organised by the European Central Bank in Frankfurt, June 2005.

Jonsson, G. (1997) 'Monetary Politics and Unemployment Persistence' *Journal of Monetary Economics*, 39: 303–25.

Katzenstein, P. (1985) *Small States in World Markets*, Ithaca: Cornell University Press.

Krugman, P. and M. Obstfeld (2003) *International Economics – Theory and Policy*, Boston, Mass.: Addison-Wesley.

Lohmann, S. (1993) 'Electoral Cycles and International Policy Coordination', *European Economic Review*, 37: 1373–91.

Lora, E. (2000) 'What Makes Reforms Likely? Timing and Sequencing of Structural Reforms in Latin America', *Inter-American Development Bank Working Paper* 424, Washington.

Mélitz, J. (1997) 'The Evidence about the Costs and Benefits of EMU', *Swedish Economic Policy Review*, 4: 191–234.

Nicoletti, G., S. Golub, D. Hajkova, D. Mirza and K.-Y. Yoo (2003) 'Policies and International Integration: Influences on Trade and Foreign Direct Investment', *OECD Economics Department Working Papers* 359.

Nickell, S. (2005) 'Comments on Duval, R., Elmeskov, J. "The Effects of EMU on Structural Reforms in Labour and Product Markets"', mimeo, paper prepared for the Conference on 'What Effects is EMU Having on the Euro Area and its Member Countries?' organised by the European Central Bank in Frankfurt (June 2005).

OECD (2005) *Economic Policy Reforms. Going for Growth*, Paris: OECD.

Ozkan, F.G., A.C. Sibert and A. Sutherland (1997) 'Monetary Union, Entry Conditions and Economic Reform', *CEPR Discussion Paper* no. 1720, London.

Pitlik, H. and S. Wirth (2003) 'Do Crises Promote the Extent of Economic Liberalisation?', *European Journal of Political Economy*, 19: 565–581.

Pitlik, H. (2004) 'Are Less Constrained Governments Really More Successful in Executing Market-Oriented Policy Changes?', *Diskussionsbeiträge aus dem Institut für Volkswirtschaftslehre der Universität Hohenheim 255/2005*, University Hohenheim, Stuttgart.

Reinhart, C.M. and K.S. Rogoff (2002) 'The Modern History of Exchange Rate Regime Arrangements: A Reinterpretation', *NBER Working Paper* no. 8963, National Bureau of Economic Research. Cambridge, Mass.

Rodrik, D. (1996) 'Understanding Economic Policy Reform', *Journal of Economic Literature*, 34, 9–41.

Saint-Paul, G. and S. Bentolila (2000) 'Will EMU Increase Eurosclerosis? International Macroeconomics and Labour Economics', *CEPR Discussion Paper* no. 2423, London.

Sibert, A.C. and A. Sutherland (1997) 'Monetary Regimes and Labour Market Reform', *CEPR Discussion Paper* no. 1731, London.

Simmons, B.A. (1994) *Who Adjusts? – Domestic Sources of Foreign Economic Policy During the Interwar Years*, Princeton: Princeton University Press.

Svensson, L. (1997) 'Optimal Inflation Targets, "Conservative" Central Banks, and Linear Inflation Contracts', *American Economic Review*, 87, 98–114.

van Poeck, A. and A. Borghijs (2001) *EMU and Labour Market Reform: Needs, Incentives and Realisations*, Oxford: Blackwell Publishers.

World Bank (2002) *World Development Indicators*, Washington, DC: World Bank Publications.

Discussion

F. Gulcin Ozkan

It was widely acknowledged that high unemployment in a number of candidate countries in the run up to the formation of European Monetary Union (EMU) was one of the major challenges facing policy-makers. Most observers agreed that structural reform was essential in removing labour and product market distortions which brought about low labour force participation and low employment. Therefore, whether the realisation of monetary union would help or hinder structural reform in the participant countries has formed a crucial aspect of the debate on the desirability of EMU.

Motivated by the continuing significance of reforms in European economies, Belke, Herz and Vogel attempt to quantify the correlation between the degree of monetary autonomy and the reform effort in Europe. On a more theoretical level, this question can be re-phrased as: what is the role of monetary discipline as an incentive for structural reforms?

The findings of the two separate literatures – one on the time inconsistency of optimal monetary policies and the other on optimum currency areas – suggest that the answer to the above question depends critically on the relevance of inflationary bias *vis-à-vis* the possibility of monetary union member countries being hit by asymmetric shocks. In general, it is expected that monetary union would eliminate or reduce the inflationary bias thus reducing the incentive to carry out costly reform. On the other hand, it could be argued that when individual countries can no longer use their monetary instrument, as is the case under monetary union, there would be greater incentives for structural reforms in order to facilitate adjustment in the face of shocks. Therefore, depending upon which argument is more relevant in Europe, EMU might reduce or increase the possibility of reform in the member countries.

The authors adopt a roundabout way of testing this relationship for EMU by estimating the link between monetary discipline and the propensity to reform in a wider set of countries. They also consider a wider set of reforms including reforms of financial markets and product markets and a reduction in government size. In relating the reform propensity to the monetary regime, Belke *et al.* use another simplification. Instead of identifying the type of monetary framework, they use the type of exchange-rate regime as an indicator for this. Given that the greater the flexibility of the exchange rate, the greater the scope for monetary autonomy, a positive correlation between exchange-rate flexibility and reform intensity would support the view that reforms are slower under monetary unions. This relationship between exchange-rate flexibility and the reform effort is then tested in a sample of 23 OECD countries and 178 world countries for the period 1980–2000. Overall, they find some support for the role of discipline on the reform effort, but this support is not robust to varying samples or models.

The first important issue regarding the analysis in the paper is related to the way reform is defined. The authors utilise the 'Economic Freedom of the World' (EFW) index as their measure of the extent of economic liberalisation and the change in this index as a measure of reforms. Although obviously a rise in economic freedoms and liberalisation should indicate some kind of reform, it is questionable whether this would include the type of labour and product-market reforms that underpin much of the theoretical literature that establishes the relationship between the monetary regime and the incentive to reform. The fact that the significance of the exchange-rate flexibility variable varies considerably in explaining the changes in different types of reform indicates the relevance of this point. The authors do not address why the hypothesised relationship between monetary discipline and labour-market reforms should also hold for other types of reform.

A second issue regarding the estimation is related to the choice of the world sample of 178 countries. Given that the total number of countries in the world was about 200 in 2000, this sample must involve a large number of countries with potentially very diverse sets of economic and institutional structures. Unless these differences are accounted for, which is not obvious, one would worry about the potential implications for the estimated coefficients. This is especially the case given the level of generality used in defining the reform indices.

Another important issue is the potential implications of using exchange-rate flexibility as synonymous with monetary autonomy. It is possible for an individual country in the sample to be adopting some other form of nominal anchor such as monetary targeting or inflation targeting while operating under a flexible exchange rate regime. In the current framework these countries would be, wrongly, considered as having a lack of monetary discipline. The authors provide additional evidence by utilising other forms of monetary commitment in measuring monetary discipline as a robustness check for their main results. The change in the results highlights the importance of measuring monetary discipline appropriately.

What do these results imply for the incentives to reform in eurozone countries? If one needs to identify one of the samples as more relevant for

EMU members, it would obviously be the OECD sample. As the sign and the size of the coefficients of the monetary regime vary considerably in estimations using the OECD sample, it is not possible to confidently declare the direction of this relationship one way or the other.

Notwithstanding these concerns, this chapter studies an important relationship on which there is very little empirical work. Given that eurozone economies continue to be characterised by distortions that clearly affect their economic performance, understanding the determinants of reform efforts in these economies remains a highly relevant policy issue.

9

The Euro and Financial Integration

*Philip R. Lane and Sébastien Wälti**

Introduction

The goal of this chapter is to provide a quantitative review of the impact of European Monetary Union (EMU) on international financial integration. The degree of financial-market integration can be measured along several different dimensions and there is no widespread agreement about a single correct measure (Adam *et al.*, 2001; Baele *et al.*, 2004). *De jure* measures of financial market integration rely on the dating of financial-market liberalisations initiated by policy-makers. The effects of such liberalisation episodes are typically examined using event-study methodologies. *De facto* measures focus instead on the outcomes of such liberalisations. In so far as the impact of policy decisions will develop into outcomes gradually over time, it is likely that *de jure* and *de facto* measures will provide different views about the extent of financial-market integration. Moreover, *de facto* measures rely either on quantities, be it stocks or flows of equity, debt or foreign direct investment, or on asset prices or returns. Finally, some studies make use of conditional asset-pricing models and assess the relative importance of regional and local risk factors in explaining expected returns (Bekaert and Harvey, 1995; Hardouvelis *et al.*, 2006): a greater degree of market integration results when expected returns are increasingly explained by regional risk factors and less by local risk factors.

In this chapter, we consider both volume-based indicators of financial integration and the evidence from asset prices. We find that both approaches generally provide clear evidence that the launch of the euro has led to a remarkable degree of financial integration among the member

---

*Prepared for 'The Travails of the Eurozone' conference, Heriot-Watt University, 24 March 2006. We thank David Cobham, Robbie Mochrie and the conference participants for helpful comments. Email: plane@tcd.ie; waltis@tcd.ie. Agustin Benetrix and Vahagn Galstyan provided excellent research assistance. Lane thanks the IRCHSS and the HEA-PRTLI grant to the IIIS for financial support.

countries. However, we also argue that a parallel trend has been a contemporaneous increase in financial globalisation – financial linkages among all countries (inside and outside the euro area) have been growing rapidly in recent years – and that EMU has not been the only force shaping financial integration.

The structure of the rest of the chapter is as follows. First, we examine volume-based indicators of financial integration, before turning to an analysis of asset returns. The international financial role of the euro is then discussed, while some conclusions are offered in a final section.

Volume-based indicators of financial integration

In this section, we first discuss the impact of the euro on the volume of asset trade in debt and equity securities markets, before examining its impact on the banking sector. Finally, we briefly review the evidence concerning the effect of EMU on foreign direct investment.

Securities markets

In this subsection, we first consider the money and bond markets before turning to equity markets.[1] EMU has naturally led to a very high degree of integration of the money and bond markets, as a result of the unification of the monetary environment. By combining the individual markets of the

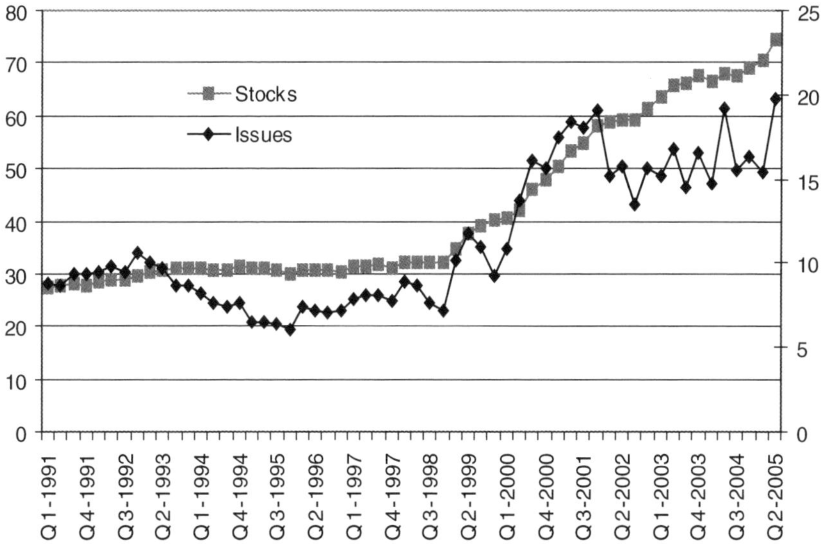

Figure 9.1 Euro area: securities issues (as a ratio to GDP)
Source: Lane (2006b), based on ECB data.

member countries, a much larger and more liquid market has been created. In turn, this has prompted a significant increase in bond issuance by the corporate sector – a market segment that historically had lagged far behind the United States. For instance, Figure 9.1 shows a trend break in the volume of corporate bond issuance which is clearly linked to the formation of EMU.

One way to capture the scale of integration of the euro area bond market is to examine bilateral patterns in cross-border bond holdings – are EMU members more likely to hold each other's bonds than is the case for other country pairs? To address this question, Lane (2006b) examines the bond portfolio allocations of a sample of investor countries that includes 11 EMU member countries and 11 other high-income countries from outside the euro area *vis-à-vis* over 90 destination countries.[2] By contrasting the behaviour of members and similar non-members, it is possible to investigate whether a country pair where both are members of the euro area has a different investment pattern from other country pairs. The general specification employed in that study is given by:

$$\log(BOND_{ij}) = \phi_i + \phi_j + \beta EURO_{ij} + \rho Z_{ij} + \varepsilon_{ij},\ i = \{HIGH - INC\} \qquad (9.1)$$

where the dependent variable is the level of source country j's bond or equity holdings in destination country i and the pair-wise dummy $EURO_{ij}$ takes the value 1 if both the source and destination countries are members of the euro area and zero otherwise. The other explanatory variables include the level of bilateral imports, bilateral exchange rate volatility, an EU membership dummy, a border dummy, bilateral distance, colonial and common language dummies, the bilateral correlation in growth rates, a tax treaty dummy and a dummy for common origin of legal institutions. The regression results estimated by Lane (2006b) indicate that common membership of the euro area raises bilateral bond holdings by about 100 per cent in a levels specification and by about 85 per cent in a first-differences specification. In addition, employing a similar specification, Lane and Milesi-Ferretti (2005a) find that common membership of the euro area raises bilateral portfolio equity holdings by 62 per cent.

However, it is not clear that the increase in intra-EMU financial holdings provides much diversification against country-specific shocks. First, the abolition of national currencies means that the country component in bond returns has largely been eliminated. Second, as we shall discuss further later, national stockmarket indices do not necessarily provide much exposure to national risk factors, since the global and sectoral components in returns have increased in relative importance.

Lane and Milesi-Ferretti (2006) and Lane (2006a) emphasise that the scale of global asset trade has also increased rapidly in recent years. To the extent that member countries hold different global portfolios, this may actually serve to reduce the internal coherence of the euro area, since it implies asymmetric exposures to external financial shocks. Indeed, this was cited by HM Treasury (2003) as an important barrier to the United Kingdom's participation in EMU, in view of the particularly strong financial linkages between the United Kingdom and the United States.

The banking sector

At a qualitative level, the introduction of a single currency should contribute to further cross-border banking integration among the participating countries. The elimination of currency risk fosters greater transparency and should lead to more competition. More integrated markets should allow banks to exploit economies of scale and to develop more diversified activities, thereby enhancing the stability of the financial system. There is also mounting evidence showing that financial integration brings about a more efficient allocation of capital and enhances economic growth.

Clearly, other factors will also contribute to the evolution of cross-border banking integration. The liberalisation of international capital movements and gradual deregulation in the European banking industry should facilitate the cross-border provision of financial services and should lead banks to hold a significant proportion of their assets outside their own jurisdiction. Technological innovation not only reduces the costs of the banking industry, such as the collection and the processing of financial information, but also allows banks to expand the number of services that they provide. Moreover, technological innovation lowers the effect of other types of impediments to cross-border banking integration such as geographical distance. Overall, the combination of free capital movements, a single currency and technological innovation should lead to greater European banking integration.[3]

Walkner and Raes (2005) distinguish between three forms of cross-border banking integration, namely organic growth through the creation of foreign branches and subsidiaries, consolidation through mergers and acquisitions, and the cross-border provision of banking services. We consider each aspect of banking integration in turn, providing some evidence about the degree of integration and discussing the remaining obstacles that prevent further integration.

Foreign branches and subsidiaries

Walkner and Raes (2005) argue that foreign branches should be more widespread than subsidiaries. Current EU legislation facilitates organic growth through the creation of a foreign branch that is subject to the home-country supervision. In contrast, the establishment of subsidiaries involves supervision in each of the host countries and would therefore appear to be less practical and more costly. Yet, European Central Bank (2005b) shows that around half of the foreign presence in EU countries consists of subsidiaries. Overall, the market share of foreign branches and subsidiaries accounts for around 25 per cent of the total EU25 assets.

Walkner and Raes (2005) list several reasons behind the apparently disproportionate share of subsidiaries in the overall market share of foreign branches and subsidiaries. In particular, the creation of foreign branches requires extensive knowledge of the local market in so far as the relationship between banks and potential customers is typically characterised by asymmetric information. Borrowers typically know more about their own creditworthiness than banks do. Consequently, long-term relationships remain crucial since they provide banks with a track record of their customers. The creation of a foreign branch must overcome the lack of knowledge about local market conditions, as well as the generally weak incentives for customers to break a long-term relationship with their banks.

Mergers and acquisitions

Mergers and acquisitions should develop as banks exploit economies of scale and they should contribute to the consolidation of the European banking industry. They also represent a possible solution to the problems inherent in establishing foreign branches. European Central Bank (2005a) shows that the number of credit institutions in the euro area has actually declined from 9,500 in 1995 to 6,400 in 2004. This one-third reduction can be interpreted as evidence that the European banking industry is going through a process of consolidation. However, Walkner and Raes (2005) and the European Central Bank (2005a) show that more than three-quarters of mergers and acquisitions are conducted at the national level, and not across borders. Even though it appears that consolidations within countries have been slowing down, while consolidations across countries have increased, it remains true that consolidations involving only domestic credit institutions represent a large proportion of all mergers and acquisitions.

This evidence has raised questions about the likely welfare impact of mergers and acquisitions. Consolidation at the national level would mean greater concentration, possibly leading to less competition and preventing consumers from reaping the benefits of further consolidation. Walkner and Raes (2005) provide estimates of concentration indices and show that competition has actually decreased in most countries, except for the three Scandinavian countries. In this sense, further cross-border banking integration is more likely to bring benefits for consumers than within-border consolidation.

Several studies have identified remaining impediments to further cross-border banking integration. Local regulations still differ despite successive efforts at harmonising legislation across the European Union. Cultural differences in banking practice imply different work practices, different management procedures, different technological solutions and possibly different languages. As a result, the integration of two financial institutions requires overcoming significant obstacles. Taxation remains a national prerogative and different national tax systems create costs and uncertainty for cross-border financial institutions. Finally, and importantly, some governments have resisted cross-border mergers and acquisitions on strategic grounds. Recent examples involve various sectors of the economy, in particular the energy sector and the banking sector. The French government blocked a bid made by Enel, the leading Italian energy company, for Suez, a French competitor, by forcing the state-owned Gaz de France and Suez to merge, thereby marking the birth of yet another national champion. The Spanish government has recently expressed discontent after E.ON, a German energy company, made a bid for the leading Spanish energy firm Endesa. The Governor of the Bank of Italy was forced to resign after blocking bids by a Spanish bank and a Dutch bank for two Italian banks.

These examples suggest that protectionism is returning to the forefront of the industrial policy agenda. Special public control rights allow states to intervene directly into the economy. The strategy appears to consist of encouraging consolidation at the new national level in order to reach a critical mass which then allows foreign acquisitions to be undertaken, or mergers in which the national firm is a leader. It must be noted that this strategy has not been universally adopted in so far as some major countries such as the United Kingdom have not resisted mergers and acquisitions. Understanding the reasons behind the different views about mergers and acquisitions is beyond the scope of this chapter; yet, it means that removing legal obstacles will not fully achieve cross-border banking integration since some countries pursue their own interests at the expense of the development of a truly integrated banking industry.

Cross-border provision of financial services

The international expansion of banking activity may also arise from the cross-border provision of financial services. European Central Bank (2005b) shows that cross-border holdings of interbank loans and securities amount to around 45 per cent of total holdings in the euro area. Therefore, it seems that banking integration is relatively high at the wholesale level (Cabral *et al.*, 2002). However, integration remains very low at the retail level and shows no sign of a change since the introduction of the single currency. Another indication of the small degree of integration in retail banking is the large difference between fees charged for cross-border financial transactions and those charged for domestic transactions.

The weak integration at the retail level partly reflects the nature of banking relationships at that level. Banks have traditionally developed at the local level to overcome the problem of asymmetric information inherent in the activity of banking. In this respect, selling financial services abroad remains difficult insofar as banks do not have strong knowledge of local markets. Again, asymmetric information would suggest that mergers and acquisitions are the easiest way to overcome the asymmetric information problem. Another obstacle to the cross-border provision of financial services is that European contract law diverges across member states, so that banks must establish different contracts in each member state. This legal problem means that banks cannot apply the same model to all countries equally, and that cross-border transactions entail significant costs due to the multiplication of contracts and procedures. Moreover, the absence of a unified private law at the European level creates problems in other areas. For example, the nature and the extent of the protection of consumers remains heterogeneous across countries. Such divergences in rules imply that banks cannot offer identical products everywhere in the EU, and that they cannot fully exploit the economies of scale.

Banking integration and financial supervision

At a general level, a greater degree of cross-border banking integration will have significant macroeconomic effects. Notwithstanding the higher degree of concentration at the national level, further cross-border integration is likely to raise competition and to deliver the usual benefits to consumers. However, further integration also means a greater potential for systemic turbulence insofar as banks are increasingly interdependent. This is especially true at the wholesale level, which is relatively integrated. The possibility of systemic effects raises new challenges for financial supervision, in particular in the light of the current home and host arrangements.

Gonzalez-Paramo (2006) focuses on banking supervision and crisis management. On the first issue, sharing information about cross-border institutions should involve all relevant parties, both during tranquil times and episodes of turbulence. Greater coordination of supervisory measures will arise from the Capital Requirements Directive, which aims to strengthen and clarify supervisory relationships between home and host countries. On the second issue, coordination is even more difficult in so far as banking crises involve not only financial supervisors, but also central banks and finance ministries. Timely information sharing is a necessary condition for a prompt reaction to systemic developments. Financial market turbulence can be severely contagious when emerging turbulence is not contained rapidly and in a coordinated manner. Stress-testing exercises and further cooperation through Memoranda of Understanding have enhanced coordination among all relevant parties.

Summary

In this subsection, we have emphasised that there are still many real and policy barriers which prevent the full integration of the banking sector. While banks in the euro area are linked together through the wholesale money markets, it is policy decisions at the EU level that are most important for European banking integration. Indeed, some of the most important cross-border mergers and acquisitions in Europe have involved non-members of the euro area (for example the formation of Nordea in

Scandinavia, the entry of Spanish banks into the UK banking sector). The supervisory and regulatory challenges at the levels of the euro area and the broader European Union are significant, in view of the variable geometry of the current policy regimes.

Foreign direct investment

In principle, it is ambiguous whether EMU should raise or lower FDI flows between member countries – the increase in trade permitted by a reduction in trade costs may be a substitute or a complement for direct investment. However, the evidence is that the net impact has been positive: De Sousa and Lochard (2005) estimate that the euro has raised intra-EMU FDI flows by 62 per cent and FDI stock positions by 17 per cent. Along another dimension, Barr *et al.* (2003) find suggestive evidence that EMU has tilted direct investment flows away from those EU countries that have not joined EMU and towards those that have, such that the intra-European exchange rate stability offered by the euro area is proving to be attractive for export-platform multinational activity.

Evidence from asset pricing

This section focuses on stockmarket-return correlations and examines whether the adoption of the euro has affected the pattern of correlations across countries and over time. The introduction of the euro should affect stockmarket-return correlations for several reasons. First, the existence of a single currency means that currency risk disappears completely among the participating countries, and consequently the barriers to cross-border investment arising from the costs of hedging currency risk are fully eliminated. Second, the common monetary policy inherent in the single currency and the convergence of long-term interest rates arising from the convergence of inflation expectations have brought about almost perfectly correlated real risk-free rates (Cappiello, Engle and Sheppard, 2003). Almost identical risk-free rates will in turn mean a more homogeneous valuation of stocks across the participating countries. Third, the process of monetary integration induces closer real convergence in the form of enhanced trade integration and greater business cycle synchronisation. Consequently, it is likely that expectations of real dividends will become more synchronised across countries.

Taken together, these three reasons explain why asset return correlations should increase after the adoption of the euro, with important implications for both financial-market participants and policy-makers. Higher cross-country stockmarket correlations would mean that the traditional approach to portfolio diversification across countries is not the most appropriate one anymore. There is strong evidence that the relative importance of country effects has decreased, and there is some evidence that industry effects are now prevailing among EMU participating countries. We follow the flexible approach of Adjaoute and Danthine (2003, 2004) and provide the latest evidence on both types of effects. We find evidence that supports the prevalence of industry effects over country effects in the early period after the introduction of the single currency. Cross-sectional measures of dispersion are higher across industries than across countries. However, this shift appears to be only temporary since cross-sectional standard deviations converge in 2004. These results suggest that the common currency has contributed to an increase in intra-industry trade, thereby increasing return correlations across industries.

Bond spreads

Table 9.1 shows that spreads on ten-year government bonds are minimal across the member countries. These low spreads underline the high degree of substitutability across these bonds, signalling the effective unification of the government debt market.[4] Similarly, the evidence from the corporate bond market is that spreads are determined by the sectoral and credit-risk attributes of issuers, with only a minor role for country factors (Baele *et al.*, 2004; Pagano and von Thadden, 2004).

Evidence on stock market return correlations

This section presents evidence on the magnitude of stockmarket-return correlations. We make use of Datastream stockmarket indices expressed in US dollars and obtain returns through log differentiation. The time period ranges from April 1988 to December 2005 and data are retrieved at the

Table 9.1 Spreads on ten-year government bonds

Country	*Spread*
Austria	0.1
Belgium	1.8
Finland	–6.9
France	–0.5
Germany	0.0
Greece	20.1
Ireland	–1.8
Italy	20.0
Luxembourg	8.1
Netherlands	–6.2
Portugal	–0.8
Spain	0.3

Note: End of January 2006.

Source: Authors' calculations based on data drawn from global financial data.

weekly frequency, unless otherwise noted. Daily data remain problematic because of non-synchronous trading hours. Monthly data may not provide enough information to the extent that the computation of correlations requires a significant amount of data.

Preliminary evidence

Figure 9.2 shows correlation coefficients between the returns of individual countries and the return on an EMU index, both before the creation of the euro and afterwards. The sample consists of ten EMU countries (Luxembourg and Portugal are excluded) and four European non-EMU countries (the United Kingdom, Sweden, Denmark and Switzerland), which should be seen as a control group. The return on the EMU index is computed as a weighted average of the returns of the ten EMU countries above, excluding the country with respect to which the correlation coefficient is calculated. Thus, the EMU return used to calculate the correlation with the return of country *j* is given by:

$$r_{EMU,t} = \frac{1}{\sum\limits_{k \neq j} w_{k,t}} \left[\sum_{k \neq j} w_{k,t} r_{k,t} \right] \tag{9.2}$$

The weights for each country are obtained as the ratio of this country's market capitalisation to the total market capitalisation of the ten EMU countries. The hypothesis that the euro has brought closer stock market integration should translate into higher correlations between EMU partici-

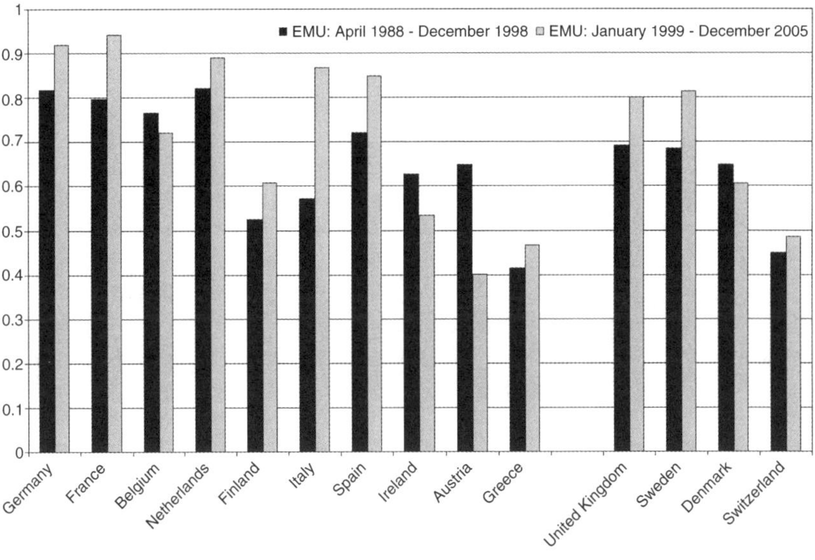

Figure 9.2 Return correlations to an EMU return for two sub-periods

pants' returns and the EMU return after the creation of the euro, and relatively stable correlations for European non-EMU countries across both sub-periods.

For most countries, correlation coefficients between the returns of individual EMU participants and the EMU return increased after the introduction of the euro.[5] These results could be interpreted as evidence that the euro has indeed led to a greater level of financial integration. However, a higher degree of financial market integration could also arise from a more general tendency towards free capital movements and financial liberalisation at the global level. Consequently, it remains crucial to consider other European countries that do not belong to the euro area as a control group. Figure 9.2 shows that correlations between the returns of the United Kingdom, Sweden and Switzerland, and the EMU return have also increased after the introduction of the euro. This result casts doubt on the validity of the interpretation that the single currency is the cause of higher correlations for EMU participants.

This analysis can be extended by considering the correlation coefficients of individual countries not only with an EMU return but also with the return on a world index. In such a way, we hope to determine whether the correlations of the returns of European countries with a world return have also increased. Figure 9.3 presents correlations between the returns of

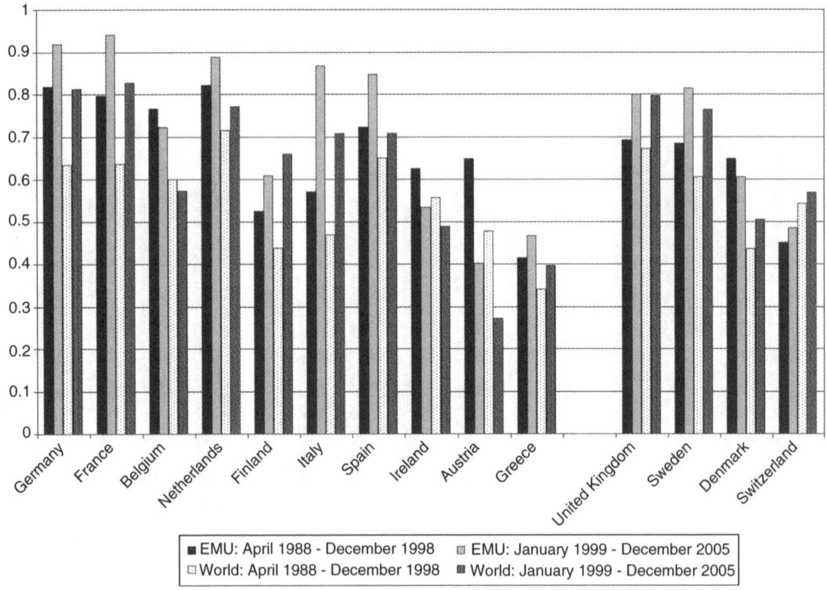

Figure 9.3 Return correlations to two returns for two sub-periods

individual countries and the same EMU return as above as well as the world return, for the same two sub-periods. Correlations with the return on the world index have increased for all countries since the introduction of the euro, except for Belgium, Ireland and Austria. Further evidence (not presented here) shows that Belgium and Ireland exhibit higher correlations with a US return after the introduction of the euro. Finally, it should be noted that correlations with the world return are almost as high as those with the EMU return. Overall, we conclude that the interpretation that the creation of the single currency has increased raw correlations in returns between member countries is not supported by the data.

Time-varying correlations

Two potential issues arise in the estimation of correlations across two sub-periods. First, we have arbitrarily chosen the first week of January 1999 as the turning point and we have then computed correlations for each country in two sub-periods. In fact, it is unclear whether the first week of January 1999 is the right turning point. For example, Fratzscher (2002) concludes that stockmarket integration has risen during the convergence period that preceded the introduction of the euro, that is from around 1996. Second, many studies (for example Cappiello *et al.*, 2006) have shown that correlations are time-varying, even at relatively high frequencies. As a result, the computation of mean correlations over several years may not provide an adequate characterisation of financial-market integration in so far as mean statistics could hide significant time variation.

The time-varying nature of financial-market integration is captured through rolling correlation coefficients, whereby the correlation coefficient is computed over a moving period of ninety weeks leading up to the date under consideration.[6] For instance, the correlation for the first week of January 1990 is calculated over the period from mid-April 1988 until the first week of January 1990 inclusive. Other studies focus on correlation coefficients centred around two windows corresponding to a number of weeks before the date under consideration, and the same number of weeks after that date. This alternative calculation remains problematic if significant events occur during the latter window and capture a pattern of integration that does not yet exist at the date under consideration. One particular example in our context is the occurrence of the 1992/93 crisis of the Exchange Rate Mechanism. The latter approach would exhibit rising correlations in the summer of 1991 already when the crisis really started in the summer of 1992.

Figure 9.4 depicts correlation coefficients for four EMU countries and two European non-EMU countries. The correlations are clearly time-varying, as shown by Cappiello *et al.* (2006). In particular, Belgium exhibits high variability but it is as integrated as France and Germany by the end of the sample period. Clearly, computing means over long periods of time can be

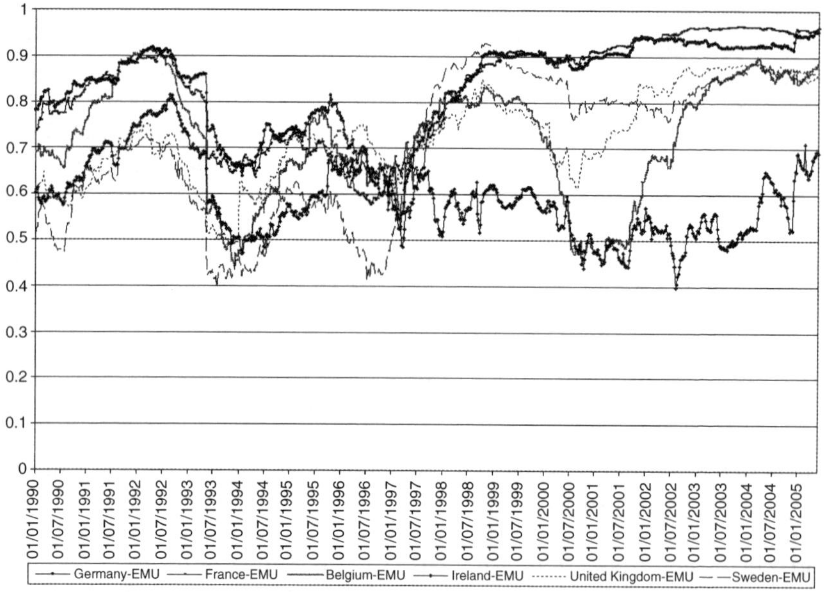

Figure 9.4 Time-varying correlations to an EMU return

misleading! In general, all countries exhibit rising correlations in the period leading up to the 1992/93 ERM crisis, possibly as a result of the removal of controls on capital movements in the late eighties and the early nineties. The correlations decreased in the aftermath of the crisis and remained somewhat lower until they started rising in a highly synchronous manner, except for Ireland. Interestingly, the correlations have been rising since early 1997 for all countries, whether forthcoming EMU participants or not. Since the turn of the century, with the exception of Ireland which has seen higher correlations with the United States, correlations have been very high. Consequently, we would conclude that European financial markets are now very highly integrated. Yet, this does not seem to depend heavily on EMU participation.

Figure 9.5 provides the mean for each week of the correlations for two groups of countries, respectively ten EMU countries and four European non-EMU countries. Financial-market integration seems to be slightly higher among the group of EMU participants but this is the case throughout the whole sample period, not only after the introduction of the single currency. Again, this casts doubt on the hypothesis that the euro has led to greater financial integration. Another interesting pattern is the similarity of the time-varying pattern of correlations across the two groups. This observation suggests that the correlations could be affected by a factor common to both EMU and non-EMU members, thereby hiding the effect of the introduction of the common currency.

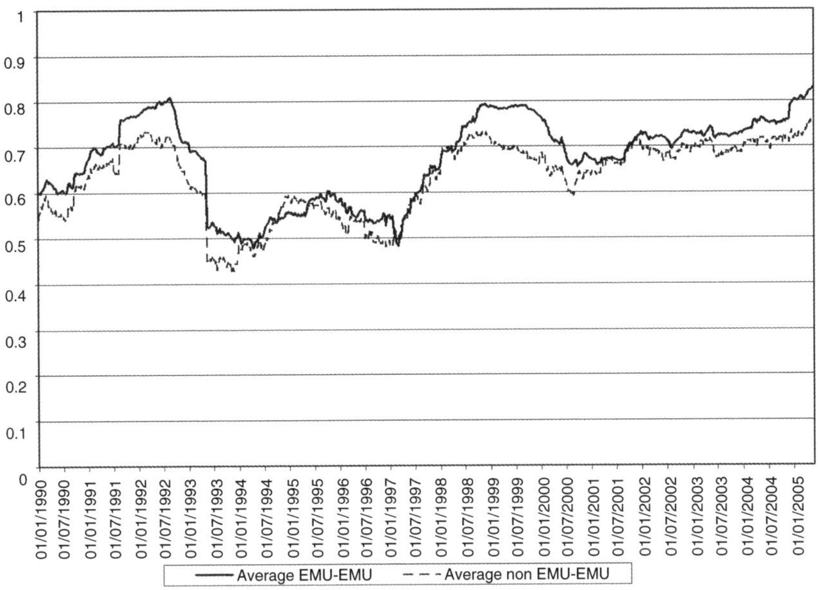

Figure 9.5 Means of time-varying correlations to an EMU return

Correlation coefficients and common shocks

Country-specific stock market returns, denoted as r_{it} can be decomposed into a time-varying common factor, denoted as D_t, and a time-varying idiosyncratic factor, denoted as ε_{it}. Hence,

$$r_{it} = \beta_t D_t + \varepsilon_{it} \tag{9.3}$$

Correlation coefficients could be high because the contribution of the common factor to explaining returns could be large relative to that of the idiosyncratic factor. Such common factors include not only international influences such as the level of oil prices, the level of international interest rates, global risk appetite or a drive towards more homogeneous monetary and fiscal policies, but also common European legislation or free capital movements among EU member states. The effect of the single currency could be hidden by common factors, that is factors common to EMU as well as non-EMU European countries, and it may therefore be desirable to abstract from such factors in order to pin down the Euro effect more precisely.[7]

There are two equivalent ways in our simple framework to decompose returns into common and idiosyncratic effects. On the one hand, we could simply pool all country returns over time in a panel-data framework, and estimate equation (9.3) using time dummies. The coefficient β_t would indicate the magnitude and the direction of the impact of the factor for each week. On the other hand, we could simply calculate the mean return across countries for each week. Indeed, this is precisely what the coefficient β_t is capturing in a panel regression. The identified common factor is then subtracted from the country-specific returns to obtain estimates of the idiosyncratic factor for each week. We also reconstruct our EMU returns focusing only on the idiosyncratic component. Correlation coefficients are obtained using the idiosyncratic component of each country's return and the EMU return based on idiosyncratic components.

Figure 9.6 depicts the mean for each week of the correlations for each group of countries, namely EMU countries and non-EMU countries. It shows clearly that once we have extracted the component of returns common to both EMU and non-EMU countries, the former group exhibits significantly higher correlations than the latter group from the time of the introduction of the single currency onwards, *other common things equal*. Indeed, the disconnect between the correlations of the two groups starts at the beginning of 1998, a time when the group of countries that would eventually participate in the monetary union became known with almost complete certainty. Adjaoute *et al.* (2000) collect poll data on expected participation in the monetary union and find that all future members were expected to join with a probability greater than 0.95 by January 1998.

Our conclusion is that stockmarket-return correlations are a useful indicator to measure the degree of financial-market integration. Yet, financial

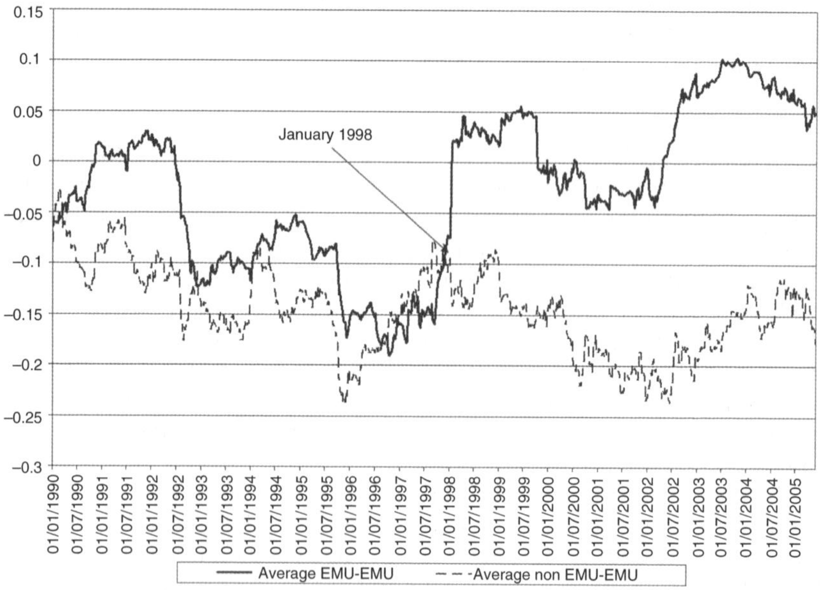

Figure 9.6 Means of time-varying correlations based on idiosyncratic components

integration is affected by a wide variety of factors and isolating the euro effect remains a difficult task. Our approach is to abstract from common factors affecting the returns of all countries, including the non-EMU economies, and to compute time-varying correlation coefficients, so that we do not have to choose an arbitrary turning point. Our evidence shows a rapid, significant and persistent disconnect of correlations in early 1998. To the extent that the future members of the monetary union were more or less known at that time, it was logical that the effect of the common currency on financial markets could start at that time.

Implications for international investors

The correlation coefficients between the returns of countries participating in the monetary union and an EMU return have increased over time. It remains unclear whether the euro is the main explanation or whether it contributed marginally. However, cross-country correlations have definitely increased and this has important implications for international investors. The traditional approach to portfolio diversification has been to allocate wealth firstly across countries and secondly within each country. There is indeed widespread historical evidence that country factors dominate industry factors in explaining stockmarket returns (Heston and Rouwenhorst, 1994; Griffin and Karolyi, 1998; Rouwenhorst, 1999). Nevertheless, higher stockmarket-return correlations across countries would imply lower benefits of portfolio diversification across countries and would mean that an investment strategy based on diversification across industries may become more appealing. Several studies have documented the fall in the dominance of country factors over time (for example Brooks and Del Negro, 2004) and some studies conclude that the introduction of the euro coincides with a greater dominance of industry factors (Brooks and Del Negro, 2002; Isakov and Sonney, 2004; Flavin, 2004). Isakov and Sonney (2004) emphasise that the shift in the relative importance of country and industry factors has led financial institutions to reorganise their research departments in terms of industries rather than countries.

Most studies use the methodology advanced by Heston and Rouwenhorst (1994) to determine the relative importance of country and industry effects. Stockmarket returns are regressed on a set of industry-specific and country-specific factors captured by dummy variables and their relative importance is assessed by calculating the relative variances of the estimated factors at each frequency of the data. However, this approach has been criticised on several grounds (Adjaoute and Danthine, 2003; Moerman, 2004). In particular, firms are restricted to belong to only one industry and also to only one country, thereby not depending on other industries and/or other countries. This feature remains largely inadequate in so far as economic activity is partly multinational and multisectoral. Moreover, the approach assumes that all assets from a given industry or country have the same sensitivity to that industry or country.

Adjaoute and Danthine (2003, 2004) rely on an alternative view about the respective role of industry effects and country effects. They calculate standard deviations of sectoral returns and country returns, respectively, for each month over a given time period. Although diversification benefits are typically related to correlations, Solnik and Roulet (2000) show that there is a direct and inverse relationship between correlations and cross-sectional measures of dispersion. Higher cross-sectional standard deviations should therefore correspond to lower correlations. This alternative measure to correlations is useful in so far as the relative importance of country and industry effects could exhibit significant time variation.

Monthly sectoral returns are computed for ten broad sectors, namely energy, materials, industrials, consumer discretionary goods, consumer staples, health care, financials, information technology, telecommunications and utilities, and the data are retrieved from the MSCI's Global Industry Classification Standard. We also make use of MSCI's stockmarket indices to compute monthly country returns. The time period ranges from February 1995 until December 2005. Figure 9.7 shows cross-sectional standard deviations for both country returns and industry returns, as well as corresponding 18-month moving averages to identify the underlying trends. We have also replicated this analysis using the Hodrick–Prescott filter and the results remain unaffected.

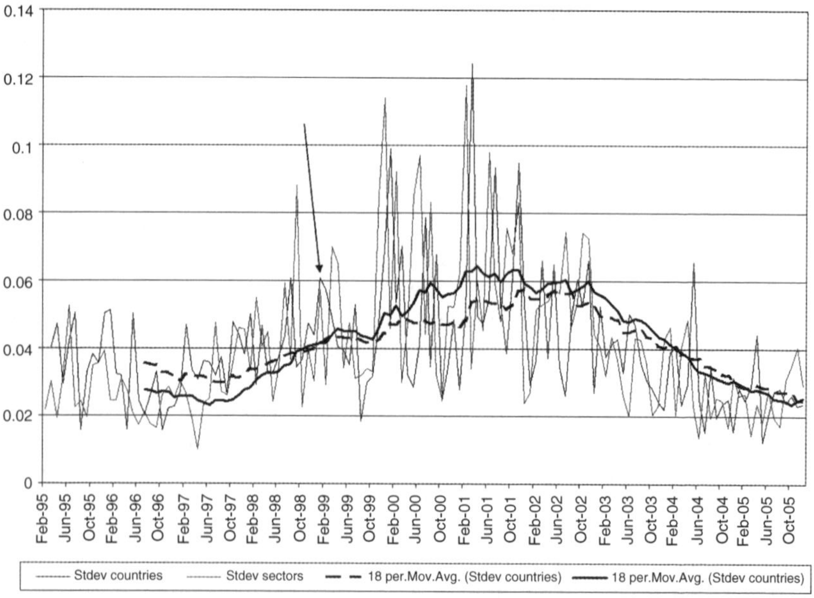

Figure 9.7 Cross-sectional dispersions for country and industry returns

We confirm previous evidence (Brooks and Del Negro 2002; Isakov and Sonney 2004; Flavin 2004) that industry effects have become relatively more important than country effects during the convergence period and after the introduction of the euro. The cross-sectional standard deviation of industry returns becomes relatively higher around the second half of 1998. However, the change in the relative importance of country and industry effects appears to be only temporary since the cross-sectional standard deviations revert in the first half of 2004. The two dispersion measures are almost equal by the end of 2005.

Our evidence suggests that although the importance of country factors has decreased, it is also the case that industry factors become less significant. Further economic integration leads to higher cross-country return correlations, but also to higher cross-industry return correlations in the last part of our sample period. It is possible that the higher level of economic openness associated with the creation of the monetary union (see Baldwin, 2005, for a review) implies that broad economic sectors could be affected by global shocks to a greater extent. The temporary rise in the standard deviation of industry returns could also be due to the bubble in the information technology sector, bringing about higher dispersion of returns across industries. Overall, our results would suggest that portfolio diversification across industries only is unlikely to yield the highest benefits for international investors. To the extent that both country and industry effects become similar, an investment strategy that yields superior gains would be to diversify across both countries and industries (Adjaoute and Danthine, 2004; Moerman, 2004). This being said, it remains true that the traditional top-down approach to portfolio diversification has become inadequate for the purpose of international investment in Europe.

The international financial role of the euro

After the US dollar, the euro is the world's second most important currency. Table 9.2 shows that the euro is heavily represented in global foreign exchange transactions, while Table 9.3 underlines the importance of the euro in international debt markets.[8] However, Table 9.4 also shows that the euro still takes only a small share of 'external' transactions – only 6.2 per cent of loans made by banks outside the euro area to borrowers outside the euro area are denominated in euro, while the euro accounts for only 8.4 per cent of deposits in banks outside the euro area held by non-banks outside the euro area. Table 9.5 shows that one-quarter of global reserves are denominated in euros: however, this share is far behind the dollar's dominant position. However, Dominguez (2006) emphasises that the euro has established a significant regional presence – it is highly important in the external financial transactions of the countries in Central and Eastern Europe and the Community of Independent States.

Table 9.2 The euro in foreign exchange markets

Share of the euro in:	
Total foreign exchange turnover	37.2%
Daily settlements	43.0%

Source: Derived from European Central Bank (2005c).

Table 9.3 The euro in international debt markets

Share of the euro in:	
Stock of debt securities	27.30%
Broad stock of international debt securities	46.60%
Narrow stock of international debt securities	31.50%
Issues of international bonds and notes	34.90%
Issues of international money market instruments	37.10%
Bond portfolio	30%
Portfolios in the United States and Canada	0.70%
Portfolios in non-euro area Europe	26.20%

Source: Derived from European Central Bank (2005c).

Table 9.4 The euro in international loan and deposit markets (%)

Share of the euro in:	
Loans from euro area banks to external borrowers	37.4
Loans from external banks to non-bank borrowers in the euro area	54.1
Loans from external banks to external non-bank borrowers	6.2
Deposits of external non-banks in banks in the euro area	50.6
Deposits of euro area non-banks in external banks	51.5
International deposits of external non-banks in external banks	8.4

Note: External refers to entities outside the euro area.

Source: Derived from European Central Bank (2005c).

Table 9.5 The euro in third countries

Number of euro trackers	50
Share in global reserves	24.9%
Cumulative net external shipments of euro banknotes	55.0 billion
Total external stock of euro-denominated bank deposits	68.0 billion

Source: Derived from European Central Bank (2005c).

It is well-understood that network externalities and hysteresis effects mean that the dollar, as the leading currency, can command a disproportionate share in international transactions and global reserve holdings. However, by the same token this situation can shift rapidly if a 'tipping point' is reached that turns the euro into a truly global currency that can rival the dollar. The large current-account deficits of the United States in recent years have raised the probability of this scenario, since holders of dollar assets face substantial depreciation risk to the extent that a dollar weakening is a necessary component of the adjustment process that the United States must undertake in order to engineer an improvement in its trade balance (Gourinchas and Rey, 2005; Lane and Milesi-Ferretti, 2005b). For instance, Chinn and Frankel (2005) estimate that the euro could surpass the dollar as the leading reserve currency by 2022, if the euro area is enlarged to include the United Kingdom and dollar depreciation risk remains important.

More generally, growth in the international role of the euro will reflect the pace of development in the euro area's financial markets – the most important difference between the dollar and the euro is that dollar markets are much deeper and more liquid than the euro markets, which is an especially important criterion in the reserve allocation decisions of central banks. For instance, European Central Bank (2006) reports that the total dollar bond market is $21.4 trillion, with the euro area's bond market less than half its size at $10.3 trillion. Since it is still early days in the development of the European corporate bond market, the gap may be expected to narrow in the coming years – especially if the United Kingdom were to join the euro area.

Finally, another dimension of the international role of the euro is in the exchange-rate regime choices made by other countries. Table 9.5 records that 50 countries attach some weight to the euro in their exchange-rate targets. To the extent that greater bilateral nominal exchange rate stability *vis-à-vis* the euro promotes trade and financial linkages, this may carry additional benefits both for the member countries and the trackers. However, it also alters the monetary transmission mechanism, since the interest rate choices by the European Central Bank have a direct spillover effect on the tracking currencies (Honohan and Lane, 1999), and it may carry some risk to the extent that a tracking country experiences difficulty in maintaining its currency target.

Conclusions

This chapter has reviewed the impact of the euro on international financial integration. We have found considerable evidence that the euro has significantly reshaped the European financial system, especially with respect to the securities markets. This is evident both in the data on the volume and direction of asset trade and in regard to the patterns in asset-return comovements. However, the real and policy barriers to integration in the retail and corporate banking sectors remain significant, even if the wholesale end of banking has been largely integrated. Finally, while the international financial role of the euro is significant, it does not yet closely rival the dollar in world financial markets.

The financial integration induced by EMU has had a significant macroeconomic impact. Dvorak (2005) finds that EMU has raised the investment rate by five percentage points. As is highlighted by Lane (2006a), the unification of the debt market and the elimination of national currency and liquidity risk premia has allowed some peripheral countries to experience significant lending booms and run sizeable current-account deficits. This relaxation of credit constraints helps lagging countries to accelerate the convergence process (Blanchard and Giavazzi, 2002). However, an excessive lending boom may lead to overvaluation and attendant adjustment problems (Blanchard, 2006). An unresolved issue for the euro area is how it would cope with a systemic problem in the banking sector, given the lack of a European-level financial supervisory authority and the uncertainty about the relative roles of the European Central Bank and national fiscal authorities in addressing distress in the banking system. The policy framework supporting financial integration remains incomplete.

Notes

1 The line of argument in this subsection draws on Lane (2006a).

2 These are the US, the UK, Denmark, Sweden, Switzerland, Norway, Japan, Canada, Iceland, Australia and New Zealand. These countries are advanced economies that are structurally similar to the EMU member countries and as such form a natural comparator group. Luxembourg is excluded as a source country due to its special status as an offshore centre.

3 These forces also operate on the integration of European (and global) capital markets. For instance, the Euronext platform now combines the stock exchanges in Amsterdam, Brussels, Paris and Lisbon, while there are have been multiple attempts to seek a merger between the London Stock Exchange and other major exchanges in Germany and the United States.

4 The evidence shows that the spreads are positively related to the ratio of government debt to GDP – but the slope is quite flat. Indeed, there is a debate about whether risk in this market is underpriced, with some market participants expecting that the ECB would bail out a government that faced repayment difficulties.

5 Correlations have decreased for Belgium, Ireland and Austria.

6 Forbes and Rigobon (2002) and Cappiello *et al.* (2006) have noted that correlation coefficients may exhibit a bias in the presence of heteroscedastic stockmarket returns. Forbes and Rigobon (2002) propose a correction for the correlation coefficient that works only under certain conditions. Cappiello *et al.* (2006) make use of GARCH estimations to calculate conditional correlation coefficients. We have implemented the correction of Forbes and Rigobon (2002) and the main results remain unchanged.

7 Corsetti, Pericoli and Sbracia (2005) construct a single-factor model and derive a measure of financial-market interdependence that allows for changes in the rela-

tive variance of common and idiosyncratic shocks, as well as changes in the country-specific factor loadings. We do not follow this approach in this chapter for practical reasons. Again, our aim is to extract any information common to both EMU and non-EMU participating countries to focus narrowly on the idiosyncratic components of returns.

8 Table 9.3 also shows that euro-denominated bonds form only a trivial proportion of the portfolios of North American institutions.

References

Adam, K., T. Jappelli, A. Menichini, M. Padula and M. Pagano (2001) 'Analyse, Compare, and Apply Alternative Indicators and Monitoring Methodologies to Measure the Evolution of Capital Market Integration in the European Union', European Commission Report.

Adjaoute, K., L. Bottazzi, J.P. Danthine, A. Fischer, R. Hamaui, R. Portes and M. Wickens (2000) *EMU and Portfolio Adjustment*, CEPR Policy Paper 5.

Adjaoute, K. and J.P. Danthine (2003) 'European Financial Integration and Equity Returns: A Theory-Based Assessment', in V. Gaspar, P. Hartmann and O. Sleijpen (eds), *The Transformation of the European Financial System*, Frankfurt: ECB, pp. 185–245.

Adjaoute, K. and J.P. Danthine (2004) 'Equity Returns and Integration: is Europe Changing?', *Oxford Review of Economic Policy*, 20: 555–70.

Baele, L., A. Ferrando, P. Hördahl, E. Krylova and C. Monnet (2004) 'Measuring Financial Integration in the Euro Area', ECB Occasional Paper no. 12.

Baldwin, R.E. (2005) 'The Euro's Trade Effects', mimeo, Graduate Institute for International Studies.

Barr, D., F. Breedon and D. Miles (2003) 'Life on the Outside: Economic Conditions and Prospects outside Euroland', *Economic Policy*, 18: 573–613.

Bekaert, G. and C. Harvey (1995) 'Time-Varying World Market Integration', *Journal of Finance*, 50, 403–44.

Blanchard, O. (2006) 'Adjustment Within the Euro Area. The Difficult Case of Portugal', mimeo, MIT.

Blanchard, O. and F. Giavazzi (2002) 'Current Account Deficits in the Euro Area. The End of the Feldstein Horioka Puzzle?', *Brookings Papers on Economic Activity* 2, 147–209.

Brooks, R. and M. Del Negro (2002) 'International Stock Returns and Market Integration: a Regional Perspective', IMF Working Paper no. 202.

Brooks, R. and M. Del Negro (2004) 'The Rise in Comovement Across National Stock Markets: Market Integration or IT Bubble?', *Journal of Empirical Finance* 11, 649–80.

Cabral, I., F. Dierick and J. Vesala (2002) 'Banking Integration in the Euro Area', ECB Occasional Paper no. 6.

Cappiello, L., R. Engle and K. Sheppard (2003) 'Asymmetric Dynamics in the Correlations of Global Equity and Bond Returns', ECB Working Paper no. 204.

Cappiello, L, P. Hördahl, A. Kadareja and S. Manganelli (2006) 'The Impact of the Euro on Financial Markets', ECB Working Paper no. 598.

Chinn, M. and J. Frankel (2005) 'Will the Euro Eventually Surpass the Dollar as Leading International Reserve Currency?', NBER Working Paper no. 11510.

Corsetti, G., M. Pericoli and M. Sbracia (2005) 'Some Contagion, Some Interdependence: More Pitfalls in Tests of Financial Contagion', *Journal of International Money and Finance* 24, 1177–99.

De Sousa, J. and J. Lochard (2005) 'Does the Single Currency Affect FDI?', mimeo, University of Paris 1.

Dominguez, K. (2006) 'The ECB, the Euro and Global Financial Markets', mimeo, University of Michigan.
Dvorak, T. (2005) 'The Impact of the Euro on Investment', Sectoral Evidence, Mimeo, Union College.
European Central Bank (2005a) *ECB Monthly Bulletin*, May.
European Central Bank (2005b) *EU Banking Structures*, October.
European Central Bank (2005c) *Review of the International Role of the Euro*, December.
European Central Bank (2006) 'The Accumulation of Foreign Reserves', ECB Occasional Paper No. 43.
Flavin, T. (2004) 'The Effect of the Euro on Country Versus Industry Portfolio Diversification', *Journal of International Money and Finance* 23, 1137–58.
Forbes, K. and R. Rigobon (2002) 'No Contagion, Only Interdependence: Measuring Stock Market Comovements', *Journal of Finance* 57, 2223–61.
Fratzscher, M. (2002) 'Financial Market Integration in Europe: on the Effects of EMU on Stock Markets', *International Journal of Finance and Economics* 7(3), 165–93.
Gonzalez-Paramo, J.M. (2006) 'Cross-border Banking in the EU: Developments and Emerging Policy Issues', speech in Hong Kong, 24 February.
Gourinchas, P.-O. and H. Rey (2005) 'International Financial Adjustment', NBER Working Paper no. 11155.
Griffin, J. and G. Karolyi (1998) 'Another Look at the Role of the Industrial Structure of Markets for International Diversification Strategies', *Journal of Financial Economics* 50, 351–73.
Hardouvelis, G., D. Malliaropulos and R. Priestley (2006) 'EMU and European Stock Market Integration, *Journal of Business* 79, 365–92.
Heston, S. and K. Rouwenhorst (1994) 'Does Industrial Structure Explain the Benefits of International Diversification?', *Journal of Financial Economics* 36, 3–27.
HM Treasury (2003) *EMU Study*, London.
Honohan, P. and P.R. Lane (1999) 'Pegging to the Dollar and the Euro', *International Finance* 2, 379–410.
Isakov, D. and F. Sonney (2004) 'Are Practitioners Right? On the Relative Importance of Industrial Factors in International Stock Returns', *Swiss Journal of Economics and Statistics* 140, 355–79.
Lane, P.R. (2006a) 'The Real Effects of EMU', IIIS Discussion Paper no. 115.
Lane, P.R. (2006b) 'Global Bond Holdings and the Euro', *International Journal of Central Banking*, forthcoming.
Lane, P.R. and G.M. Milesi-Ferretti (2005a) 'The International Equity Holdings of Euro Area Investors', IIIS Discussion Paper no. 104.
Lane, P.R. and G.M. Milesi-Ferretti (2005b) 'Financial Globalisation and Exchange Rates', IIIS Discussion Paper no. 44.
Lane, P.R. and G.M. Milesi-Ferretti (2006) 'The External Wealth of Nations Mark II', IIIS Discussion Paper no. 126.
Moerman, G. (2004) 'Diversification in Euro Area Stock Markets: Country Versus Industry', ECB Working Paper no. 327.
Pagano, M. and E.L. Von Thadden (2004) 'The European Bond Market Under EMU', *Oxford Review of Economic Policy* 20, 531–54.
Rouwenhorst, K. (1999) 'European Equity Markets and EMU', *Financial Analysts Journal* 55, 57–64.
Solnik, B. and J. Roulet (2000) 'Dispersion as Cross-sectional Correlation', *Financial Analysts Journal* 56, 54–61.
Walkner, C. and J. P. Raes (2005) 'Integration and Consolidation in EU Banking – an Unfinished Business', *European Economy, Economic Papers* 226.

Discussion

Robert I. Mochrie

Lane and Wälti begin their chapter by stating that 'The goal ... is to provide a quantitative review of the impact of European Monetary Union on international financial integration.' That is, the authors claim that they will review the extent to which unitary financial markets and institutions have emerged as a result of the creation of the eurozone. Hence, they consider the behaviour of institutions and markets, looking for systematic differences across the eurozone and other countries. They take two approaches, firstly reviewing existing work on financial integration on the eurozone, based on work that Philip Lane is currently engaged in; and then outlining some ongoing work on the effects of eurozone membership on co-movements of securities prices.

The breadth of the survey is impressive. They provide a considerable amount of evidence relating to the impact of eurozone membership, some indicating strong effects, while the remainder indicates very little. Yet, I cannot help feeling that had they been less ambitious in scope, the overall result might have been more effective. The survey in the first part lacks sufficient detail to be compelling, while the analysis in the sequel has the feel of a preliminary essay. No doubt in future work it will be possible for them to overcome this concern.

The form of study that we are considering here always suffers from a risk of looking for the emergence of systematic differences, and arguing, when they are found, for membership of the eurozone causing them, rather than being correlated with them. The authors have been careful to avoid this trap here, but there are some methodological problems that they might have addressed more precisely. For example, it is not clear to me, at least, how one should define the comparator countries. Should they be European countries that are not participating in stage 3 of EMU? If so, does it matter if they are members of the European Union, or of the European Economic Area?

Quite separately, it also seems problematic that we are here trying to identify variables that might affect the evolution of relatively short series of stochastic processes. Given that the authors have chosen not to present much in the way of econometric evidence, as a relatively casual reader

I found myself scrutinising graphs quite closely. Figure 9.4 is the best illustration of my concerns. This shows the correlation of stockmarket returns in six European markets, compared with the returns on an EMU-wide market. Concentrating on the three largest countries – Germany, the UK and France – it appears from this diagram that the evolution of the correlation measure is very similar in all three countries. I am not certain how to interpret this outcome, other than to conclude that it suggests that membership of the eurozone is not the main explanatory factor at work here.

The novelty in this chapter is in its analysis of co-movements of securities prices. It includes a very helpful discussion of the problems of defining the turning point used to divide the period into two sections, and also the length of sub-periods for which correlations are measured. The authors suggest that descriptive data do not indicate that eurozone membership has immediately apparent effects, and so move on to more sophisticated analytical techniques.

The method that they use is to strip out the common component of external factors on returns, giving their measure of the idiosyncratic shock for each market in each week. Using a panel-data regression, the authors identify the idiosyncratic shock as the difference between the mean return on all markets in any week and the return in any one market. The results presented suggest that for members of the eurozone there is a zero mean correlation between the returns of individual and combined eurozone markets, while for non-members there is a negative correlation in returns. It is not clear whether this is simply chance, a statistical artefact, or a significant difference. For what follows, a fuller explanation of this result could be important.

The chapter then turns to consider the implications of the formation of the eurozone on portfolio diversification. Here, again, there are very interesting and substantial results, with a helpful description of their derivation and possible limitations. The conclusion that in the last 18 months, both sectoral and national variability in returns across industries have fallen, with variability in sectoral returns dipping lower, is interesting. Yet, the commentary does not convince me that this outcome flows from the formation of the eurozone. For example, the authors do not explore the effects of increasing globalisation or the impact of the dotcom boom in 1999 and 2000 on both industry and market volatility.

The authors are to be commended for cramming so much into their chapter. The analysis of the correlation in returns in stockmarkets seems to be both novel and important. Not only does this seem to be the most substantial result that they have presented here, it is also the one that is most clearly helpful to their thesis that membership of the eurozone has led to a measurable and, indeed, substantial increase in financial integration. The other results are interesting, but they seem to provide an interesting commentary on the main thesis.

10

The Impact of the Euro Changeover on Inflation: Evidence from the Harmonised Index of Consumer Prices

*Marco G. Ercolani and Jayasri Dutta**

Introduction

Although anecdotal evidence has emerged to suggest that the prices of some goods did rise substantially at the time euro notes and coins were introduced, there have been few studies that have attempted to test this formally. Here we present formal statistical tests for the occurrence of a sudden increase in the aggregate price level for the 12 countries that undertook the changeover to euro notes and coins on 1 January 2002. Any sudden increase in the price level can also be detected as a temporary but substantial one-period rise in the rate of inflation. We use the countries that did not participate in the euro-changeover – Denmark, Sweden and the UK – as a control group for the formal statistical tests. We find that although the results are sensitive to the estimation method and to how the data are treated, there is weak evidence of a slight temporary increase in aggregate inflation (EuroStat code cp00) in January 2002 for the countries that did join the euro compared to those that did not. The data we use are from the New Cronos HICP (2005) monthly Harmonised Index of Consumer Prices (HICP) as supplied by EuroStat and cover the period 1995 to 2005.

Those studies that have formally tested for the inflationary effects of the euro-changeover have focused almost exclusively on the restaurant sector. The tests carried out on the aggregate price index are therefore repeated for the restaurant sector (EuroStat code cp1111). We confirm for the restaurant sector the presence of a significant increase in prices and a temporary increase in inflation as suggested by past studies. These results suggest that the significant price increases during the euro changeover may have taken place only for a small sub-set of product groups. In combination these sub-

*We would like to thank Michael Biggs for his helpful comments. Any shortcomings are our own.

sectors may have caused the barely perceptible price deviations detected in the aggregate price index. Our statistical procedures fully control for the existence of seasonal effects and therefore any price changes that would fall within the bounds for seasonal variation are not misinterpreted as being due to the euro changeover. For completeness, summary tests on a euro-changeover effect in inflation for 129 other product and service sub-categories are also discussed.

Although the EuroStat data we analyse cannot directly identify the reasons why some sectors are more susceptible to price changes following the euro changeover, they may suggest possible explanations. Three possible explanations emerge: 'menu costs', 'asymmetric information (rounding-up)' and 'rounding-off'. The details of these are discussed below and the sectors in which the substantive price changes occur suggest which of these explanations are more plausible.

The chapter proceeds as follows. In the next section a literature survey is presented which highlights existing statistical tests for the euro-changeover effect. Some of the issues raised are then discussed and possible time-series patterns for euro-changeover-induced inflation are proposed. We present time-series plots for the price indices and the rates of inflation, to allow comparisons with the patterns suggested. Formal statistical tests are then presented, including tests for persistent changes in the levels of prices and for temporary increases in the rate of inflation. A final section concludes.

Background and literature survey

Folkertsma (2001) provided possibly the earliest prediction for the occurrence of a euro-changeover-induced increase in prices, a prediction which was based as much on the theory of 'rounding up' prices as that of 'menu costs'. The idea of menu costs as a theoretical explanation for a sudden increase in prices gained prominence just after the euro changeover. Much of the research that has followed this has consisted largely in attempts to identify any price jumps empirically and the theoretical underpinnings for this have been based on the theory of menu costs.

The theory of menu costs suggests that the euro changeover creates a synchronisation mechanism for retailers to increase prices on the same date. This synchronisation occurs because although retailers could have posted prices in euros at almost any time they were obliged to do so by 1 January 2002 at the latest. Obviously, the theory of price rounding-up also suggests that the euro-changeover creates a synchronisation mechanism for retailers to increase prices. Typically a price index appears to increase smoothly because each index is an aggregation of individual sellers' prices and sellers tend to change their prices asynchronously. A theoretical construct to support the claim that in equilibrium prices adjust asynchronously is provided by Bhaskar (2002) in the context of menu costs and imperfect competition. The extent of this synchronisation may depend on the magnitude of menu costs. The duration of the deviation from the expected trend may depend on the degree of market competition. In addition to the sudden jump in an aggregate price index the theory of menu costs also predicts that one may observe a very short period of non-changing prices in the lead up to the euro-changeover date. A rigorous theoretical and empirical treatment of both the *synchronisation* effect that causes the jump and the *horizon* effect that causes a short pre-period of price stagnation can be found in Hobijn *et al.* (2004).

Much of the debate over euro-changeover-induced inflation stems from the observation that consumers' expectations of inflation increased substantially around January 2002. The earliest evidence of this was investigated by Forsells and Kenny (2002), who found that consumers' expectations of inflation only deviated systematically from the true values in the short run.

A number of studies have been carried out that use micro-level data, most of which have focused either on the 'all products' price index or on the restaurant sector. The reason for this is that given this is a story of menu costs the restaurant sector seems a natural starting point. Adriani *et al.* (2004) examine the inflationary consequences of the euro-changeover in theoretical and empirical models of the restaurant sector, and show that the changeover acts as a coordination device which shifts restaurants to a high-price equilibrium. Their data is collected from the *Michelin Red Guide* and it supports the prediction that a permanent change in relative prices took place in euro-changeover countries. Gaiotti and Lippi (2005) also focus on the restaurant sector, collecting an original unbalanced panel of data for 2,500 Italian restaurants in Italy over the period 1998–2004. The sources of their data are the two guides *Guida dei ristoranti d'Italia* and *Guida dei ristoranti di Roma*. They find that the euro changeover can explain about a 3–4 per cent additional increase in this sector but that consumers possibly attributed the entire increase to the euro changeover. The authors suggest that this 3–4 per cent additional increase may be attributed to the presence of menu costs and the short-run lack of competition in this sector.

Some research has found the evidence for a euro-changeover-induced increase in prices to be at best weak or non-existent. Angelini and Lippi (2005) present a simple theoretical model in which the relationship between aggregate ATM withdrawals and aggregate expenditure is not homogeneous of degree one in the price level. They collect data from the analysis of cash withdrawals from ATMs and compare these to expenditures. Their analysis does not find evidence to support the hypothesis that the euro changeover generated inflation that was not detected by official statistics. Anderton *et al.* (2003) use pre-euro-changeover data to investigate the idea that monetary union may result in faster cross-border transmission of price movements. Their findings suggest that the euro changeover would homogenise price movements across the member countries of the eurozone. Although this is interpreted as evidence of the 'law of one price' it may also be taken to be evidence of increased market collusion and higher prices. Most notably, research by the European Central Bank clearly stated that no evidence of a euro-changeover-induced increase in aggregate prices could be found and that any variation in food prices was due to seasonal factors. However, the ECB concedes that there *may* have been price movements in some service sectors that were related to the changeover:

> While a strong increase in overall inflation was observed at the beginning of 2002 this was largely due to exceptional and short-lived factors. For example, adverse weather conditions in some parts of the Euro area led to increases in unprocessed food prices; in addition there were anticipated influences of indirect taxes and base effects resulting from developments in energy prices. Price increases were also registered for some specific items in the services sector, which could have been related to the changeover. However, while it is extremely difficult to isolate the inflationary impact of the changeover from other factors with any degree of precision, there was no evidence of a significant impact on prices at the aggregate level as a result of the Euro cash changeover. (ECB, 2002, p. 43)

Possible euro-changeover effects

In the light of the aforementioned research papers, it is apparent that the euro changeover might lead to a time-series pattern in the log of the price level of the kind illustrated in Figure 10.1. The solid lines represent the euro-changeover-induced path for the log of the price level, annual inflation and monthly inflation. The dashed lines represent the paths under no currency changeover. The salient feature of this pattern is the large upward jump in January 2002, the magnitude of which is captured by the EUROJUMP variable in the empirical analysis. A secondary feature of this pattern is the slight stagnation of prices just before January 2002, this is captured by the PRE-EURO variable in the empirical analysis.

Taking the first difference of the log-level generates a monthly inflation series and taking the twelfth difference generates an annual inflation series, both of which are illustrated in the lower part of Figure 10.1. The monthly inflation series demonstrates the substantial jump in January 2002 which is captured by the EUROSPIKE variable in the empirical analysis. The pre-January 2002 dip in inflation is captured by the PRE-EURO variable. The twelfth difference strips out of the data any seasonal unit roots and the same EUROSPIKE and PRE-EURO variables are used to capture the euro-changeover effect.

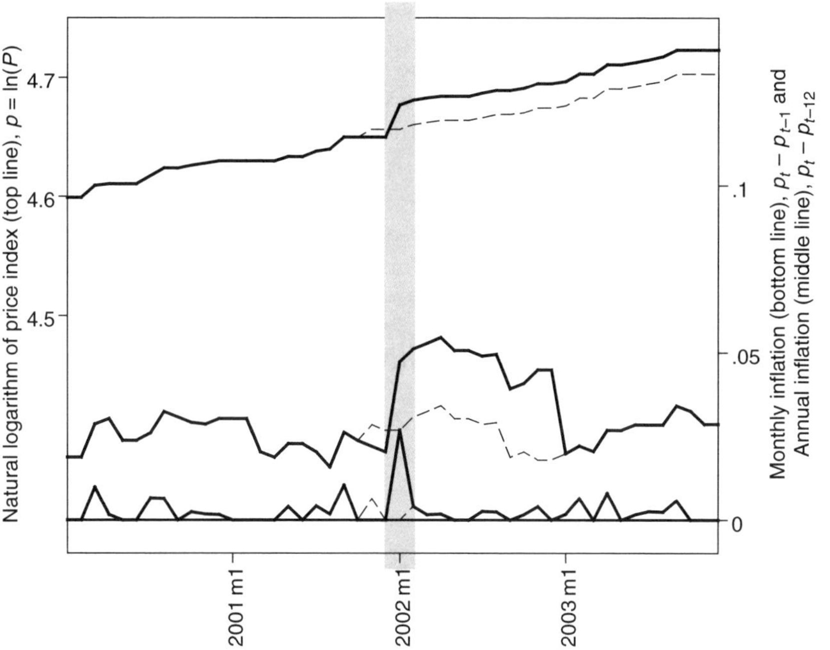

Figure 10.1 Suggested euro-changeover-induced patterns for log of price level, annual inflation and monthly inflation.

The data and time-series plots

In this section we present time-series plots of the data for the all-items HICP and for a sub-set of product categories selected on the basis of the material found in the literature survey and on the basis of the statistical results reported in the statistical analysis section.

The broad pattern that emerges from these figures is that, as expected, there is no evidence of an increase in prices in January 2002 for the three countries that did not join the euro at that time, whereas some of the countries that underwent the euro changeover in January 2002 exhibit substantive price increases at that point in time. The countries where these price increases are more evident are the larger ones with normally less volatile price indices such as France, Germany, Italy and Spain. The Netherlands exhibits a distinct pattern with substantive price increases one year before the euro changeover in January 2001. In some countries, particularly Greece, the seasonal variations are too volatile to discern any euro-changeover effect on prices from the figures. For this reason the analysis needs to be substantiated by the statistical results reported in the statistical analysis section.

Each figure illustrates the time-series plots for the 12 countries that joined the euro in January 2002 and for three EU countries that did not: Denmark, Sweden and the UK (the 'non-euro countries'). Each country's sub-panel illustrates three time-series: the natural logarithm of the price level $p_t = \ln(P_t)$, the monthly inflation rate based on first differences

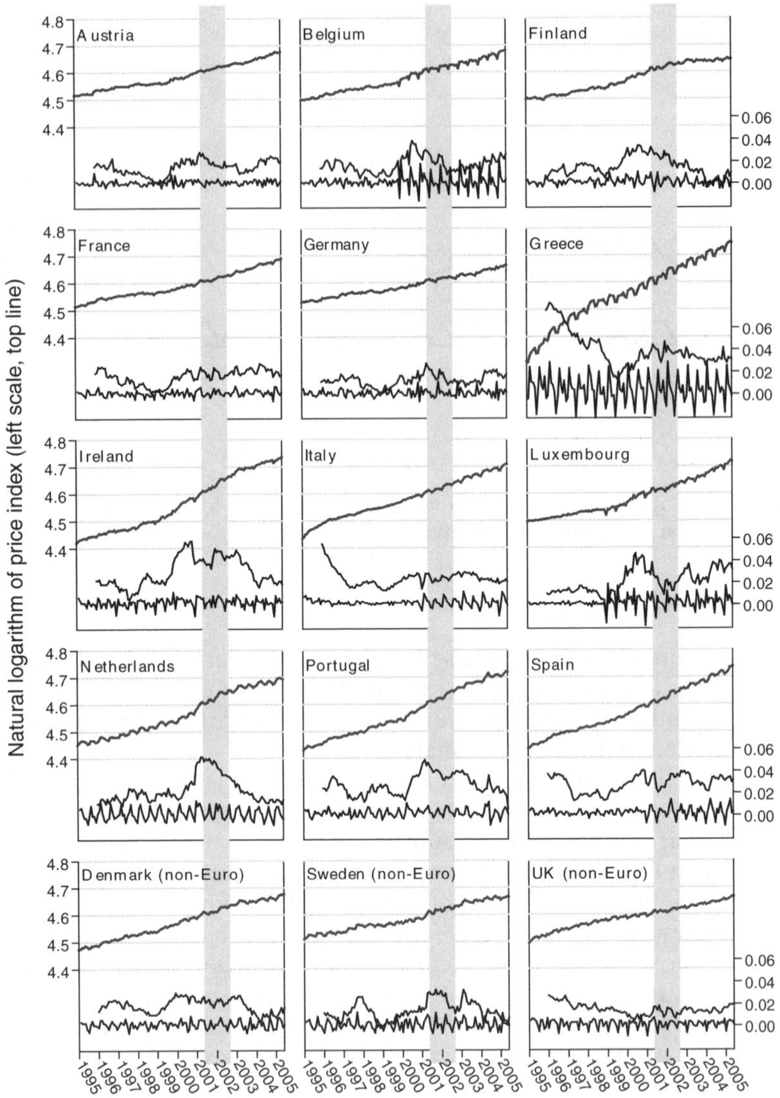

Figure 10.2 Natural logarithm of price level, annual inflation and monthly inflation: all products (cp00)

$\Delta p_t = p_t - p_{t-1}$ and the annual inflation rate based on twelfth differences $\Delta_{12} p_t = p_t - p_{t-12}$.[1]

Figure 10.2 illustrates the aforementioned time-series for the all products HICP (cp00); the grey vertical lines are centred on January 2002. Figure 10.2

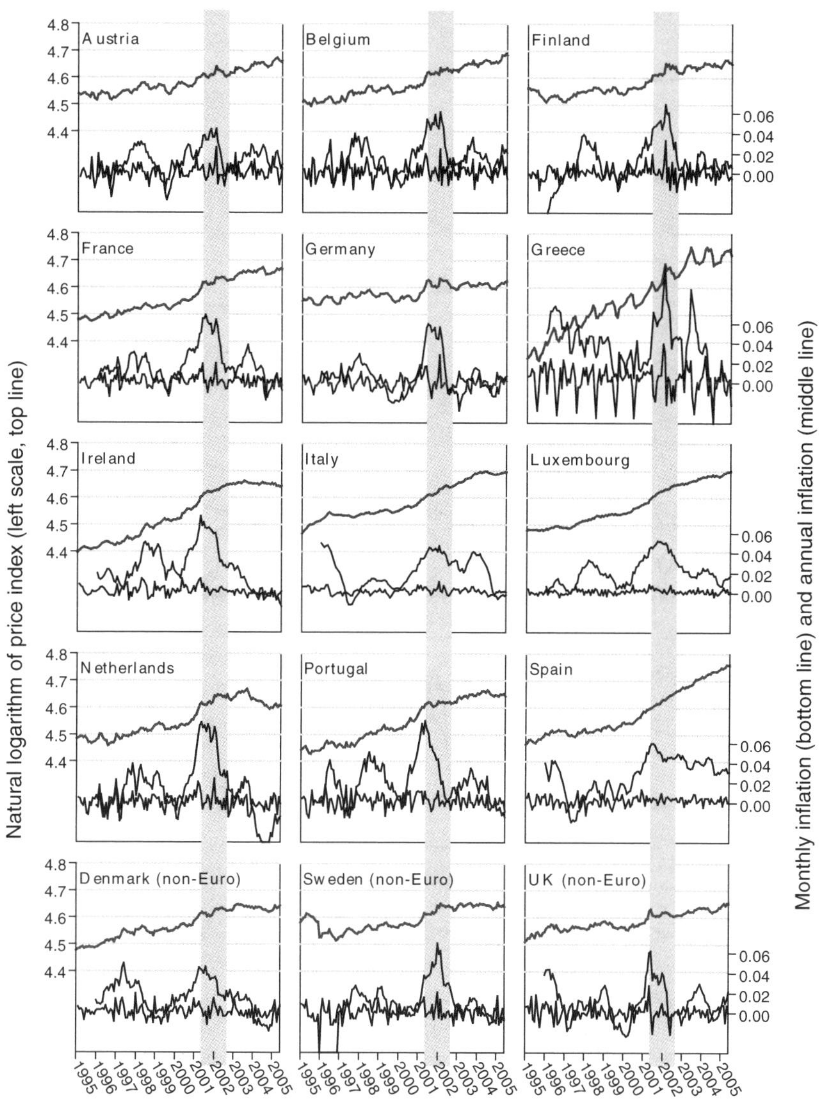

Figure 10.3 Natural logarithm of price level, annual inflation and monthly inflation: food and non-alcoholic beverages (cp01)

shows that there is no apparent visual evidence of a substantial increase in prices in January 2002. In particular, the series for monthly inflation in each case would demonstrate a significant 'spike' in January 2002 if there had been a substantial increase in the price level on this date. Hahn (2002)

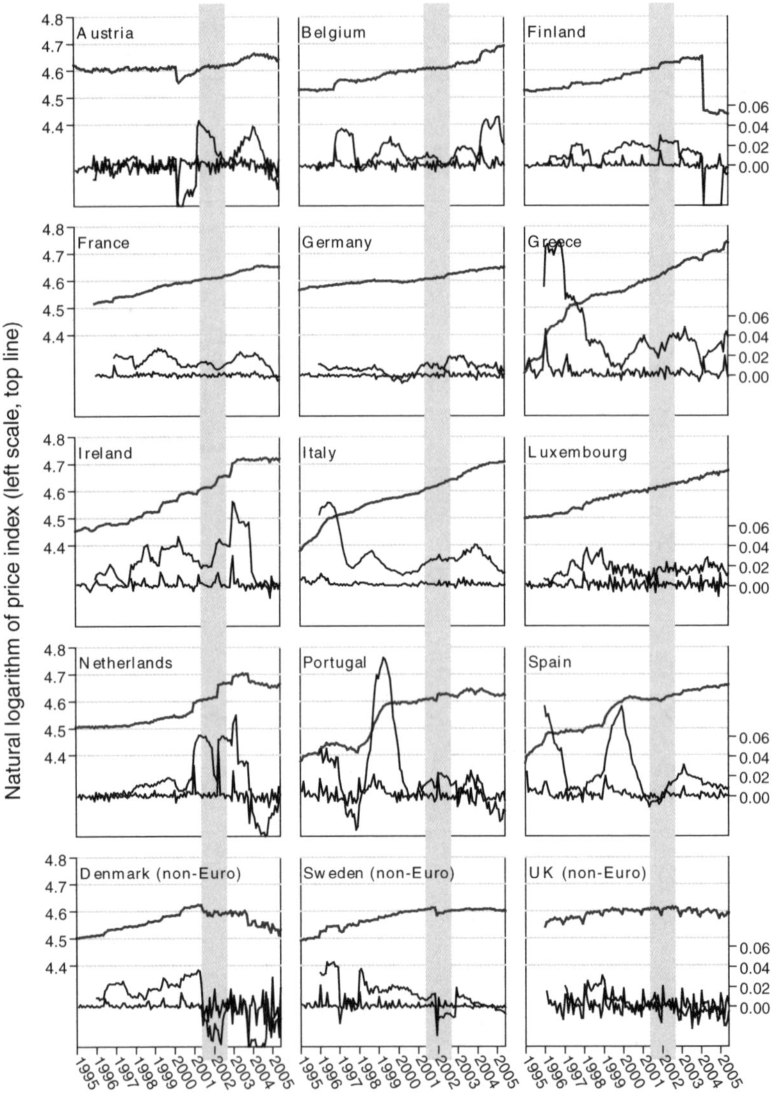

Figure 10.4 Natural logarithm of price level, annual inflation and monthly inflation: alcoholic beverages (cp021)

advocates analysing the price index for all products that excludes seasonal food and energy (EuroStat code xeseas). This is due to the high seasonal variation in food prices and the stochastic nature of energy prices. We have examined this measure also and, as we found for the HICP all products index, there seems no obvious evidence of a euro-changeover effect.

Figure 10.3 illustrates the time-series for food and non-alcoholic beverages (cp01). Here the pattern is a mixed one with substantial price increases occurring in all countries but over a full year before the euro is introduced. Rather than a once and for all increase in the price level, this seems to be a sustained increase in the rate of inflation. This pattern is most evident for Spain where there is an increase in the slope of the log-price level from 2000 onward.

Figure 10.4 illustrates the time-series for alcoholic beverages (cp021). Although the later empirical results lend some support to the presence of a euro-changeover effect on prices one should be cautious in interpreting the price movements for the sub-categories in alcoholic beverages, tobacco and narcotics (cp02). The reason for this caution is that the price of these goods is largely governed by taxes. Figure 10.4 is a case in point as it illustrates the dramatic cut in taxes that was applied to alcoholic beverages. Recently Sweden cut its duties on wine by 20 per cent in December 2001, Denmark cut alcohol duties by nearly 50 per cent on 1 October 2003 and Finland slashed alcohol duties on 1 March 2004. An appropriate modelling strategy is required for these product categories otherwise severe bias due to variable omission may occur. Figure 10.4 suggests that there were no particular price increases in January 2002 for the alcoholic beverages category; on the contrary, there may well have been price falls following tax cuts in response to opening up of trade following the euro changeover.

Figure 10.5 illustrates the time-series for actual rentals for housing (cp041). From the plots there are obvious price movements, the significance of which is picked up in the *F*-tests reported in the statistical section but these price movements do not appear to be associated with the euro changeover in January 2002. Austria and Ireland actually experienced a fall in the rate of price increase around January 2002. The Netherlands and Portugal display price increases that suggest the existence of a heavily regulated rental market. Hence, any statistical significance in these price movements should not be interpreted as being due to the euro changeover.

Figure 10.6 illustrates the time-series for electricity (cp0451). Again, there are obvious price movements the significance of which is picked up in the *F*-tests reported in the empirical section. However, these price movements also do not appear to be associated with the euro changeover in January 2002. The step changes observed in most countries suggest the existence of another highly regulated market and any statistical significance should not be interpreted as being due to the euro changeover. The only country that shows no evidence of step changes is the UK. Note that Ireland is one

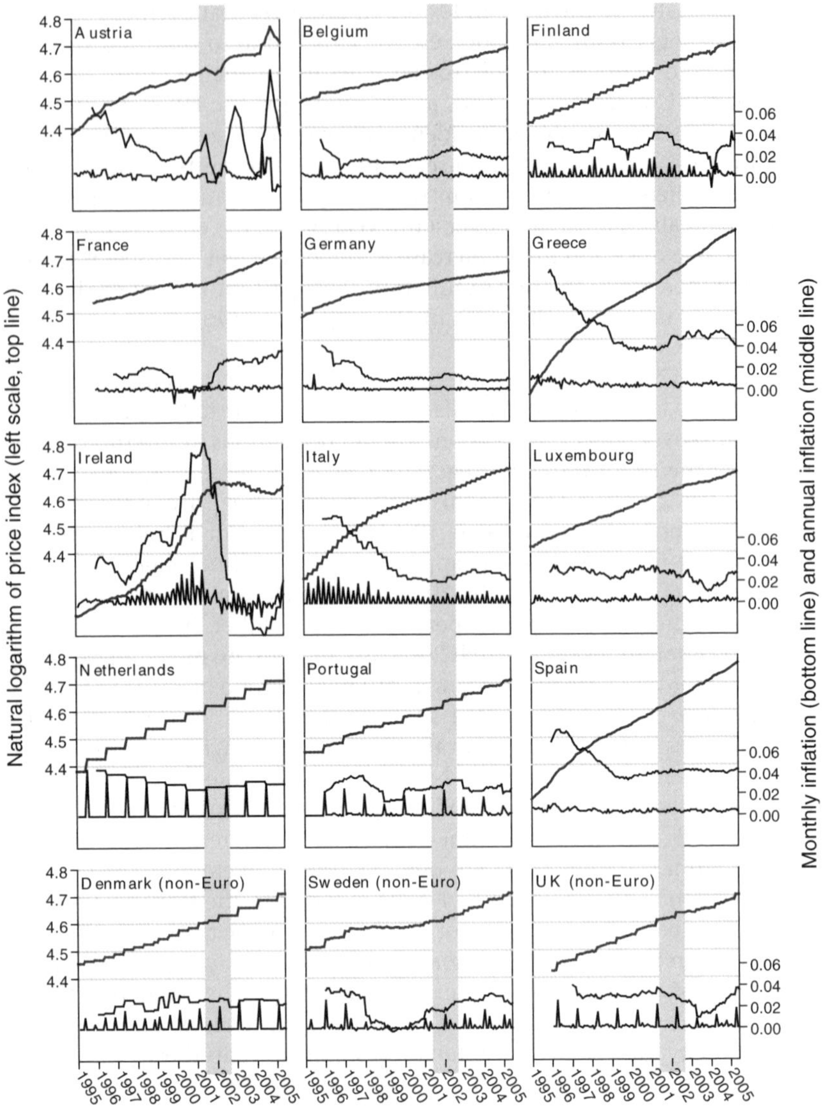

Figure 10.5 Natural logarithm of price level, annual inflation and monthly inflation: actual rentals for housing (cp041)

country where on the advent of the euro changeover substantial step increases in electricity prices begin.

Figure 10.7 illustrates the time-series for health (cp06). There are obvious price movements the significance of which is picked up in the *F*-tests

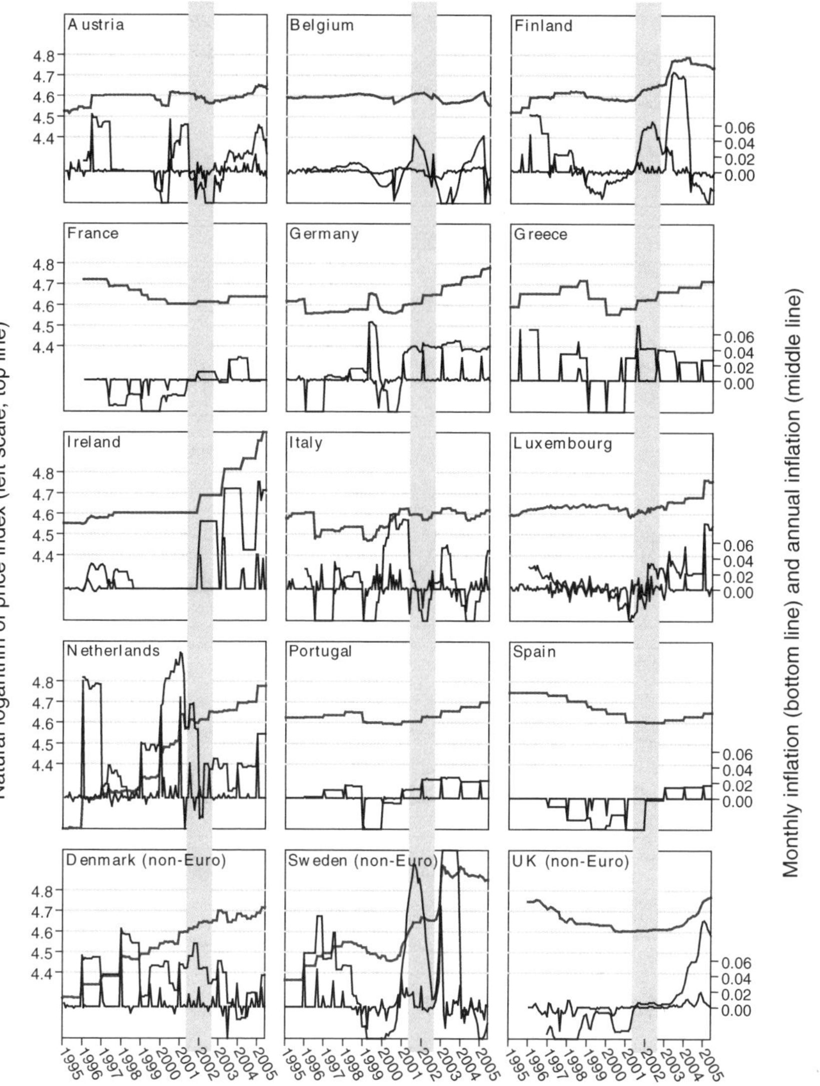

Figure 10.6 Natural logarithm of price level, annual inflation and monthly inflation: electricity (cp0451)

reported in the statistical section, but these price movements also do not appear to be associated with the euro changeover. The price movements seem to be so substantive that they are more likely to be associated with legislative changes with regard to government health policy. The statistically significant results should therefore be treated with caution. The only

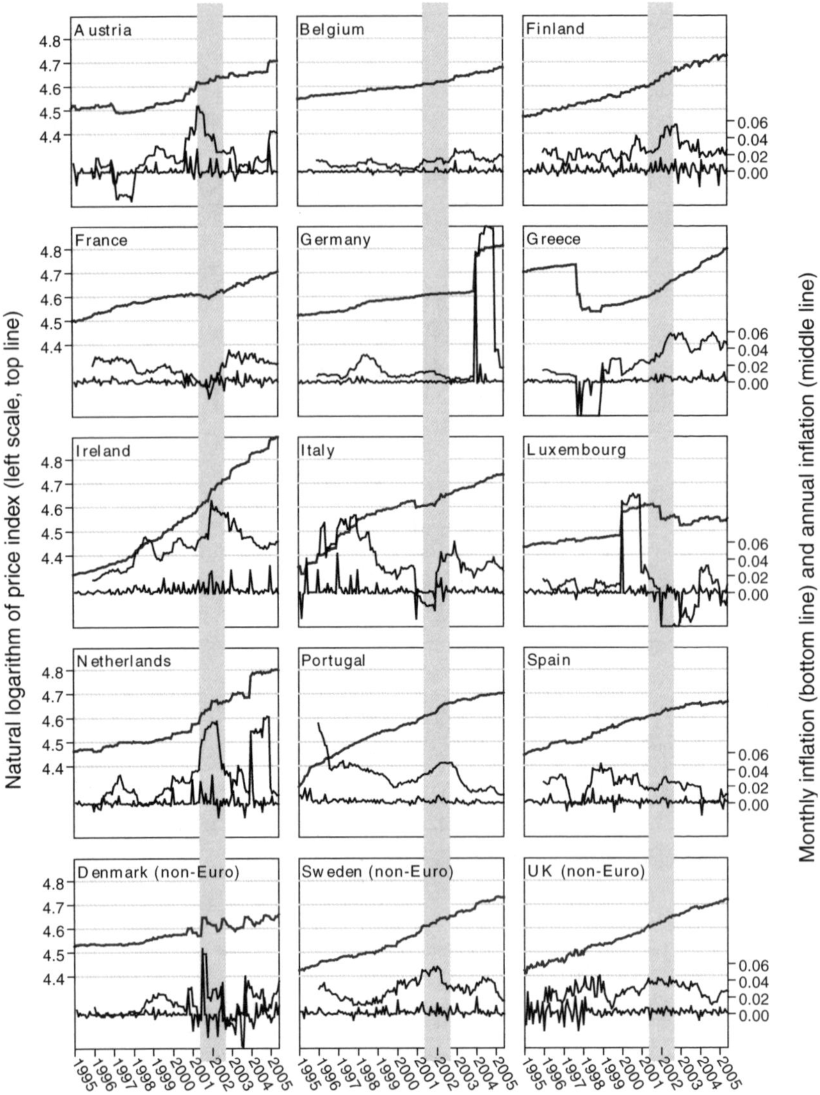

Figure 10.7 Natural logarithm of price level, annual inflation and monthly inflation: health (cp06)

country to exhibit a substantive price increase at the time of the euro changeover is Ireland.

Figure 10.8 illustrates the time-series for the purchase of vehicles (cp071). Here there are slight price movements whose significance is still picked up

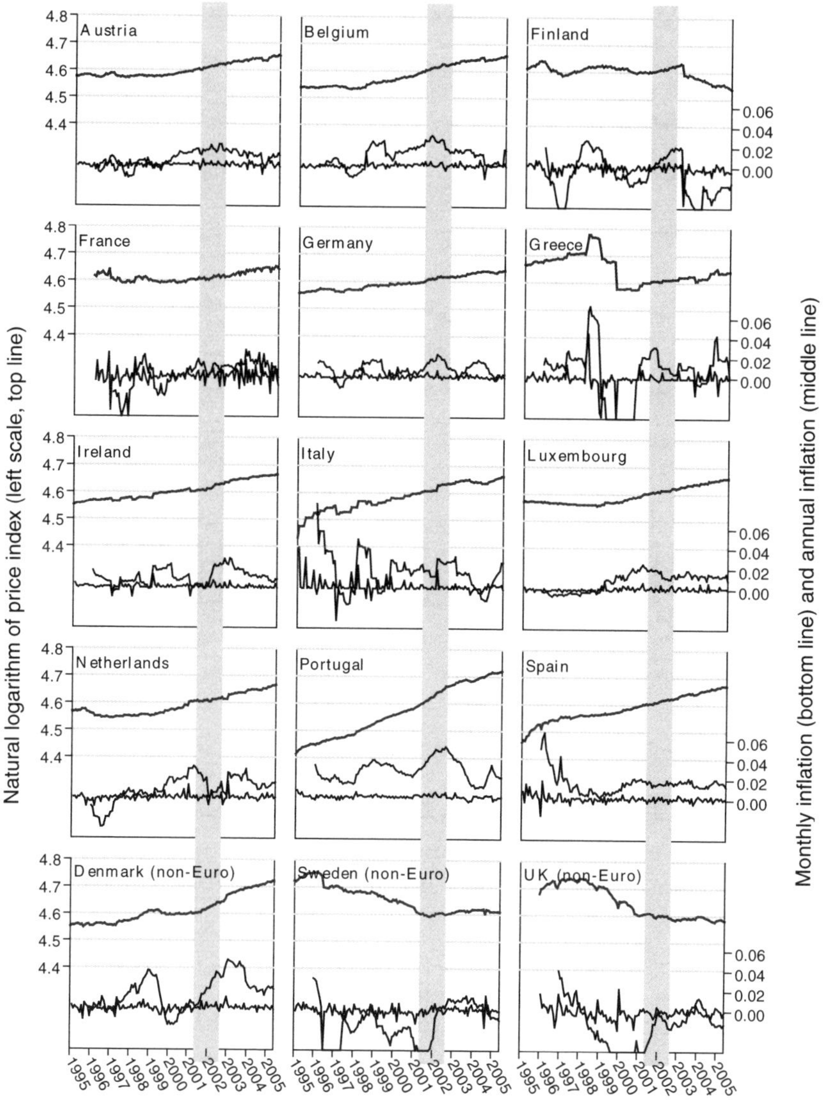

Figure 10.8 Natural logarithm of price level, annual inflation and monthly inflation: purchase of vehicles (cp071)

in the *F*-tests reported in the empirical section. In Germany, Ireland and Italy January 2002 coincides with very small but uncharacteristic increases in the price indices. In Greece and Luxembourg January 2002 corresponds with small falls in the price indices.

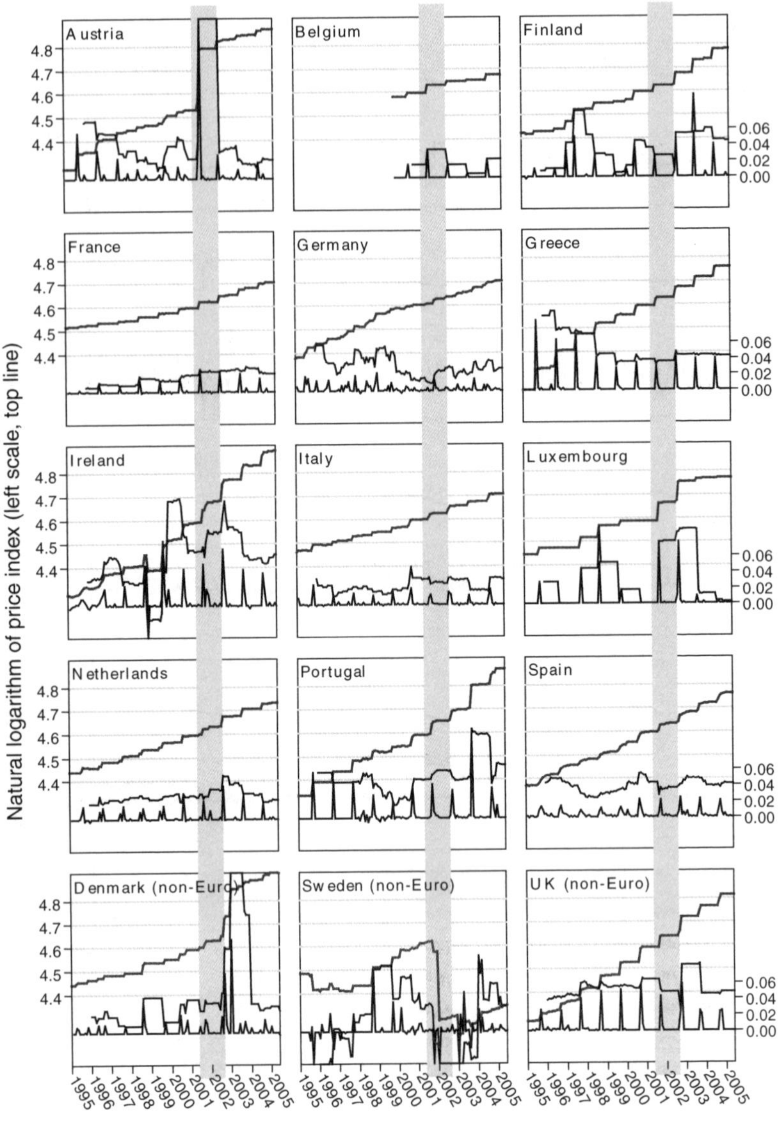

Figure 10.9 Natural logarithm of price level, annual inflation and monthly inflation: education (cp10)

Figure 10.9 illustrates the time-series for education (cp10). The step changes suggest the presence of another highly regulated market. These step changes appear to occur each September coinciding with the academic year. Very careful visual inspection reveals additional small increases in

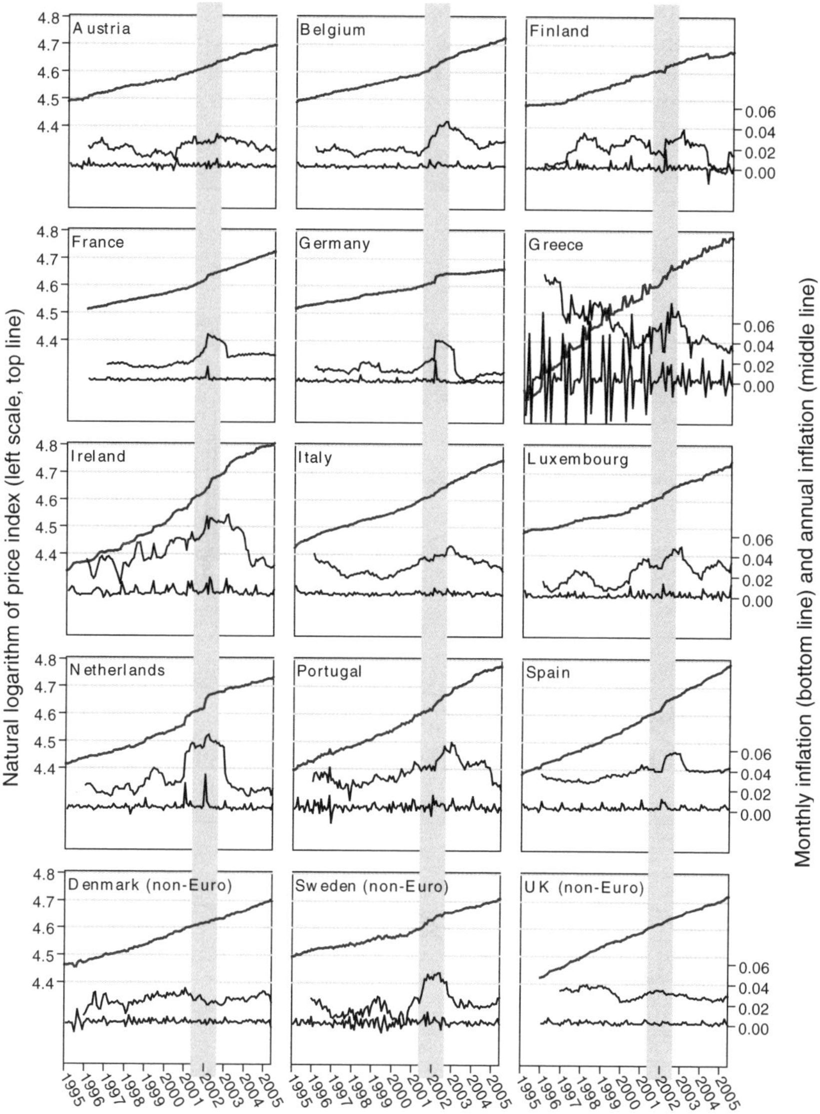

Figure 10.10 Natural logarithm of price level, annual inflation and monthly inflation: restaurants and the like (cp1111)

January 2002 for Germany, Ireland and the Netherlands. The significance of these is picked up in the *F*-tests reported in the empirical section. The most striking price change is the substantial price drop observed in Sweden in January 2002. The significance of this too is picked up in the *F*-tests.

Figure 10.10 illustrates the time-series for restaurants, cafés and the like (cp1111). In this sector there appear to be distinct euro-changeover-induced price increases for Finland, France, Germany, Ireland, Luxembourg, the Netherlands and Spain. Denmark and the UK exhibit no such price rise and

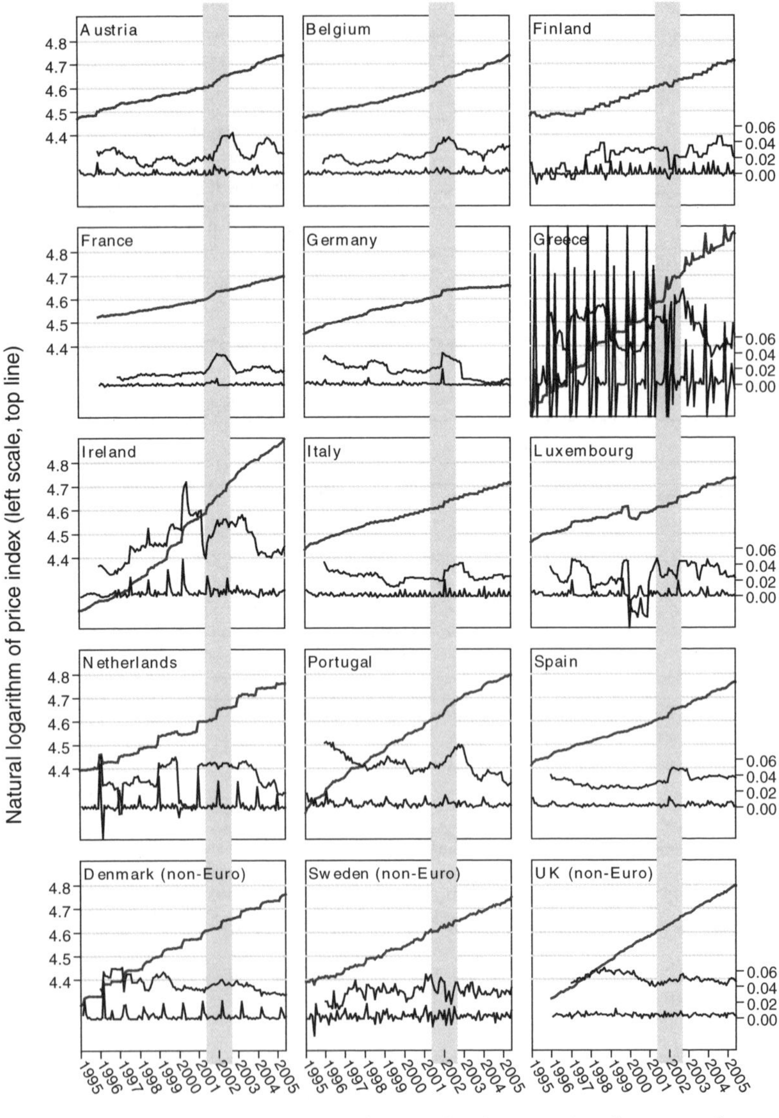

Figure 10.11 Natural logarithm of price level, annual inflation and monthly inflation: hairdressing and personal grooming salons (cp1211)

Sweden's price increase pre-dates the euro changeover by about six months. The strength of this euro-changeover effect is demonstrated by the joint *F*-tests reported in Table 10.7.

Figure 10.11 illustrates the time series for the hairdressing salons and personal grooming establishments sector (cp1211). In this service sector too there appear to be distinct euro-changeover-induced price increases for Finland, France, Germany, Italy and Spain. The non-euro countries do not exhibit uncharacteristic price increases in January 2002. Again, the strength of this euro-changeover effect is demonstrated by the joint *F*-tests reported in the empirical section.

Statistical analysis

The hypothesis that the euro changeover induced a significant increase in prices is tested using *F*-tests across Seemingly Unrelated Regression Estimations (SURE). SURE is chosen for a number of reasons. Firstly, it permits each country to possess its own dynamic structure in terms of lags, seasonals, trend and euro-specific dummies. Secondly, it permits joint cross-country *F*-tests on these euro-specific dummies. Thirdly, it allows for some degree of cross-country interdependence in terms of the covariance structure. Complete regression results and joint *F*-tests for all products (EuroStat code cp00) and the restaurant sector (EuroStat code cp1111) are presented in Tables 10.1 to 10.6. The results of the joint *F*-tests on only the euro dummies are reported in Table 10.7 for some more of the sub-sectors.

Estimation procedure

The data in the figures suggests that three alternative SURE equation specifications are possible. The first is presented in equation (10.1) which represents the equation in log-levels of the price index $p_{it} = \ln(P_{it})$. The country is indexed by the i subscripts, therefore each SURE system is made up of 15 equations. The EUROSHIFT dummy equals zero up to December 2001 and equals one from January 2002 onwards, so it captures a shift in the price index at the time of the euro changeover. The PRE-EURO dummy equals one in December 2001 and zero everywhere else, it therefore captures any possible negative (or positive) deviation from trend just before the euro changeover. Equation (10.1) also allows for each country to have its own trend t its own intercept term β_{i0}, its own dynamics in terms of lagged dependent variables and its own deterministic seasonal captured by eleven monthly dummies M_m.

$$p_{it} = \alpha_{i0}\text{EUROSHIFT} + \alpha_{i1}\text{PRE} - \text{EURO} + \tau_i t + \beta_{i0} + \sum_{l=1}^{12} \beta_{i,l}\, p_{i,t-l} + \sum_{m=2}^{12} \mu_{i,m} M_m + \varepsilon_{it} \qquad (10.1)$$

$$\Delta p_{it} = \alpha_{i0}\text{EUROSPIKE} + \alpha_{i1}\text{PRE} - \text{EURO}$$
$$+ \tau_i t + \delta_i p_{i,t-1} + \beta_{i0} + \sum_{l=1}^{12} \beta_{i,l}\Delta p_{i,t-l} + \sum_{m=2}^{12} \mu_{i,m} M_m + \varepsilon_{it} \tag{10.2}$$

$$\Delta_{12} p_{it} = \alpha_{i0}\text{EUROSPIKE} + \alpha_{i1}\text{PRE} - \text{EURO}$$
$$+ \tau_i t + \delta_i p_{i,t-1} + \beta_{i0} + \sum_{l=1}^{12} \beta_{i,l}\Delta_{12} p_{i,t-l} + \sum_{m=2}^{12} \mu_{i,m} M_m + \varepsilon_{it} \tag{10.3}$$

Equation (10.2) represents a time-series model of monthly inflation ($\Delta p_{it} = p_{it} - p_{it-1}$). This differs from equation (10.1) insofar as the EUROSHIFT dummy is replaced by a EUROSPIKE dummy that equals one on January 2002 and zero everywhere else. Equation (10.2) also includes one lag of the log-level, so the significance values on the parameters δ_i constitute augmented Dickey–Fuller (ADF) (1979) tests for the presence of unit roots. Critical values for these ADF tests must be the ones based on the presence of an intercept and a slope parameter but these are only approximate as they do not accommodate the presence of the structural dummies such as EUROSPIKE and PRE-EURO.

The specification presented by equation (10.3) represents a time-series model of annual inflation given by $\Delta_{12} p_{it} = p_{it} - p_{it-12}$. This specification differs from equation (10.2) only insofar as the price data have been differenced by a lag of 12 thus removing any seasonal unit roots. The effect of this can be seen in Tables 10.3 and 10.6 where for each country the month dummies are found to be jointly insignificant by the *F*-tests. Again the parameters on the lag of the log-levels δ_i constitute tests for the presence of unit roots at the zero frequency. Tests for the presence of seasonal unit roots as proposed by Dickey *et al.* (1984), Osborn *et al.* (1988), Hylleberg *et al.* (1990, aka HEGY), Franses (1991) or Beaulieu and Miron (1993) are not practical for such short runs of data. The 12 lags of the dependent variable therefore allow for the presence of seasonal unit roots though they do not allow this structure to be identified. Also impractical for these data are panel unit-root tests as first proposed by Levin and Lin (1992), given the seasonality and the heterogeneity between the various countries.

SURE estimation is implemented as a variant of Feasible Generalised Least Squares (FGLS) where each equation is estimated individually but the covariance structure spans across equations. The estimator is defined by:

$$\hat{\beta} = [\mathbf{X}'\Omega^{-1}\mathbf{X}]\mathbf{X}'\Omega^{-1}\mathbf{y} \tag{10.4}$$

where $\hat{\beta}$ is a staked vector of each parameter vector for each country. **X** is a matrix of matrices, with the X matrix for each country along the diagonal sub-matrices and zeros everywhere else. **y** is a stacked vector of dependent variables for each country and Ω is the disturbance covariance matrix defined by $\mathbf{E}[\varepsilon'\varepsilon|\mathbf{X}]=\Omega$. An estimable Ω is required for SURE regression to be feasible hence making SURE a FGLS procedure. Further details can be seen in various sources such as Greene (2003, ch. 14.2), the estimation procedure adopted is Stata's *sureg* with the small sample correction options *small* and *dfk2*.

Estimates for the overall price index

SURE results for the all products price index are reported in Tables 10.1, 10.2 and 10.3. The broad picture is that for the 12 countries which adopted the euro in January 2002 there is a statistically significant but quantitatively very small increase in prices, for the three countries that did not join the euro there is no statistical evidence of an uncharacteristic price change on January 2002.

Considering more closely the results for the log-level of the all products price index reported in Table 10.1, we see at the bottom of this table that for the euro-changeover countries the joint *F*-test has a density in the tail of 0.0059. This implies a rejection of the hypothesis that the EUROSHIFT dummies are jointly insignificant for the euro-changeover countries, and suggests a statistically significant increase over and above existing trends in the price indices in January 2002. The same *F*-test for the three non-euro countries has a density in the tail of 0.4457 indicating a non-rejection of the hypothesis that the EUROSHIFT dummies are jointly insignificant. This suggest that there was no particular deviation in the price index for these three countries in January 2002. Looking more closely at the parameter estimates for the EUROSHIFT dummies we note that the countries with the significant EUROSHIFT dummies are Italy and Spain. The joint *F*-tests for the PRE-EURO dummies show that these are jointly insignificant for both the 12 euro-changeover and the three non-euro countries at *p*-values of 0.2289 and 0.2118. The *F*-tests for the lagged dependent variables and the month dummies suggest that both these sets of variables are important for all countries and the Q-statistics suggest that there is no remaining residual autocorrelation.

The SURE results in Table 10.2 shed more light by considering the monthly inflation rate at the time of the euro changeover. The joint *F*-test of the EUROSPIKE dummies for the euro-changeover countries has a *p*-value of 0.0257 suggesting an (only just) significant increase in the monthly inflation rate in January 2002. Closer inspection of the EUROSPIKE parameters reveals values ranging from 0.008 to –0.001 indicating rather modest increases of 0.8 per cent to –0.1 per cent above any expected increases. Such modest increases in the aggregate price indices could be due to increases in a very small number of sub-sectors, and the *F*-test reported in Table 10.2 confirms this hypothesis. The joint *F*-test of the EUROSPIKE dummies for the non-euro countries has a *p*-value of 0.0998 suggesting (only just) insignificant EUROSPIKE dummies for January 2002. Paradoxically, the most significant EUROSPIKE dummy for the non-euro countries is the negative one for Sweden at –0.005 suggesting a fall in monthly inflation. Again, the PRE-EURO dummies are jointly insignificant for both the euro-changeover and the non-euro countries with *p*-values of 0.4056 and 0.3369.

The SURE results for the annual inflation rate in Table 10.3 are broadly in line with the results for the monthly inflation rate. The joint *F*-tests for the

Table 10.1 SURE on natural logarithm of price level $p = \ln(P)$ for all products (cp00)

Dependent variable: p	*Austria*	*Belgium*	*Finland*	*France*	*Germany*	*Greece*	*Ireland*	*Italy*	*Luxembourg*	*Netherlands*	*Portugal*	*Spain*	*Denmark*	*Sweden*	*UK*
*Parameter estimates:**															
EUROSHIFT	0.001	–0.001	–0.001	0.002	0.000	0.002	0.002	0.002	0.001	0.004	0.003	0.003	0.001	0.001	0.001
	(0.55)	(0.59)	(0.81)	(1.93)	(0.40)	(1.23)	(1.55)	(2.59)	(0.58)	(1.71)	(1.88)	(2.67)	(1.40)	(0.59)	(0.94)
PRE-EURO	–0.001	–0.003	–0.001	–0.002	0.005	0.002	0.006	–0.002	–0.004	0.002	0.002	0.001	0.004	0.001	–0.001
	(0.38)	(0.70)	(0.49)	(0.82)	(1.63)	(0.73)	(1.90)	(0.71)	(0.96)	(0.52)	(0.68)	(0.28)	(2.03)	(0.24)	(0.28)
Trend	0.007	0.022	0.003	0.008	0.011	0.029	0.024	0.037	0.019	0.029	0.032	0.030	0.028	0.014	0.011
	(1.19)	(1.92)	(0.45)	(2.30)	(1.33)	(2.53)	(3.46)	(3.24)	(2.49)	(3.00)	(2.71)	(3.21)	(3.06)	(1.84)	(1.60)
Constant	0.215	0.469	0.058	0.237	0.372	0.404	0.327	0.761	0.340	0.556	0.526	0.495	0.618	0.411	0.417
	(1.01)	(1.45)	(0.35)	(2.30)	(1.16)	(2.85)	(3.26)	(3.36)	(1.95)	(2.83)	(2.70)	(3.24)	(3.11)	(1.64)	(1.95)
R^2	0.9979	0.9954	0.9979	0.9984	0.9964	0.9992	0.9994	0.9992	0.9970	0.9990	0.9993	0.9992	0.9991	0.9972	0.9984
Obs.	114	114	114	114	114	114	114	114	114	114	114	114	114	114	114
Diagnostics:															
Lagged dependent variables' joint significance tests, ~ $F_{12,1305}$.															
F-test	71.04	28.50	144.84	178.31	32.50	77.80	169.19	169.19	67.93	110.28	66.78	85.46	87.83	43.28	31.97
p-value	0.00	0.00	0.00	0.00	0.00	0.00	0.00	0.00	0.00	0.00	0.00	0.00	0.00	0.00	0.00
Month dummies' M_2 to M_{12} joint significance tests, ~ $F_{11,1140}$.															
F-test	3.29	3.71	7.36	6.16	6.21	22.12	10.46	10.46	2.70	8.98	4.85	3.01	12.84	6.96	13.15
p-value	0.00	0.00	0.00	0.00	0.00	0.00	0.00	0.00	0.00	0.00	0.00	0.00	0.00	0.00	0.00
Residual autocorrelation Portmanteau/Q tests, ~ χ^2_1.															
e_{t-1}	0.13	0.13	0.11	0.16	0.03	0.01	0.12	0.12	0.10	0.08	–0.03	0.17	0.02	0.11	0.01
Q-stat	1.94	1.86	1.29	3.06	0.08	0.02	1.63	1.63	1.12	0.66	0.08	3.35	0.05	1.45	0.02
p-value	0.16	0.17	0.26	0.08	0.78	0.88	0.20	0.20	0.29	0.42	0.78	0.07	0.83	0.23	0.90

Tests for joint significance of EUROSHIFT and PRE-EURO dummies across countries.
EUROSHIFT dummies in the 12 euro countries. $F_{12,1305} = 2.33$, *p*-value = 0.0059
EUROSHIFT dummies in 3 non-euro countries. $F_{3,1305} = 0.89$, *p*-value = 0.4457
PRE-EURO dummies in the 12 euro countries. $F_{12,1305} = 1.27$, *p*-value = 0.2289
PRE-EURO dummies in three non-euro countries. $F_{3,1305} = 1.50$, *p*-value = 0.2118

Note: *p*-values are densities in the tail of each distribution. Absolute value of *t*-statistics given in (parentheses). * Individual parameter estimates on lagged dependent variables and month dummies not reported; see *F*-tests.

Table 10.2 SURE on monthly inflation ($\Delta p = p_t - p_{t-1}$), for all products (cp00)

Dependent variable: p	*Austria*	*Belgium*	*Finland*	*France*	*Germany*	*Greece*	*Ireland*	*Italy*	*Luxembourg*	*Netherlands*	*Portugal*	*Spain*	*Denmark*	*Sweden*	*UK*
*Parameter estimates:**															
EUROSHIFT	0.002	0.003	0.006	0.005	0.005	0.008	0.005	0.002	–0.001	0.007	0.001	0.005	0.002	–0.005	0.002
	(1.14)	(0.86)	(2.30)	(2.45)	(1.93)	(2.29)	(1.70)	(0.99)	(0.13)	(2.47)	(0.31)	(1.86)	(1.06)	(1.69)	(1.01)
PRE-EURO	–0.001	–0.002	–0.000	–0.002	0.003	0.002	0.006	–0.002	–0.005	0.000	0.000	–0.001	0.004	0.000	–0.000
	(0.47)	(0.43)	(0.00)	(0.88)	(1.03)	(0.64)	(1.99)	(0.93)	(1.08)	(0.11)	(0.13)	(0.36)	(1.75)	(0.16)	(0.21)
Trend	0.010	0.035	0.016	0.007	0.018	0.030	0.023	0.026	0.021	0.017	0.016	0.021	0.024	0.012	0.010
	(2.02)	(3.29)	(3.15)	(1.92)	(2.63)	(2.58)	(3.75)	(2.59)	(2.63)	(2.86)	(1.98)	(2.65)	(2.79)	(2.10)	(1.59)
p_{t-1}	–0.055	–0.184	–0.089	–0.030	–0.131	–0.089	–0.063	–0.105	–0.075	–0.062	–0.054	–0.068	–0.113	–0.074	–0.076
	(1.76)	(3.17)	(3.42)	(1.41)	(2.53)	(2.69)	(3.77)	(2.51)	(2.16)	(2.94)	(1.99)	(2.44)	(2.86)	(2.13)	(1.62)
Constant	0.248	0.819	0.395	0.133	0.593	0.378	0.267	0.465	0.329	0.275	0.237	0.298	0.503	0.332	0.339
	(1.76)	(3.15)	(3.40)	(1.38)	(2.54)	(2.61)	(3.67)	(2.51)	(2.12)	(2.98)	(1.99)	(2.43)	(2.87)	(2.11)	(1.59)
R^2	0.4118	0.7994	0.6382	0.5444	0.6173	0.9549	0.7399	0.7746	0.6977	0.8180	0.6087	0.7442	0.7586	0.7104	0.8474
Obs.	113	113	113	113	113	113	113	113	113	113	113	113	113	113	113
Diagnostics:															
Lagged dependent variables' joint significance tests, ~ $F_{11,1275}$.															
F-test	0.94	11.41	2.80	0.94	2.08	2.09	1.07	1.07	4.06	1.58	2.12	11.20	1.03	0.85	0.74
p-value	0.51	0.00	0.00	0.50	0.02	0.02	0.38	0.38	0.00	0.09	0.01	0.00	0.42	0.60	0.71
Month dummies' M_2 to M_{12} joint significance tests, ~ $F_{11,1275}$.															
F-test	3.55	3.72	5.21	6.82	3.03	4.97	4.66	4.66	3.21	4.27	3.44	2.54	6.40	5.79	5.30
p-value	0.00	0.00	0.00	0.00	0.00	0.00	0.00	0.00	0.00	0.00	0.00	0.00	0.00	0.00	0.00
Residual autocorrelation Portmanteau/Q tests, ~ χ^2_1.															
e_{t-1}	0.00	0.07	0.10	0.19	0.06	0.02	0.16	0.16	0.10	0.08	–0.06	0.17	0.02	0.13	0.02
Q-stat	0.00	0.60	1.19	4.12	0.37	0.04	2.84	2.84	1.23	0.66	0.42	3.32	0.07	2.04	0.05
p-value	0.98	0.44	0.28	0.04	0.54	0.84	0.09	0.09	0.27	0.42	0.52	0.07	0.79	0.15	0.82

Tests for joint significance of EUROSHIFT and PRE-EURO dummies across countries.
EUROSHIFT dummies in the 12 euro countries. $F_{12,1275} = 1.95$, *p*-value = 0.0257
EUROSHIFT dummies in 3 non-euro countries. $F_{3,1275} = 2.09$, *p*-value = 0.0998
PRE-EURO dummies in the 12 euro countries. $F_{12,1275} = 1.04$ *p*-value = 0.4056
PRE-EURO dummies in three non-euro countries. $F_{3,1275} = 1.13$ *p*-value = 0.3369

Note: *p*-values are densities in the tail of each distribution. Absolute value of *t*-statistics given in (parentheses). * Individual parameter estimates on lagged dependent variables and month dummies not reported; see *F*-tests.

Table 10.3 SURE on annual inflation ($\Delta_{12} p = p_t - p_{t-12}$), for all products (cp00)

Dependent variable: p	*Austria*	*Belgium*	*Finland*	*France*	*Germany*	*Greece*	*Ireland*	*Italy*	*Luxembourg*	*Netherlands*	*Portugal*	*Spain*	*Denmark*	*Sweden*	*UK*
*Parameter estimates:**															
EUROSHIFT	0.004	0.013	0.010	0.011	0.009	0.016	0.009	0.002	0.013	0.000	0.000	0.010	0.006	0.000	0.005
	(1.09)	(2.93)	(2.92)	(3.97)	(2.86)	(3.70)	(2.30)	(0.60)	(2.31)	(0.01)	(0.07)	(3.38)	(1.94)	(0.06)	(1.86)
PRE-EURO	–0.003	0.005	0.003	0.000	0.002	0.005	0.013	0.002	0.002	0.004	–0.000	0.001	0.004	0.005	0.001
	(0.91)	(1.07)	(1.00)	(0.05)	(0.72)	(1.24)	(3.64)	(0.56)	(0.35)	(0.86)	(0.07)	(0.29)	(1.56)	(1.00)	(0.31)
Trend	0.005	0.009	0.027	–0.008	–0.009	0.021	0.027	0.004	–0.005	0.024	0.019	0.016	–0.006	–0.007	–0.015
	(0.56)	(0.65)	(2.66)	(1.20)	(0.81)	(0.88)	(2.33)	(0.25)	(0.37)	(2.08)	(1.14)	(1.29)	(0.36)	(0.63)	(1.36)
P_{t-1}	–0.010	–0.035	–0.143	0.071	0.081	–0.063	–0.071	–0.012	0.059	–0.082	–0.062	–0.037	0.026	0.044	0.126
	(0.17)	(0.45)	(2.71)	(1.75)	(0.99)	(0.93)	(2.25)	(0.21)	(1.02)	(2.06)	(1.18)	(0.88)	(0.33)	(0.66)	(1.47)
Constant	0.045	0.159	0.637	–0.320	–0.364	0.280	0.309	0.057	–0.262	0.363	0.272	0.166	–0.110	–0.196	–0.568
	(0.17)	(0.45)	(2.71)	(1.76)	(0.99)	(0.94)	(2.25)	(0.22)	(1.02)	(2.07)	(1.18)	(0.90)	(0.32)	(0.65)	(1.47)
R^2	0.8648	0.7769	0.9198	0.8962	0.8014	0.8931	0.9556	0.8167	0.8468	0.9455	0.8935	0.9087	0.8789	0.8236	0.7524
Obs.	102	102	102	102	102	102	102	102	102	102	102	102	102	102	102
Diagnostics:															
Lagged dependent variables' joint significance tests, ~ $F_{12,1110}$.															
F-test	29.77	20.37	53.17	31.05	21.18	42.09	131.67	131.67	22.13	88.88	47.69	38.31	34.95	22.98	18.54
p-value	0.00	0.00	0.00	0.00	0.00	0.00	0.00	0.00	0.00	0.00	0.00	0.00	0.00	0.00	0.00
Month dummies' M_2 to M_{12} joint significance tests, ~ $F_{11,1110}$.															
F-test	0.21	0.91	0.72	0.59	0.33	0.19	0.57	0.57	0.44	0.26	0.20	0.77	0.22	0.08	0.31
p-value	1.00	0.53	0.72	0.84	0.98	1.00	0.86	0.86	0.94	0.99	1.00	0.67	1.00	1.00	0.98
Residual autocorrelation Portmanteau/Q tests, ~ χ^2_1.															
e_{t-1}	0.24	0.05	0.16	0.24	0.13	0.10	0.22	0.22	0.16	0.19	–0.04	0.20	0.17	0.23	0.17
Q-stat	5.91	0.32	2.54	6.20	1.72	1.03	4.94	4.94	2.69	3.65	0.14	4.30	3.08	5.50	3.21
p-value	0.02	0.57	0.11	0.01	0.19	0.31	0.03	0.03	0.10	0.06	0.71	0.04	0.08	0.02	0.07

Tests for joint significance of EUROSPIKE and PRE-EURO dummies across countries.

EUROSPIKE dummies in the 12 euro countries. $F_{12,1110} = 2.92$, *p*-value = 0.0005
EUROSPIKE dummies in 3 non-euro countries. $F_{3,1110} = 2.18$, *p*-value = 0.0888
PRE-EURO dummies in the 12 euro countries. $F_{12,1110} = 2.21$, *p*-value = 0.0098
PRE-EURO dummies in 3 non-euro countries. $F_{3,1110} = 0.91$, *p*-value = 0.4362

Note: *p*-values are densities in the tail of each distribution. Absolute value of *t*-statistics given in (parentheses).

EUROSPIKE dummies suggest a significant increase in inflation for the euro-changeover countries with a *p*-value of 0.0005 and an insignificant effect for the non-euro countries with a *p*-value of 0.0888. The joint *F*-tests for the PRE-EURO dummies suggest a significant increase in inflation in December 2001 for the euro-changeover countries with a *p*-value of 0.0098 and an insignificant effect for the non-euro countries with a *p*-value of 0.4362. Looking more closely at the individual results for the PRE-EURO dummies, we note that the only country with a significant PRE-EURO dummy is Ireland and this is driving the significant result for the joint *F*-test. The other diagnostics suggest that the lagged dependent variables are significant, the deterministic seasonal dummies are not significant and for Austria, Ireland, Italy and Spain there is some unexplained residual autocorrelation.

Estimates for the restaurant sector

SURE results for the restaurants and the like price index (EuroStat code cp1111) are reported in Tables 10.4, 10.5 and 10.6. This sector has been singled out for analysis because it has received particular attention in past research and in the popular press. The pattern that emerges for this sector matches very closely the pattern one would expect from the presence of substantive menu costs and the occurrence of a currency changeover. For the 12 countries that adopted the euro in January 2002 there is a statistically significant and quantitatively large increase in prices, while for the three countries that did not join the euro there is no statistical evidence of an uncharacteristic price change. In addition, the PRE-EURO parameter appears to be negative for just over half of the euro-changeover countries.

Table 10.4 reports the SURE results for the log-levels of the price indices and in this case the EUROSHIFT parameters appear to be positive and significant for most euro-changeover countries and jointly significant with a *p*-value of 0.0000. The EUROSPIKE parameters for the non-euro countries are jointly insignificant with a *p*-value of 0.7593. Similarly, the PRE-EURO parameters are jointly significant for the euro-changeover countries with a *p*-value of 0.0481 and jointly insignificant for the non-euro countries with a *p*-value of 0.9925.

Table 10.5 reports the SURE results for monthly inflation. The EUROSPIKE parameters appear to be positive and significant for most euro-changeover countries and they are jointly significant with a *p*-value of 0.0000. The largest parameter estimate is 0.026 for the Netherlands, suggesting a substantive 2.6 per cent increase in monthly inflation over and above what one would have expected. The lowest parameter estimate is –0.010 for Greece; although this is insignificant it suggests a fall in monthly inflation, contrary to what one would have expected. The PRE-EURO parameters are jointly significant for the euro-changeover countries with a *p*-value of 0.0006 and jointly insignificant for the non-euro countries with a *p*-value

Table 10.4 SURE on natural logarithm of price level $p=\ln(P)$, for restaurants and the like (cp1111)

Dependent variable: p	*Austria*	*Belgium*	*Finland*	*France*	*Germany*	*Greece*	*Ireland*	*Italy*	*Luxembourg*	*Netherlands*	*Portugal*	*Spain*	*Denmark*	*Sweden*	*UK*
*Parameter estimates:**															
EUROSHIFT	0.002	0.002	0.002	0.000	0.006	0.010	0.004	0.002	0.002	0.006	0.005	0.003	–0.001	–0.000	–0.000
	(1.92)	(1.95)	(1.49)	(0.12)	(4.77)	(2.68)	(2.03)	(2.73)	(1.85)	(2.60)	(3.56)	(4.53)	(1.07)	(0.14)	(0.09)
PRE-EURO	–0.002	–0.000	–0.002	0.003	0.001	–0.009	0.006	0.001	0.001	0.002	–0.005	0.002	–0.000	–0.001	–0.000
	(1.01)	(0.24)	(0.57)	(1.73)	(0.42)	(1.07)	(1.39)	(0.37)	(0.35)	(0.43)	(1.76)	(1.15)	(0.18)	(0.25)	(0.07)
Trend	0.019	0.016	0.025	0.002	0.041	–0.063	0.054	0.017	0.017	0.048	0.046	0.047	0.040	0.015	0.011
	(2.75)	(3.46)	(1.58)	(0.64)	(5.83)	(1.52)	(2.97)	(3.35)	(2.63)	(3.83)	(4.13)	(5.34)	(2.62)	(1.36)	(1.04)
Constant	0.424	0.309	0.560	0.027	1.427	–0.155	0.474	0.256	0.296	0.660	0.548	0.513	0.650	0.237	0.165
	(2.77)	(3.15)	(2.01)	(0.32)	(6.12)	(0.53)	(3.02)	(3.43)	(2.48)	(3.83)	(4.34)	(5.32)	(2.47)	(0.89)	(1.21)
R^2	.9992	.9997	.9973	.9996	.9979	.9970	.9994	.9998	.9992	.9989	.9995	.9999	.9995	.9978	.9998
Obs.	102	102	102	102	102	102	102	102	102	102	102	102	102	102	102
Diagnostics:															
Lagged dependent variables' joint significance tests, ~ $F_{12,1125}$.															
F-test	61.36	196.18	50.98	265.48	46.09	21.35	57.76	57.76	111.67	107.40	84.22	148.70	26.78	23.37	100.21
p-value	0.00	0.00	0.00	0.00	0.00	0.00	0.00	0.00	0.00	0.00	0.00	0.00	0.00	0.00	0.00
Month dummies' M_2 to M_{12} joint significance tests, ~ $F_{11,1125}$.															
F-test	0.50	1.98	1.07	2.62	0.37	3.28	0.85	0.85	2.15	3.92	3.26	13.24	1.14	0.96	2.75
p-value	0.90	0.03	0.38	0.00	0.97	0.00	0.59	0.59	0.02	0.00	0.00	0.00	0.33	0.48	0.00
Residual autocorrelation Portmanteau/Q tests, ~ $\chi 21$.															
e_{t-1}	0.02	0.02	0.06	–0.05	0.08	0.10	0.11	0.11	0.03	0.04	–0.17	0.20	0.19	–0.00	–0.04
Q-stat	0.07	0.07	0.44	0.22	0.70	1.10	1.29	1.29	0.12	0.21	3.26	4.51	4.30	0.00	0.15
p-value	0.79	0.79	0.50	0.64	0.40	0.29	0.26	0.26	0.73	0.64	0.07	0.03	0.04	0.98	0.70

Tests for joint significance of EUROSHIFT and PRE-EURO dummies across countries.

EUROSHIFT dummies in the 12 euro countries. $F_{12,1125} = 5.85$, p-value = 0.0000
EUROSHIFT dummies in 3 non-euro countries. $F_{3,1125} = 0.39$, p-value = 0.7593
PRE-EURO dummies in the 12 euro countries. $F_{12,1125} = 1.77$, p-value = 0.0481
PRE-EURO dummies in 3 non-euro countries. $F_{3,1125} = 0.03$, p-value = 0.9925

Note: *p*-values are densities in the tail of each distribution. Absolute value of *t*-statistics given in (parentheses).

Table 10.5 SURE on monthly inflation ($\Delta p = p_t - p_{t-1}$), for restaurants and the like (cp1111)

Dependent variable: p	*Austria*	*Belgium*	*Finland*	*France*	*Germany*	*Greece*	*Ireland*	*Italy*	*Luxembourg*	*Netherlands*	*Portugal*	*Spain*	*Denmark*	*Sweden*	*UK*
*Parameter estimates:**															
EUROSHIFT	0.004	0.004	0.017	0.011	0.020	–0.010	0.003	0.004	0.008	0.026	0.006	0.003	–0.002	0.002	–0.001
	(1.99)	(2.37)	(5.16)	(13.12)	(17.12)	(1.10)	(0.58)	(2.99)	(3.38)	(8.13)	(2.02)	(2.10)	(1.00)	(0.62)	(0.78)
PRE-EURO	–0.003	–0.001	–0.003	0.003	–0.001	–0.015	0.004	–0.000	–0.000	0.000	–0.007	0.000	0.001	–0.002	–0.000
	(1.56)	(0.85)	(1.00)	(3.00)	(1.03)	(1.69)	(0.95)	(0.33)	(0.07)	(0.14)	(2.39)	(0.27)	(0.30)	(0.40)	(0.05)
Trend	0.011	0.009	0.007	0.005	0.010	–0.017	0.043	0.010	0.009	0.015	0.017	0.016	0.050	0.020	0.020
	(1.77)	(2.48)	(0.43)	(2.37)	(3.32)	(0.42)	(2.94)	(2.34)	(1.55)	(2.02)	(1.77)	(2.38)	(3.12)	(2.53)	(2.17)
P_{t-1}	–0.045	–0.032	–0.037	–0.013	–0.067	0.008	–0.077	–0.030	–0.026	–0.040	–0.040	–0.034	–0.193	–0.075	–0.066
	(1.67)	(2.25)	(0.58)	(1.60)	(3.59)	(0.11)	(2.98)	(2.29)	(1.31)	(2.14)	(1.81)	(2.17)	(3.09)	(2.38)	(2.27)
Constant	0.201	0.143	0.170	0.058	0.301	0.003	0.332	0.134	0.118	0.183	0.181	0.152	0.858	0.335	0.290
	(1.68)	(2.25)	(0.59)	(1.65)	(3.61)	(0.01)	(3.02)	(2.30)	(1.34)	(2.25)	(1.88)	(2.26)	(3.10)	(2.37)	(2.30)
R^2	.2667	.5147	.4002	.8277	.8357	.8437	.3401	.4689	.5221	.7260	.5409	.7612	.4766	.3067	.5852
Obs.	101	101	101	101	101	101	101	101	101	101	101	101	101	101	101
Diagnostics:															
Lagged dependent variables' joint significance tests, ~ $F_{12,1095}$.															
F-test	1.14	2.24	0.70	0.86	1.62	6.94	1.97	1.97	1.85	1.42	0.95	1.34	2.91	1.60	1.22
p-value	0.32	0.01	0.76	0.58	0.08	0.00	0.02	0.02	0.04	0.15	0.50	0.19	0.00	0.09	0.26
Month dummies' M_2 to M_{12} joint significance tests, ~ $F_{11,1095}$.															
F-test	0.59	2.36	0.72	1.90	0.98	3.27	0.55	0.55	2.17	3.13	3.78	4.33	1.24	1.00	1.82
p-value	0.84	0.01	0.72	0.04	0.46	0.00	0.87	0.87	0.01	0.00	0.00	0.00	0.25	0.44	0.05
Residual autocorrelation Portmanteau/Q tests, $\chi 21$.															
e_{t-1}	–0.01	0.03	0.09	0.01	–0.05	0.02	0.15	0.15	0.01	–0.01	–0.03	–0.00	0.24	–0.04	–0.07
Q-stat	0.00	0.10	1.04	0.00	0.26	0.03	2.66	2.66	0.00	0.01	0.14	0.00	6.83	0.17	0.44
p-value	0.96	0.75	0.31	0.95	0.61	0.86	0.10	0.10	0.94	0.92	0.71	0.97	0.01	0.68	0.51

Tests for joint significance of EUROSPIKE and PRE-EURO dummies across countries.

EUROSPIKE dummies in the 12 euro countries. $F_{12,1095} = 57.91$, *p*-value = 0.0000
EUROSPIKE dummies in 3 non-euro countries. $F_{3,1095} = 0.69$, *p*-value = 0.5557
PRE-EURO dummies in the 12 euro countries. $F_{12,1095} = 2.89$, *p*-value = 0.0006
PRE-EURO dummies in 3 non-euro countries. $F_{3,1095} = 0.09$, *p*-value = 0.9642

Note: *p*-values are densities in the tail of each distribution. Absolute value of *t*-statistics given in (parentheses).

of 0.9642. The broad pattern is one of negative or insignificant PRE-EURO parameters for the euro-changeover countries with the one exception of France. In the case of France the PRE-EURO parameter is positive and significant, suggesting that monthly inflation began to rise before the euro was introduced. This is confirmed by the plot in Figure 10.10.

Table 10.6 reports the SURE results for annual inflation. These results are broadly in line with those from Table 10.5. The EUROSPIKE parameters are jointly significant for the euro-changeover countries with a *p*-value of 0.0000 and they are jointly insignificant for the non-euro countries with a *p*-value of 0.9205. On the other hand, the PRE-EURO parameters are borderline insignificant for the euro-changeover countries with a *p*-value of 0.0537, and they are strongly insignificant for the non-euro countries with a *p*-value of 0.8454.

Joint F-tests for product categories and sub-categories

Presented in Table 10.7 are the joint *F*-tests for some of the 129 product sub-categories tested (a complete listing for all 129 sub-categories is available from the authors upon request). The picture that emerges from these results is a mixed one, with very weak evidence of a euro-changeover effect on increased prices in the all-items HICP (cp00). However, there is some evidence of a very strong increased price effect in January 2002 for euro-changeover countries for some service sectors. The obvious interpretation is that the euro changeover caused substantive price increases in some sub-sectors, mainly services, and that some of this effect has fed-through to the all items HICP.

Given the large number of results, no individual parameter estimates are reported. These results are intended to give a broad picture of price movements on January 2002 but should be treated with caution and subjected to the same degree of scrutiny as the results already presented. In particular, there are some sub-sectors where prices are either closely regulated by governments (such as public transport) or are dominated by tax rates (such as alcohol and tobacco). Another potential pitfall is that in some countries substantial price *reductions* may have occurred for some product sub-categories and these too would register as significant price changes according to the *F*-tests.

In Table 10.7, for each product (sub-)category, two joint *F*-tests on the EUROSHIFT parameters are reported for the log-price-level regressions $p = \ln P$, the first *F*-test is for the 12 euro-changeover countries and the second is for the three non-euro countries. The third and fourth *F*-tests in Table 10.7 measure the joint significance of the EUROSPIKE parameters on the monthly inflation rates given by $\Delta p_t = p_t - p_{t-1}$. In practice, it is these third and fourth *F*-tests that give the clearest indication of the price movements in January 2002. The fifth and sixth *F*-tests measure the joint significance of the EUROSPIKE parameters on the annual inflation rates given by $\Delta_{12} p_t = p_t - p_{t-12}$.

Table 10.6 SURE on annual inflation ($\Delta_{12} p = p_t - p_{t-12}$), for restaurants and the like (cp1111)

Dependent variable: p	Austria	Belgium	Finland	France	Germany	Greece	Ireland	Italy	Luxembourg	Netherlands	Portugal	Spain	Denmark	Sweden	UK
*Parameter estimates:**															
EUROSHIFT	0.003	0.004	0.018	0.015	0.024	–0.017	0.015	0.005	0.007	0.010	0.003	–0.000	–0.001	0.003	–0.001
	(1.06)	(1.62)	(3.99)	(8.82)	(8.46)	(1.67)	(2.95)	(2.44)	(2.01)	(1.80)	(0.71)	(0.15)	(0.19)	(0.53)	(0.37)
PRE-EURO	–0.003	–0.002	–0.004	0.003	–0.002	–0.022	0.002	–0.002	0.001	0.001	–0.006	0.001	–0.002	–0.002	–0.000
	(0.95)	(0.68)	(0.80)	(1.73)	(0.77)	(2.18)	(0.43)	(0.81)	(0.38)	(0.22)	(1.36)	(0.64)	(0.85)	(0.39)	(0.02)
Trend	0.028	0.007	–0.110	0.009	–0.003	0.017	0.035	0.016	0.017	0.033	0.019	0.021	0.056	0.023	0.025
	(1.93)	(0.88)	(2.89)	(1.67)	(0.30)	(0.32)	(1.27)	(1.59)	(1.50)	(1.55)	(0.85)	(1.53)	(1.29)	(1.47)	(1.20)
P_{t-1}	–0.110	–0.018	0.419	–0.019	0.012	–0.055	–0.067	–0.048	–0.031	–0.082	–0.043	–0.043	–0.214	–0.070	–0.087
	(1.68)	(0.60)	(2.84)	(0.96)	(0.19)	(0.57)	(1.39)	(1.62)	(0.83)	(1.57)	(0.86)	(1.42)	(1.29)	(1.12)	(1.32)
Constant	0.489	0.079	–1.847	0.085	–0.054	0.258	0.284	0.212	0.138	0.356	0.189	0.187	0.951	0.311	0.391
	(1.68)	(0.61)	(2.83)	(0.95)	(0.19)	(0.62)	(1.40)	(1.62)	(0.84)	(1.58)	(0.88)	(1.43)	(1.30)	(1.12)	(1.35)
R^2	.8679	.9705	.8860	.9794	.9543	.7242	.9374	.9703	.9355	.9485	.9088	.9673	.8029	.9014	.9411
Obs.	90	90	90	90	90	90	90	90	90	90	90	90	90	90	90
Diagnostics:															
	Lagged dependent variables' joint significance tests, ~ $F_{12,930}$.														
F-test	25.64	121.59	12.99	141.49	76.40	8.39	62.87	62.87	73.92	80.10	39.88	131.24	16.05	38.20	48.34
p-value	0.00	0.00	0.00	0.00	0.00	0.00	0.00	0.00	0.00	0.00	0.00	0.00	0.00	0.00	0.00
	Month dummies' M_2 to M_{12} joint significance tests, ~ $F_{11,930}$.														
F-test	0.13	0.18	0.26	1.00	0.85	0.32	0.36	0.36	0.21	0.07	0.11	0.33	0.19	0.04	0.24
p-value	1.00	1.00	0.99	0.45	0.59	0.98	0.97	0.97	1.00	1.00	1.00	0.98	1.00	1.00	1.00
	Residual autocorrelation Portmanteau/Q tests, ~ $\chi 21$.														
e_{t-1}	0.17	–0.03	0.24	0.13	0.26	0.13	0.14	0.14	0.13	0.06	–0.10	–0.04	0.24	0.00	0.12
Q-stat	2.96	0.09	5.93	1.62	6.84	1.69	2.11	2.11	1.66	0.43	1.14	0.18	6.06	0.00	1.29
p-value	0.09	0.77	0.01	0.20	0.01	0.19	0.15	0.15	0.20	0.51	0.28	0.67	0.01	0.97	0.26

Tests for joint significance of EUROSPIKE and PRE-EURO dummies across countries.

EUROSPIKE dummies in the 12 euro countries. $F_{12,930} = 12.19$, *p*-value = 0.0000
EUROSPIKE dummies in 3 non-euro countries. $F_{3,930} = 0.16$, *p*-value = 0.9205
PRE-EURO dummies in the 12 euro countries. $F_{12,930} = 1.74$, *p*-value = 0.0537
PRE-EURO dummies in 3 non-euro countries. $F_{3,930} = 0.27$, *p*-value = 0.8454

Note: *p*-values are densities in the tail of each distribution. Absolute value of *t*-statistics given in (parentheses).

Table 10.7 *F*-tests for EUROSHIFTS and EUROSPIKES for various categories and sub-categories (*p*-values in italics)

		F-test for EUROSHIFT on log-levels index $p_t = \ln(P_t)$		*F*-test for EUROSPIKE on monthly inflation $\Delta p_t = p_t - p_{t-1}$		*F*-test for EUROSPIKE on annual inflation $\Delta_{12}p_t = pt - p_{t-12}$	
EuroStat code	*Description*	*Euro 12*	*Non-Euro*	*Euro 12*	*Non-Euro*	*Euro 12*	*Non-Euro*
cp00	All-items HICP	2.33 *0.0059*	0.89 *0.4457*	1.95 *0.0257*	2.09 *0.0998*	2.92 *0.0005*	2.18 *0.0888*
cp01	Food and non-alcoholic beverages	0.87 *0.5782*	3.93 *0.0083*	3.44 *0.0001*	3.23 *0.0217*	2.89 *0.0006*	3.20 *0.0228*
cp0113	Fish and seafood	1.54 *0.1041*	0.86 *0.4602*	2.18 *0.0110*	3.64 *0.0125*	0.92 *0.5290*	2.97 *0.0309*
cp0117	Vegetables	3.41 *0.0001*	1.38 *0.2479*	3.62 *0.0000*	4.99 *0.0019*	4.41 *0.0000*	6.17 *0.0004*
cp021	Alcoholic beverages	2.13 *0.0131*	0.06 *0.9810*	1.83 *0.0388*	1.30 *0.2747*	1.61 *0.0834*	0.65 *0.5819*
cp03	Clothing and footwear	3.31 *0.0001*	4.39 *0.0044*	1.92 *0.0286*	2.64 *0.0483*	6.17 *0.0000*	4.77 *0.0026*
cp041	Actual rentals for housing	4.70 *0.0000*	1.98 *0.1158*	4.66 *0.0000*	1.11 *0.3428*	3.85 *0.0000*	0.27 *0.8477*
cp0451	Electricity	4.11 *0.0000*	2.03 *0.1083*	12.61 *0.0000*	0.72 *0.5372*	25.32 *0.0000*	0.86 *0.4600*
cp05	Furnishings, household equipment	0.81 *0.6418*	0.47 *0.7061*	1.34 *0.1895*	1.49 *0.2161*	1.02 *0.4288*	0.33 *0.8052*
cp06	Health	5.42 *0.0000*	3.44 *0.0164*	6.70 *0.0000*	0.88 *0.4517*	9.90 *0.0000*	0.55 *0.6484*

Table 10.7 *F*-tests for EUROSHIFTS and EUROSPIKES for various categories and sub-categories (*p*-values in italics) – *continued*

F-test for EUROSHIFT		*F*-test for EUROSPIKE on log-levels index $p_t = \ln(P_t)$		*F*-test for EUROSPIKE on monthly inflation $\Delta p_t = p_t - p_{t-1}$		on annual inflation $\Delta_{12} p_t = pt - p_{t-12}$	
EuroStat code	*Description*	*Euro 12*	*Non-Euro*	*Euro 12*	*Non-Euro*	*Euro 12*	*Non-Euro*
cp071	Purchase of vehicles	2.08 *0.0161*	4.25 *0.0054*	3.00 *0.0004*	0.63 *0.5981*	3.58 *0.0000*	2.32 *0.0736*
cp10	Education	3.64 *0.0000*	79.97 *0.0000*	2.54 *0.0031*	66.21 *0.0000*	1.21 *0.2806*	2.53 *0.0579*
cp1111	Restaurants, cafés and the like	5.85 *0.0000*	0.39 *0.7593*	57.91 *0.0000*	0.69 *0.5557*	12.19 *0.0000*	0.16 *0.9205*
cp112	Accommodation services	2.93 *0.0005*	1.06 *0.3632*	1.79 *0.0458*	0.63 *0.5971*	1.45 *0.1385*	0.34 *0.7945*
cp1211	Hairdressing salons and personal care salons	7.92 *0.0000*	0.89 *0.4436*	25.67 *0.0000*	1.23 *0.2967*	7.45 *0.0000*	1.14 *0.3316*

An inspection of Table 10.7 reveals that among the food categories (cp011–cp0119) most display a price increase for the euro-changeover countries but not the non-euro ones. However, the overall price index for food (cp01) shows a significant increase in monthly inflation for both the euro-changeover countries and the non-euro ones. The only two categories where a substantial price increase is registered for the non-euro countries are fish and seafood (cp0113) and vegetables (cp0017). Among the non-alcoholic beverages (cp012–cp0122) there seems to be no consistent pattern to indicate substantial price increases on January 2002.

The results for alcoholic beverages, tobacco and narcotics (cp02–cp022) all indicate significant price increases for the euro-changeover countries and insignificant ones for the non-euro countries. However, these results must be interpreted with a degree of caution as in some countries a large component of these products' prices are made up of taxes.

In the case of clothing and footwear (cp03–cp032) the results are mixed, some sub-categories suggesting more significant price increases in the euro-changeover countries and others suggesting more significant price increases in the non-euro countries. The overall clothing and footwear price index (cp03) suggests significant price increases for both groups of countries in January 2002.

The overall price index for housing, water, electricity, gas and other fuels (cp04) suggests significant price increases for the euro-changeover countries but not the non-euro ones. Closer inspection of the sub-categories reveals that this is driven by differences for a few product groups, namely actual rentals for housing (cp041) and electricity (cp0451) which experienced significant increases in the euro-changeover countries.

The results for furnishings, household equipment and routine maintenance of the house (cp05) suggest overall insignificant price increases on January 2002 in both the euro-changeover and the non-euro countries. Closer inspection of the sub-categories (cp051–cp0561) reveals that though some categories experience substantial price increases in January 2002, this seems independent of whether the price changes occurred in the euro-changeover countries or the non-euro ones.

The categories relating to healthcare (cp06, cp0611 and cp0612–613) show a strong euro-changeover effect with very significant joint *F*-tests for a substantial increase in prices in January 2002. Conversely, all but one of the joint *F*-tests suggest no substantial increase in healthcare prices in January 2002 for the three countries that did not undertake the euro changeover. These price data relate only to healthcare products and services that are charged for at the point of delivery and therefore exclude a large component of publicly provided healthcare.

Although the overall price index for transport (cp07) shows little evidence of substantive price increases for either the euro-changeover or the non-euro countries, there is evidence of substantial changes for some sub-categories. One sub-category where substantial price changes are observed at the time of the euro-changeover is the purchase of vehicles (cp071), while this price increase is not evident in the non-euro countries. There is further evidence of this euro-changeover effect for other transport sub-categories.

In communications (cp08–cp083) and recreation and culture (cp09–cp096) there is no systematic evidence of a euro-changeover effect. In some cases euro-changeover countries demonstrate a substantial price increase in January 2002 and in some cases this price increase is evident in the non-euro countries. However, the pattern is largely random and suggestive of one that would arise from a purely random draw.

The results for the education sector (cp10) are rather puzzling with a strong price increase for the euro-changeover countries but also a very strong price effect for the non-euro countries. This category is not available at a lower level of disaggregation and it is therefore difficult to investigate these results. The time-series plots illustrated in Figure 10.9 do indicate small, uncharacteristic price increases for Germany, Ireland and the Netherlands in January 2002. Figure 10.9 also indicates a substantial price drop for Sweden in January 2002, which would explain the very large *F*-tests reported for the non-euro countries.

The results for restaurants and hotels (cp11–cp0112) also show a strong euro-changeover effect. In all cases the joint *F*-test is significant for a price increase in the euro-changeover countries and is insignificant in all but one product category and transformation (cp0112, annual inflation) for the non-euro countries. Recall that the sub-category for restaurants and the like (cp1111) has already been analysed in detail in the previous sub-sections.

Most sub-categories in miscellaneous goods and services (cp12–cp127) show no systematic patterns with regard to the euro-changeover and non-euro countries. The one exception is hairdressing salons and personal grooming establishments (cp1211) where all three pairs of *F*-tests suggest the presence of significant euro-changeover effects.

Further unreported *F*-tests for alternative product categories released by EuroStat were also carried out. EuroStat produces these categories to facilitate alternative analyses of price movements at a disaggregated level. No evidence of a euro-changeover effect was found in the aggregate overall index that excludes services (EuroStat code goods). The regressions in log-levels and monthly inflation produce *F*-tests that indicate no substantial price increases in January 2002. However, the regressions for annual inflation indicate substantial price increases for both euro-changeover countries and non-euro countries.

The only categories where a statistically significant euro-changeover effect on increased prices is detected are these: processed food including alcohol (foodproc), services related to recreation, including repairs and personal care (servrp), services related to recreation and personal care, excluding package holidays and accommodation (servrp-oth), services related to package holidays and accommodation (servrp-pha), services related to transport (servtrans), overall index excluding alcohol and tobacco (xalco-tob), the overall index excluding housing, water, electricity, gas and other fuels (xhousing) and the overall index excluding education, health and social protection (xeduheasoc).

The only sector where the results are the opposite to what one would expect from a euro-changeover effect is that of services related to housing (servhouse). However, even in this case the SURE regression in log-levels generates *F*-tests that suggest a positive euro-changeover effect.

The overall impression from these results is that there is insignificant evidence of a euro-changeover effect on increased prices in the aggregate but that there is stronger evidence of a euro-changeover effect in some service sub-sectors.

Conclusion

We have presented a multitude of tests for the presence of a euro-changeover-induced temporary increase in inflation, using countries that did not join the euro as a comparative control group. We have found that for each country's Harmonised Index of Consumer Prices (HICP) the evidence of a euro-changeover-induced increase in inflation is at best weak but not non-existent. Given past research and anecdotal evidence, we also focused on the restaurant sector where we have found, like others before us, strong evidence of a temporary increase in inflation that coincides with the euro-changeover date of January 2002.

Further tests on 129 other sub-sectors highlight the existence of possible temporary increases in inflation on January 2002 for 'hairdressing salons and personal care establishments' and 'cultural services' which includes cinemas. There is some evidence that these temporary increases in inflation may have been associated with sectors which deal mainly with the provision of recreational services rather than products. Products, even seasonal ones, show no strong evidence of an increase in inflation that may be attributed to the euro-changeover. Although price increases were substantial for some seasonal goods, these were in line with their expected seasonal pattern and we use seasonal controls for these in the statistical tests.

We conclude that the euro-changeover coincided with temporary increases in inflation for a select few sub-sectors whose output is largely associated with the provision of services rather than products. In the country-level aggregated inflation rates for all products this effect largely disappears due to aggregation effects. Possible explanations for this temporary increase in inflation include 'menu costs' of reposting prices or 'rounding up' of prices. We find no real evidence that inflation fell in the month before the euro-changeover, evidence of which would have lent greater support to the theory of menu costs.

The results presented here also highlight other directions for further research. An obvious extension is to deal more directly with the issue of non-deterministic seasonal unit roots and their statistical significance. Some sectors need more careful modelling, particularly alcohol and tobacco where substantial tax-cuts in some countries produce large price variations on specific dates. The Netherlands is notable for exhibiting two surges in sectoral inflation, one on the euro-changeover date and another one exactly one year earlier in January 2001. Some countries such as Greece exhibit very volatile seasonal price patterns while others such as France exhibit very smooth price patterns, this suggests further modelling strategies to account for this differing volatility (heteroscedasticity). Finally, some countries instituted policies aimed directly at discouraging price increases on January 2002, so substantive price changes outside these regulated periods warrant closer attention.

Note

1 Although these measures of inflation do not strictly correspond to the institutional measures of monthly inflation $(P_t - P_{t-1})/p_{t-1}$ and annual inflation $(P_t - P_{t-12})/p_{t-12}$ they do provide a convenient methodology for dealing with non-stationarity. In addition, the strictest definition of inflation is the rate of increase in prices, or the time-derivative of the price index and it is not immediately apparent which of these discrete approximations dominates.

References

Adriani, F., G. Marini and P. Scaramozzino (2004) 'The Inflationary Consequences of a Currency Changeover: Evidence from the Michelin Red Guide', *Royal Economic Society Annual Conference*: 45.

Anderton, R., R. Baldwin and D. Taglioni (2003) 'The Impact of Monetary Union on Trade Prices', Working paper no. 238, European Central Bank.

Angelini, P. and F. Lippi (2005) 'Did inflation Really Soar after the Euro Cash Changeover? Indirect Evidence from ATM Withdrawals', Discussion Paper no. 4950, CEPR.

Beaulieu, J.J. and J.A. Miron (1993) 'Seasonal Unit Roots in Aggregate U.S. Data'. *Journal of Econometrics*, 55: 305–28.

Bhaskar, V. (2002) 'On Endogenously Staggered Prices', *Review of Economic Studies*, 69: 97–116.

Dickey, D.A. and W.A. Fuller (1979) 'Distributions of the Estimators for Autoregressive Time Series with a Unit Root', *Journal of the American Statistical Association*, 74: 427–31.

Dickey, D.A., D.P. Hasza and W.A. Fuller (1984) 'Testing for Unit Roots in Seasonal Time Series', *Journal of the American Statistical Association*, 79: 355–67.

ECB (2002) 'Evaluation of the 2002 Cash Changeover', Technical report, European Central Bank.

Folkertsma, C. (2001) 'The Euro and Psychological Prices: Simulations of the Worst-case Scenario', WO Research Memoranda no. 659, Netherlands Central Bank, Research Department.

Forsells, M. and G. Kenny (2002) 'The Rationality of Consumers' Inflation Expectations: Survey-based Evidence for the Euro Area', Working Paper no. 163, European Central Bank.

Franses, P.H. (1991) 'Seasonality, Non-Stationarity and the Forecasting of Monthly Time Series', *International Journal of Forecasting*, 7: 199–208.

Greene, W.H. (2003) *Econometric Analysis*, 5th edn. New Jersey: Pearson Education/ Prentice-Hall.

Gaiotti, E. and F. Lippi (2005) 'Pricing Behaviour and the Introduction of the Euro: Evidence from a Panel of Restaurants', Discussion Paper no. 4893, CEPR.

Hahn, E. (2002) 'Core Inflation in the Euro Area: Evidence from the Structural VAR Approach', Technical Report 2001/09, Center for Financial Studies.

HICP (1995–2005) *New Cronos, Harmonised Index of Consumer Prices, University of Manchester*. European Communities, EuroStat.

Hobijn, B., F. Ravenna and A. Tambalotti (2004) 'Menu Costs at Work: Restaurant Prices and the Introduction of the Euro', Staff Reports no. 195, Federal Reserve Bank of New York.

Hylleberg, S., R.F. Engle, C.W.J. Granger and B.S. Yoo (1990) 'Seasonal Integration and Cointegration', *Journal of Econometrics*, 44: 215–38.

Levin, A. and C.-F. Lin (1992) 'Unit Root Tests in Panel Data: Asymptotic and Finite-Sample Properties', Working Paper no. 92–23, University College of San Diego.

Osborn, D.R., A.P.L. Chui, J.P. Smith and C.R. Birchenhall (1988) 'Seasonality and the Order of Integration for Consumption', *Oxford Bulletin of Economics and Statistics*, 50: 361–77.

Discussion

Manfredi La Manna

As the only contributor blessed with total ignorance of anything remotely related to the macroeconomics of the euro, I shall examine the Ercolani-Dutta chapter from a microeconomic perspective and more specifically as a challenge to explore the microfoundations of price adjustment from an industrial organisation angle.

When are menu costs not menu costs

Ercolani-Dutta take the concept of menu costs as a primitive and refer to the paper by Hobijn, Ravenna and Tambalotti (2004) for a theoretical explanation. Let me quote from the latter:

> Prices are sticky because firms in each sector *i* face a (stochastic) fixed cost of adjusting their prices. The magnitude of this cost is drawn independently for each firm in each period. We denote its value in terms of units of labor by ξ_{kt}, where *k* indexes the firm and *t* time. Such a fixed cost is generally referred to as a 'menu cost'. There are many different factors that are claimed to make up menu costs. However, for the restaurant sector it seems appropriate to take the term 'menu costs' literally, to mean the costs associated with printing new menus whenever prices need to be changed. With this interpretation of menu costs, the assumption that the adoption of a new currency must be accompanied by a reformulation of the menu is very natural. However, even if we thought that menu costs are primarily those associated with the need to gather the necessary information to choose prices optimally, it would still be reasonable to assume that firms would decide to incur those costs and reoptimise their prices when they adopt a new currency. (2004, p. 12)

According to Hobijn *et al.* it is self-evident that menu costs are relevant to restaurants, as they claim that: 'Where else would menu costs be more applicable [to explain price increases] than in the restaurant sector?!' (p. 2)

I would argue the exact opposite: I cannot think of a sector where the 'literal' menu-cost explanation for sticky prices is less appropriate than the restaurant sector. The reason is obvious: typically restaurants have to change menus (and 'print' them) even if prices remain constant and therefore 'the costs associated with printing new menus whenever prices need to be changed' are effectively nil. Of course, the non-literal interpretation of menu costs may still apply to price stickiness in restaurants, but not with any greater force than for any other sector.

This bring me to another, and in my view far more important, reason why menu costs are likely to be the *least* plausible explanation for any one-off price increases following the euro changeover in *any* sector. Ignoring the issue of timing and assuming for simplicity a fixed changeover point (say 1 January 2002), any cost associated with currency conversion fails a major criterion in order to qualify as a micro-economically significant cost, namely that it should be *avoidable.*

This poses a conundrum: in sectors such as restaurants how can one account for the significant monthly price increases in the euro area in January 2002, increases that in the literature have been explained largely in terms of menu costs?

When the issue is examined from an oligopoly theory perspective the answer is reasonably straightforward: what is needed is a model that yields a menu of price adjustments in terms of fundamentals (for example, demand, costs, competitiveness, shocks) both for positive and zero menu costs. What follows is perhaps the simplest such model.

A simple Bertrand duopoly with(out) menu costs

As in Hobijn *et al.* (2004), this a static, partial-equilibrium model. Nominal price, P_i, is set before trade takes place (when demand is fully satisfied) and at the initial Nash equilibrium $P_i^* = P_i^* N^e$, where P_i^* is price in real terms and N^e is the expected value of the nominal scale variable N. It is natural to assume that stochastic nominal shocks affect N. On the (fixed) date of currency changeover a new realization of N is drawn and each firm decides whether to adjust its nominal price in view of the new N. Whether price adjustments involve a fixed nominal menu cost μ depends on the interpretation of 'menu cost' in the presence of currency conversion costs. If μ is interpreted (as in Hobijn *et al.*, 2004) as the cost of printing the new menus, then it will play no role in the decision whether to adjust because it has to be incurred anyway. Only if μ includes costs specifically associated with price adjustments will it enter into the firm's decision to adjust or not.[1]

Let demand for good i be:

$$q_i = \alpha - \beta p_i + \varepsilon p_j;\ i \neq j = 1,2,\ \alpha,\beta > 0$$

Goods i and j are substitutes (complements) if $\varepsilon > 0$ ($\varepsilon < 0$) and the absolute size of e is an index of strategic interaction. Assume marginal cost to be constant and normalized to zero. The best-response functions are given by:

$$pi(pj) = \frac{\alpha + \varepsilon p_j}{2\beta}$$

and therefore at a symmetric Nash equilibrium:

$$P_i^* = P_j^* = \frac{\alpha}{2\beta - \varepsilon} \Rightarrow \pi_i(P_i^*, P_j^*) = \pi_j(P_i^*, P_j^*) = \frac{\alpha^2\beta}{(2\beta - \varepsilon)^2}$$

Of course, firms set *nominal* prices: $P_i^* = P_j^* = p^* N^e$.

Faced with a realization $N_t (\lesseqgtr N^e)$ each firm has to decide whether to incur the menu cost μ and adjust its price or keep its nominal price fixed at the now sub-optimal level. In the duopoly case the payoff matrix is as follows, where $\sigma \equiv N^e/N_t$ is the size of the shock at time t; see Table 10D.1. Using the linear structure outlined above, it is fairly straightforward to establish the pattern of price adjustments in terms of 'fundamentals', that is, menu costs (μ), degree of strategic interaction (ε) and sign and size of the shocks (σ); as in Table 10D.2.

This simplest of models is not meant to capture the complexities and subtleties of price adjustments in the euro changeover, but merely (i) to point to some problems with the micro-foundations of models that do attempt to explain pricing behaviour in January 2002 in terms 'menu costs', and (ii) to hint at possible explanations for the industry-specific pricing policies highlighted in the Ercolani-Dutta chapter.

1 Some of the industrial sectors with significant temporary price inflation at the time of the euro changeover (for example, restaurants, cinemas, and so on) fit not too uncomfortably into the 'local oligopoly' stereotype and thus (at a stretch!) into the Bertrand story sketched above. This, combined with the absence of proper menu costs, may explain why,

Table 10D.1 Payoff matrix

		Firm 2	
		adjusted	**fixed**
Firm 1	**adjusted**	$\pi_1 (p_1^{**}, p_2^{**}) - \mu$, $\pi_2 (p_1^{**}, p_2^{**}) - \mu$	$\pi_1 (p_1^{**}, p_2^{*}\sigma) - \mu$, $\pi_2 (p_1^{**}, p_2^{*}\sigma)$
	fixed	$\pi_1 (p_1^{*}\sigma, p_2^{**})$, $\pi_2 (p_1^{*}\sigma, p_2^{**}) - \mu$	$\pi_1 (p_1^{*}\sigma, p_2^{*}\sigma)$, $\pi_2 (p_1^{*}\sigma, p_2^{*}\sigma)$

Table 10D.2 Price adjustment

<table>
<tr><th></th><th></th><th colspan="2">ε > 0
substitutes</th><th colspan="2">ε < 0
complements</th></tr>
<tr><th></th><th></th><th>μ = 0</th><th>μ > 0</th><th>μ = 0</th><th>μ > 0</th></tr>
<tr><td rowspan="2">Inflationary shock σ < 1</td><td>'small'</td><td rowspan="2">Full Flex</td><td rowspan="2">Full Flex, Full Rigid</td><td rowspan="2">Full Flex</td><td>Full Flex, Full Rigid</td></tr>
<tr><td>'large'</td><td>Partial Flex</td></tr>
<tr><td rowspan="2">Deflationary shock σ > 1</td><td>'small'</td><td>Partial Flex</td><td>Partial Flex</td><td>Partial Flex</td><td rowspan="2">Partial Flex</td></tr>
<tr><td>'large'</td><td>Full Flex</td><td>Full Flex, Full Rigid</td><td>Fully Flex</td></tr>
</table>

Note: Full Rigid, Full Flex and Partial Flex refer respectively to the cases where the equilibrium outcome is for neither firm to adjust prices, for both firms to adjust prices, and for one firm to adjust its price while its rival does not.

irrespective of the sign of any cross-price effects and almost irrespective of the type of shocks, these sectors can be expected to display greater price flexibility.

2 As Table 10D.2 shows and common-sense suggests, the pattern of price adjustments is quite different depending on the substitutability/complementarity of the products involved. How is this captured in models (such as Ercolani–Dutta) that work with sector data?

3 Given that the pattern of price adjustment is different for inflationary, as opposed to deflationary, shocks, is it possible that different sectors may entertain different expectations?

Note

1 Notice that the common interpretation of menu costs adopted by Hobijn *et al.*, namely, that 'menu costs are primarily those associated with the need to gather the necessary information to choose prices optimally' cannot affect the decision to adjust prices optimally because in this case menu costs would have to be incurred irrespective of whether prices are adjusted at all.

Reference

Hobijn, B., F. Ravenna and A. Tambalotti (2004) 'Menu Costs at Work: Restaurant Prices and the Introduction of the Euro', Federal Reserve Bank of New York Staff Report, no. 195.

11

Issues and Problems Related to Eurozone Entry of the New Accession Countries: An Analytical Review

Miroslav Beblavý

Introduction

This chapter focuses on issues related to the entry to the eurozone of eight new EU member states from Central and Eastern Europe (the Czech Republic, Estonia, Hungary, Latvia, Lithuania, Poland, Slovakia and Slovenia). It does not deal with the two new member states that have not undergone the transition from a centrally planned economy to a market-based one (Cyprus and Malta).

As part of their accession process, all eight former communist countries of Central and Eastern Europe agreed to adopt the single currency and join the eurozone after their accession. There is no transitional period, permanent derogation or waiver, but an official expectation that they will join once they have achieved 'a sufficient degree of sustainable nominal convergence... examined by means of the Maastricht convergence criteria' (Issing, 2005, p. 1). This is embodied in Article 4 of the Treaty of Accession, whereby all new member states received the status of 'Member States with derogation' regarding EMU membership (European Commission, 2004, p. 2).

Even though these countries share, in addition to this commitment, many macroeconomic and structural similarities, the expected dates for their entry into the eurozone vary from 2007 to the yet unknown. The differences are not related to popular attitudes towards the EU or the euro, but to the underlying structural strengths and weaknesses of the respective economies as well as the domestic political will to deal with the problems.

Since eventual EMU accession is a *fait accompli* in the new member states, this chapter does not concern itself with optimum currency theories or other ways of determining whether monetary integration is a suitable recipe for the eight new member states. Rather, it will look into factors underlying the differences between their environments and the consequences for monetary policy in the run-up to EMU. After briefly examining monetary policy frameworks and exchange rate strategies during the transition, and looking at drivers of popular opinion on the euro, we turn to an analysis of the five Maastricht criteria.

The core of the chapter then examines which of the Maastricht criteria has been a binding constraint for the economic policy of each country and how policy-makers have been dealing with these constraints and their influence on the expected entry date. While the debt or interest rate criteria have not generally been a major problem and the exchange rate stability criterion is treated as an afterthought, the fiscal deficit and inflation criteria will be documented as the real challenges.

Background to monetary and exchange-rate developments since the late 1990s

Even though all the countries in question are former postcommunist countries that embarked on the transition to a market economy at the same time in the 1989–91 period, their initial macroeconomic and microeconomic conditions differed substantially. Nonetheless, despite widely varying initial conditions, all the countries have been able to implement rapid reforms and achieve successful structural adjustment. After the initial depression in the early 1990s that was associated with the beginning of transition, the break-up of the Soviet Union and the introduction of economic liberalisation, they have enjoyed relatively strong growth performance with the exception of one further slowdown, which occurred for each country at a different time, but was associated with the Russian and Asian crises as well as with the accumulated micro- and macroeconomic debris of reform. As we can see from Table 11.1, the second pause did not involve a sustained period of decline in output (with the exception of the Czech Republic). These countries therefore entered the EU in May 2004 with both an experience and an expectation of growth.

Table 11.1 Real GDP growth, eurozone and new member states (%)

	1997	*1998*	*1999*	*2000*	*2001*	*2002*	*2003*	*2004*	*2005*
Eurozone	2.7	3.0	3.0	3.9	1.9	1.2	1.2	2.4	1.6
Czech Republic	–0.7	–1.1	1.2	3.9	2.6	1.5	3.2	4.7	6.0
Estonia	11.1	4.4	0.3	7.9	6.5	7.2	6.7	7.8	9.8
Latvia	8.3	4.7	4.7	6.9	8.0	6.5	7.2	8.5	10.2
Lithuania	7.0	7.3	–1.7	3.9	6.4	6.8	10.5	7.0	7.5
Hungary	4.6	4.9	4.2	6.0	4.3	3.8	3.4	4.6	4.1
Poland	7.1	5.0	4.5	4.2	1.1	1.4	3.8	5.3	3.2
Slovenia	4.8	3.9	5.4	4.1	2.7	3.5	2.7	4.2	3.9
Slovakia	4.6	4.2	1.5	2.0	3.8	4.6	4.5	5.5	6.0

Source: Eurostat.

On their transition path, the eight countries shared several features of their economic and political environments that shaped their monetary policy choices. A brief summary follows (for more detail, see Beblavý, 2006).

All the countries had a high and increasing level of economic openness. While in the case of trade the transition period built on trade flows inherited from the communist period, financial flows started from a very limiting regulatory environment and correspondingly low base but increased rapidly. In terms of the regulatory environment, the countries studied covered the same path to financial liberalisation in 12 years that the developed countries took 50 postwar years to achieve.

In terms of inflation developments, the countries experienced an uncommonly large role played by those factors influencing price developments that were unrelated to monetary or fiscal policies as such. Both regulated prices and supply-determined prices, such as those of food and commodities, have had a much higher share of the consumer basket than in developed economies, making much of the development of prices directly unresponsive to monetary policy. Additionally, the transition countries started transition with a combination of structural deficiencies in the economy and price regulation which led to imbalances in relative prices and to prices that did not clear the market. The results were a low price level and a burst of inflation upon price liberalisation that continued to reverberate for much of the transition. Shifts in relative prices accompanying the adjustment process created an upward and persistent pressure on inflation in transition countries above and beyond their direct influence.

Consequently, initial conditions, inflationary pressures unrelated to monetary and fiscal policies and fiscal looseness in some countries led to a high initial and often continuing level of inflation. Due to high levels of financial openness and other factors, monetary policy in these countries faced a paradox not unusual in small, open economies – while the overall objective was related to disinflation, the actual policy was driven primarily by considerations of external (im)balance. The reason is that imbalances between aggregate supply and aggregate demand tended to lead to the deterioration of the current account, while the inflationary impact was felt only later when measures taken to address the current account problems increased inflation. In economies with a longer history of such problems (in particular Hungary, to some extent Poland), awareness of the issue caused a spillover of external imbalances directly into heightened inflation expectations. Additionally, the working of the interest-rate channel of monetary policy was often scrambled due to dysfunctionalities in the financial sector and peculiarities in its relationship with the real economy, so the exchange rate was the strongest and the most immediate channel of transmission.

The reaction of policy-makers and their various monetary policy frameworks and exchange-rate strategies are contained in the following six brief sketches that encompass all eight countries. A summary is provided in Table 11.2.

Estonia and Lithuania established currency boards shortly after their independence and the hard peg has remained their exchange rate regime as well as monetary policy framework ever since, with a shift from the dollar to the euro as the anchor currency in Lithuania. This approach was justified by the low credibility of their monetary policy and their essentially non-existent currency reserves after the break-up of the Soviet Union. At the same time, both countries introduced unlimited convertibility of their currencies and free movement of capital.

Their policy framework remained unaffected by ERM II entry as currency boards are seen as an acceptable modification of the ERM II framework provided the euro is the sole reserve currency and multilateral obligations of other members of ERM II are not different from what they would be under normal circumstances. Both countries entered ERM II at the earliest opportunity (less than two months after the EU accession) and planned on the earliest possible date for the adoption of the euro – 1 January 2007 – though Estonia had to give this up recently because it did not fulfil the inflation criterion.

Their Baltic neighbour, Latvia, has practiced a little less rigour and, since 1994, has had in place an intermediate exchange rate regime – a peg to the SDR with a very narrow band of 1 per cent. In practice, the difference in monetary policy has been minuscule as this narrow peg was accompanied by a complete liberalisation of the capital account. ERM II entry in May 2005 meant only a shift of the anchor currency to the euro and the expected date for the adoption of the euro is 1 January 2008.

The Czech Republic and Slovakia had a soft peg tied mainly to the deutschmark and the dollar until 1997, a heritage of their joint Czechoslovak policy started in 1991. After several years with just one devaluation in Slovakia (in 1993) and none in the Czech Republic, both abandoned their soft pegs under the pressure of currency crises, in 1997 and 1998 respectively. Since then, they have pursued inflation-targeting coupled with managed floats. In the Czech case, this framework had an explicit form of direct inflation-targeting, whereas in the Slovak case the inflation-targeting was implicit in the way the central bank set and announced its targets, but there was no medium-term framework and no clear commitment to a medium-term inflation target until 2005. In November 2005, Slovakia entered ERM II with the target date of euro adoption on 1 January 2009. In the Czech Republic, there is not yet an official target date though the government has announced that it sees 1 January 2010 as the likely date.

Slovenia pursued a policy of a heavily managed float after its independence in 1991. The exchange rate also served as the intermediate target of monetary policy, with the central bank applying a policy of gradual and

Table 11.2 Summary of monetary policy frameworks in new member states

	Monetary policy framework in place from early 1990s until ERM II entry	*ERM II entry date*	*Monetary policy framework in place after ERM II entry*	*Official expected euro adoption date*
Czech Republic	Exchange rate target: peg to basket of dollar and deutschmark (until 1997); direct inflation target and managed float (since 1998)	–	–	1 January 2010
Estonia	Exchange rate target: currency board to deutschmark between 1992 and 1999, to euro since 1999	28/6/2004	Unchanged	1 January 2007
Latvia	Exchange rate target: peg to SDR (since 1994)	2/5/2005	Exchange rate target: peg to euro with 1% band	1 January 2008
Lithuania	Exchange rate target: currency board to dollar between 1994 and 2002, to euro since 2002	28/6/2004	Unchanged	1 January 2007
Hungary	Exchange rate target: crawling peg to basket of currencies gradually moving towards euro (until 2001); direct inflation target and ERM II-like peg to euro since 2001	–	–	1 January 2010
Poland	Exchange rate target: crawling peg with gradually widening band from 1991 until 2000 to basket of currencies gradually moving towards euro; direct inflation target and managed float (since 2000)	–	–	–
Slovenia	Exchange rate target: heavily managed float	28/6/2004	Exchange rate target: ERM II	1 January 2007
Slovakia	Exchange rate target: peg to basket of dollar and deutschmark (until 1998); managed float and implicit inflation targeting (between 1999 and 2005); switch to explicit inflation targeting prior to ERM II entry in 2005	25/11/2005	Exchange rate target: ERM II and inflation target	1 January 2009

Source: European Commission, central bank websites.

continuous depreciation. Since both a floating currency and a continuous depreciation are incompatible with ERM II, Slovenia changed its exchange rate policy with ERM II entry in June 2004 and stabilised the exchange-rate close to the new parity, where it has remained ever since. Slovenia plans to switch to the euro on 1 January 2007 and is likely to fulfil all the criteria.

Hungarian monetary policy has some echoes of the Slovenian approach though via different means. After a policy of discretionary and frequent devaluation between 1991 and 1994, Hungarian policy-makers switched to a crawling peg mechanism in 1994. The rate of crawl was gradually decreased until, in 2001, the crawling peg was transformed into a fixed peg. In preparation for eventual ERM II entry, a new 15 per cent band was also adopted at the same time. Since then, Hungary has followed a shadow ERM II regime, though it has adjusted the parity several times. The official Hungarian target for euro adoption is 1 January 2010.

Poland also adopted a crawling peg in the early 1990s, but later chose a different exit strategy from Hungary. Combining a decrease in the rate of crawl and an extension of the permissible trading band around the parity, it gradually moved towards a lightly managed floating currency, completing the shift in 2000. In 1998, it also introduced direct inflation targeting. Poland is the only country not to have an expected date for entry into the eurozone.

Overall, the countries analysed here have been able, despite the heritage of the command economy and other challenges, to achieve macroeconomic stability and, by the early 2000s at the latest, to successfully reduce inflation to single-digit levels. Even though they have not always avoided currency crises, these have not had a significant impact on their long-term growth prospects. The challenge of the Maastricht inflation criterion, however, is proving to be trickier for some as will be shown below.

Popular attitudes towards the euro

To understand the political economy of euro adoption in the new member states, it is useful to understand popular views on the subject. As we can see from Table 11.3, popular enthusiasm for the introduction of the euro is quite subdued in the new member states and the level of support is dropping. The citizens of the three Baltic states are most sceptical with approval rates in the 21–25 per cent range. At the other end of the spectrum, Hungary and Slovenia are now the only new member states where supporters outweigh opponents. The Czech Republic and Poland are between the two extremes. Slovakia is an interesting case which would have been firmly in the pro-euro camp a year ago, but has now moved to the other side.

There is a universally accepted worry about the abuse of the changeover by merchants to increase prices, though the numbers for Hungary and Slovenia are again notably lower. There is a clear statistical link between

Table 11.3 Views on euro adoption in new member states, September 2005

	Are you personally happy about euro replacing national currency?				*Are you afraid of abuse of prices during the changeover?*	*What will be the likely effect of the euro on prices?*	
	happy	***change since September 2004***	***unhappy***	***change since September 2004***	***yes***	***contribute to price stability***	***increase inflation***
Czech Republic	33	–6	58	+3	66	18	43
Estonia	24	–5	64	+7	66	17	61
Latvia	21	–2	64	+5	69	15	61
Lithuania	25	–9	69	+11	78	14	71
Hungary	49	–7	37	+4	53	39	26
Poland	34	–6	54	+5	85	24	51
Slovenia	58	–8	34	+7	43	36	49
Slovakia	42	–8	50	+8	75	20	46
average	36	–6	53	+6	75	24	48

Source: EOS Gallup Europe, September 2005.

views on the likely effect of the euro on prices and attitudes towards the single currency. While the correlations between expectations of price abuse during the changeover and attitudes towards euro adoption are relatively high (–0.65 for those for the single currency and 0.68 for those against), they are dwarfed by the link between the overall impact of the euro on prices and the desirability of euro adoption. The correlation between the percentage in each country which is happy about the introduction of the single currency and the percentage which believes the euro will contribute to price stability is 0.89 and the inverse correlation between those unhappy about euro adoption and those who believe the euro will be a force for stable prices is –0.95.

Padfield and Verdun note that policy-makers in the Czech Republic and Hungary do not feel 'that public opinion had a direct impact on the time-frame and method of euro adoption' (Padfield and Verdun, 2005, p. 28). However, they do feel that 'the fiscal requirements for euro adoption would be complicated because of negative public opinion regarding cutbacks to social spending' (*ibid.*).

Consequently, one can posit a model in which expectations of price stability or inflation under the euro drive popular sentiment concerning the single currency, but that in itself is not what concerns policy-makers the most. In countries with significant fiscal problems, it is the expectation of resistance to structural reforms necessary to fulfil the Maastricht criteria that worries the elites (see below).

The ability to fulfil the Maastricht criteria

This section examines which of the Maastricht criteria has been a binding constraint for the economic policy of each country and how policy-makers have been dealing with these binding constraints and their influence on the expected entry date. There are five Maastricht criteria, concerning public debt and fiscal deficits, inflation and long-term interest rates as well as exchange-rate stability. We leave the criterion of exchange-rate stability for the next section. Here, we start with the criteria concerning debt and long-term interest rates, which do not pose a major problem, and then proceed to the two binding constraints – the inflation and fiscal deficit criteria. (The criteria are set out in two protocols to the Treaty establishing the European community: the Protocol on the convergence criteria referred to in Article 109j of the Treaty establishing the European Community and the Protocol on the excessive deficit procedure. They can be found *inter alia* on the ECB website.)

Article 2 of the Protocol on the convergence criteria states that to consider a member state in compliance with the deficit and debt criteria, it must be true that 'at the time of the examination the Member State is not subject of a Council decision under Article 104c(6) of this Treaty that an

Table 11.4 Government debt levels, eurozone and new member states (% of GDP)

	1997	*1998*	*1999*	*2000*	*2001*	*2002*	*2003*	*2004*	*2005*
Eurozone	74.3	73.6	72.2	69.6	69.3	68.1	69.3	69.8	70.8
Czech Republic	12.2	12.9	13.4	18.2	26.3	28.8	30.0	30.6	30.5
Estonia	6.4	5.6	6.0	4.7	4.7	5.5	6.0	5.4	4.8
Latvia	n.a.	9.8	12.6	12.9	15.0	13.5	14.4	14.6	11.9
Lithuania	15.2	16.5	23.0	23.8	22.9	22.3	21.2	19.5	18.7
Hungary	64.2	61.9	61.2	55.4	52.2	55.0	56.7	57.1	58.4
Poland	44.0	39.1	40.3	36.6	36.7	39.8	43.9	41.9	42.5
Slovenia	n.a.	23.6	24.9	27.4	28.4	29.7	29.1	29.5	29.1
Slovakia	28.6	28.6	43.8	49.9	49.2	43.3	42.7	41.6	34.5

Source: Eurostat.

excessive deficit exists'. 'Excessive deficit' has two components – public debt and fiscal deficits. The debt criterion focuses on whether the ratio of government debt to gross domestic product exceeds a reference value of 60 per cent.

It is clear from Table 11.4 that the debt criterion is not a binding constraint on eurozone entry in the new member states with the possible exception of Hungary. The three Baltic states have had low and stable debt levels. The Czech Republic and Slovakia experienced rapid increases in their debt/GDP ratios in the late 1990s and early 2000s, but these changes generally reflected the conversion of implicit transitional liabilities into explicit ones rather than a real increase in government liabilities. Since then, they have kept their debt on sustainable trajectories. Poland and Slovenia managed to stabilise their debt at medium levels between 30 per cent and 45 per cent of GDP.

Only in Hungary was the Maastricht ceiling of debt at 60 per cent of GDP exceeded (in the mid-1990s), due to the high level of debt inherited from the Communist period (Orban and Szapary, 2004). The subsequent fiscal restraint and significant privatisation revenues drove the debt down (*ibid.*), but the absence of either has pushed it up again since 2002. The real problem of Hungary, however, is an irresponsible fiscal policy which, via high fiscal deficits and interest rates, also pushes up debt. A return to a sustainable and credible fiscal policy path would also mean a solution to this problem; so in this sense, the debt criterion is not really the binding constraint for Hungary either.

The criterion on the convergence of interest rates means, according to Article 4 of the protocol on the convergence criteria, that

> a Member State has had an average nominal long-term interest rate that does not exceed by more than 2 percentage points that of, at most, the

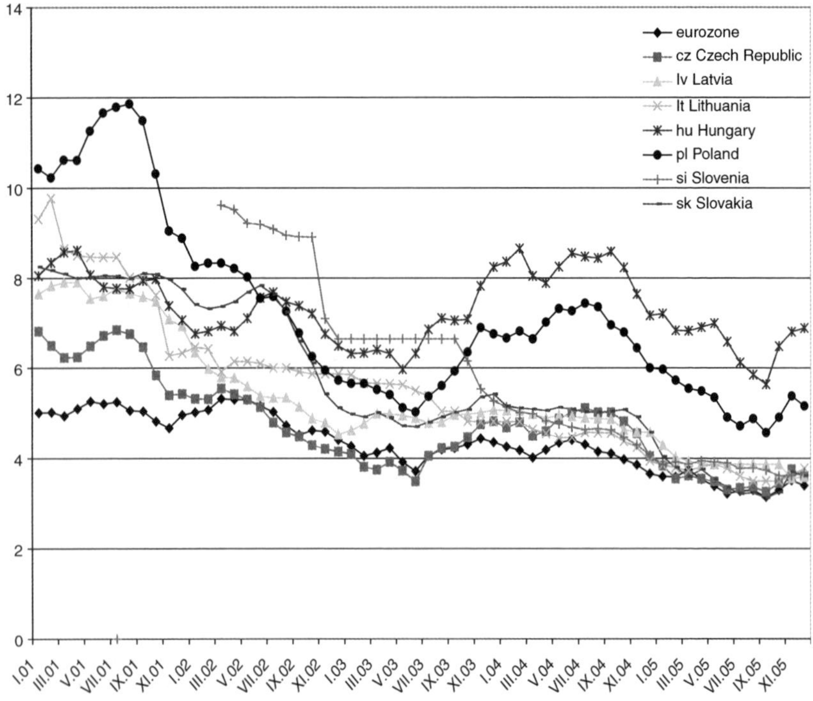

Figure 11.1 Long-term bond yields in the eurozone and new member states, 2001–05 (%)
Source: Eurostat.

three best performing Member States in terms of price stability. Interest rates shall be measured on the basis of long term government bonds or comparable securities.

Long-term interest rates (see Figure 11.1) have converged to the eurozone level from highly variable initial levels, with the exception of Hungary and Poland. This convergence reflected in part a decrease in inflation and inflation expectations in some countries, but also the credibility of their expected eurozone entry with financial markets. The two countries where the rates have not converged with the eurozone are the ones where there is either no date set for entry into the eurozone (Poland), or the date set is not credible (Hungary) and for which markets expect the latest entry out of all the new member states in the sample.

After dealing with the debt and interest-rate criteria, let us proceed to inflation. The protocol on the convergence criteria stipulates in Article 1 that a member state fulfils the price-convergence criterion, if it

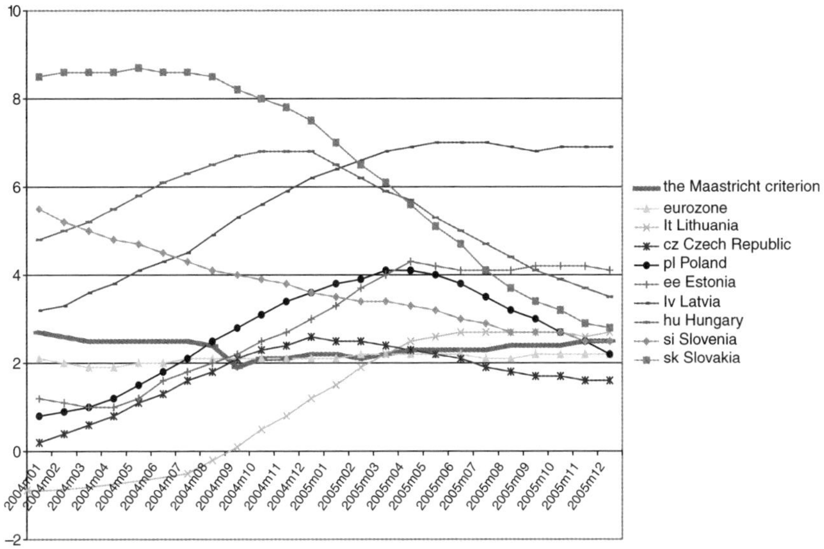

Figure 11.2 Inflation in the eurozone and new member states, 2004–05 (%)
Source: Eurostat.

has a price performance that is sustainable and has an average rate of inflation, observed over a period of one year before the examination, that does not exceed by more than 1.5 percentage points that of, at most, the three best-performing Member States in terms of price stability.

Figure 11.2 shows the convergence of headline inflation towards the required level in most of the new member states during 2004 and 2005. Despite this, the Maastricht criterion concerning inflation has been the key binding constraint. The fact that the reference value is set at a rather low level, given an inevitable dispersal of inflation rates, makes achievement of this criterion something of a roulette. If one takes into account the fact that supply-driven prices, such as oil and food, have a greater impact on overall inflation in the less developed economies of new member states, the roulette does not provide very good odds.

This is particularly so given the fact that the three reference countries on which it is based do not have to be, and indeed quite often tend not to be, members of the eurozone. Indeed, during 2004 and 2005, five out of the ten states that served as reference countries at some point during the two years were not members of the eurozone. Therefore, it is not surprising that during 2004 and 2005 the eurozone as a whole was very close to the maximum reference values and even exceeded it once.

On the positive side, the inability to achieve the required inflation in a given year has no permanent consequences; it only requires one to play again the following year. Therefore, countries with particularly negative external shocks to prices can wait for a year and then qualify. However, countries with rigid nominal exchange rates might experience repeated problems in qualifying because of the interaction of their exchange rate regime with rapid real exchange rate appreciation and one-time inflationary shocks.

Real exchange rates have been appreciating strongly in all the eight countries since the beginning of the transition process. The trend has been particularly strong for the Baltic countries, which opted for a highly undervalued currency following their independence from the Soviet Union and then saw appreciations of their equilibrium real exchange rates of nearly 300 per cent during the 1992–98 period according to some estimates (De Broek and Slok, 2001). However, even in the Central European group, trend appreciation has been demonstrated for the 1993–2001 period though the trend has been extremely uneven (Beblavý, 2006). The appreciation has generally continued in the more recent period in the run-up to EU membership and since then.

The appreciation is usually attributed to what Halpern and Wyplosz call 'rapid gains in efficiency once markets drive prices and allocation of resources' (Halpern and Wyplosz, 1997, p. 458). These include:

- the 'investment demand channel' where 'rising productivity in any sector raises the equilibrium capital stock in the economy and thus raises investment demand which in turn increases prices' (Fischer, 2002, p. 27);
- a 'brand improvement' effect with increases in international prices of domestically produced tradables due to the gradual establishment of reputation and penetration of western markets and capital accumulation in the tradables sector (Lipschitz and McDonald, 1990); and
- the Balassa–Samuelson (B–S) effect, present in fast-growing countries, which increases the equilibrium real foreign exchange rate due to differing productivity growth in the traded and the non-traded sector (Balassa, 1964).

While there is a general consensus that, for the eight acceding countries, there has been an appreciation of the equilibrium exchange rate (Egert *et al.*, 2002), relating the actual real exchange-rate appreciation convincingly to the theories presented above has been quite difficult (Mihaljek, 2002). At the same time, it is not accidental that the two countries with the largest problems with the inflation criterion (Estonia and Latvia) combine very high levels of growth in production and productivity with currency boards. If high growth pushes the real exchange rate upwards, the currency board regime transforms this appreciation into higher inflation. In other words, while the Czech Republic, Poland and Slovakia have been able to use nominal appreciation to manage the impact of real exchange rate appreciation on inflation, this route is closed to countries with currency boards.

At the same time, there is nothing inevitable about higher inflation for Estonia and Latvia. Not only did they have lower inflation at times of equally strong growth performance in the past, but neighbouring Lithuania with an equally impressive growth performance and a similar though not identical fixed exchange rate has had a much lower inflation rate. However, it is likely that this policy mix makes it difficult to react decisively to additional inflationary impulses, such as those caused by world energy prices or other supply-side shocks.

In other words, fixed nominal exchange rates make it more difficult to achieve the Maastricht inflation criterion under conditions of rapid productivity growth and inflationary shocks.

The fourth criterion explored in this section is the fiscal deficit. It focuses on whether the ratio of the planned or actual government deficit to gross domestic product exceeds a reference value of 3 per cent.

Table 11.5 provides a recent history of fiscal deficits in the eurozone and new member states. When one examines this table, it becomes clear that fiscal deficits are the norm rather than the exception in all the new member states other than Estonia. At the same time, Latvia and Lithuania had significant fiscal deficits only in the aftermath of the Russian crisis of 1998 and have since brought them down significantly. Slovenia has also been successful in sustained deficit reduction. However, it is also clear that fiscal indiscipline is the binding constraint in terms of the Maastricht criteria for the Central European four (the Czech Republic, Hungary, Poland and Slovakia) and that the deficit is of a structural nature (Dabrowski, 2005, p. 42).

Several questions then emerge: Why is this so? What can one expect in the future? In trying to explain the reasons why it is so difficult to contain

Table 11.5 Fiscal deficits in the eurozone and new member states (% of GDP)

	1997	*1998*	*1999*	*2000*	*2001*	*2002*	*2003*	*2004*	*2005*
Eurozone	–2.6	–2.2	–1.3	0.2	–1.9	–2.5	–3.0	–2.8	–2.4
Czech Republic	–2.5	–4.2	–3.4	–3.7	–5.9	–6.8	–6.6	–2.9	–2.6
Estonia	1.9	–0.3	–3.7	–0.6	0.3	1.0	2.4	1.5	1.6
Latvia	n.a.	–0.6	–4.9	–2.8	–2.1	–2.3	–1.2	–0.9	0.2
Lithuania	–1.1	–3.0	–5.6	–2.5	–2.0	–1.4	–1.2	–1.5	–0.5
Hungary	–6.8	–8.0	–5.6	–3.0	–3.5	–8.4	–6.4	–5.4	–6.1
Poland	–4.0	–2.1	–1.4	–0.7	–3.7	–3.2	–4.7	–3.9	–2.5
Slovenia	n.a.	–2.2	–2.1	–3.5	–3.9	–2.7	–2.9	–2.3	–1.8
Slovakia	–5.5	–4.7	–6.4	–12.3	–6.6	–7.7	–3.7	–3.0	–2.9

Source: Eurostat.

the fiscal deficit in the Central European four compared to their peers, it quickly becomes clear that the obvious explanations do not fit.

First of all, it is difficult to explain the issue in terms of their limited ability to raise revenue. Hungary, the Czech Republic and Poland have a revenue/GDP ratio that is close to the eurozone average and higher than for any of the Baltic countries (Table 11.6). Given their status, globally, of high middle-income countries, the revenue is certainly at the high end of the spectrum. In the Czech and Hungarian cases, it is also not declining, but stable or mildly rising. In the Polish case, there was a significant drop during the economic slowdown of 2000–01, but from a high level.

The deficit is also clearly not of a cyclical nature as all the countries, with the possible exception of Poland, have witnessed strong growth close to or even above their potential for several years.

It is the expenditure side of fiscal policy that is much more useful in explaining the persistent deficit issue. Hungary has an expenditure/GDP

Table 11.6 The revenue/GDP ratio in the eurozone and the new member states (%)

	1997	*1998*	*1999*	*2000*	*2001*	*2002*	*2003*	*2004*	*2005*
Eurozone	46.6	46.2	46.8	46.3	45.6	45.2	45.2	44.9	45.3
Slovenia	n.a.	n.a.	n.a.	44.3	44.7	45.4	45.2	45.3	44.9
Hungary	n.a.	n.a.	44.4	44.3	44.7	43.7	43.4	44.1	44.3
Czech Republic	40.0	38.8	39.2	38.5	39.1	40.4	41.1	41.7	40.8
Poland	41.7	40.0	40.8	39.6	40.0	41.0	39.9	38.6	40.5
Estonia	40.9	39.1	39.1	37.9	37.4	37.8	39.1	37.9	38.5
Latvia	38.3	40.6	37.0	34.7	33.7	33.4	33.5	34.9	37.7
Slovakia	58.8	57.1	49.8	47.6	37.2	36.1	36.0	36.7	34.9
Lithuania	39.6	37.4	37.5	35.8	33.1	32.9	31.9	31.9	34.2

Source: Eurostat.

Table 11.7 The expenditure/GDP ratio, eurozone and new member states (%)

	1997	*1998*	*1999*	*2000*	*2001*	*2002*	*2003*	*2004*	*2005*
Hungary	n.a.	n.a.	49.9	47.4	48.2	52.0	49.8	49.5	50.4
Eurozone	49.2	48.4	48.0	46.2	47.4	47.8	48.3	47.7	47.7
Slovenia	n.a.	n.a.	n.a.	48.1	49.0	48.0	48.1	47.6	46.7
Czech Republic	42.4	43.8	42.9	42.1	45.0	47.3	47.7	44.6	43.4
Poland	46.4	44.3	42.7	41.0	43.7	44.2	44.6	42.5	43.0
Slovakia	65.0	60.8	56.9	59.9	43.8	43.8	39.8	39.8	37.9
Latvia	36.8	41.3	42.4	37.5	35.8	35.6	34.6	35.9	37.5
Estonia	39.2	39.5	42.8	38.3	37.1	36.8	36.7	36.4	36.9
Lithuania	50.9	40.4	40.3	39.3	35.1	34.3	33.2	33.4	34.7

Source: Eurostat.

ratio of 50 per cent, above the eurozone average (Table 11.7). Poland and the Czech Republic have ratios hovering around 45 per cent. This is still ten percentage points above the average for the Baltic countries (35.1 per cent in 2004). As Von Hagen (2004) notes, the Central European governments appear comparatively oversized for their *per capita* income levels even if their openness is taken into account.

At the same time, it is worth noting that Slovenia and the Czech Republic have high employment rates of 64–65 per cent of the 15–64 population, higher than the employment rate in the eurozone (Table 11.8). The Baltic states have employment rates that are lower, but between 61 and 63 per cent are close to the eurozone level. Slovakia, Hungary and Poland have witnessed significantly worse performance, below 60 per cent.

In other words, the Baltic states have implemented a model of limited but fiscally prudent government. Hungary, the Czech Republic and Poland have implemented a model of a post-communist welfare state, but without the fiscal ability or political will to fully fund it. Slovenia and Slovakia are outliers. Slovenia has managed to implement a fiscally prudent post-communist welfare state due largely to its ability to retain high employment and consequently a large fiscal base, while Slovakia has tried to shift between the groups – from Central Europe to the Baltics.

In terms of future expectations, Slovakia seems on track to consolidate its public finances at a much lower level of redistribution, while the Czech Republic and Poland have recently been able to squeeze their deficits below 3 per cent on the back of strong cyclical performances. Hungary, with its low employment rate, mediocre GDP growth and structural fiscal problems, seems unlikely to be able to fulfil the deficit criterion on a sustainable basis without major structural reforms. Consequently, the ambitions of the Czech Republic, Hungary and Poland to emulate Slovenia might require

Table 11.8 Employment rate, 15–64 age group, in the eurozone and new member states (%)

	1998	*1999*	*2000*	*2001*	*2002*	*2003*	*2004*
Slovenia	62.9	62.2	62.8	63.8	63.4	62.6	65.3
Czech Republic	67.3	65.6	65.0	65.0	65.4	64.7	64.2
Eurozone	59.3	60.6	61.7	62.2	62.4	62.6	63.0
Estonia	64.6	61.5	60.4	61.0	62.0	62.9	63.0
Latvia	59.9	58.8	57.5	58.6	60.4	61.8	62.3
Lithuania	62.3	61.7	59.1	57.5	59.9	61.1	61.2
Slovakia	60.6	58.1	56.8	56.8	56.8	57.7	57.0
Hungary	53.7	55.6	56.3	56.2	56.2	57.0	56.8
Poland	59.0	57.6	55.0	53.4	51.5	51.2	51.7

Source: Eurostat.

more or less structural reform, but there is no indication as yet of any ambition to change the fiscal paradigm.

ERM II entry and exchange-rate management

So far, we have ignored the last Maastricht criterion of exchange-rate stability. Article 3 of the Protocol on the convergence criteria states the following:

> The criterion on participation in the exchange rate mechanism of the European Monetary System...shall mean that a Member State has respected the normal fluctuation margins provided for by the exchange-rate mechanism of the European Monetary System without severe tensions for at least the last two years before the examination. In particular, the Member State shall not have devalued its currency's bilateral central rate against any other Member State's currency on its own initiative for the same period.

Within ERM II, a currency of the participating member state has a fixed central parity with the euro. There is a fluctuation band of 15 per cent around the parity and both the member state and the ECB are, in principle, committed to unlimited interventions to preserve the parity. However, this is not an ironclad commitment as the ECB does not have to intervene if such a step would threaten price stability (Folsz, 2003, p. 5), a provision used by the Bundesbank when it refused to rescue the British pound in 1992.

The new member states tend to see participation in ERM II either as an irrelevance (those with currency boards or soft pegs) or as a potentially dangerous inconsistency in their monetary policy framework (all others). Backé *et al.* (2005, p. 6) provide a succinct summary of their attitudes:

> Most acceding countries regard ERM II as an institutional requirement for the adoption of the euro that cannot be avoided, but whose appropriateness as an exchange rate policy framework is questionable. Overall, they perceive ERM II as a 'waiting room' that offers at best little value-added and may even entail certain risks.

It is not surprising that those countries that have had a difficult (Poland) or disastrous (the Czech Republic, Slovakia) experience with soft pegs are wary of another commitment, especially since it may easily clash with their price stability objective and/or the Maastricht inflation criterion. According to Folsz, there is indeed 'a risk that in practice the new exchange rate system might work as a unilateral fixed exchange rate mechanism, and, as such, it might leave the member states' currencies highly vulnerable to speculative attacks' (Folsz, 2003, p. 11). For Estonia, Latvia and Lithuania, with currency boards or long-standing narrow pegs, it is an irrelevance because the ECB and the old member states have agreed to accept their exchange rate regimes as compatible with ERM II so, for them, entry presents no actual change.

On the other hand, the view from Frankfurt is quite different, at least in principle. According to Issing (2005), the two-year participation in ERM II is not so much a dangerous or an irrelevant waiting room, but a necessary testing room, designed to check the actual ability of new member states to participate in the eurozone through the ability to maintain an unchanged central parity for two years. The ECB as a whole sees participation in ERM II as useful in terms of ensuring fiscal discipline, enhancing exchange rate credibility as well as adjustability and providing multilateral support for the exchange rate regime (ECB, 2003).

However, in real life even the ECB urges caution in joining ERM II: 'It is important to undertake major necessary policy adjustments – for example with regards to price liberalisation and fiscal policy – in the pre-ERM II phase' (Issing, 2005, p. 4). Therefore, there is very little pressure on new member states to join ERM II more than two and a half years before their expected date for the switch to the single currency. (Two and a half years is necessary because the decision on whether a country will join the single currency needs to be made at least six months prior to entry for a variety of technical reasons.) Estonia, Lithuania and Slovenia joined ERM II in June 2004 with the objective of adopting the euro on 1 January 2007. Latvia followed them in May 2005 and its expected euro date is 1 January 2008. Only Slovakia, with the euro target date of 1 January 2009, moved sooner than necessary in November 2005.

Consequently, the view of ERM II as a largely redundant but inevitable waiting room has prevailed in practical policy-making.

Conclusion

We have reviewed some issues related to eurozone entry of the eight new EU member states from Central and Eastern Europe. They have all pledged themselves to adopt the single currency and join the eurozone as soon as they are ready and to work steadily towards this objective. The front-runners are expected to join on 1 January 2007, while the rest of the group is spread out well into the next decade.

The chapter has examined which of the Maastricht criteria has been a binding constraint for the economic policy of each country and how policy-makers have been dealing with these binding constraints and their influence on the expected entry date. While the debt or interest rate criteria have not generally been a major problem and the exchange rate stability criterion is treated as an afterthought, the fiscal deficit and inflation criteria have been the real challenges.

The inflation criterion continues to present an unpredictable challenge to all who hope to join the eurozone simply because it is low given the recent high variability of inflation. It has become a roulette in which both supply-driven prices (such as energy prices) and the moving target of the average inflation in the three countries with the lowest inflation in the EU can be more influential in whether countries hit the target in a given year than the actual conduct of monetary or fiscal policy. Ironically, high growth coupled with a truly stable currency can also become a winner's curse, as appreciation in the real exchange rate punishes what is usually regarded as a winning combination. This is the case in Estonia and Latvia.

The fiscal deficit criterion provides a benchmark that has been achieved by some (Baltic states, Slovenia), but is proving nearly impossible to surmount for others (Central Europe). The differences are not due to asynchronous business cycles, but are based on widely differing expenditure ambitions and abilities to finance them. Slovenia has managed to implement a fiscally prudent post-communist welfare system. The Baltic states have implemented a model of government with limited redistributive ambition, but with a very developed sense of fiscal responsibility. The Central Europeans have attempted to emulate a fully fledged welfare state, but do not seem to have the fiscal ability or political will to fully fund it. However, this group is breaking up, with Slovakia heading towards the Baltic model, while the other three attempt to emulate Slovenia.

The exchange-rate stability criterion calls for member states to complete at least two years in ERM II without parity devaluation. The policy-makers in the new member states see the exchange-rate mechanism as an inevitable but either irrelevant or potentially dangerous precondition for the eurozone entry. As a consequence, the timing of ERM II entry has been decided as an afterthought to the overall euro adoption strategy, with the intention of spending the least time necessary in it. So far, only Slovakia has committed itself to participating in ERM II sooner than absolutely necessary, but only for six months longer.

References

Backé, P., C. Thimann, O. Analibel, O. Calvo-Gonzalez, A. Mehl and C. Norlich (2004) 'The Acceding Countries' Strategies Towards ERM II and the Adoption of the Euro: An Analytical Review', Occasional Paper, no. 10 European Central Bank, Frankfurt.

Balassa, B. (1964) 'The Purchasing Power Parity Doctrine: A Reappraisal', *Journal of Political Economy*, 72: 684–96.

Beblavý, M. (2006) *Monetary Policy in Central Europe*. London: Routledge, forthcoming.

Dabrowski, M. (2005) 'A Strategy for EMU Enlargement', *CASE Studies and Analyses*, no. 290 CASE, Warsaw.

De Broek, M. and T. Slok (2001) 'Interpreting Real Exchange Rate Movements in Transition Countries', IMF Working Paper, no. 56, International Monetary Fund, Washington DC.

Egert, B., I. Drine and Ch. Rault (2002) 'On the Balassa–Samuelson Effect in the Transition Process: A Panel Study', mimeo Modem, Nantoppe University, and Eurequa, Sorbonne University.

EOS Gallup Europe (2005) 'Introduction of the Euro in the New Member States, Survey and Report', September–October.

European Central Bank (2003) *Policy Position of the Governing Council of the European Central Bank on Exchange Rate Issues Relating to the Acceding Countries*. Frankfurt: European Central Bank.

European Commission (2004) 'Convergence Report 2004 – Technical Annex', European Commission Services Working Paper, European Commission, Brussels.

Fischer, C. (2002) 'Real Currency Appreciation in Accession Countries: Balassa-Samuelson and Investment Demand', BOFIT Discussion Paper, no. 8, Bank of Finland, Helsinki.

Folsz, A. (2003) 'The Monetary Framework after Accession – a Political Economy Analysis of ERM II', *European Integration Online Papers*, 7(2), available at http://eiop.or.at/eiop/texte/2003–002a.htm.

Halpern, L. and C. Wyplosz (1997) 'Equilibrium Exchange Rates in Transition Economies', *IMF Staff Papers*, 44(4), International Monetary Fund, Washington DC.

Issing, O. (2005) 'The Enlargement of the EU and the Euro Zone', Speech at the Spring 2005 World Economic Outlook Conference, April 27 Frankfurt am Main.

Lipschitz, L. and D. McDonald (eds) (1990) 'German Unification: Economic Issues', Occasional Paper no. 75, International Monetary Fund, Washington, DC.

Mihaljek, D. (2002) 'The Balassa-Samuelson Effect in Central Europe: A Disaggregated Analysis', paper presented at the 'ICEG – European Center Conference: Exchange Rate Strategies During the EU Enlargement', 27–30 November 2002, Basel.

Orban, G. and G. Szapary (2004) 'The Stability and Growth Pact from the Perspective of New Member States', mimeo, University of Michigan.

Padfield, M. and A. Verdun (2005) 'The Politics and Economics of Joining EMU: The Cases of the Czech Republic and Hungary', paper presented at 'The European Union and the World: Asia, Enlargement and Constitutional Change', IPSA-RC 3 Conference, 5–6 May 2005, Beijing.

Von Hagen, J. (2004) 'Fiscal Policy Challenges for EU Acceding Countries', paper presented at the ECSA Conference, February 2004, Vienna.

Discussion

Atanas Christev

The new accession countries are committed, via the process of EU enlargement, to adopting the single currency after a period of time in which they fulfil a set of nominal (Maastricht) convergence criteria. The dilemma faced by the policy-makers now is not whether these economies should become fully-fledged participants in the eurozone, but how soon they will become ready to adopt the euro. The timing of entry is of the essence and widely debated. What 'trials and tribulations' they encounter along the way is the subject of Miroslav Beblavý's chapter. It is one of the few existing sources that carefully examines and compares both the challenges and the policy developments, however disparate, of all eight new EU members from Central and Eastern Europe. The chapter clearly discusses the Maastricht criteria and the achievements to date and offers an evaluation of the current state of affairs. This is indeed a timely contribution to the ongoing processes of profound change associated with the currency union.

Beblavý's chapter presents an informative analysis and provides sufficient detail on the relevant policy developments in the new accession countries. It illustrates how binding a constraint for monetary and economic policy the Maastricht criteria appear to be in these countries' experiences. The current polemic on this topic has largely overlooked this issue or not found much room for it in previous work. The findings suggest that the public debt and interest rate criteria have not turned out to be major concerns, while the fiscal deficit and inflation criteria, together with that on exchange rate stability, or perhaps even because of it, have proven to be harder to tackle. The explanations for such outcomes are also not surprising.

One well-documented aspect deals with the influence of the Balassa–Samuelson hypothesis. Another takes into account the legacy of central planning and the difficulties these economies faced in confronting their unique 'transformational recessions' of the early 1990s. The Maastricht criteria may ignore some essential features of the new accession countries as suggested by Nuti (2002). The existence of quasi-fiscal deficits and debt (as well as external debt commitments) and the lack of institutional convergence in most of these economies point to the ongoing enormous systemic transformation to a market economy which had started a decade earlier. The new accession countries are still in the process of transforming their economies, and their initial conditions are of particular importance. Especially slow progress in some sectors of the economy and delayed restructuring in the banking and financial sectors in particular prompts the informed policy-maker to consider, for example, the influence of non-performing loans in state-owned banks or existing (hidden) subsidies or the low share of credit available to the private sector (perhaps even a credit crunch) (Nuti, 2003). In addition, the Maastricht criteria need to be scrutinised in the light of the established low capitalisation and liquidity of the emerging capital markets and the extraordinary volatility of the rates of return in some of these countries as well.

However, ultimately evaluating these criteria and the expected future date of entry is an empirical question. As more data become available, it will be of considerable interest to know how well the Maastricht parameters for debt, deficits, interest rates and inflation perform as indicators of the degree of monetary, real (financial) and institutional convergence *before* and *after* the decision to join the EU. These influences should be deemed endogenous and serve as a unifying framework for understanding the variety of different paths, institutions and policy developments in the accession countries as discussed in the chapter. Crafts and Kaiser (2004) analyse empirical results for the medium-term growth prospects of the transition economies and find a significant gap in institutional quality between the countries with EU commitments and the rest. The existence of the Maastricht criteria changes governments' current and future behaviour in ways that would not have been possible, without this credible constraint.

In this context, surprisingly little research has been done on the welfare consequences of the loss of monetary flexibility. Woodford (2003) proposes that there may be great benefits in analysing the effects of alternative monetary regimes on the welfare gains and losses of private agents on the basis of explicit microeconomic foundations. This gives certain advantages in understanding the importance of government budget constraints and the persistence of different technological and other shocks experienced by these economies. The current chapter evaluates alternative policies only in terms of the *ad hoc* external (Maastricht) objectives for various macroeconomic indicators, which may not allow us to see the broader context of dynamic adjustment necessary for the adoption of the single currency. For example, Devereux and Engel (2003) observe that in the presence of local-currency pricing the optimal monetary policy is that of a fixed exchange rate, even in the presence of country-specific shocks, contrary to perceived wisdom. These results may suggest useful policy advice for the new and future accession countries, perhaps even for the current members of the EU.

Finally, Beblavý's chapter discusses some rare but valuable evidence from surveys of public perceptions and popular attitudes towards the adoption of the euro in the new member states. As it is evident from these findings, it is essential that the winners of this large-scale institutional and economic change find the proper mechanisms to compensate the losers (Nuti, 2003, argues in favour of redistribution to overcompensate). Otherwise, the fulfilment of the Maastricht criteria will be fraught with difficulties and uncertainty and may lead to opposition to eurozone entry. Future expectations of the benefits from the single currency and the actual structural reforms required for its implementation will suffer, if negative public perceptions and opinion against the euro become well-entrenched.

References

Crafts, N. and K. Kaiser (2004) 'Long-Run Growth Prospects in Transition Economies: A Reappraisal', *Structural Change and Economic Dynamics*, 15: 101–18.

Devereux, M. and C. Engel (2003) 'Monetary Policy in the Open Economy Revisited: Price Setting and Exchange Rate Flexibility', *Review of Economic Studies*, 70: 765–84.

Nuti, M. (2002) 'The Costs and Benefits of Euroization in Central and Eastern Europe Before or Instead of EMU Membership', in M.I. Blejer and M. Skreb (eds), *Financial Policies in Emerging Markets*. Cambridge, Mass.: MIT Press.

Nuti, M. (2003) 'Not "Just Another Accession"', WSPiZ Distinguished Lecture Series no. 3, April.

Woodford, M. (2003) *Interest and Prices: Foundations of a Theory of Monetary Policy*. Princeton: Princeton University Press.

12

A Portfolio-Based Analysis of Movements in the Euro-Dollar Rate

*Ali Al-Eyd, Ray Barrell and Dawn Holland**

Introduction

Since its inception on 1 January 1999, the euro, as measured against the US dollar, has experienced a period of sustained weakness followed by a period of sustained strength. After weakening slightly since the beginning of 2005, the euro is currently hovering around its initial value. Conventional models of exchange-rate behaviour (see Isard, 1995) rely on underlying economic fundamentals to explain exchange-rate paths. However, as De Grauwe (2000) discusses, these models do not provide clear guidance for an analysis of the factors driving the fluctuations in the euro, as speculative market activity or other noise can dominate the role of fundamentals in the short term. The movements of the euro/dollar exchange rate are not easily explained, as it is difficult to disentangle the roles of economic fundamentals and 'news' from 'pure noise' (a random walk).

Studies of real exchange-rate movements encounter similar difficulties.[1] Lane and Milesi Ferretti (2004) suggest that it is possible to draw some conclusions on real exchange rates using measures of a country's net external position. In this chapter, we draw upon the ideas set out in Lane and Milesi Ferretti (2004), as well as in Cavallo and Ghironi (2002) and Obstfeld and Rogoff (1995), which find that a country's net foreign asset position provides information that relates to the value of the home currency. We investigate if this information can be exploited in a systematic way. As our study is concerned with the nominal exchange rate rather than the real exchange rate we do not need to constrain ourselves to the analysis of fundamentals. We also consider the roles of factors that affect nominal developments.

*National Institute of Economic and Social Research, 2 Dean Trench St., Smith Square, London, SW1P 3HE. Emails: aaleyd@niesr.ac.uk; rbarrell@niesr.ac.uk; dholland@niesr.ac.uk. We would like to thank David Cobham, Jacques Mélitz and conference participants for their comments. Errors remain ours.

Many explanations for the initial and sustained decline of the euro have been advanced in the literature, including those relating to structural weaknesses in the euro area, uncertainty over the correct equilibrium value of the euro (both in De Grauwe, 2000), market uncertainty over the future course of ECB policy, and productivity gains and hence stronger profitability and growth in the US (Corsetti and Pesenti, 1999). Meredith (2001) draws upon this latter view and attributes much of the initial weakness in the euro to a strengthening dollar, which came on the heels of a surge in equity market capitalisation in the US starting in the mid-1990s. In line with the evidence of strong wealth channels in US consumption (as found in Al-Eyd, Barrell and Holland, 2006), this stockmarket dynamic gave rise to a large positive demand shock and this contributed to the strength of the dollar. Brooks *et al.* (2001) also find evidence supporting a portfolio-based view over this period where net flows from the euro area into US stocks closely track movements in the euro/dollar exchange rate.

Since 2001, there has been a reversal of FDI and equity flows between the US and the euro area and a subsequent strengthening of the euro. This study seeks to shed some empirical light on the movements of the euro by adopting a portfolio-based approach. Our framework is couched within the familiar uncovered interest parity (UIP) relation where the implied excess on the bilateral exchange rate (part of which can be described as a risk premium related to portfolio composition) relates to characteristics of both the host and home country. It is argued that the US-based component of the premium is the same regardless of the geographic location of the external portfolio manager, but that this specific location will have different effects on the overall premium. As such, we define a closed *portfolio bloc* – consisting of the US, the UK and the euro area[2] – and simultaneously estimate a set of bilateral risk premium adjusted arbitrage equations and examine the properties of the unexplained (or random) components for stationarity. In addition, we investigate the possibility that this random component may be the result of 'news' that becomes available subsequent to the time at which the exchange rate is set.[3] Specifically, we derive estimates of 'news' based upon innovations in monetary policy – as encapsulated in the changes in the term structure of interest rates – and on the implications of changes in fiscal policy – as encapsulated in historical NIESR forecasts – to explain a substantial portion of this random component of the excess on the estimated US/euro area arbitrage equation. As a result, we are able to decompose the component not explained by the arbitrage condition into both systematic and pure random components.

Understanding the reasons for movements in exchange rates is very important for policy makers since it is possible that a fall in the euro could lead to an increase in inflationary pressure, and hence require a monetary response from the Central Bank. However, as Al-Eyd, Barrell and Pomerantz (2005) argue, the effects of a movement in a bilateral exchange rate will depend upon its causes. A perceived loosening in the monetary policy stance in the US will weaken the dollar and raise inflation prospects there, but it may have little other than transitory implications for inflation in the Euro Area, and hence may require no monetary response, while other sources of shocks with the same nominal outcome may require significant responses.

The chapter is structured as follows. The next section discusses some of the literature examining the causes of the observed fluctuations in the euro/dollar exchange rate and also summarises the theoretical discussions on the determinants of nominal exchange rates. The discussion stresses that fluctuations in the euro/dollar exchange rate can be driven by events on either side of the Atlantic and that a portfolio-model approach is useful in capturing these features. We then develop our methodology and provide estimates of the systematic component of the risk premium – or the contribution of the net foreign asset position to the observed excess on the bilateral arbitrage conditions. We then seek to explain the remainder of this excess through the arrival of 'news' relating to monetary and fiscal policy. A final section concludes.

Background

It was widely expected among policy-makers, economists and market participants alike that the launch of the euro would give rise to its strengthening since the benefits of monetary union would be realised, attracting both capital flows and foreign direct investment (see for example Krugman, 1998). In addition many central bank analysts (Arrowsmith *et al.*, 1999, is

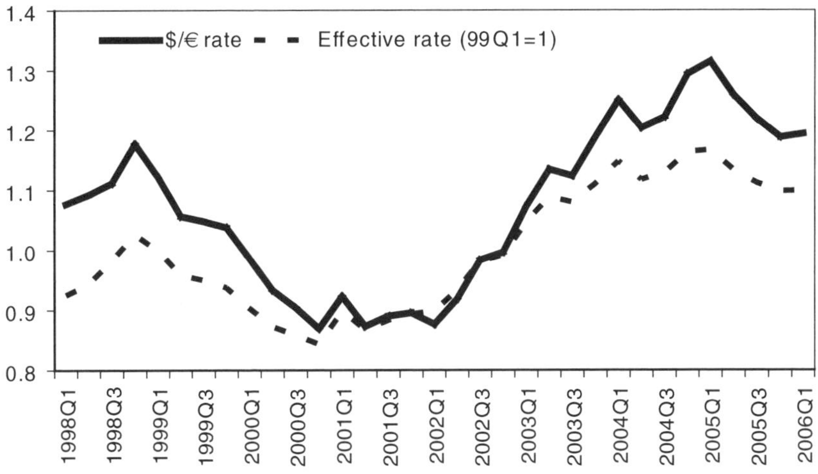

Figure 12.1 Dollar–euro exchange rate and euro effective exchange rate
Source: NiGEM Database.

an example) presumed that international reserve holdings would shift into the euro on its formation and that this would strengthen the currency noticeably. However, in its first 18 months in existence the euro promptly lost nearly 25 per cent of its value against the dollar (Figure 12.1). The effective exchange rate of the euro also fell markedly during this period, although not by as much as the euro/dollar rate, reflecting a modest strengthening of the euro against the currencies of other trading partners.

Exchange rates are determined in a complex set of markets, and can move for many reasons. Conventional models of exchange-rate behaviour such as the flexible price and sticky price monetary models (Dornbusch, 1976) relate movements in the nominal exchange rate to economic fundamentals, including inflation rates, the balance of payments, interest differentials and output growth.[4] In a world with liberalised and sophisticated financial markets the bilateral exchange rate, defined as domestic currency per unit of foreign currency, will depend on the interest differential between the two countries and the exchange rate expected next period, along with a risk premium on the assets of one of the countries. The current exchange rate may shift because exchange rates are expected to be different in the future or because the risk premium has changed. A move in the expected exchange rate could be generated by an expected change in the real rate of return or by an expected change in nominal interest rate differentials driven by expected developments in monetary policy.

Under this type of model, the observed movements in the euro/dollar rate could be driven by a number of possible factors. A positive productivity shock in the US, as discussed in Barrell and Holland (2004a), might weaken the dollar and worsen the US current-account deficit. A shift in the expected stance of monetary policy, as discussed in Barrell and Pain (2000), Laxton *et al.* (1998), Erceg *et al.* (2004) and Barrell and Holland (2004b), should also impact on the current value of the euro/dollar exchange rate. In addition, a rise in the risk premium on dollar assets, as discussed in Al-Eyd, Barrell and Pomerantz (2005), could weaken the dollar. Each of these fundamental developments could produce a shift in the euro/dollar exchange rate, with sharply different consequences for the US and euro area economies.

A common strand of analysis when looking at exchange-rate behaviour is the portfolio-balance approach, where an agent's desire for portfolio diversification plays a large role in the determination of exchange rates. As with standard monetary models, portfolio-balance models also relate the balance of payments to the exchange rate. However, unlike monetary models, portfolio-balance models do not view home currency and foreign currency securities as perfect substitutes. The assumption of imperfect substitutes introduces a measure of risk. Meredith (2001) and Brooks *et al.* (2001) find support for the portfolio channel in explaining movements in the euro/dollar exchange rate, but little support for a fundamentals-based explanation. As noted in De Grauwe (2000), the current account plays a prominent role in portfolio-balance models because it measures the change in the net foreign asset position of nations. In turn, changes in the net foreign asset position influence the risk premia attached to investments in different currencies.

Exchange rates and external balances are clearly linked, although this relationship may not be as straightforward as it first appears. External deficits can exist if the currency moves above its sustainable real exchange rate, and in this case a real depreciation can remove such a deficit. Deficits caused by exchange-rate movements are likely to be more temporary than those that either emerge for long-term structural reasons or result from structural imbalances in the economy. A structural deficit can be the consequence of low domestic saving or high domestic government borrowing. If domestic investment is very profitable then even high levels of domestic saving may result in a savings shortfall, and the high returns may induce a structural capital inflow, which will produce a sustainable current account deficit as a consequence.

The US current account deficit began to deteriorate in 1997, and in the wake of a large fiscal stimulus in 2001 and a corresponding fall in US national saving it has continued to erode to the present (Figure 12.2). The euro area current account also deteriorated in the late 1990s, but from 2001 it began to improve despite a strengthening exchange rate and rising oil prices and their implications for the current account. Figure 12.2 confirms that the emergence of a sustained deficit does not automatically necessitate a fall in the exchange rate, and a fall in the exchange rate may not correct

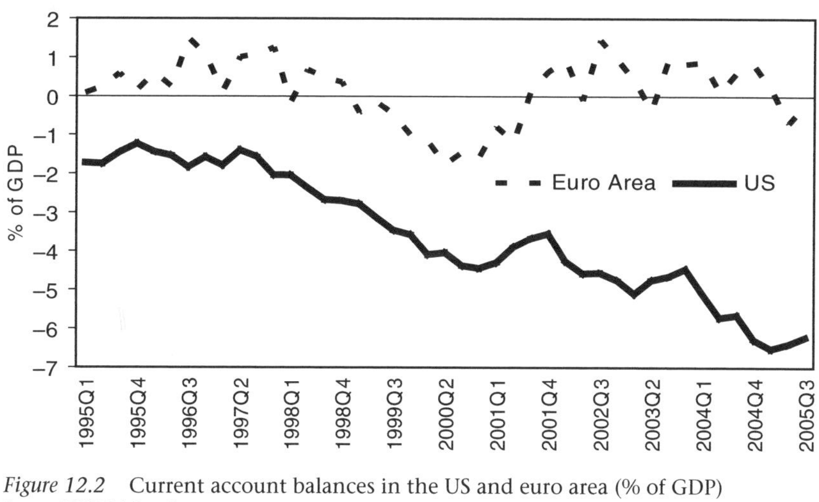

Figure 12.2 Current account balances in the US and euro area (% of GDP)
Source: NiGEM Database.

such a deficit. From 1995 to 2001, the euro area and US current account balances follow very similar paths, although the euro weakened by nearly 50 per cent against the dollar over this period. From 2002 the euro area current account balance stabilised and the US deficit deteriorated by a further 2.5 per cent of GDP, while the dollar weakened by nearly 30 per cent against the euro.

A current-account deficit is the difference between national savings and national investment. Depending on the source of the imbalance, a deficit can be viewed as either sustainable or unsustainable, or, more commonly, productive or unproductive. The driving factors behind the US current-account deficit have shifted in recent years. Beginning in the mid-1990s we saw a steady rise in net investment as a share of GDP. Moderate national savings were coupled with large inflows of foreign savings which sustained the rising investment. Starting in 1997 and accelerating in 2001 we see a fall in national savings. Inflows of foreign savings moderate from 2001, accompanied by falling levels of investment.

The difference between the second half of the 1990s and the first half of the following decade is crucial. In the former case, the widening current account deficit reflected productive behaviour in the form of expected future income generation. Expected future income growth from currently rising investment may ensure that a country displays intertemporal solvency and may enable a nation to service current debt obligations. Both consumption and investment in the US were able to grow simultaneously during the second half of the 1990s because capital flows appeared to be based on expected future returns. Since 2001, the deterioration of the deficit has reflected reduced national savings and investment alongside

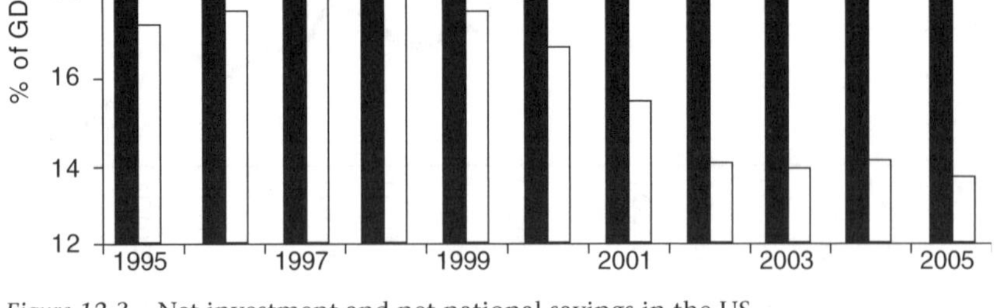

Figure 12.3 Net investment and net national savings in the US
Source: OECD Economic Outlook Database.

rising consumption, rather than investment in the productive capacity of the US economy. As a result, capital flows have moved from being sustaining (FDI and equities) to accommodating (bank and other short-term borrowing). From Figure 12.3 it is immediately clear that the large and growing current account deficits of the recent years are a direct result of the drop in the level of national saving, which has pulled down investment.

Savings and investment as a share of GDP in the euro area have exhibited less volatility than we have seen in the US, but the improvement in the current-account balance since 2001 has coincided with a small decline in the net investment ratio. This suggests that the improvement may be related to a downward revision to expected growth in the euro area. The observed pattern would be consistent with a temporary upward revision to growth expectations in 1999–2000, which was subsequently corrected when anticipated spillovers from the rise in US productivity growth did not materialise and global share prices dropped.

The drop in national saving in the US since 2001 is largely attributable to the increase in government borrowing, as shown in Figure 12.4. As Summers (2004) reports, the federal deficit now absorbs three-quarters of the private saving generated by the US economy. We have also seen a drop in household savings over this period, while corporate sector savings have risen since 2001. The converse is true of the euro area, where government borrowing is generally more restrained than before the signing of the Stability and Growth Pact in 1997, as we can see from the chart. If debt is not neutral then a widening budget deficit impacts on savings and invest-

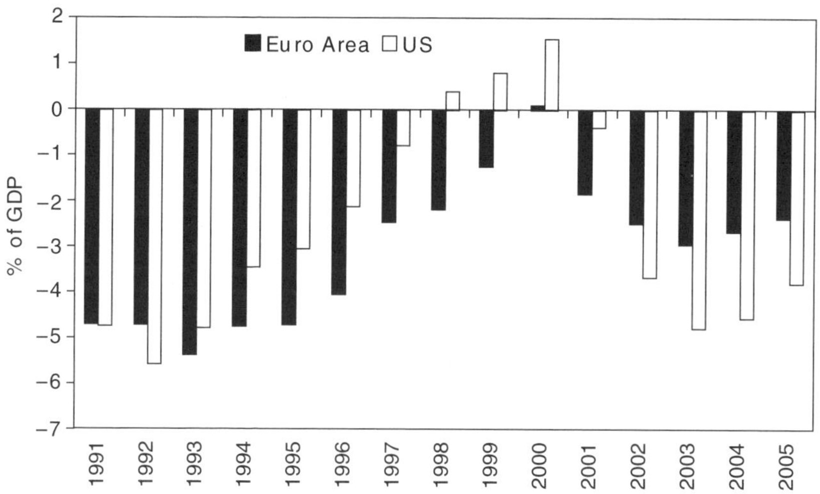

Figure 12.4 Government budget balances (including UMTS revenue)
Source: NiGEM Database.

ment decisions and produces a link between government dissaving, lower national saving and a widening current-account deficit, as is discussed by Pomerantz and Weale (2005). This is clearly the case in the US today as net household savings have been declining since the early 1990s while national savings as a whole began to deteriorate substantially only in 2001.

Given a fiscal expansion one would expect to find rising domestic interest rates not only to balance financial markets, but also to compensate lenders for an increasing risk associated with holding a larger stock of US debt. The increase in the interest rate that would follow from a looser fiscal stance would depend upon the reactions of the central bank. As long as it was perceived that an increase in demand would put upward pressure on inflation and the central bank was concerned about this, rates would rise. Higher interest rates would move to dampen consumption and increase savings and investment and, thus, lead to an improvement in the current account deficit. However, US interest rates have not risen as might have been expected, and this is partly attributable to a shift in the sources of finance of the US current-account deficit.

Figure 12.5 plots the shares of US foreign investment by asset class. It is clear from examining the sources of finance of the US current-account deficit that increasingly the imbalance is less about investment and more about financing current consumption. Since 1999, FDI and foreign investment in US corporate equities have declined as a share of foreign investment, while inflows into both private and public debt securities have risen, as well as short-term speculative flows into banking assets. This marks a

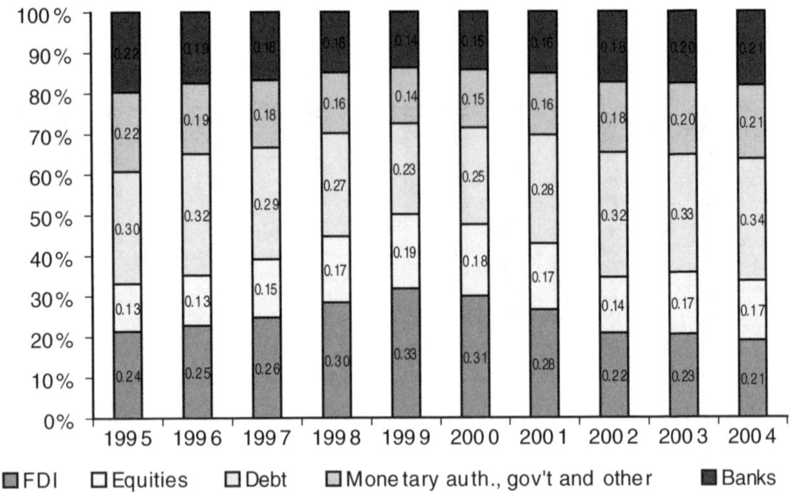

Figure 12.5 Shares of foreign investments into US by asset class
Source: IMF, *International Financial Statistics*.

shift in behaviour in the second half of the 1990s, when an increase in US productivity and the underlying potential of the economy encouraged large inflows of capital. As a result, the US was able to finance its growing current account deficit with these inflows of foreign savings, thereby alleviating pressure on the exchange rate.

The US government has increasingly relied on foreigners to finance its government deficit, as the proportion of the federal debt held by foreigners increased from 32 per cent in 1995 to 49 per cent in 2003. As the inflow of FDI and foreign investment in equity began to dry up, foreign central banks, notably those in Asia, became the main source of financing for current US federal deficits. In an attempt to maintain competitive exchange rates *vis-à-vis* the dollar, Asian central banks, pursuing quasi-fixed exchange rate regimes, have been buying large amounts of official US securities. Their actions have helped slow down the adjustment in interest rates we would expect, with noticeable foreign-exchange market intervention being conducted in emerging Asia, led by China. The combination of low long-term interest rates and weak Asian currencies exacerbates the deterioration in the US current account as consumers continue to buy cheap imported goods and face no incentives to raise savings.

Figure 12.6 plots the shares of euro area foreign investment by asset class, which show a somewhat different picture. There has been a rising share of investment in the form of FDI, while investment in banking assets has come down since 1999. Similarly to the US, the euro area has seen some

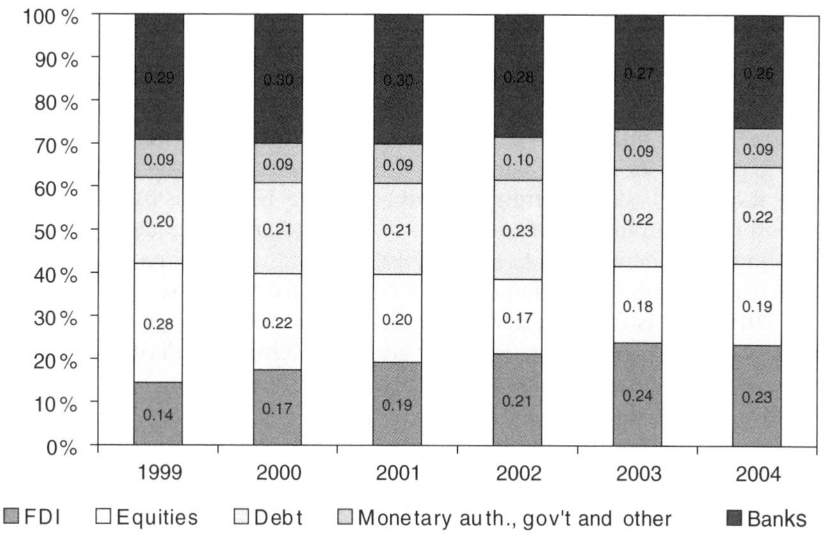

Figure 12.6 Shares of foreign investments into euro area by asset class
Source: IMF, *International Financial Statistics*.

shift from equities toward private-sector debt. As the euro has strengthened there has been a slight change in the composition of the inflow, and since 2003 we have seen an increase in the total of FDI and equity flows, so that in 2004 they amounted to 42 per cent of the total stock as compared to 39 per cent in 2000 and 2001. The shift of FDI flows from the US to the euro area may be one reason for the recent strengthening of the euro, although it is unlikely to be the major factor.

Methodology and empirical analysis

The analysis presented below is couched within the familiar uncovered interest parity (UIP) relation whereby the expected change in the exchange rate is given by the difference in the interest earned on assets held in local and foreign currencies. However, there is an extensive empirical literature rejecting the standard UIP (see for example Froot and Thaler, 1990). In addition, due to the high level of short-term noise in exchange rates, there are only weak empirical links between economic fundamentals and exchange-rate movements, and the seminal work by Meese and Rogoff (1983) shows that a random walk forecast typically outperforms a perfect foresight fundamentals-based forecast.[5] We seek to improve on the random-walk model by disaggregating deviations from UIP into systematic factors associated with risk, unexpected information ('news') about relevant economic variables or policies and pure noise.

Following accepted convention (for example Wadhwani, 1999) we augment the UIP relation with a risk premium (rp_t) and a random component (w_t):

$$e_t = e_{t+1}\left(\frac{1 + r_t^*}{1 + r_t}\right) + rp_t + w_t \tag{12.1}$$

where e_t is the bilateral exchange rate at time t (defined as domestic currency per unit of foreign currency), r_t is the short-term nominal interest rate at home, r_t^* is the interest rate abroad, and rp_t is taken as the systematic *ex post* risk premium. In the next section we build on this model, extracting the impact of 'news' from the pure noise in the random component.

In a similar spirit, Brigden *et al.* (1997) seek to decompose the excess on the UIP over historical periods. However, their methodology differs from ours in that the decomposition they employ attempts to identify the contribution of interest-rate expectations – net of the currency risk premium and the expected terminal exchange rate – to a change in the current spot exchange rate. Specifically, the authors identify 'news' as the unexpected change in the spot rate and seek to explain this through observable forward interest rate differentials, subject to a specified terminal date. The remainder of the 'news' not explained by the forward interest differential is attributed to the change in the expected nominal value of the currency (at the chosen terminal date) and the net change in the currency risk premium (up to the chosen terminal date); however, neither of these components are observables, so they are treated as a pure residual in their analysis.

Given (12.1), we can explore rp_t in an attempt to capture any of its systematic components. In a world with perfect foresight, the risk premium would of course be a constant over time with associated random fluctuations around that constant, as there would be no systematic deviation from the UIP relation. Without perfect foresight, in a portfolio based description of behaviour we might expect to find risk premia that are systematically related to observables. For example, risk premia may rise as more of an asset has to be held as compared to other assets in the portfolio. This may reflect increasing perceptions of default risk as the gross portfolio increases or it may reflect administrative constraints on the types of assets people are allowed to hold.[6] We augment the standard UIP with the net asset position, to determine if the risk premium is systematically related to the net asset position.

Risks on investments in the US that are associated with the US net asset position will be common to portfolio managers in other countries, such as the UK and the euro area. Conversely, risks associated with the euro area net asset position will be common to portfolio managers in the UK and the US. A build-up of assets by the UK or the euro area will reduce their currency risk premiums *vis-à-vis* the US, for instance, and a fall in US assets will raise the US risk premium in its bilateral rates with other countries. Hence we estimate the joint impact of the net foreign asset (NAR) positions of the US, the euro area and the UK on their respective bilateral risk premiums.[7] Although there has been much theoretical work on defining currency risk premiums, econometric studies have failed to find decisive

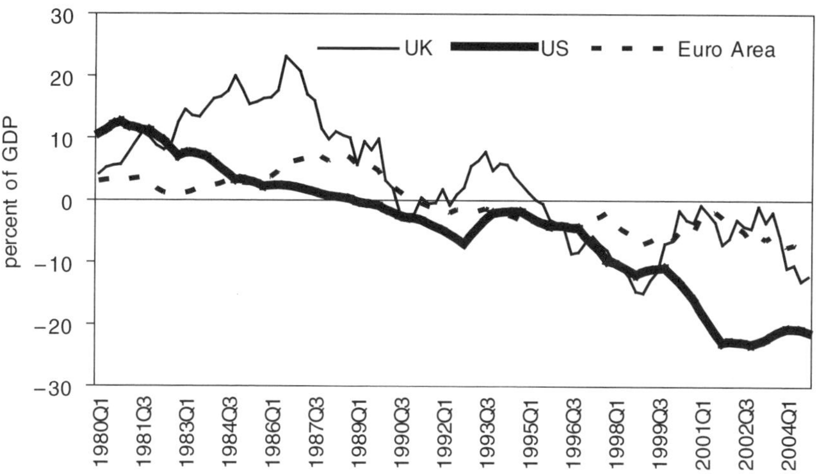

Figure 12.7 Net asset positions for US, UK and euro area
Source: NiGEM Database.

support for the role of assets. This reflects both the inherent difficulty in explaining forward looking markets, and also the fact that the emergence of a net debtor position in one country has to be matched by net creditor positions in others. We plot the evolution of these ratios over our estimation period in Figure 12.7, and we note that the US position has been declining over time. The UK position declined steadily from the mid-1980s to the end of the 1990s, but seems to have stabilised since the turn of the century. The euro area position has been broadly stable and close to balance since the mid-1990s.[8]

We estimate a balanced multivariate regression (SUR) to test how, if at all, net foreign assets as a share of a country's GDP contribute to risk premiums, to gauge the role that this has played in recent fluctuations in the euro/dollar exchange rate. Simultaneously determining the risk premia across the three relevant pairings, we estimate the following for each of the three pairings along the lines of the US-euro area (EA) link below:

$$rp_t^{US\text{–}EA} = C + \alpha_{EA}NAR_{EA} - \alpha_{US}NAR_{US} \tag{12.2}$$

where C is a constant term, NAR_{EA} is the net foreign assets as a share of GDP in the euro area and NAR_{US} is the corresponding net foreign asset position of the US. We constrain the coefficients to be the same size in each of the pair of bilaterals where they appear, so that α_{US} in the US–EA risk premium is equal to α_{US} in the US–UK risk premium. We would expect the home country in each pair to have a negative sign (more assets lowers risk) and the other party to have a positive sign (more assets reduce the risk on this country relative to its bilateral partner). As we take the arbitrage condition as given we have only current dated information on the right hand side, and hence we do not need to instrument our regressors.

Table 12.1 highlights the results, where the small size of the coefficients reflects the scaling of the variables. Overall we can see that the decline in the US net asset position has been associated with a rise in the risk premium on US assets, and to a lesser extent the same is true for the UK. Given our priors, the net asset ratios do appear to help explain the risk premia over time, and all of the coefficients are significant. The equation set passes the standard panel cointegration tests relatively easily, but there is some slight evidence of serially correlated errors in the two equations containing the euro area net asset position. This serial correlation is of the first order, and a standard LM test for serial correlation up to order four suggests that it is absent. The potential first-order serial correlation may reflect some systematic time variation in the risk premium associated with the formation and hardening of the Exchange Rate Mechanism over this time period.[9] Figure 12.8 plots the three sets of residuals over the estimation period.

The results as summarised in Table 12.1 are broadly consistent with those obtained by Gagnon (1996) and by Obstfeld and Rogoff (1995), both of whom present empirical results confirming a positive correlation between net

Table 12.1 Results from a multivariate regression model of the risk premium

	Equation	*Equation*	*Equation*
Determinants	US–EA	US–UK	UK–EA
NAR_{US}	–0.0014	–0.0014	
	(3.5)	(3.5)	
NAR_{EA}	0.0014		0.0014
	(4.2)		(4.2)
NAR_{UK}		0.0007	–0.0007
		(4.5)	(4.5)
Std. error	0.047	0.041	0.035
R-squared	0.083	0.22	0.13
DW	1.55*	1.66	1.57*
LM(4) *F*-test	1.67	1.41	1.48
	prob. (0.16)	prob. (0.24)	prob. (0.22)
Sample 1980Q1 to 2004Q4			
Panel cointegration null:			
Common unit root Levin Lin Chu		–15.30 (prob. 0.000)	
Individual unit roots Im Pesaran Shin		–13.20 (prob. 0.000)	
No unit root Hadiri *Z* stat		–1.11 (prob. 0.8660)	

Note: We used a dummy variable for 1992Q3 in the UK equations to exclude the ERM crisis episode from the sterling exchange rate. A * on the DW indicates potential significance at the 5% level (but not 1%).

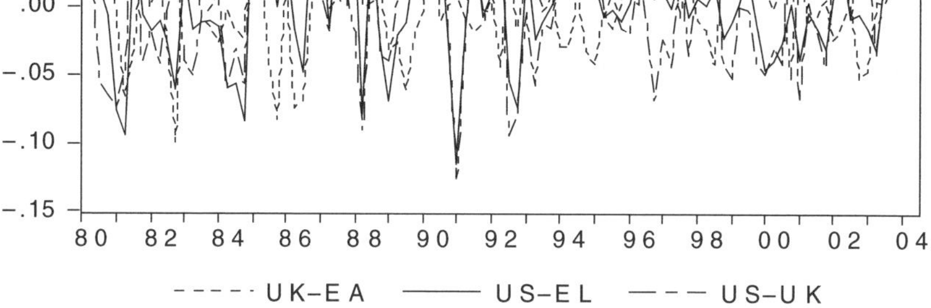

Figure 12.8 Individual regression residuals

foreign assets and the real exchange rate. Our regression results suggest that when the euro area net foreign asset position deteriorates by 1 per cent of euro area GDP, it will increase the associated dollar risk premium by 0.14 percentage points, putting downward pressure on the euro and raising euro area interest rates relative to those elsewhere. However, the net foreign asset position of the other countries is just as important to the trajectory of euro risk. In particular, the coefficients on the US net foreign assets and those of the euro area are the same, implying a doubling in the rise of the euro area risk premium *vis-à-vis* the dollar from a deteriorating euro area net foreign asset position that was accompanied by an equivalent rise of US net foreign assets. Taken in conjunction with similar findings in the recent literature, the evidence above points to a distinct relationship between the net asset position of the euro area and the excess (or *ex post*) 'risk' associated with the euro/dollar exchange rate.

Fiscal and monetary policy news

Conventional models of exchange-rate behaviour which have included actual measures of economic fundamentals have also sought to relate *unexpected components* of these fundamentals to movements in the exchange rate (for example Goodhart and Figliuoli, 1991; Brigden *et al.*, 1997; and De Boeck, 2000). The unexpected components of economic fundamentals are referred to as 'news'. For example, an innovation in monetary policy realised after the current period exchange rate is set will influence the value of the next period's exchange rate. Indeed, in a perfect foresight world, this implies that innovations in 'news' about economic fundamentals are the only things that can change the exchange rate at a given point in time. It would be possible to repeat our regression above augmented with news on the factors that have affected the risk premia and on monetary policy over the whole period. Whilst the latter is relatively easy to construct, the former is beyond the scope of this chapter, and we choose to undertake an additional regression of the errors on the net asset adjusted arbitrage equation over a shorter period of time.

We can assume that the current exchange rate depends upon expectations of future net assets, interest rates and other factors. After the exchange rate is set in a period, news becomes available about the future. An expected rise in the US interest rate in any period in the future, will, by forward recursion, cause the US exchange rate to jump now, all else equal. Conversely, news about the euro area interest rate will have an impact with the opposite sign to the US. Equally, news about the net asset ratio that is expected in the future will cause the exchange rate to jump now. There are a variety of sources of news about the future net asset position, but the most obvious one is the potential impact of changes in projected budget deficits. NIESR has been constructing forecasts of the world economy using its NiGEM model for two decades, and these forecasts contain projections of budget deficits for the future. These are available for the US over a relatively long period, but they are only available for the euro area from its inception in 1999. The news on deficits and on long rates are discussed below. Once we have constructed the series we can evaluate whether they are orthogonal to the regressors included in Table 12.1. If they are, then it is possible to undertake a regression decomposition of the impact of news on the unexplained component of this regression.

Budget deficits and the net asset position

In a world with complete Ricardian equivalence there are clearly no impacts of announced changes in government borrowing on the current-account deficit in future and hence no impact on the net asset position and hence on the exchange rate. However, the conditions for such equivalence are strong and well-known. Pomerantz and Weale (2005) undertake a panel data analysis of the impact of government borrowing in the euro area since its inception on net saving and they suggest that there is some offset, estimating that a 1 per cent of GDP increase in the deficit will produce a –0.23 per cent worsening of the current account. Their results are supported by the analysis in OECD (2005).

Therefore, news about changes in the future course of the budget deficit in the US or the Euro Area will impact on the expected future net asset position and the expected risk premia, and hence by forward recursion will impact on the current exchange rate. In addition, we know that the accounting scandals that built up from the collapse of Enron to the collapse of Worldcom in June 2002 impacted on portfolio flows in the private sector and should have raised the projected risk premium significantly, and hence we include this event as a dummy in our regression.

We utilise budget forecasts published in NIESR *Quarterly Reviews* for the period 1999Q1 to 2005Q4, and we plot the average deficit for the five years from the forecast date as quarter-by-quarter projections in Figure 12.9. The NIESR projections tend to move with the rest of the 'market', and hence as we can see the major changes in US budget projections come after the election of President Bush in late 2000, after 11 September in 2001 and after the invasion of Iraq in 2003. The need for such changes in projections became immediately obvious, but the basis for NIESR projections was (and remains) plans approved by Congress, and hence the impact of the potential deterioration in the public sector accounts caused by these two events came up to six months before the change in forecasts. Therefore, where they are significant we include these events as dummies as well. The euro area budget projections move more slowly over time, but there are signs of successive deteriorations. We also plot the euro/dollar exchange rate where, despite having more inertia than suggested by the news, we can see that this relation tends to move in line with changes in budget projections.

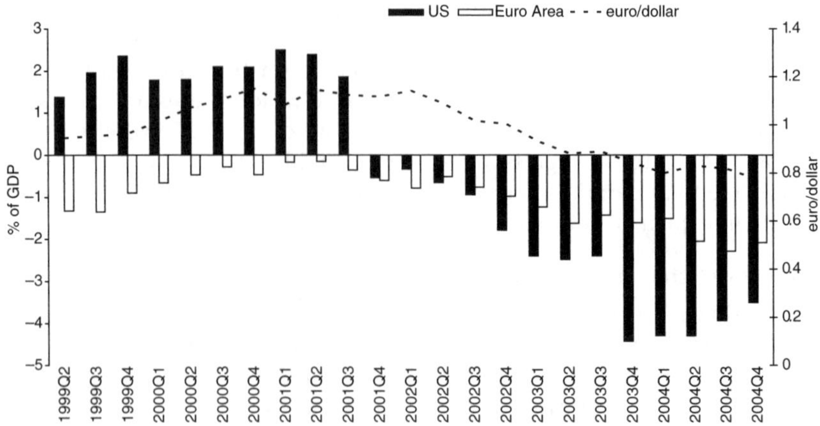

Figure 12.9 Quarter-by-quarter forecasts for US budgets and euro area budgets (5-year-ahead average) and euro/dollar exchange rate
Source: National Institute Economic Review, NIESR forecasts.

Long interest rates

In a nominal framework, monetary policy news is perhaps easier to evaluate than fiscal policy news. The exchange rate will jump because of movements in anticipated interest rates, and these will be fully encapsulated in the yield curve, as is discussed in Brigden *et al.* (1997). We utilise data for 10-year government bonds, and we plot the changes in US (*LR**) and in euro area (*LR*) long rates between adjacent quarters from 1999Q1 when the

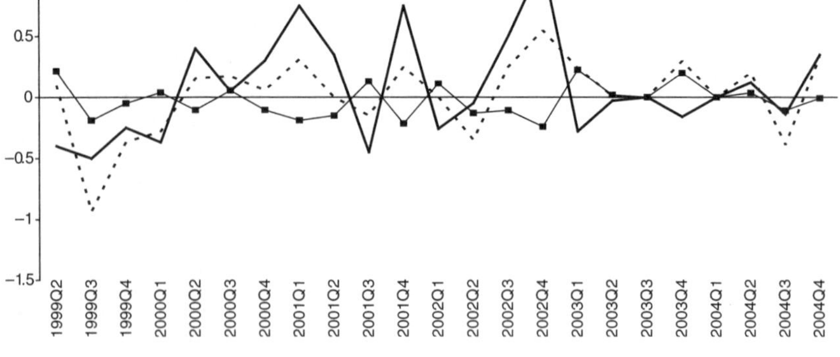

Figure 12.10 US and euro area long rates (change)

euro was formed. This information on bond rates can be used to calculate the monetary policy news as $(1+LR^*)/(1+LR)$ and we plot this in Figure 12.10 as well (where it has been scaled by 10 for clarity). The variation in US long rates is almost twice as great as that of euro area long rates, and the variances of these series are 0.1811 and 0.1028 respectively. We would expect that our long-rate news would be completely reflected in changes in the exchange rate, and hence if we include it as a regressor to explain the residual from Table 12.1 it should have a unit coefficient.

Although it is difficult to associate news over a five-year period with the long-run movements in the exchange rate, we can undertake a partial decomposition as long as the news is orthogonal to the regressors in Table 12.1, and this is the case. The correlations between the *US NAR* and *US Budget* deficit news ($Fiscal\ News_{US}$) and between EA NAR and euro area budget deficit news ($Fiscal\ News_{EA}$) between 1999Q2 and 2004Q4 are 0.39 and 0.1, which are not significant at the 95 per cent level. The correlations between the pairs *US NAR* and MP_{News} and *EA NAR* and MP_{News} are –0.66 and 0.12, which are also not significant at the 95 per cent level. Hence, as US net assets and the news on US net assets and on monetary policy are orthogonal (and the same for the euro area), we can undertake a simple

Table 12.2 Euro area–US residual regression ($EA–US_{Res}$)

Variable	*Coefficient*	*T-Statistic*
Constant	–0.021	2.7
$Fiscal\ News_{US}$	0.23	0.3
$Fiscal\ News_{EA}$	1.65	3.1
MP News	–0.96	2.0
$d00Q4_{Bush}$	0.07	2.1
$d02Q2_{World\ Com}$	0.10	3.0
$d03Q3_{Iraq\ War}$	0.07	2.2
Std. error	0.03	
$\bar{R}^2$	0.44	
LM(4) *F*-test	2.3 prob. (0.12)	
Sample	1999Q3 to 2004Q4	
Series statistics:	ADF(1)	Regressors
$EA–US_{Res}$	5.2*	Constant, trend
$NAR_{US\ News}$	4.5*	Constant
$NAR_{EA\ News}$	3.5*	
MP_{News}	6.5*	Constant

Note: * In absolute values; pass at 1%, MacKinnon (1996) values.

regression of the residual from the risk-premium-adjusted arbitrage condition on the dummies we have discussed and on the two budget-related sets of news about assets, as well as about monetary policy news.

Table 12.2 provides the results, and we find that the coefficient on monetary policy news is almost exactly one, as we would expect from our discussion. The three US dummies are significant, and as a result there appears to be no independent news in our budget forecasts for the US. The euro area budget forecast news is significant and of the correct sign with a worsening of the budget deficit causing a rise in the dollar exchange rate and hence a depreciation of the euro, reflecting the increased risk premia that are associated with higher budget deficits. These variables taken together explain approximately 44 per cent of the variation of the error on the euro/dollar arbitrage and risk-premium-based equation. We should of course proceed with caution as we have fewer than 24 degrees of freedom in the regression. Moreover, these factors are only some amongst a long list of possible contributions, and we do not presume that the changes are exactly represented by the news items we calculate. In general, however, over this period, it is US events that appear to be driving the unexplained component from the arbitrage adjusted exchange rate path.

Conclusion

This study investigates the observed movements in the euro/dollar exchange rate by drawing upon ideas encompassed in a standard portfolio-balance model. A closed portfolio bloc between the euro area, the US and the UK is defined, permitting us to decompose deviations from bilateral open arbitrage conditions into systematic and random components. Beginning with a multivariate framework, the former component is defined by changes in these countries' net foreign asset positions, but we find that this constitutes only a small portion of the *ex post* deviations from the arbitrage condition. The latter random component, constituting the remainder of this deviation, is to some extent explained by 'news' relating to innovations in monetary and fiscal policy. However, a substantial portion of the deviation from the bilateral euro area/US open arbitrage condition reflects pure noise which cannot be accounted for in our framework. The analysis does, nevertheless, suggest that events in the US – changes in the net asset position and US monetary policy news – largely drive movements in the euro/dollar relation.

Notes

1 The discussion of FEERs in Driver and Wren Lewis (1998) provides some guidance to modelling real exchange rates.

2 Gross portfolio flows and stocks from these three regions dominate global financial markets.

3 We use a quarterly dataset for our estimation, and this refers to 'news' that becomes available between the data points.

4 See Isard (1995) for an overview of these monetary models and the portfolio model discussed below.
5 Over time, however, one would expect that fundamentals-based models would become more accurate predictors of exchange rate movements. For example, see Rogoff (1996).
6 Such restrictions vary from country to country, but it is common, at least within the euro area, to constrain pension funds, for instance to hold mainly domestic assets.
7 We concentrate only on the dollar/euro, dollar/sterling and sterling/euro rates in part for expositional clarity. When we include Japan and Canada in our system, we do not find significant net asset-related risk premiums for these countries, which we should not find surprising. The build up of Canadian liabilities reflects its role as a natural resource producer, and does carry increased risk. The rise in the risk premium on Japanese assets over the last 20 years has been independent of the growth of the positive net asset position of that country.
8 The US net asset position is not itself a perfect indicator of the balance of income flows, and net factor income has not followed the same downward trend. We see this as a change in the rate of return rather than a hidden asset position. This is discussed in greater detail by Higgins *et al.* (2005).
9 The euro only came into existence in 1999, and before 1996 we would not expect it to have a unique risk premium but rather one associated with the variance of risks across currencies as well. It is, however, useful to utilise the whole data period as this is used in most ECB work in this area (see Fagan *et al.*, 2005).

References

Al-Eyd, A., R. Barrell and D. Holland (2006) 'The Role of Financial Markets' Openness in the Transmission of Shocks in Europe', Paper presented to Finprop conference Brussels, 2006.

Al-Eyd, A., R. Barrell and O. Pomerantz (2005) 'Dollars and Deficits: the US Current Account Deficit and its Exchange Rate Consequences', *National Institute Economic Review*, 191: 31–6.

Arrowsmith, J., R.J. Barrell and C. Taylor (2000) 'Managing the Euro in a Tri-Polar World', in M. Artis and C. Hennessy (eds), *The Euro: A Challenge an Opportunity for Financial Markets*. London: Routledge.

Barrell, R., and N. Pain (2000) 'Monetary and Fiscal Policy in Europe', *National Institute Economic Review*, 174: 63–7.

Barrell, R. and D. Holland (2004a) 'The Dollar, the Jobless Recovery and Technical Progress', *National Institute Economic Review*, 188: 13–15.

Barrell, R. and D. Holland (2004b) 'Are Current Exchange Rates Sustainable?', *National Institute Economic Review*, 187: 11–15.

Brigden, A., B. Martin and C. Salmon (1997) 'Decomposing Exchange Rate Movements According to the Uncovered Interest Rate Parity Condition', *Bank of England Quarterly Bulletin*, 37, 377–89.

Brooks, R., H. Edison, M. Kumar and T. Slok (2001) 'Exchange Rates and Capital Flows', IMF Working Paper no. 01/190, International Monetary Fund, Washington DC.

Cavallo, M., and F. Ghironi (2002) 'Net Foreign Assets and the Exchange Rate: Redux Revisited', Working Paper, Boston College.

Corsetti, G. and P. Pesenti (1999) 'Stability, Asymmetry, and Discontinuity: The Launch of the European Monetary Union', *Brookings Papers on Economic Activity*, 2, 295–358.

De Boeck, J. (2000) 'The Effect of Macroeconomic 'News' on Exchange Rates: a Structural VAR Approach', mimeo, University of Leuven.

De Grauwe, P. (2000) 'Exchange Rates in Search of Fundamentals: the Case of the Euro/dollar Rate', University of Leuven, Economics Paper 109.

Dornbusch, R. (1976) 'Expectations and Exchange Rate Dynamics', *Journal of Political Economy*, 84, 1161–76.

Driver, R. and S. Wren-Lewis (1998) 'Exchange Rates for the Year 2000', in S. Wren-Lewis and R. Driver (eds), *Real Exchange Rates for the Year 2000: Policy Analysis in International Economics*, Washington: International Institute for International Economics.

Erceg, C., L. Guerrieri and C. Gust (2004) 'Sigma: a New Open Economy Model for Policy Analysis', US Federal Reserve Board, unpublished manuscript.

Fagan, G., J. Henry and R. Mestre (2005) 'An Area-Wide Model for the Euro Area', *Economic Modelling*, 22: 39–59.

Froot, K.A., R. Thaler (1990) 'Foreign Exchange', *Journal of Economic Perspectives*, 4, 179–92.

Gagnon, J. (1996) 'Net Foreign Assets and Equilibrium Exchange Rates: Panel Evidence', Board of Governors of the Federal Reserve System, International Finance Discussion Papers, no. 574.

Goodhart, C.E. and L. Figliuoli (1991) 'Every Minute Counts in the Foreign Exchange Markets', *Journal of International Money and Finance*, 10, 23–52.

Higgins, M., T. Klitgaard and C. Tille (2005) 'The Income Implications of Rising US International Liabilities', Federal Reserve Bank of New York, *Current Issues in Economics and Finance*, 11(12), 1–8.

Isard, P. (1995) *Exchange Rate Economics*. Cambridge: Cambridge University Press.

Krugman, P. (1998) *Exchange Rate Instability*. Cambridge, MA: MIT Press.

Lane, P.R. and G.M. Milesi–Ferretti (2004) 'The Transfer Problem Revisited: Net Foreign Assets and Real Exchange Rates', *Review of Economics and Statistics*, 86, 841–857.

Laxton, D., P. Isard, H. Faruqee, E. Prasad and B. Turtelboom (1998) 'Multimod Mark III', Occasional Paper no. 164, IMF, Washington, DC.

Lettau, M. and S. Ludvigson (2004) 'Understanding Trend and Cycle in Asset Values: Re-evaluating the Wealth Effect on Consumption' *American Economic Review* 94, 276–299.

MacKinnon, J. (1996) 'Numerical Distribution Functions for Unit Root and Cointegration Tests', *Journal of Applied Econometrics*, 11, 601–18.

Meese, E. and K. Rogoff (1983) 'Empirical Exchange Rate Models of the Seventies: Do They Fit Out of Sample?' *Journal of International Economics*, 14: 3–24.

Meredith, G. (2001) 'Why has the Euro Been so Weak?' IMF WP/01/155, International Monetary Fund, Washington DC.

Obstfeld, M. and K. Rogoff (1995) 'The Intertemporal Approach to the Current Account', in S. Grossman and K. Rogoff (eds), *Handbook of International Economics*. Amsterdam: North Holland Press.

Pomerantz, O. and M. Weale (2005) 'Are we Saving Enough? The Macroeconomics of the Savings Gap', *National Institute Economic Review*, no. 191, 79–93.

Rogoff, K. (1996) 'The Purchasing Power Parity Puzzle', *Journal of Economic Literature*, 34, 647–68.

Summers, L. (2004) 'The United States and the Global Adjustment Process', Third Annual Stavros S. Niarchos Lecture, Institute for International Economics, Washington, DC.

Wadhwani, S.B. (1999) 'Sterling's Puzzling Behaviour', *Bank of England Quarterly Bulletin* 39, 416–427.

Discussion

Jacques Mélitz

Al-Eyd, Barrel and Holland (ABH in what follows) provide new evidence of the interest of the old portfolio-balance approach to the exchange rate. They show that the respective net foreign asset positions of the US and the EA (euro area) help explain the quarterly deviations from *ex post interest-rate parity* (open interest-rate parity after we replace the expected exchange rate of the dollar/euro with its observed future value) in 1980–2004. This evidence indeed favours portfolio-balance analysis and is contrary to open interest-rate parity (based on the expected exchange rate rather than its observed future value). If open interest-rate parity was correct, these deviations would not depend on the composition of international portfolios between dollars and euros (and the predecessors of the euro in 1980–99). They would simply reflect errors in expectations or news, and random events. ABH also bolster their emphasis on portfolio balance by exhibiting the impact of various sorts of news. Some of these news items clearly would not explain *ex post* deviations from interest rate parity in 1999Q3–2004Q4, as ABH say, at least in any simple way, in the presence of open interest-rate parity. This refers to the impact of the projections of higher US deficits following President Bush's election and the invasion of Iraq in 2003 on the dollar/euro exchange rate. It is easiest to explain both of these news items' effect on the exchange rate, as ABH do, on the basis of the adverse consequences for the US current-account balance and net US foreign assets.

But not all of the news that appears as important in ABH's econometric analysis supports their emphasis on portfolio balance. For example, the impact of the news about monetary policy would follow just the same if agents were perfectly risk-neutral and open interest-rate parity was correct. Likewise, news of the 'accounting scandals that built up from the collapse of ENRON to the collapse of Worldcom in 2 June 2002' could have had the same effect if agents were risk-neutral. The information about the scandals then could still have lowered the expected return on dollar assets and therefore necessitated a rise in the nominal interest rate on dollars relative to euros (as adjusted in their way). But if not all the deviations from *ex post* interest-rate parity that ABH treat can be seen as relating to a risk premium, they still present a variety of support for their emphasis on the portfolio-balance model and successfully reinforce recent efforts to bring back the model to centre-stage in explaining exchange-rate behaviour (compare Blanchard, Giavazzi and Sa, 2005, in particular).

Based on the portfolio-balance model, however, ABH's treatment raises one important question: How valid it is to analyse the dollar/euro strictly in terms of US and EA behaviour? The US is now a huge debtor (with net foreign debt equal to 25 per cent of GDP). Its two leading creditors (in terms of *net* debt) are China and Japan. Surely, if China and Japan had not expanded their holdings of dollars in recent years as much as they did, the euro would have risen further relative to the dollar. To test the idea, I propose that the right way to proceed would be to have, instead of ABH's equation (12.2), the following:

$$rp^{US\text{-}EA} = c_1 + \alpha_{EA}NAR_{EA} + \alpha_{US}NAR_{US} + \alpha_{ROW}NAR_{ROW} + \varepsilon^{US\text{-}EA}$$

$$\alpha_{EA} > 0 \qquad \alpha_{US} < 0 \qquad \alpha_{ROW} \mp 0 \qquad \alpha_{EA} + \alpha_{US} + \alpha_{ROW} = 0$$

where ROW refers to the rest of the world or any section of it (and $\varepsilon^{US\text{-}EA}$ is a disturbance term). Instead, ABH merely impose $\alpha_{ROW} = 0$. But is this correct? If the rest of the world had a preference for dollars relative to euros (i.e. it wanted to hold a larger proportion of its portfolio in dollars than in euros), α_{ROW} would be negative. (That would be my assumption as regards China and Japan.) In the opposite case, or if the rest of the world had a preference for euros, then α_{ROW} would be positive. It is only if the rest of the world has a preference for neither, as ABH assume, that α_{ROW} will be zero. Interestingly enough, ABH actually test the assumption of an identical preference for dollars and euros when the rest of the world consists of the UK and they confirm it. (That, I believe, is the right interpretation of their test procedure and results in Table 12.1: the UK wants to hold equal shares of euros and dollars and has a preference for neither.) However, ABH do not test the condition for other countries. Or rather, when they do test it, as they do for Canada and Japan according to note 7, the condition fails. But instead of concluding from this that $\alpha_{CAN}NAR_{CAN}$ and $\alpha_{JAP}NAR_{JAP}$ belong in the equation for $rp^{US\text{-}EA}$, that is in the *ex post* deviation of the interest-rate differential between the US and the EA from interest-rate parity, they conclude the opposite: that it is correct to disregard both countries.

In sum, I believe it would be interesting if ABH extended their analysis to allow for more third-country influences on the dollar/euro.

Reference

Blanchard, O., F. Giavazzi and F. Sa (2005) 'International Investors, the U.S. Current Account, and the Dollar', *Brookings Papers on Economic Activity*, 1: 1–49.

Index